"THIS IS NO DRILL"

Titles in the series

"NO ONE AVOIDED DANGER"
NAS KANEOHE BAY AND THE JAPANESE ATTACK OF 7 DECEMBER 1941

Pearl Harbor Tactical Studies Series

J. Michael Wenger, Robert J. Cressman, and John F. Di Virgilio, editors

More than three-quarters of a century has passed since 7 December 1941, and yet no comprehensive tactical history exists for the Japanese attacks on the island of Oʻahu. Much of the material and documentary evidence relating to the attacks has become generally available to historians and researchers only within the last two decades. This material not only spans far-flung repositories in the United States and Japan, it also bridges a vast chasm separating two very different cultures, complicating the material's use.

The Pearl Harbor Tactical Studies series seeks to fill this wide gap in military history by exploring the deepest levels of practical, personal, and tactical details. The goal of these works is to promote a deeper understanding of the events of 7 December 1941 and to convey the chaos and magnitude of the disaster on Oʻahu as experienced by individuals. A careful survey of the available records and accounts from both sides has resulted in comprehensive accounts that document the epic American-Japanese struggle on and over Oʻahu and the intensely human tragedy of that day.

THE HISTORY OF NAS PEARL HARBOR AND THE JAPANESE ATTACKS OF 7 DECEMBER 1941

"THIS IS NO DRILL"

J. MICHAEL WENGER, ROBERT J. CRESSMAN, AND JOHN F. DI VIRGILIO

NAVAL INSTITUTE PRESS

Annapolis, Maryland

Naval Institute Press
291 Wood Road
Annapolis, MD 21402

Library of Congress Cataloging-in-Publication Data
Names: Wenger, J. Michael, author. | Cressman, Robert, author. | Di Virgilio, John F., author.
Title: "This is no drill" : the history of NAS Pearl Harbor and the Japanese attacks of
    7 December 1941 / J. Michael Wenger, Robert J. Cressman, and John F. Di Virgilio.
Other titles: History of NAS Pearl Harbor and the Japanese attacks of 7 December 1941
Description: Annapolis, Maryland : Naval Institute Press, [2018] | Series: Pearl harbor
    tactical studies series | Includes bibliographical references and index.
Identifiers: LCCN 2018016044 | ISBN 9781682471814 (hardcover : alk. paper)
Subjects: LCSH: Pearl Harbor (Hawaii), Attack on, 1941. | Pearl Harbor (Hawaii),
    Attack on, 1941—Sources.
Classification: LCC D767.92 .W466 2018 | DDC 940.54/26693—dc23
    LC record available at https://lccn.loc.gov/2018016044

♾ Print editions meet the requirements of ANSI/NISO z39.48-1992
(Permanence of Paper).
Printed in the United States of America.

26 25 24 23 22 21 20 19 18   9 8 7 6 5 4 3 2 1
First printing

To the servicemen and civilians
on Ford Island
on 7 December 1941

CONTENTS

PREFACE

The story of the attacks on Naval Air Station (NAS) Pearl Harbor on 7 December 1941 is at least vaguely familiar to most Americans and certainly to those interested in the military history of the Pacific War. Located on Ford Island, the station was at the epicenter of the greatest disaster the U.S. Navy has ever suffered. Sailors and Marines on that small island witnessed the first bomb strikes on the seaplane base and the first torpedo strikes against the Pacific Fleet. Those men were no mere observers of the tragic events that unfolded about them; they played prominent roles in the fierce defense of their base and the harbor outside Ford Island's shores. Naval aviators attached to squadrons based at NAS Pearl Harbor were the first Americans to take to the air and search for the Japanese invaders. Indeed, the vast majority of American aerial searches throughout the day originated from there. In the evening hours, the men unwittingly participated in a tragic friendly fire incident that ended a fear-filled day.

Unlike the newer American military airfields on Oʻahu that came under attack, NAS Pearl Harbor boasted a long history. The aviation facilities on Ford Island resembled the "joint base" strategy of recent decades in that both the Army and the Navy occupied the island and shared the landing field there, albeit with separate hangars, maintenance facilities, and housing. Both services had maintained a presence there since World War I, although the Army began air operations before the Navy did. Both services played defining roles in the development of Ford Island over the span of two decades. Some knowledge of the history of Ford Island prior to World War II will put the events of 7 December 1941 into context.

The authors were keenly aware that the full story of NAS Pearl Harbor on 7 December 1941 needed to be told well before they began work on this volume, but it was not until we delved into the voluminous materials bequeathed to us by the defenders (and attackers) that we appreciated the intricacy of the full story and the difficulties we would encounter in writing it. Our desire to do the defenders of NAS Pearl Harbor full justice led us to take on this challenging task. It is our hope that the reader will look back upon those sailors and Marines and remember their gallantry and heroism on that infamous day.

—J. Michael Wenger, Robert J. Cressman,
John F. Di Virgilio
22 August 2016

ACKNOWLEDGMENTS

A book such as this is necessarily the product of the supporting labors of many, from trained archival specialists to friends and colleagues in the field and those who lived through these momentous events. Some no longer work in the archives in which we began our research more than forty years ago, but our indebtedness to them remains. Nearly all of the veterans with whom we talked or corresponded have since died.

In particular, this work stands on the shoulders of two individuals without whose resources any work dealing with Pearl Harbor would fall woefully short of the mark. Dr. Gordon W. Prange's papers remain an unparalleled source of information. We especially thank Jennie A. Levine at the University of Maryland and Dr. Donald M. Goldstein, Marianne Kasica, and Michael Dabrishus of the University of Pittsburgh for making Dr. Prange's materials available. Similarly, Walter Lord's work is practically synonymous with Pearl Harbor studies. Access to his interviews, questionnaires, and correspondence came to us via archivist Curtis Utz of the Naval History and Heritage Command.

Archivists and reference specialists at a number of institutions and repositories provided help and guidance. The National Archives and Records Administration (NARA II) in College Park, Maryland, has provided access to records over many years, and we thank Jim Trimble, Holly Reed, Theresa Roy, and Sharon Culley of the Still Picture Branch; Nathaniel Patch of the Textual Branch; and Andrew Knight and Alice Rosser of the Cartographic Branch for their assistance. The generous staff at the Naval History and Heritage Command (formerly the Naval Historical Center) in Washington, D.C., helped us over the span of a generation, particularly Charles R. Haberlein, Agnes F. Hoover, and Mike Walker. Hill Goodspeed at the National Naval Aviation Museum (now a part of the Naval History and Heritage Command enterprise in Pensacola, Florida) gave generously of his time, resources, and materials. Lisa Fox of the University of North Texas supplied copies of interviews from that institution's oral history program. NAVFAC Hawaii assisted in locating architectural plans. Our research at the National Archives and National Personnel Records Center in St. Louis, Missouri, would not have been possible without the energy and advice of Scott A. Levins, Bryan McGraw, Barbara Bauman, Whitney Mahar, Eric Kilgore, Dean Gall, Donna Noelken, Jennifer Moll, Amy Reckmann, Angela Miller, Mary Parker Biby, and Jaclyn Ostrowski.

The following individuals assisted with translation of Japanese documents, books, articles, and monographs: Dr. Kataoka Hiroko (formerly of North Carolina State University), Oka Akio, Sugahara Kan, Dr. Kawamoto Minoru, Sam Tagaya, and D. Y. Louie. In particular, Mr. Sugahara was instrumental in evaluating our translation of the Japanese aircrew rosters from the attacks on Oʻahu.

Shibata Takehiko and Kageyama Kōichirō at the War History Office of the Japanese Defense Agency offered expertise, documents, and analysis and served as our liaison with Japanese veterans.

Access to U.S. Marine Corps service records at the National Personnel Records Center would have been impossible without the help of Annette D. Amerman of the Marine Corps History Division.

Fellow historians and researchers extended generous offers of assistance. Capt. Roger Pineau, Cdr. Chihaya Masataka, and Capt. Uesaka Yasushi aided research in Japan. Other individuals provided documents, materials, and valuable advice, including John B. Lundstrom, James C. Sawruk, Kamada Minoru, John W. Lambert, John Burdette, Geoff Gentilini, William M. Cleveland, Todd Pederson, Jeffrey Dodge, James Lansdale, Nancy Casey, Dorinda Nicholson, Ron Werneth, Yoshida Jirō, David Aiken, and Richard F. Barnes. Dr. Timothy P. Mulligan made available copies of the fragmentary codebooks recovered from Japanese aircraft wreckage. David Born and Ike Copperthite of the Historic Preservation Division, Prince William County, Virginia, located a critical wartime photograph of then–lieutenant commander Richard B. Black. Institutions and individuals in Japan supplied documents and photographs: War History Office of the Japanese Defense Forces, Murooka Yasuo of *Maru* magazine, Todaka Kazunari, Tanaka Shōichi, and Kamada Minoru. Osamu "Sam" Tagaya secured pictures of Japanese aircrews from Dr. Izawa Yasuo. Mr. Takahashi of Konnichi no Wadai-sha also made one key photograph available.

Extended families and acquaintances of American veterans provided accounts, photographs, and other personal papers (with the veteran's name and 1941 rank in brackets): Linda Black [Lt. Richard B. Black]; Michael, Mimi, and Anthony Bolser and Shannon Gault [Lt. (jg) Gordon E. Bolser]; Daniel Closser [1st Lt. Daniel P. Closser]; Paul "Doc" Doolittle [BM1c Elliot Milliken]; Jim Duty and Ann Barnhill [RM3c Glenn E. Pennock]; Joan Earle [Maj. Adolph Zuber]; Perry and Andy Edwards [Ens. John P. Edwards]; Toni Espinoza [SM1c Charles A. Flood]; Lynne Erdahl, Carol Fauber, and Tracy Rossello [AMM1c Robert S. Fauber]; Janice Fiore and Robert Hanson [RM2c Harry R. Mead]; Rick Gano [AMM1c Hubert D. Gano]; Bill Knight [Pvt. Ray A. Knight Jr.]; Niles and Bruce Larson [Ens. Nils R. Larson]; Janet K. Lesher [AMM1c David John Lesher]; Allan MacKay [CRM (PA) Allan G. MacKay]; Donald Morton [AOM1c Theodore W. Croft]; Tom Richards [Lt. Cdr. Thomas G. Richards]; Debbie Sherrard [PhM1c Paul J. Sherrard Sr.]; Roger and Richard Switzer and Joanne Herrera [AMM2c David L. Switzer]; Diane Clark and Christopher Waalkes [AMM1c William P. Evans]; and Daniel Young [AMM2c Ralph B. Young]. CWO3 Audrey G. Coslett (Ret.); Rich Lane; Walter Lord; Al Makiel; Todd Pederson; Dr. Gordon W. Prange (via Dr. Donald M. Goldstein); Kathy Weeks. Authors J. Michael Wenger, Robert J. Cressman, John F. Di Virgilio also provided photographs.

As we began concerted work began on this volume relatively recently, we came in sustained contact with few veterans and had to rely on articles, reminiscences, interviews, and materials passed to us by their extended families. However, Mr. Jack Rogo, a veteran of NAS Pearl Harbor, provided superb details and analysis in his interviews. Similarly, Cdr. Wesley H. Ruth, USN (Ret.) of VJ1 and Capt. Charles P. Muckenthaler, USN (Ret.) of VP11 were generous in providing interviews and personal papers to Wenger. The following Japanese aviators contributed materially to our understanding of Japanese ordnance, tactics, and the events of 7 December 1941: Abe Zenji, Fujita Iyozō, Harada Kaname, Satō Zenichi, and Ushijima Shizundō.

Beth Oldham Design assisted with graphic overlays.

The following individuals on the staffs of World War II Valor in the Pacific National Monument and Pacific Historic Parks have supported our research and work for many years: Tom Shaw, Marjorie Shaw, Daniel Martinez, Scott Pawlowski, and Patty Brown.

We would like to express gratitude to our families for their suggestions, patience, and support as we made our way toward completion of this work.

Finally, we wish to thank Richard Russell, Glenn Griffith, Emily Bakely, and Robin Noonan of the Naval Institute Press for their continued interest in the authors' work, specifically in the Pearl Harbor Tactical Studies series.

NOTES ON NAMES

U.S. Navy, U.S. Army, and Japanese Aircraft Names

The U.S. Navy, by and large, did not often use the popular nicknames approved in October 1941 for its planes. The U.S. Army, however, did tend to use such nicknames. The Imperial Japanese Navy designated its types of aircraft in a very particular way, and we refer to them as it did. The reader thus will not find the anachronistic "Val" or "Kate" in the text because those names would not be used until November 1942.

U.S. NAVY

Unless otherwise specified, all U.S. Navy ship names will be understood as being preceded by USS (United States ship); a USN ship's alphanumeric identification number will be used only at the ship's first mention. All times and dates are those observed locally by a ship or station unless otherwise specified and are rendered military fashion (e.g., 1000 for 10:00 a.m., 1300 for 1:00 p.m., etc.).

▷ Brewster F2A-3 Buffalo
▷ Consolidated PBY-1, PBY-2, PBY-3, PBY-5 Catalina
▷ Curtiss SOC Seagull
▷ Douglas SBD-2, SBD-3 Dauntless
▷ Douglas TBD-1 Devastator
▷ Grumman F4F-3, F4F-3A Wildcat
▷ Grumman J2F-1, J2F-2, J2F-3, J2F-4 Duck
▷ Vought OS2U-3 Kingfisher
▷ Vought SB2U-3 Vindicator

U.S. ARMY

▷ Boeing B-17D Flying Fortress
▷ Douglas B-18 Bolo

IMPERIAL JAPANESE NAVY

▷ Aichi D3A1 Type 99 carrier bomber (*kanbaku*) ("Val")
▷ Mitsubishi A6M2 Type 0 carrier fighter (*kansen*) ("Zero")
▷ Nakajima B5N2 Type 97 carrier attack plane (*kankō*) ("Kate")

Japanese Personal Names

We follow the Japanese fashion for names, with the surname first and the given name last. Romanization of Japanese names from *kanji* characters, however, is an inexact science, so after translating the names herein we consulted with historian Sugahara Kan of Japan, who offered corrections and alternative readings. Owing to the nature of Japanese personal names, there will never be a last word in this matter, but with the help of Mr. Sugahara the rosters of the Japanese participants are as authoritative as practicality allows.

Japanese Terms

chūtai: Japanese aviation unit of six to twelve aircraft, usually three *shōtais*

kanbakutai: Japanese aviation unit of Type 99 carrier bombers

kankōtai: Japanese aviation unit of Type 97 carrier attack planes

kansentai: Japanese aviation unit of Type 0 carrier fighters

kidō butai: a Japanese term (literally, "mobile force") that referred to any naval force that contained an aircraft carrier and was capable of independent operation. In terms of the Hawaiian Operation, *Kidō Butai* was a euphemism for "Carrier Striking Force."

Hawaiian Place-Names

Except for the names of military bases and public buildings and quotes from contemporary correspondence, Hawaiian place-names are rendered in the orthography of that language.

National Personnel Records Center

For two generations, the term "National Personnel Records Center" has been synonymous with the former Page Avenue facility in St. Louis, Missouri, that held all the Official Military Personnel Files (OMPFs) from the World War II period and other eras. In recent years, however, the volume of records being released for public use has increased, and the facility in St. Louis has become two institutions in one building operating under the umbrella of the National Archives and Records Administration, each with its own separate research room and procedures. The National Personnel Records Center administers nonarchival records (those closed to the public), and the National Archives administers archival records (those open to the public).

Primary sources accessed through the research room in the Records Center are cited as residing in "NPRC, St. Louis." Open material accessed through the research room in the National Archives is cited as residing in "NARA, St. Louis." The custody of records in St. Louis relating to World War II changes daily, passing increasingly to the National Archives. The citations herein refer to the custodian of records *at the time of the authors' research* and may no longer be valid.

ABBREVIATIONS

AA	antiaircraft; acting appointment, when used as a suffix to a chief petty officer rating	CAP	chief aviation pilot
		CarDiv	carrier division
		CEAG	Commander Enterprise Air Group
AV(G), USNR	commissioned aviation officers designated naval aviators and qualified for general duty afloat or ashore	CECV(S)	commissioned civil engineer
		CG	commanding general
		ChC	Chaplain Corps
AV(N), USNR	commissioned aviation flight officers detailed to active duty in the aeronautic organization of the Navy immediately following the completion of training and designation as naval aviators	ChCV(G), USNR	commissioned chaplains qualified for general detail afloat or ashore
		CinCAF	Commander-in-Chief, U.S. Asiatic Fleet
		CinCPac	Commander-in-Chief, U.S. Pacific Fleet
		CinCUS	Commander-in-Chief, U.S. Fleet
AV(S), USNR	commissioned aviation officers qualified for specialist or ground duties	CNO	Chief of Naval Operations
		CO	commanding officer
		ComAirBatFor	Commander Aircraft, Battle Force
AWS	Aircraft Warning Service, Hawaii	ComAirScoFor	Commander Aircraft, Scouting Force
BAR	Browning automatic rifle		
BatDiv	battleship division	ComBatDiv	Commander Battleship Division
BOQ	bachelor officer quarters		
BuNo	bureau number		
BuSandA	Bureau of Supplies and Accounts	ComCruBatFor	Commander Cruisers, Battle Force

ComCruScoFor	Commander Cruisers, Scouting Force	IMI	request to repeat message
ComPatWing	Commander Patrol Wing	MAG	Marine aircraft group
ComScoFor	Commander Scouting Force	MarDet	Marine detachment
ComTF	Commander Task Force	MC	Medical Corps
Com14	Commandant, 14th Naval District	MCV(S)	commissioned medical officers qualified for specialist duties or qualified to fill general mobilization assignments
ComUtron	Commander Utility Squadron		
CV(S)	commissioned communication officers qualified for specialist duties	MTBron	motor torpedo boat squadron
		NAP	naval aviation pilot
		NAS	naval air station
CXAM-1	an early air search radar, one of the first such detection devices to see widespread use in the U.S. Navy	NASPH	Naval Air Station Pearl Harbor
		NCO	noncommissioned officer
		NOB	naval operating base
		NTS	naval training station
DC	Dental Corps	OinC	officer in charge
DesRon	destroyer squadron	OOD	officer of the day (or deck)
DV(G), USNR	deck officers, commissioned or warranted, qualified for general detail afloat or ashore	OpNav	Office of the Chief of Naval Operations
DV(S), USNR	commissioned deck officers qualified for specialist duties	PA	permanent appointment, when used as a suffix to a chief petty officer rating
EV(P)	commissioned engineer officers (general service) appointed in probationary status and, after qualification and transfer to EV(G), available for general detail, afloat or ashore	PatWing	patrol wing
		ROTC	Reserve Officer Training Corps
		SC	Supply Corps (Navy); Signal Corps (Army)
		SCV(G), USNR	supply officers, commissioned and warrant, including pay clerks qualified for general detail afloat or ashore
F-4-C	Fleet Reserve class comprising men transferred to Fleet Reserve upon completion of sixteen years who were serving in the regular Navy on 11 July 1925, and men who reenlisted under continuous service immediately thereafter upon completion of sixteen years	SCV(P), USNR	supply officers (general service), commissioned in probationary status and, after qualification and transfer to SCV(G), available for general detail afloat or ashore
FAB	fleet air base	SCV(S), USNR	commissioned supply officers qualified for specialist duties
HAD	Hawaiian Air Depot	SecNav	Secretary of the Navy
HC	Hospital Corps	shōtai	Japanese aviation unit of two to four aircraft, usually three
HMS	His/Her Majesty's ship		

TF	task force
T.H.	Territory of Hawaii
USAT	United States Army transport
USCG	U.S. Coast Guard
USMC	U.S. Marine Corps
USMCR	U.S. Marine Corps Reserve
USN	U.S. Navy
USNR	U.S. Naval Reserve
USS	United States ship
V6	Naval Reserve class wherein enlisted men are required for mobilization, in addition to other classes of Volunteer Reserve
XO	executive officer

Standard Nomenclature for U.S. Navy Ships

AD	destroyer tender
AE	ammunition ship
AG	miscellaneous auxiliary
AM	minesweeper
AO	fleet oiler
AT	fleet tug
AV	seaplane tender
AVD	auxiliary seaplane tender
BB	battleship
BM	monitor
CA	heavy cruiser
CL	light cruiser
CM	minelayer
CV	aircraft carrier
DD	destroyer
PE	patrol vessel, Eagle
SS	submarine

Standard Nomenclature for District Craft

YFB	ferryboat
YG	garbage lighter
YSD	seaplane wrecking derrick

Squadrons

VB	bombing squadron
VCS	cruiser scouting squadron
VF	fighting squadron
VJ	utility squadron
VMF	fighting squadron, Marine
VMJ	utility squadron, Marine
VMSB	scout bombing squadron, Marine
VO	observation squadron
VP	patrol squadron
VS	scouting squadron
VT	torpedo squadron

American Ranks and Ratings

ACOM	aviation chief ordnanceman
ACM	aviation chief metalsmith
ACMM	aviation chief machinist's mate
ActPayClk	acting pay clerk; a warrant officer
ADC	aviation machinist's mate chief petty officer (postwar)
Adm.	admiral
Aerog	aerographer, a warrant officer
AMM1c, 2c, 3c	aviation machinist's mate first class, second class, third class
AM1c, 2c	aviation metalsmith first class, second class
AOM1c, 2c, 3c	aviation ordnanceman first class, second class, third class
AS	apprentice seaman
ATC	aviation electronics technician chief petty officer (postwar)
AvCdt	aviation cadet
BM1c, 2c	boatswain's mate first class, second class
Bosn	boatswain; a warrant officer
CAerog	chief aerographer; a warrant officer
Capt.	captain (USN and USMC)
Carp	carpenter; a warrant officer

CBM	chief boatswain's mate
CCStd	chief commissary steward
Cdr.	commander
ChGun	chief gunner; a warrant officer
ChMach	chief machinist; a warrant officer
ChPayClk	chief pay clerk; a warrant officer
CMM	chief machinist's mate
Cox.	coxswain
CP	chief photographer
CPhM	chief pharmacist's mate
Cpl.	corporal (USMC)
CQM	chief quartermaster
CRM	chief radioman
CSF	chief shipfitter
CSK	chief storekeeper
Elect	electrician; a warrant officer
Ens.	ensign
1st Lt.	first lieutenant (USMC)
F1c, 3c	fireman first class, third class
GM3c	gunner's mate third class
Gun	gunner; a warrant officer
HA1c	hospital apprentice first class
Lt.	lieutenant
Lt. (jg)	lieutenant (junior grade)
Lt. Cdr.	lieutenant commander
Mach	machinist; a warrant officer
Maj.	major (USMC)
Midn.	midshipman
PFC	private first class (USMC)
PhM1c, 2c, 3c	pharmacist's mate first class, second class, third class
P1c, 2c	photographer first class, second class
Pvt.	private (USMC)
RadElec	radio electrician; a warrant officer
Rear Adm.	rear admiral
RM1c, 2c, 3c	radioman first class, second class, third class
Sea1c, 2c	seaman first class, second class
SK2c, 3c	storekeeper second class, third class
Vice Adm.	vice admiral
Y3c	yeoman third class

Japanese Ranks and Ratings

The Imperial Navy's aviation ratings did not correspond with those of the U.S. Navy. For commissioned ranks, American equivalents are used. For the sake of simplicity, Japanese noncommissioned and enlisted ranks are presented as follows: WO (warrant officer), PO1c, 2c, 3c (petty officer first, second, third class), and Sea1c (seaman first class). See the table with corresponding Japanese terminology and translation below:

Adm.	*Taishō*	admiral
Vice Adm.	*Chūjō*	vice admiral
Rear Adm.	*Shōshō*	rear admiral
Capt.	*Taisa*	captain
Cdr.	*Chūsa*	commander
Lt. Cdr.	*Shōsa*	lieutenant commander
Lt.	*Tai-i*	lieutenant
Lt. (jg)	*Chū-i*	sub-lieutenant
Ens.	*Shō-i*	ensign
WO	*Hikō Heisōchō*	flight warrant officer
PO1c	*Ittō Hikō Heisō*	flight petty officer first class
PO2c	*Nitō Hikō Heisō*	flight petty officer second class
PO3c	*Santō Hikō Heisō*	flight petty officer third class
Sea1c	*Ittō Hikōhei*	flight seaman first class

PHOTO CREDITS

Many of the photographs and illustrations in this book are official U.S. Navy documents from the collections of the National Archives and Records Administration (NARA II or NARA, St. Louis), the Naval History and Heritage Command (formerly the Naval Historical Center, NHHC), National Personnel Records Center (NPRC, St. Louis), National Naval Aviation Museum (NNAM), and Historic American Buildings Survey (HABS); some are from private collections. Photos marked 19-N, 71-CA, 72-AC, RG-77, RG-80, 80-CF, 80-G, 111-SC, 208-PU, and 226-P can be found at NARA II in College Park, Maryland. The NHHC's photos are distinguished by the NH prefix. Photos with a USAR prefix are from World War II Valor in the Pacific National Monument. Photos loaned or given by individuals are indicated by the donor's last name. Photos marked BKS can be found at the War History Library (Senshi bu) of the Japan Defense Agency, War History Section (Bōeichō Kenshūjo Senshishitsu). Photos marked PWC are from the Historic Preservation Division, Prince William County, Virginia.

Chapter One

"AN ISLAND IN PEARL RIVER COVERED WITH GOATS, HOGS, AND RABBITS"

Native Hawaiians knew Ford Island, "an irregular particle of land, no more than a mile and a quarter long and half as wide," as "Moku'ume'ume." Translation of that name is uncertain. One source has it as "island of strife," but a far more picturesque rendition is "island [*Moku*] of attraction ['*ume'ume*]," with the reduplicated element referring to a fertility rite—short-term mate swapping—sanctioned by tribal chieftains. By the 1820s, however, after the arrival of missionaries and with the increasing Western influence, the tradition of '*ume'ume* had diminished.[1]

Probably the first Western inhabitant of the island was Francisco de Paula Marín, a Spaniard born near Cádiz who deserted the Spanish navy and reached the Sandwich Islands (Hawai'i) subsequent to 1792. Marín experimented with animal husbandry and agriculture and is credited with the introduction of melons, bananas, and pineapples to Hawai'i. Fluent in several languages, he acted as an interpreter and adviser to King Kamehameha I, who presented Moku'ume'ume to Marín in about 1810, although subsequently, ownership likely reverted to the crown. In 1818 Peter Corney, an

English explorer and sailor, wrote that Marín "had an island in Pearl River . . . [Pearl Harbor] covered with goats, hogs, and rabbits."[2]

Moku'ume'ume received a new name in 1825 during a visit by HBMS *Blonde*—a forty-six-gun frigate under the command of Captain the Right Honorable George Anson, Lord Byron. While a party surveyed "Pearl River," naturalist Andrew Bloxam visited the island, hunting the abundant wild ducks and feral rabbits. After compiling a map based on the study, Lt. Charles R. Malden renamed the isle "Rabbit Island."[3]

In 1826, during a search for mutineers from the American whaler *Globe*, the U.S. Navy schooner *Dolphin*, Lt. Cdr. John Percival commanding, dropped anchor off O'ahu and fired the first U.S. salute to a reigning Hawaiian monarch—Kamehameha III—when he visited the ship. Lt. Hiram Paulding from the *Dolphin* was probably the first American to set foot on Rabbit Island. He chronicled the experience in his journal: "After breakfast we [set] off in our boat to visit a small island near the seashore, it was a half mile long, level and over grown with high weeds[;] an old

Spaniard, by the name of Menini [Marín] who had settled at Omavoora [Honolulu], put one or more pairs of rabbits upon this small island and prevailed upon the chiefs to taboo them."[4]

While America's interest lay in Pearl Harbor itself rather than the island at its center, when the U.S. Exploring Expedition, Lt. Charles Wilkes, commanding, touched at the Sandwich Islands in early 1840, Kamehameha III asked Wilkes to survey the Pearl River and the Oʻahu coastline as far as "Barbours Point." Wilkes obliged, sending Lt. James Alden and a party in two boats to carry out the work. The surveyors concluded that "ample depth" existed for large ships, "and room for any number of them." Deepening a channel into "Pearl River Harbour" would render it "the best and most capacious harbor in the Pacific."[5]

In a complicated series of transactions, Rabbit Island was sold at public auction in 1865. James I. Dowsett, the high bidder, paid $1,040 for it but a few weeks later, on 28 December 1865, sold the island to Caroline "Carrie" Jackson for the sum of $1.[6]

More than a decade before these events took place, Dr. Seth Porter Ford, a prominent Boston physician, and his wife, Maria Fowler, traveled to Hawaiʻi in the clipper ship *R. B. Forbes* to assume medical positions at the Hawaiian Insane Asylum and the U.S. Marine Hospital. Circumstances forced Dr. Ford to declare bankruptcy and file for divorce. By 1864, however, he had resumed practice and finalized his divorce. Ford met and courted Carrie Jackson and married her in June 1866. After marrying Carrie, Dr. Ford assumed ownership of Rabbit Island and supposedly renamed it Ford Island to honor his minor son, Seth Porter Ford Jr., although the timing of the name change is unclear. On 13 November 1866, only months after his wedding, Dr. Ford died, leaving behind a pregnant widow. Seth Jr. received the island in a trust upon his father's death and took possession of it in 1885 when he came of age. He sold the land to the John

Papa ʻIʻi estate in 1891. By 1899 the ʻIʻi estate had leased the island to the Oahu Sugar Company.[7]

America's involvement in the affairs of Hawaiʻi continued in the ensuing years. The United States emerged as a world power after defeating Spain in 1898 and gaining territory in the Pacific. U.S. Navy ships frequented Honolulu rather than Pearl Harbor in the opening decade of the twentieth century, but naval strategists were aware of its potential importance.

With the coming of war in Europe in July 1914, concerned Americans cast "a watchful eye to security in the Pacific"—a gaze that presaged the end of civilian ownership of Ford Island. A purchase price of $236,000 was arranged for "the transfer of Ford Island to the U.S. government for military purposes"; $170,000 went to the ʻIʻi estate and $65,000 to the Oahu Sugar Company as lessee of the majority of the island. The government gave custody of the northwestern half to the U.S. Army, which began developing an airfield there shortly thereafter.[8]

Dr. Seth Porter Ford
Pearl Harbor Naval Library, USN, via Daniel Martinez

On 9 January 1917 the War Department directed Capt. John F. Curry, junior military aviator (SC), to proceed to Fort Kamehameha on Oʻahu "to organize and command the 6th Aero Squadron." Curry arrived in Hawaiʻi on 13 February. On 23 February telegraphic instructions from the Adjutant General's Department directed that fifty enlisted men of the Signal Corps' Aviation Company A at Rockwell Field, California, under Capt. John B. Brooks (SC) be sent to Fort Kamehameha. The unit departed Rockwell on 28 February, took passage from San Francisco in the USAT *Sheridan*, and reported to Fort Kamehameha on 13 March. Orders from the War Department activated the 6th Aero Squadron that same day, and Captain Curry assumed command. Less than one month later the United States entered World War I.[9]

The unfortunate lack of aircraft obliged the squadron to remain in the fort on the windward side of the Pearl Harbor entrance channel for many months, taking "trips around the Island to occupy their time." In that interim period, however, construction began on Ford Island of two seaplane ramps, two hangars, and a hard-surfaced road leading northeast alongside twenty large garrison tents.

Not until seven months after the squadron's arrival did it take possession of the field on Ford Island, with the move occurring 25–26 September 1918 under the command of Maj. Hugh J. Knerr (AS). In the squadron's charge at that time was a three-seat Curtiss HS-2L (No. 437) single-engine flying boat and several single-seat Curtiss R-6 seaplanes. The HS-2L was the first aircraft to occupy the newly constructed hangars on the far western tip of Ford Island.[10]

Additional construction continued into 1919. The island "covered with sugar cane and coral" with decrepit cottages transitioned from "a pleasant tropical locality" into "a great landing field." By the end of January 1919 another hangar and other buildings, along with a leveled and sodded landing field, supported land planes. Officers occupied the old ʻIʻi Brown cottages while the NCOs and enlisted men still lived under canvas. On 1 May 1919, in accordance with Headquarters, Hawaiian Department, General Orders No. 7, the Army named its facility on Ford Island Luke Field to honor

1st Lt. John F. Curry, circa 1915
NARA II, 342-FH-4A-07485

1st Lt. John B. Brooks, circa 1915
NARA II, 342-FH-4A-06911

Maj. Hugh J. Knerr, 12 March 1927
NARA II, 342-FH-4A-09620

Luke Field, circa 26 June 1924. A hangar line is in place for the field's land planes. Seaplanes were already operating from Luke, one of which is visible parked in front of the left bay of the hangar at center; each hangar had two bays, giving a total storage capacity of four flying boats.
NARA II, 342-FH-3B-19548

deceased 2nd Lt. Frank Luke Jr. of the 27th Aero Squadron. President Woodrow Wilson awarded two Distinguished Service Crosses for Luke's air actions earlier in September 1918 and (posthumously) the Medal of Honor for his air action of 29 September. Luke also received a posthumous promotion to first lieutenant.[11]

Paralleling the Army's efforts to establish its airfield on Ford Island, the Navy developed its aviation presence in Hawai'i as well. Six days before Christmas 1919, Naval Air Station (NAS) Pearl Harbor began operations with Lt. Cdr. Robert D. Kirkpatrick in command. Nine officers and fifty-five enlisted men—the Pacific Air Detachment—were billeted in the Pearl Harbor Navy Yard. The location of the station itself lay near the future location of the yard's repair basin.[12]

2nd Lt. Frank Luke Jr., Rattentaut, France, 19 September 1918
NARA II, 111-SC- 23127

A joint board that met "to consider the subject of the joint use by the Army and Navy of Ford's Island as an aviation base" recommended, on 17 April 1920, joint tenancy of the island by the Army and the Navy. The recommendation presaged the transfer of the Navy's aviation assets to the island at a later date.[13]

Robert Dudley Kirkpatrick—NAS Pearl Harbor's first commanding officer—was born on 28 July 1891 in the Williamson County seat of Georgetown, Texas, and graduated with the Naval Academy class of 1913. From there he went to the *Maryland* (Armored Cruiser No. 8) and continued sea duty as executive officer and chief engineer of the *Hull* (Destroyer No. 7) off the west coast of Mexico. He reported to NAS Pensacola for flight training on 1 April 1916 and, after qualifying in both heavier- and lighter-than-air craft, received the designation naval aviator no. 48 on 7 June 1917. In November he reported to the Navy Department as officer in charge of detail and training naval aviation personnel. From September 1918 until after the armistice Kirkpatrick served in the U.S. Naval Headquarters in London. In February 1919 he transferred to NAS San Diego to become its executive officer. He then assumed command of the Pacific Air Detachment, a post he held until October 1922. While in Hawai'i he supervised the building of the air station on Ford Island, made the first aircraft flights at Midway Island and Palmyra Island, and conducted the first aerial photographic surveys of those two strategic locations.[14]

NAS Pearl Harbor on 29 October 1920, looking southwest across the Southeast Loch toward the buildings and torpedo boat piers of the Navy Yard. At left are the naval air station's two canvas Bessonneau hangars—Hangar 1 (Building 804) at right for the N-9s and Hangar 2 (Building 805) at left for the larger HS-2Ls. The monitor *Monterey* (BM 6) moored at Pier 2 at the end of Second Street served as a station ship for the Pearl Harbor Naval Station.

NARA II, 71-CA-165A-PH53

At the outset the detachment had only two Curtiss HS-2L flying boats and two Curtiss N-9H floatplanes. They were sheltered in portable Bessonneau hangars of canvas and wood construction with components cobbled together with wooden plates, steel brackets, and bolts.[15] The hangars' flimsy, baggy appearance reflected their primary shortcoming—namely, the inability to hold up in rough weather. Kirkpatrick's detachment continued operations from the station's temporary base in the Navy Yard while he supervised the work on Ford Island.[16]

The Navy's initial construction projects included the prerequisites for conducting air operations: a seaplane ramp and hangar facility (Hangar 6). Other support buildings followed, including a motor test building (Building 8), water tower, wharf, the spacious Enlisted Barracks (Building 18), and bungalows for the station's senior petty officers just west of the new Bachelor Officer Quarters (Quarters D) at the north end of Ford Island. Later, a greatly enlarged fuel system for the station was constructed with connections, fuel lines, and a pumping station that integrated the large Fuel Pier and an array of nine aboveground storage tanks. The four western

Lt. (jg) Robert D. "Kirk" Kirkpatrick (naval aviator no. 48), 8 January 1917
NARA II, 80-G-452728

tanks (nos. 56–58 and 64) provided storage for aviation gasoline, fed by lines on the west end of the pier. Lines from the opposite end fed motor fuel into five tanks to the east (nos. 59–63). The completion of the enhanced fuel storage capabilities brought the "first generation" construction of NAS Pearl Harbor to a close.[17]

Hangar 1 (Building 804) circa late 1920, with an HS-2L (No. 42) resting on beaching gear on the apron in front
NARA II, 80-G-410826, cropped

The *Eagle 40* (PE 40) moored at NAS Pearl Harbor's timber wharf, 17 April 1923, portside to. The vessel served as a seaplane tender (note the roundel to the right of her hull number) during the early years of the Pacific Air Detachment. The storeship *Hermes*—originally a schooner-rigged, diesel-powered, German-owned yacht—opposite the tender served as an auxiliary with the Pacific Air Detachment.
NARA II, 71-CA-154F-4638, cropped

Floatplane No. 11 (BuNo A2448), one of 124 Burgess-built Curtiss N-9H aircraft, lies dismantled on board the *Eagle 40*, 13 September 1921, secured on the fantail for a voyage to Palmyra Island. Note the temporary boom unique to this particular *Eagle* boat.
NARA II, 80-G-454233

Hosting a delegation from the Imperial Japanese Navy's training fleet,
Lieutenant Commander Kirkpatrick inspects an HS-2L along with his
guest, Vice Adm. Saitō Hanroku, 7 September 1921.
NARA II, 80-G-454232

Hangar 6, looking northeast, 3 December 1922,
and the apron south of the hangar
NARA II, 71-CA-153E-4382

The station's timber wharf, 2 July 1923. As completed the wharf proved inadequate, and within a year the Navy nearly tripled its length, extending it approximately 150 feet to the north, as seen here. Note the storeship *Hermes* at left center, with the *Eagle 40* at upper left, the minesweeper *Pelican* (AM 27) inboard, and the tug *Navajo* (AT 52) astern.
NARA II, 71-CA-153A-4689, cropped

Bachelor Officer Quarters D, 5 June 1922
NARA II, 71-CA-154B-4126

CPO bungalows, 7 September 1924
NARA II, 71-CA-154B-1-PH5287

NAS Pearl Harbor's Fuel Pier, 25 March 1925, showing the fueling lines. Two *Lapwing* (AM 1)–class minesweepers employed as auxiliary aircraft tenders lie inboard. At left, the seaplane tender *Wright* (AV 1) lies moored on the opposite side of the pier.
NARA II, 71-CA-154F-5361

Reserve Gasoline Tank 58 during the last stages of construction, 6 April 1925. A retaining wall about six feet tall surrounds the aviation fuel tank, but the protective earthen berms from the period just prior to the attacks on Hawai'i are not yet in place. The station plan from June 1941 shows only fencing erected, although aerial photographs from late 1941 show earthen berms surrounding groups of tanks and individual tanks. Tank 58 disappeared from the station plans sometime during late 1936 to early 1937.
NARA II, 71-CA-152F-PH13627

The fuel storage system on Ford Island, 6 May 1925. Although only one month has elapsed since the previous image, the nine tanks are all painted white. No berms are apparent—only chain-link fencing. Note the *Langley* (CV 1) moored to the Fuel Pier and a nest of decommissioned vessels astern of her.
NARA II, 71-CA-152F-PH13202

On 28 September 1922 Kirkpatrick relinquished command of NAS Pearl Harbor to Cdr. John Rodgers and reported for duty on the staff of Adm. Samuel S. Robison, Commander-in-Chief, Battle Fleet—the first aviation officer to hold such a position—in the armored cruiser *Seattle* (CA 11).[18]

Three months after Kirkpatrick's departure, Rodgers decided to move the Pacific Air Detachment to Ford Island, "entering in joint occupancy with the Army's Luke Field." Apprised of a tropical storm approaching O'ahu, Rodgers ordered the planes transferred to Hangar 6 during the second week of January 1923. After three years at the station's temporary base at the Navy Yard, the detachment left the Bessonneau hangars behind under a steadily darkening sky, happy to take possession of their more substantial hangar and quarters for the officers and enlisted men.[19]

The tropical storm swept through the islands from the morning of 13 January 1923 through the evening hours of 16 January, with the weather station in Honolulu recording gale-force winds of fifty-six miles per hour. The storm, accompanied by several light earthquake shocks, caused considerable damage on O'ahu. High winds shredded the Bessonneau hangars, vindicating Rodgers' decision to move his planes to Ford Island. As the weather moderated, Rodgers commissioned the station's Ford Island facility on 17 January 1923. The new naval air station on Ford Island was ready to support development of its air arm on O'ahu.[20]

The Army had not been idle during the construction at NAS Pearl Harbor. During 1920–23 Luke Field underwent considerable expansion. By 1923 the hangar line was essentially complete, as were the technical buildings at the southwest end of the island. They were sorely needed because the 5th Group (Composite)—originally assigned to the Hawaiian Department as the 2nd Observation Group—had among its component units the 6th Pursuit Squadron and the 23rd and 72nd Bombardment Squadrons.[21]

Less than five years after NAS Pearl Harbor's activation, the Navy was questioning whether the space allotted to it provided sufficient room for anticipated growth in the station's mission. As spacious as Ford Island appeared to be, with both the Army and the Navy expanding their operations it seemed clear that the available real estate could not support both services. By the late 1920s the Navy let it be known that it needed Ford Island in its entirety. In 1927 Rear Adm. William A. Moffett, chief of the Bureau of Aeronautics, noted in his annual report that "negotiations have been pending for some time with a view of obtaining possession by the Navy of the entire area of Ford Island." He went on to add, "It will become impossible to continue the very necessary planned development of the Station without encroaching on Army property."[22]

The Navy continued to augment its facilities through the remainder of the decade and the early 1930s. By mid-October 1925 site preparation was well under way for construction of Hangar 37, adjacent to and just north of Hangar 6. Although

Cdr. John Rodgers on 20 August 1923. He commanded NAS Pearl Harbor from 26 September 1922 to 1 May 1925.
NARA II, 80-G-419612

ramp access from the waters west of Ford Island was inadequate owing to the rocky shoreline and the necessarily awkward placement of the new hangar, the ramp and new seaplane hangar were in operation by March 1926.[23]

In response to the increasing demand on the station's maintenance facilities, by the early 1930s construction commenced on yet another seaplane hangar, an expanded system of ramps and parking aprons, and a new engine and aircraft overhaul facility. The steel frame of the future Hangar 38

Rear Adm. William A. Moffett, chief of the Bureau of Aeronautics, prepares for a flight over O'ahu on 18 August 1925. Note the two-star pennant attached to the strut of the DT-2 (BuNo A6422) in the background. The Navy assigned the aircraft to VT-2 on 12 December 1922.
NARA II, 80-G-465333, cropped

Hangar 37 (at right) nearly doubled the sheltered maintenance facilities at the station but at the cost of a substantial loss of apron space and the introduction of a cumbersome "single-lane" taxiway down to the new seaplane ramp. The hangar's awkward placement was due primarily to the requirement that the joint flying field in the center of the island (used principally by the Army) not be obstructed. Paving projects would improve the cramped situation on the aprons, but the matter would not be addressed satisfactorily until Hangar 37 was relocated during the late 1930s.
NARA II, 71-CA-153B-5622

took shape during late summer of 1932, with the structure reaching completion during the following year. To increase the available space the contractors drove pilings into the channel just offshore and extended the hangar out over the water prior to filling the area underneath for the hangar's floor and adjacent aprons to the southeast.[24]

As the 1920s progressed, the proximity of NAS Pearl Harbor's hangars and technical buildings to one another and limitations imposed by the presence of Luke Field were constant reminders of the inadequate parking aprons and seaplane ramp access. As planning went forward for Hangar 38, the Navy embarked on a program of major expansion of the station's system of ramps and aprons. By mid-1933 all the work related to reengineering the shore and paving was complete. The once jagged volcanic ledges in the vicinity of Hangars 6 and 37 had disappeared, replaced by paved areas that—although not called ramps—extended into the waters southwest of Ford Island. Hangars 6, 37, and 38 were now surrounded by spacious aprons and had three new ramps to service them.[25]

The new Engine and Aircraft Overhaul Shop (Building 39), begun in spring 1932 and completed later that year, further enhanced the maintenance capabilities of NAS Pearl Harbor. The segregation of engine and airframe overhaul activity into

a specialized building allowed more effective use of the hangars for minor maintenance and repairs. With the completion of the overhaul shop the station took on a more modern and permanent appearance, and the daily lives of the men on Ford Island were encapsulated increasingly in steel and concrete.[26]

The tempo of flight operations increased through the early 1930s as well, highlighting the need for other facilities. An annex to the Storehouse (Building 26) addressed the growing demand for parts and supplies, with provisions made by mid-1934 for a separate storehouse annex (sometimes referred to as Building 26-A) on the northeast side of the existing structure, connected to the latter via two passageways. Its completion in early 1935 more than doubled the capacity of the original building.[27]

Similarly, plans moved forward in 1935 to add yet another hangar (the future Hangar 54) to the seaplane base on Ford Island. The authorities cleared space for it by relocating two of the station's oldest buildings—the Carpenter Shop (Building 4) and the Machine Shop (Building 5)— the latter recently cleared of equipment and converted into a small land plane hangar. Hangar 54 was completed early in 1936.[28]

Hangar 38 and Seaplane Ramp 1, 4 August 1933. Three Martin PM-1s from VP-6 are in view, including 6-P-8 on the apron at left, 6-P-9 in the hangar bay at left center, and the squadron commander's 6-P-1 at far right. Note the beaching crew at the water's edge at right.
NARA II, 71-CA-153E-10518 and -10519 collage

Seaplane hangars on Ford Island and the Aircraft Overhaul Shop (right), looking west, during President Franklin D. Roosevelt's visit in July 1934. The once rough, jagged shoreline is now an array of aprons and five seaplane ramps. NARA II, 80-CF-797.32-FABPH

Two T4M-1 floatplanes from VP-6 aircraft undergo maintenance in the Engine and Aircraft Overhaul Shop on 2 June 1933. Shorn of its wings and engine, 6-P-9 (BuNo 7635) awaits attention in the background while two sailors (one standing on a barrel) balance the tail of 6-P-6 (BuNo 7625). A third sailor moves a hand-operated crane truck in the foreground. Note the caged shops and storage areas around the perimeter of the building in this view looking east. NARA II, 71-CA-154C-10471

Hangar 54 nears completion, circa June 1936. Building 5 and Building 4 are visible beyond the water tower at right. Building 3 (containing a small storehouse) and Building 2 (now a small landplane hangar) are in their original positions just behind Hangar 54, which today houses the principal restoration facility for the Pacific Air Museum.
NARA II, 71-CA-153B-BLDG40, cropped

Concurrent with the aforementioned expansion the Navy planned substantial housing construction for enlisted men and both noncommissioned and commissioned officers, for there had been no improvements or additions since the early 1920s. Preparatory work began following the summer of 1935. By the summer of 1937 the station boasted sixteen new senior officer quarters at the northern tip of Ford Island in the vicinity of Battery Adair (the World War I–era coastal defense emplacement) complementing the three existing residences from the base's early years. In the vicinity of the Fuel Pier the Navy constructed nine wood-frame two-story flats providing spacious quarters for the families of thirty-six married senior petty officers. For the enlisted men the Navy constructed a commodious three-story steel-and-concrete Art Deco barracks, a far cry from the termite-ridden wooden barracks to the west. In addition, the station received a modern firehouse that, in later years, featured a radio transmitter shack atop its tower. Closing out the major modifications on Ford Island, at some point prior to June 1937 the Navy demolished Reserve Gasoline Tank 58, leaving the eight remaining tanks to serve the station and its aviation units.[29]

The Senior Officer Quarters at the north end of Ford Island, circa 25 October 1939. Note the new shoreline pushed out to the north, behind which filling operations are under way.
NARA II, 71-CA-152A-13

Chief Petty Officer Housing seen from the southeast shore of Ford Island, looking roughly northeast. Each of the nine wood-framed buildings (seven are visible here) contained four flats, two on each floor. The Boathouse (Building 44) at far right has a puzzling provenance. A larger version of Building 44 (which incorporated dormitory space above the slips) once lay farther south, and it appears that the Navy incorporated its roof structure into the new building contemporary to this photo. Quarters 95 for the boat crews is behind and just to the left of the Boathouse.
NARA II, 71-CA-152C-PH312861

The new Enlisted Barracks (Building 55), circa 1936. The old wooden barracks have been cleared away and replaced by temporary tennis courts. The Scrub House (Building 19) at upper right was one of the station's first-generation structures.
NARA II, 71-CA-152B-2

The Fire Station (Building 42), 4 August 1936, held dormitory space for sixteen men. The tower was used to dry out fire-hoses after use. A battery room and ready room lay beneath the tower on the first floor. The vehicle entryway at left center is for the fire chief's car.
NARA II, 71-CA-152C-11908-PH39555

During 1937–39 the Navy finally demolished the old wooden Enlisted Barracks (Building 18) and erected tennis courts on the site. Additionally, NAS Pearl Harbor acquired a schoolhouse for the younger children of the station's service families. The modest wood-frame structure that came into use during the 1937–38 school year was named the Kenneth Whiting School in honor of NAS Pearl Harbor's very popular commanding officer (18 July 1935–4 June 1938).[30]

The prospect of the Consolidated Aircraft Corporation's much larger P2Y patrol bomber (as well as the later PBY) for the VP squadrons operating out of NAS Pearl Harbor entailed both blessings and curses. Although the range of the newer aircraft types exceeded 2,500 miles, their 100-foot wingspan raised hangar capacity and apron space issues. During late 1938, to clear an expanse north of Hangar 6, the Navy dismantled Hangar 37—completed only twelve years before—and stored its components for use elsewhere. The improved access to Hangars 6 and 54 greatly enhanced operations.[31]

The most significant change at NAS Pearl Harbor during 1939 was difficult to discern except for the absence of men and aircraft. For much of the early 1930s it was clear that elbow room on Ford Island was running out for both services. While NAS Pearl Harbor still had some open space to allow modest expansion, Luke Field had little or none. The Army's cramped, antiquated facilities barely supported the 18th Composite Wing, let alone any expanded mission. Accordingly, the military authorities decided that Luke Field on Ford Island's northwest shore, which included "240.78 acres with 116 buildings, including 28 sets of quarters," should go to the Navy, augmenting the 96 acres then in use as FAB Pearl Harbor. The Army was to occupy a new site between the Pearl Harbor Navy Yard and John Rodgers Airport—a base that was to become Hickam Field, an immense facility projected to exceed 2,500 acres. On 26 October 1936 President Franklin D. Roosevelt signed Executive Order 7215, which mandated that Ford Island's "areas of government-owned land . . . existing constructions and permanent installations"

Kenneth Whiting School (Building 73), May Day 1941. Interestingly, none of the children appear to be wearing shoes. Note the belfry straddling the ridgeline of the roof and Reserve Gasoline Tank 63 looming in the background.
Kinsman

be "set apart and assigned to the uses and purposes of naval reservations under control and jurisdiction of the Secretary of the Navy."[32]

Preliminary organizational changes presaged the Army's physical transition to Hickam. Reflecting a separation of Air Corps activity from the Hawaiian Department, the wing commander and his staff transferred from Fort Shafter to Hickam Field on 30 October 1937, to be followed by a similar wholesale transfer of the Air Corps' assets. On 23 January 1939 General Order No. 2, Headquarters, Hawaiian Department, relegated Luke Field to the status of "a sub-depot of Hickam Field" and cleared the way for the recently redesignated 18th Wing to move to the new facility. Each squadron's administrative supplies and maintenance equipment had to be crated and transported across the Pearl Harbor entrance channel as well. Component squadrons transferred to Hickam over the course of a year, with headquarters, aircraft and crews, and support personnel reporting from February 1938 through March 1939.[33]

By early 1940 all of the 18th Wing's units were in their new quarters at Hickam Field. Title to Luke Field's quarters, garages, squadron offices, enlisted barracks, and athletic facilities passed to the Navy on 31 October 1939, with the completed transfers being announced by Headquarters, Hawaiian Department, on 1 November. Owing to the shortage of officer housing at the NAS, the Navy put the Married Officer Quarters to use almost immediately, with the buildings designated as naval housing on the 30 June 1940 station plan.[34]

Ford Island, 25 October 1939, six days before the Army passed ownership of the 18th Wing's buildings to the Navy. This is the last known image of Luke Field prior to its partial transfer. Evidence of the Hawaiian Detachment's arrival at Pearl Harbor is reflected by the carrier *Enterprise* at right and the five heavy cruisers ahead of her at the mooring quays.
NARA II, 71-CA-152A-14

The southern portion of Luke Field's Married Officer Quarters, circa July 1936. Construction of the New Bachelor Officer Quarters and Hangar 175 required the demolition of six of these structures. Sixteen of the quarters (about four of which were duplexes) out of the twenty-two original quarters remained by 1941.
NARA II, 71-CA-152A-43

The Air Corps' Hawaiian Air Depot remained on Ford Island until the new depot and supply facilities at Hickam could be completed. Whereas the bombardment squadrons moved across Pearl Harbor with "only" their planes, men, bombsights, ordnance, offices, filing cabinets, and footlockers, the Hawaiian Air Depot's transfer was more complicated. The contents of twenty-four buildings had to be moved to new facilities that, while only two miles away, must have seemed much farther, given the logistics of transporting the immense quantity of bulky material.[35]

It was critical that the essentials be sent to Hickam to maintain the Douglas B-18 bombers there. Clearing of buildings and transfer of equipment proceeded according to schedule, and on 13 September 1940 Lt. Gen. Charles D. Herron, commanding general, Hawaiian Department, declared that "pursuant to instructions contained in War Department radio, 11 September 1939, the change in station of the Hawaiian Air Depot from Luke Field, T.H. to Hickam Field, T.H. is announced." The Army passed the depot's buildings to the custody of the Navy on 14 October 1940.[36]

Meanwhile, to relieve congestion near the seaplane hangars at the southern tip of the island, VJ-1, one of the Base Force's utility squadrons, relocated from Hangar 54 to the reconstructed Hangar 37. Reassembly of the hangar began during the latter months of 1939 just southwest of the site selected for the future operations building and control tower. Work on the building and new parking aprons continued into 1940, with the hangar itself completed by April of that year.[37]

Hangar 79, seen at Luke Field looking south, July 1936. Construction crews disassembled this structure in early 1941 and began reerecting it as Hangar 123 at Ewa Mooring Mast Field in late 1941.
NARA II, RG77

Hangar 37 in its new location north of the main hangar area, where the Navy intended it to serve as a maintenance facility for the Base Force Utility Wing, 15 April 1940. The restored Hangar 37 is currently the home of the Pacific Air Museum.
NARA II, 71-CA-153B-13600

As new owner of the abandoned Army facility, the Navy aggressively pursued plans to transform the north side of Ford Island into a home for carrier-based aviation. By 6 January 1941, demolition of the former Hawaiian Air Depot/18th Wing complex was almost complete, making way for parking aprons for the carrier air groups along

with new ordnance buildings and magazines. The old hangar line remained as it was for a brief time, although the next three months saw the demolition or dismantling of half of Luke Field's hangars, leaving the three largest—Hangars 70, 73, and 74—intact (renamed Hangars 134 and 133, with Building 130 as an overhaul shop). Hangar 75

The former Luke Field side of Ford Island on 6 April 1941, looking southwest. The depot and the 18th Wing areas are gone, leaving only a portion of the old hangar line intact. Paving of parking aprons and site preparation for the new land plane hangars is well under way.
NARA II, 80-G-357033, cropped

stood for a time, but by 30 June 1941 the structure no longer showed on the station's plan. Similarly, the Navy removed the old Luke Field dispensary, school buildings, athletic facilities, and nine senior officer quarters to allow construction of Hangars 175 and 176.[38]

Four major construction projects got under way during 1940 and early 1941, and three were finished by mid-1941: the Dispensary (Building 76), the Administration Building (Building 77), and the New Bachelor Officer Quarters (Building 78). Arguably the most important of the four projects, the station's control tower, was still incomplete in early December. Although the Operations Building (Building 84) was occupied by that time, the supporting structure for the control tower platform was not yet completed.[39]

The Dispensary (Building 76) nears completion on 1 December
1940, with only painting required for its exterior.
NARA II, 71-CA-152C-14009

The Administration Building (Building 77), 2 October 1941, looking northeast
along Berth F-1 toward Berth F-1½ that runs perpendicularly to the right.
NARA II, 71-CA-152C-14626

The splendid Art Deco–style New Bachelor Officer Quarters at the north end of Ford Island, 20 September 1941. The former Luke Field Officers Club is at lower right (later, as Building 100, used as an athletic gear locker). The Navy demolished four old officer quarters to make way for the New BOQ.
NARA II, 80-G-463877

The Operations Building nearing completion on 3 November 1941. The large control tower would not be finished until February 1942. The tower on the top deck of the Operations Building used in its stead was functional by 7 December. Note the J2F Duck at far left.
NARA II, USAR-14ND-Box85-TEMP NO 795

One important development that helped alleviate the cramped conditions at the foot of Ford Island was the construction of a hangar for VJ-2, the smaller of the two Base Force utility squadrons. Hangar 177 was actually a "recycled" corrugated iron holdover from Luke Field—Building T-77, a hangar the Air Corps had used for "bulk and miscellaneous storage." Although the small footprint and configuration of the building (approximately 66 by 200 feet) proved insufficient to service the squadron's four PBY-1s, there was ample room to maintain VJ-2's J2F Ducks, and the squadron moved into the "new hangar" on Saturday, 29 November. More impressive were the two new land plane hangars far to the northeast. With the completion of Hangars 175 and 176, the facilities at NAS Pearl Harbor seemed at last to have sufficient capabilities to service the Pacific Fleet's aviation assets.[40]

The land plane hangars along the northwest shore of Ford Island on 10 October 1941. The planes of the *Enterprise* Air Group are parked on the aprons in front of three former Luke Field hangars. Farther southwest, the clearing of debris from Hangar 75 is under way. Just to the left, a still incomplete Hangar 177 (the recycled Building T-77) has been moved and rotated 90 degrees to service the aircraft of VJ-2.
NARA II, 80-G-279375, cropped

Looking north from the warming-up platform toward the newly completed land plane hangars on the northwest side of Ford Island, 5 November 1941. A portion of the *Lexington* Air Group—Douglas SBD Dauntlesses of Scouting 2 and Brewster F2A-3 Buffaloes of Fighting 2—sits on the platform with Hangar 176 in the background and Hangar 175 at far right.
NARA II, 71-CA-153E-14823

In twenty-two years NAS Pearl Harbor evolved from a small temporary facility to an installation that extended the length and breadth of Ford Island. The expansion occurred none too soon. The formation of the Hawaiian Detachment on 5 October 1939—consisting of the carrier *Enterprise* (CV 6), two divisions of heavy cruisers, two squadrons of destroyers with a light cruiser flagship, a destroyer tender, and supporting ships—followed by President Franklin D. Roosevelt's order to retain the fleet in Hawaiian waters on 7 May 1940 in the

wake of Fleet Problem XXI, meant more planes and more ships. Japan's continued aggression in China had prompted President Roosevelt to see the fleet's presence at Pearl as a deterrent keeping the Tōkyō warlords in check. NAS Pearl Harbor's growth reflected its critical mission of supporting the Pacific Fleet's patrol wings, carrier-based aviation, and Base Force. The "island in Pearl River covered with goats, hogs, and rabbits" now boasted gleaming Art Deco buildings, cavernous hangars, and bustling maintenance facilities.

Chapter Two

"WE ARE FACING A VERY TOUGH PROPOSITION"

Being notified on 15 October 1940 of his orders to command Patrol Wing Two (PatWing 2), Capt. Patrick N. L. Bellinger secured first-class passage for himself, wife Miriam, and two younger daughters (Patricia and Eleanor) on board the Matson Line steamship *Lurline*, leaving older daughter Miriam and son Frederick in school on the mainland until June. Prior to his departure for the West Coast, Bellinger reported to the Navy Department in Washington for last-minute instructions from Rear Adm. John H. Towers, chief of the Bureau of Aeronautics, and Under Secretary of the Navy James V. Forrestal. He discussed the issue of housing on Oʻahu with CNO Adm. Harold R. "Betty" Stark and the advisability of moving his family to Hawaiʻi. Stark told him that there would be no problem securing suitable housing for Miriam and the children. Bellinger arrived in Hawaiʻi on 30 October, took the oath of office as a rear admiral—being sworn by Cdr. Logan C. Ramsey, PatWing 2's operations officer—and assumed command of PatWing 2 on 1 November, relieving Rear Adm. Aubrey W. "Jake" Fitch.[1]

Patrick Bellinger's career, deeply entwined with naval aviation, began when the Cheraw, South Carolina, native graduated from the Naval Academy in 1907. His aerial exploits came early. During the occupation of Veracruz, Mexico, in 1914 he was in the first-ever naval aircraft to take enemy fire. Lacking bombs, he settled on a bar of Octagon soap as a suitable response. In 1915 he reported to NAS Pensacola, and on 21 January of the following year received a designation as naval aviator no. 4. That same year he participated in the development of the aircraft catapult, and later he would pioneer long-distance and high-altitude flights. In 1916 he conducted the Navy's first live bombing tests and the following year performed the first machine-gun firing test and radio experiments from a seaplane, as well as experimenting with night operations.

The capstone of his early career was his attempted first transatlantic flight as the plane commander of the *NC-1*, one of three Curtiss flying boats (*NC-1*, *NC-3*, and *NC-4*) that took off on 8 May 1919 from NAS Rockaway in the New

Capt. Patrick N. L. Bellinger, Hampton
Roads, Va., 15 March 1940
NARA II, 80-G-454473

Adm. Harold R. Stark, Chief of Naval
Operations, on board HMS *Prince of Wales*
during the Atlantic Charter conference at
Argentia, Newfoundland, August 1941
NARA II, 80-G-26893, cropped

SS *Lurline* off Pier 10, Honolulu, during the 1930s
Wenger collection

York City borough of Queens. Only the *NC-4* completed the journey to Portugal (via Newfoundland and the Azores). Bellinger's *NC-1* landed near the Azores before sinking. Bellinger's duties during the interwar years included numerous staff positions related to aviation and command of the large seaplane tender *Wright* (AV 1), the aircraft carrier *Ranger* (CV 4), and the naval air station at NOB Norfolk. He brought with him the reputation of a true air pioneer and innovator.[2]

Bellinger had an amicable personality, got along quite well with colleagues, and was not the type of person who worried or sweated through details. He had, however, a marked penchant for stubbornness; "once he was convinced of something," a contemporary noted, "he never gave up on it, no matter what." In addition, Bellinger often presented his views directly, forcefully, and without apology. Lt. Cdr. Charles F. "Charlie" Coe—at one time PatWing 2's chief of staff, operations officer, and war plans officer—recalled that Bellinger "wrote the strongest letters to Washington" and repeatedly "beefed up" drafts of letters that Coe prepared for him. Bellinger possessed a strikingly youthful appearance and, despite his years and heavy responsibilities, "scarcely had a gray hair in his head."[3]

Bellinger's many and complex responsibilities—including those he acquired after his arrival in Hawai'i—required him to report to a wide range of authorities concerning different components of his command. For activity pertaining purely to PatWing 1 and PatWing 2, he reported to Rear Adm. John S. McCain (ComAirScoFor) in San Diego. In his duties as Commander, Naval Base Defense Air Force (acquired on 28 February 1941) he reported to Rear Adm. Claude C. Bloch, commandant of the Fourteenth Naval District (Com 14). With regard to patrol wings and seaplane tenders engaged in fleet operations he reported to Adm. Husband E. Kimmel, Commander-in-Chief, U.S. Fleet (CinCUS, later CinCPac). After Admiral

Kimmel took fleet command on 1 February 1941 Bellinger was in almost daily contact with him, either in person or by telephone.[4]

Although Bellinger exercised direct command over PatWing 2, on 14 June 1941 Admiral Kimmel placed him in operational command of PatWing 1 as well, which functioned as a component command *under* PatWing 2.[5] That overall command—later known as Hawaiian-Based Patrol Wings—vested Bellinger with authority over all patrol aircraft and their various attached tenders. Subsequently, Kimmel designated that force Task Force 9.[6] In the event of war, TF 9 was to deploy from Hawai'i to Wake Island and Midway Island in general support of the Pacific Fleet, with Bellinger making his headquarters at Midway.[7]

As Commander, Fleet Air Detachment Pearl Harbor, Bellinger exercised administrative authority over all aircraft based at Pearl Harbor, including two utility squadrons from Utility Wing 1 (VJ-1 and VJ-2), which, though assigned to the Base Force, were maintained at NAS Pearl Harbor. Similarly, that administrative authority extended

Rear Adm. John S. McCain, ComAirScoFor, circa 1941
NARA II, 80-G-182127

Rear Adm. Claude C. Bloch, 11 April 1940, reading his orders while assuming command of the Fourteenth Naval District.
NARA II, 80-G-410174

to planes from Marine Aircraft Group 21 (MAG-21) as well as such aircraft from the carrier groups, cruisers, and battleships that landed at the station. Those remained under the operational authority of Commander Aircraft, Battle Force.[8]

Bellinger also acquired responsibilities pertaining to the Fourteenth Naval District, then under the command of Rear Admiral Bloch, who had served as CinCUS from 1938 to 1940 before being succeeded by Admiral Kimmel's predecessor, Adm. James O. Richardson. Specifically, it fell to Bellinger to oversee aviation development within the district at Midway, Wake, Palmyra, and Johnston Islands.[9]

On 2 November 1940, shortly after Bellinger arrived in Hawai'i, Maj. Gen. Frederick L. Martin took command of the Hawaiian Air Force following his temporary promotion to major general on

1 October. He reported to the Hawaiian Department from Barksdale Field, Louisiana, where he had commanded the 3rd Wing, General Headquarters Air Force. Though senior to his counterpart Bellinger by one month, Martin paid a courtesy call on Bellinger first, and almost at once the two cultivated an amicable and close working relationship.[10]

When Martin suggested to Bellinger that they consider joint exercises, the latter jumped at the chance, remembering a recent conference with then–rear admiral Kimmel on board the *Honolulu* (CL 48) in which the incoming CinCUS expressed the wish "to arrange some unified air effort" between the services. Plans moved forward "to conduct joint training operations for the purpose of preparing our personnel to work together and to utilize opportunities to prepare ourselves for war."[11]

The demand for such interservice cooperation increased after Admiral Kimmel took command as CinCUS on 1 February. Following discussions with officers from the Army and Navy, Kimmel asked Bloch to assume responsibility for a new base defense command for Pearl Harbor. Although Bloch commented that he "already had a multiplicity of duties," he agreed that he "would willingly do anything that was possible."

On 15 February Kimmel issued Pacific Fleet Confidential Letter No. 2CL-41, which established the Naval Base Defense Force and named Bloch naval base defense officer. While Kimmel's letter thoroughly summarized his expectations regarding the defense of Pearl Harbor, it was just that—a summary that required additional plans and details at the tactical level. But it catalyzed a flurry of operation plans to facilitate implementation of its provisions.[12]

Bloch distributed Naval Base Defense Force Operation Plan No. 1-41 twelve days later on 27 February. The plan, which drew heavily from Kimmel's letter, outlined the threats posed to

Rear Adm. Husband E. Kimmel,
ComCruScoFor, circa 1940. Photo likely
taken on board his flagship, the light cruiser
Honolulu, looking aft from the bridge.
NARA, St. Louis

Brig. Gen. Frederick L. Martin, 4 April
1940, while commander of the 3rd Wing,
General Headquarters Air Force
at Barksdale Field, Louisiana
NARA II, 342-FH-4A-10185

Pearl Harbor—principally sabotage, mines outside the harbor's entrance channel, probable surprise submarine attacks, and possible surprise air attacks. Five subsequent annexes provided detailed instructions:

Annex A: Inshore Patrol Plan, by the commander, Inshore Patrol

Annex B: Base Defense Air Force Plan, by ComPatWing 2

Annex C: Anti-Aircraft Defense Plan, by the district Marine officer

Annex D: Harbor Control Post Plan, by the district operations officer

Annex E: Communication Plan, by the Hawaiian Department G-3.[13]

After distributing his confidential letter in mid-February, Kimmel directed Bellinger to report to Bloch "to prepare an air defense plan in conjunction with the Commanding General Hawaiian Air Force." At that time Bloch was working on his own operation plan that required an air defense annex. Shortly after Bloch unveiled his operation plan on 27 February, the parties responsible for the five annexes sent their documents to Fourteenth Naval District Headquarters. Bellinger forwarded Naval Base Defense Air Force Operation Plan No. A-1-41 (as Annex B) on 28 February.[14]

Bellinger's annex set in place the interservice order of battle for the air assets defending Hawai'i from attack. The "Air Force" plan established two air groups. The Search and Attack Group under Rear Admiral Bellinger included most land-based naval air assets in Hawai'i, including patrol squadrons plus the Hawaiian Air Force's bombardment and reconnaissance units. The Air Combat Group included all shore-based Navy and Marine fighters and Army pursuit squadrons under Hawaiian Air Force direction. Bellinger's annexed operation plan was similar to Bloch's in that it provided a general framework within which the Army's and Navy's air assets would operate in the event of hostile threats to Hawai'i.[15]

Bellinger's Annex B was a prelude to a subsequent document issued 31 March 1941 titled "Addendum I to Naval Base Defense Air Force Operation Plan No. A-1-41." The addendum's somewhat grandiose subtitle—"Joint estimate covering Joint Army and Navy air action in the event of sudden hostile action against OAHU or Fleet Units in the Hawaiian area"—summarized the contents well. The addendum was eventually better known as the Martin-Bellinger Report. Its details pertained to the air defenses of Oʻahu, assessed the current situation, surveyed the opposing sides' strengths and weaknesses, and anticipated possible actions by Japan. Such actions included an air attack by one or more carriers from inside a three-hundred-mile radius, with a dawn attack having the highest probability of complete tactical surprise.[16]

The added responsibilities associated with the Naval Base Defense Air Force and ongoing expansion training caused NAS Pearl Harbor some growing pains, particularly in the latter months of 1941. Foremost was the chronic shortage of naval aviators within the command, which precipitated an exchange of dispatches between ComPatWing 2 and OpNav. In the first message, on 29 August, Bellinger informed OpNav that while the 144 aviators then attached to the Hawaiian-based patrol squadrons were "just sufficient," only 138 were "useful for wartime missions"; further, orders were on hand to detach seven of those for expansion training and commissioning new squadrons. Unless otherwise directed, Bellinger had determined to delay detachment of any naval aviators from his squadrons.[17]

On the very next day, OpNav informed Bellinger that he had 171 naval aviators on board, not 144, which prompted Logan Ramsey, Bellinger's operations officer, to write to Cdr. Matthias B. Gardner—ComAirScoFor chief of staff and a Naval Academy classmate—on 3 September to vent his frustration. "We are facing a very tough proposition," Ramsey declared. Personnel issues lay at the top of his litany of woes because he knew very well that he had fewer than the 144 minimum required naval aviators, let alone the 171 quoted by OpNav. "The 25 [actually 27] invisible Naval aviators," Ramsey groused, "have not been much help to us," and additional duties such as transporting men and mail—a utility squadron function—exacerbated the patrol crew shortage.[18]

Shortages of critical equipment further hampered the efficiency of Bellinger's command. Sets of beaching gear proved almost impossible to find, a bad situation made worse by the large number of Dutch and British Catalinas bound for the Far East arriving at NAS Pearl Harbor for reinstrumentation through the fall of 1941. Approximately forty-eight such aircraft transitioned through the station in October and November; thirteen other sets of beaching gear went to San Diego. The shortage made it necessary to "anchor aircraft in the Pearl City Loch" every night. Keeping the less-than-watertight PBYs in the water for extended periods required crews standing by to pump water from the bilges.[19]

Lt. Cdr. Matthias B. Gardner while serving on the staff of ComAirBatFor, 30 May 1934
NARA II, 80-G-451364, cropped

Beaching gear problems notwithstanding, it was frustrating for Ramsey to watch the new PBY-5s bound for the Netherlands East Indies at a time when one "could reasonably expect [the aircraft] to be made available to us in quantity." During October through December, VP-21 and VP-22 limped along at Wake and Midway with their aging, short-winded PBY-3s, most of which were overdue for complete overhaul.[20]

The aforementioned issues had a particularly negative impact on the capability of Hawai'i's seven patrol squadrons to mount proper patrols in the event of hostile threats to the islands. Ramsey

estimated that with available aircraft and expected maintenance and downtime, the PBYs then on O'ahu could not sustain long-term search operations exceeding 144 degrees (far from the 360 degrees recommended in the Martin-Bellinger Report) without exhausting equipment and personnel, and that estimate presumed an ample supply of spare parts. The squadrons could sustain a full 360-degree search for only two days without a precipitous drop in available aircraft and crews. Further, it was Ramsey's opinion that three weeks of protracted search activity would effect a 75 percent reduction in material readiness. That

The southern foot of Ford Island, 1 October 1941. Note the three Dutch PBY-5s at upper right, distinguishable by the national insignia atop their wings. The three PBY-1s of VJ-2 at upper right are still in their silver and chrome yellow prewar paint schemes. OS2U and SOC floatplanes from the fleet's cruisers and battleships in a mixture of paint schemes are situated between Hangar 6 at center left and Hangar 38 at lower right. Four of the station's seaplane ramps are clearly numbered 2, 3, 4, and 5.
NARA II, 80-G-279370, cropped

worrisome forecast did not take into account the coming deployments to Wake and Midway. Nevertheless, Admiral Kimmel was depending on Bellinger's PBYs to uncover hostile threats advancing toward Hawai'i. For better or worse, and despite shortages in matériel and men, the security of Hawai'i and of the Pacific Fleet itself hinged on how effectively the Navy employed the diminishing tools at its disposal.[21]

Developments in Japan during October influenced PatWing 2's allocation of resources. The collapse of the Japanese government led by Prince Konoe Fumimaro's cabinet in October 1941 followed the premier's failure to arrange a summit with President Roosevelt to explore the possibility of a rapprochement with the United States. On 16 October Emperor Hirohito accepted Konoe's resignation. The United States viewed neither Konoe's exit nor the rise of General Tōjō Hideki to the position of premier as a positive development. The Japanese press was predictably bellicose. "Japan is master of its own fate," the *Japan Times and Advertiser* blustered, having "a free hand to proceed as it wills for the safeguarding of its own State. If it is necessary to fight America . . . Japan will not hesitate to defend its people and its interests."[22]

The U.S. government's alarm percolated down through the commanders of the armed services, particularly the Navy. Inevitably, the decisions, dispatches, and orders that followed affected PatWing 2 and the naval air station on Ford Island directly. Following Konoe's downfall, OpNav informed the commanders-in-chief of the Atlantic, Pacific, and Asiatic Fleets that "the resignation of the Japanese cabinet has created a grave situation." The dispatch pronounced "hostilities between Japan and Russia a strong possibility," and said that the Japanese held the United States and Great Britain responsible for Japan's "present desperate situation." OpNav advised the three fleet commanders to "take due precautions including such preparatory deployments as will not disclose strategic intention nor constitute provocative actions against Japan."[23]

Prince Konoe Fumimaro, Japanese premier, circa 1938
NARA II, 226-P-40-2206-L

General Tōjō Hideki, Konoe's successor as premier, at the time he formed his cabinet in October 1941
NARA II, 208-PU-199U-2

Dispatch 162203, Serial 10-340 from Naval Operations to CinCPac and CinCAF regarding implications of the Konoe government's collapse in Japan
NARA II, RG 80, CinCPac dispatches, PHLO

Admiral Kimmel and Rear Admiral Bloch complied immediately with OpNav's directives. On 17 October Bloch brought to alert status all outlying islands and the naval air stations at Midway, Johnson, and Palmyra Islands, as well as the Marine detachment on Wake Island. That same day, Kimmel ordered submarines operating in the vicinity of Midway and Wake to assume war patrol status within a ten- or fifteen-mile radius of the atolls respectively. In addition, he ordered Bellinger to send a squadron of PBYs "to operate from Midway until further orders," and to institute patrols within a hundred-mile radius. Kimmel cautioned that those forces were to take offensive action only if attacked or on his orders.[24]

In turn, Bellinger issued Operation Order 2.41 to VP-22, referencing Kimmel's order of only an hour and a half earlier "to locate possible enemy forces threatening the security" of the outlying bases. The PBYs were to coordinate with the submarines *Swordfish* (SS 193) and *Sturgeon* (SS 187) off Midway, identifying themselves to the submarines by lowering their wingtip floats. Should it be necessary to send half of the squadron from Midway to Wake, the planes there were to coordinate their patrols with the *Narwhal* (SS 167) and the *Dolphin* (SS 169). Bellinger scheduled a precipitous departure for VP-22 from Pearl Harbor for first light the following morning, with eight aircraft transporting beaching gear and the others

On 18 October 1941, one day after receiving the OpNav dispatch regarding the Konoe government, Admiral Kimmel (center) confers with his staff in Building 661 in the Pearl Harbor Navy Yard: Capt. Walter S. DeLany (operations officer) at left and Capt. William W. Smith (chief of staff) at right. The actual date of this image eluded the authors for a generation. Only after manipulating the image of the dispatch visible at the bottom of the photo were they able to match the *configuration and form* of the text with that of a message from 18 October—Dispatch 171730, serial unknown, from OpNav informing Kimmel of two Japanese merchant vessels expected to arrive at Honolulu Harbor in the last week of October. One ship, the *Taiyo Maru*, carried a Japanese naval spy as a passenger. Note the *National Geographic* map of the Atlantic Ocean atop Kimmel's desk.
NHHC, NH 57100

carrying fourteen men, presumably maintenance crews, spare aircrews, or both.[25]

The 16 October OpNav dispatch offered Kimmel limited options. The defensive measures CinCPac and Com 14 took, however, were judicious and conservative. Out of the public eye, American forces went on alert, with patrols by four submarines and a squadron of PBYs in the vicinities of Wake and Midway giving the Navy some chance of uncovering Japanese threats from the west.

Another strategic factor was at work, however—the reinforcement of Gen. Douglas Mac-Arthur's command in the Philippine Islands. Starting in September, the Army Air Force began a series of ferry flights that culminated in the delivery of B-17 bombers to the Philippines. The first flight, on 5 September, originated from Hickam Field. The aircraft that followed flew from California to Hickam Field, then stopping at Midway, Wake, Port Moresby (requiring overflight of the Japanese Mandates), Port Darwin, and finally Manila.

Two indispensable stopover points, Wake and Midway, had to be safeguarded at all costs. OpNav made the point succinctly in a dispatch to Kimmel on 17 October on the eve of the second mass flight to the Philippines: "Because of great importance to reenforce Philippines with long range Army bombers you are requested to take all practical precautions for the safety of airfields at Wake and Midway."[26]

The increasing tension between America and Japan made the need for the NAS Pearl Harbor–based patrol squadrons to acquire modern equipment more critical by the day. Following months of delay, transition of two of the four squadrons based at Pearl Harbor in late 1941 finally took place during October and November.

Preparations for the transition were well under way by late summer. VP-12 (soon to be redesignated VP-24), then assigned to PatWing 1, remained in San Diego through September for an extended period of "Upkeep [and] Re-Equipment of New Planes." In early July the unit tendered its PBY-3s, although the reequipping process took longer than expected. With half of its crews reassigned to VP-44, the remaining half of the squadron familiarized itself with the new planes. On 27 August the authorities assigned Pearl Harbor as VP-12's new home port, but left the men and their machines awaiting orders for the return flight to Hawai'i.[27]

Several complications delayed VP-12's return, one of which centered on the staff of PatWing 1. Although Cdr. Knefler McGinnis (ComPatWing 1) had already reported to O'ahu, most of his staff officers and the contents of their offices were still in San Diego.[28] Complicating matters further, schedules called for all of VP-12 to depart San Diego for Pearl Harbor at the same time. Moving the squadron's ground echelon and the wing command from California to Hawai'i proved no small matter, entailing probable surface transport of "non-flying personnel and bulky impedimenta."[29]

To expedite the move to Hawai'i, on 30 August Rear Admiral McCain asked Admiral Kimmel to make the seaplane tender *Wright* available to support transport of VP-12 and the PatWing 1 staff. In addition, with the extended overwater flights to and from California, the Navy needed to place seaplane tenders as plane guards along the route from San Diego to O'ahu to provide radio communication and weather reports to the PBYs en route and other assistance if required.[30]

Unexpectedly, the preparations also involved VP-11, already with PatWing 1 at Kaneohe. The squadron was to be the first Hawai'i-based patrol squadron to make the flight to San Diego to upgrade its aircraft, supported by the *Wright* as plane guard, and then returning in company with VP-12. Accordingly, the *Wright* got under way from Pearl Harbor and took station, waiting for VP-11's appearance at the midpoint of the flight early on 3 October. The aircraft arrived in San Diego early the next morning without incident.[31]

At 1558 on 17 October, ten days prior to the return flight of VP-11 and VP-12, the latter squadron's ground echelon and the command staff of PatWing 1 embarked in the *Wright* and departed San Diego. With the *Wright* and other seaplane tenders in position again as plane guards, twelve PBYs from VP-11 took off separately at 1330 on 27 October, with the crews proceeding independently to O'ahu—a more prudent and fuel-efficient option. Six crews from VP-12, having received their aircraft during the first week of August, took off at roughly the same time, bound for NAS Pearl Harbor.[32]

Lt. Cdr. John P. Fitzsimmons, skipper of VP-12 (soon to be VP-24), commanded the flight of eighteen PBYs (twelve from VP-11 and six from VP-12). Approximately one thousand miles out from Hawai'i the weather worsened considerably. As the lead engineer in his aircraft, AMM1c Maurice H. "Maury" Meister was in the "tower," the pylon that supported the PBY's wing, and noted the storm clouds building up ahead. Fitzsimmons decided to take his flight through the bad weather rather than going around it and ordered the aircraft to

The seaplane tender *Wright*, 15 October 1931
NARA II, 80-G-463531

widen intervals and change altitudes to avoid collision—a measure that scattered the squadron further. Plane commanders ordered all men to the windows to keep an eye out for the surface of the water and for other aircraft.[33]

Meanwhile, the *Wright* awaited the arrival of the PBYs that passed over from 0038 to 0137 on 28 October. VP-11 flew on to Kaneohe while the six PBYs from VP-12 continued to NAS Pearl Harbor, where, immediately on landing, the squadron changed its designation to VP-24. The first PBY-5s of PatWing 2 were in place.[34]

VP-23's transition into PBY-5s waited until early November, at which time Lt. Cdr. Francis Massie Hughes readied his squadron for the flight to the West Coast to replace its PBY-2s. Just prior to the 8 November departure, Bellinger took Hughes aside and instructed him to fly to Washington at some point and call on Rear Admiral Towers—a longtime acquaintance of Bellinger's—and ask the chief of the Bureau of Aeronautics "what was holding up the delivery of spares and material to Pearl Harbor?"[35]

PatWing 2's operating schedule called for VP-23 to travel in company with VP-14 from NAS Kaneohe Bay and to depart O'ahu on 8 November.[36] VP-14 and VP-23 departed Kaneohe and Pearl Harbor respectively and commenced the arduous flight to the West Coast, arriving at San Diego on 9 November. There the crews rested for several days while changing out their old aircraft. VP-14's crews took charge of six newer machines from VP-44 and three from VP-42, completing the upgrade with a delivery of three aircraft from the Consolidated plant in San Diego on 14 November. VP-23 took custody of its new PBY-5s following a 10 November delivery by Consolidated.[37]

Rear Adm. John H. Towers, chief of the Bureau of Aeronautics, NAS Quonset Point, R.I., 12 July 1941
NARA II, 80-G-392515, cropped

After performing rigorous flight tests, both squadrons judged the aircraft fit for service, departed San Diego on 22 November, and arrived in Hawai'i on the twenty-third. Hughes reported to Bellinger at NAS Pearl Harbor straightaway and announced mixed success. He had delivered his squadron safely and intact, but the jaunt to Washington had yielded negative results despite Bellinger's close association with Towers. No spare parts were in the offing because the Atlantic theater still had priority.[38]

By the end of November 1941, U.S. relations with Japan had reached a breaking point; "negotiations . . . looking toward stabilization of conditions in the Pacific [had] ceased." Just after midday on 27 November OpNav sent a "War Warning" message to Admiral Kimmel in Hawai'i and to Adm. Thomas C. Hart, Commander-in-Chief, U.S. Asiatic Fleet, that outlined the grave circumstances. The message was punctuated with a statement that "an aggressive move by Japan is expected within the next few days."[39]

With hostilities apparently imminent, both Wake and Midway were in desperate need of aircraft for self-defense. Most important, the islands were indispensable to the execution of American war plans and the Pacific Fleet's intended operations should war with Japan come. In addition, further shuttling of B-17s to General MacArthur in the Philippines would be impossible in the near term without the two advanced bases.[40]

Dispatch 272337, Serial 11-856, the "War Warning" dispatch sent by OpNav to Admiral Kimmel on 27 November 1941
NARA II, RG 80, CinCPac dispatches, PHLO

Well aware of the importance of the two atolls, Kimmel had laid the groundwork for shoring up their aerial defense weeks before. On 10 November he directed that Bellinger reinforce Wake Island with twelve PBYs, and that Vice Adm. William F. Halsey Jr. prepare to ferry twelve scout bombers and twelve fighters from MAG-21, then at Ewa. Similar plans called for further reinforcement of Midway with twenty-four PBYs, eighteen scout bombers, and eighteen fighters. The magnitude of the projected deployment was

staggering; it entailed the transfer of an entire patrol wing of thirty-six PBYs and the equivalent of a small carrier air group of Marine planes, totaling thirty bombers and thirty fighters. CinCPac expected the deployment to continue for six weeks. Logistical impediments were many because air group strength reinforcements for the two bases required tools, spares, equipment, fuel, ordnance, manpower, and additional facilities. As ComTF 9, Bellinger was to provide transport for most of the men and matériel via tenders.[41]

The Ewa Mooring Mast Field, home to MAG-21, on 2 December 1941, three days before eighteen SB2U-3s of VMSB-231 flew out to the aircraft carrier *Lexington* bound for Midway Island. At upper center are the utility aircraft of VMJ-252; some of the group's SBD-1s, SBD-2s, and SB2U-3s sit along the upper edge of the large parking apron at upper left. Along the lower edge are the F4F-3s of VMF-211 left behind when twelve were ferried to Wake Island on board the *Enterprise*. Hangar 123 (formerly Hangar 79 from Luke Field) is being erected at right.
MCHD, Larkin Collection, cropped

With preliminary arrangements for the reinforcement in place, at 1757 on the afternoon of 27 November Kimmel ordered Task Force 8 under Halsey, built around the *Enterprise*, to sortie immediately from Pearl Harbor screened by the heavy cruisers *Chester* (CA 27), *Northampton* (CA 26), *Salt Lake City* (CA 25), and DesRon 6. TF 8 was to sail west on a mission to reinforce Wake Island with twelve F4F-3 Wildcat fighters drawn from VMF-211 at Ewa. Minutes later at 1820 another order went out from CinCPac, this to Bellinger, directing him to move VP-22 from Midway to Wake Island on 1 December, with the squadron providing patrols to cover the advance of TF 8.[42]

Vice Adm. William F. Halsey Jr., ComAirBatFor, circa 1941
NHHC, NH 95552

The *Enterprise* moored at Berth F-9 along the northwest shore of Ford Island, 18 September 1941. Her presence there is unusual; she generally moored alongside 1010 Pier or in Berth F-2 on the southeast shore of the island.
World War II Valor in the Pacific National Monument, Fourteenth Naval District Collection

The following day, Bellinger issued Operation Order 981 to VP-21 and VP-22, outlining Halsey's operation vis-à-vis Wake Island and specifying the search patterns to be flown during the operation. The patrol plane crews were to

1. Cover the route and provide security for TF 8 while in the vicinity of Wake
2. Obtain information regarding possible enemy forces that posed a threat
3. Provide a ready strike force while the *Enterprise* launched VMF-211

Almost simultaneously Bellinger issued Operation Order 982 to VP-21 to take effect upon completion of the reinforcement of Wake. The squadron was to conduct daily searches from Midway to uncover threats to both Wake and Midway and coordinate its activities with the submarines operating near Midway.

In addition to ordering VP-21 to fill the impending PBY void at Midway (VP-22 would return to Pearl Harbor in December) Bellinger admonished the squadron to be prepared to shift its base to Wake Island. By 2 December VP-21 and VP-22 were in place at Midway and Wake.[43]

With measures in place to reinforce Wake Island, Kimmel took similar action to shore up Midway's striking capability, supplanting Lt. Cdr. George T. Mundorff Jr.'s PBY-3s. On the afternoon of 3 December Kimmel ordered Task Force 3, built around the *Lexington* (CV 2), to reinforce Midway with eighteen SB2U-3 Vindicators of VMSB-231. At 0728 on 5 December, the *Lexington* departed Pearl Harbor, screened by the heavy cruisers *Chicago* (CA 29), *Astoria* (CA 34), and *Portland* (CA 33) along with some of the destroyers from DesRon 5, and commenced the two-plus-day voyage to the vicinity of Midway. Once there the carrier was to launch the Marine bombers in the morning hours of 7 December.[44]

Sailors from VP-21 wash down aircraft 21-P-10 (BuNo 0851) in the midday sun, 19 November 1941, thirteen days prior to the squadron's deployment to Midway. One hoses off the PBY-3 while two others are swabbing the forward fuselage to prevent corrosion from salt and seawater; 21-P-8 (BuNo 0846) is in the background, with Hangar 6 just beyond. NARA II, 80-G-463661

The *Lexington* departs San Diego, 14 October 1941. Nearly her entire air group sits in an array of deck parks with seventeen F2A-3s from VF-2 on the bow, eighteen SBDs astride the elevator amidships, nine TBD-1s from VT-2 aft of the island, and seventeen more SBDs on the fantail. The carrier is in a much-weathered Measure 1 camouflage scheme with a Measure 5 false bow wave.
NARA II, 80-G-416362

Kimmel's reinforcement of America's two principal outlying bases to the west had only begun. Another of Bellinger's patrol squadrons needed to transfer to Midway to replace Lt. Cdr. Frank O'Beirne's VP-22, due to rotate back to Pearl Harbor on 5 December after an absence of about seven weeks. Kimmel wanted eighteen fighters at Midway and an additional strike force of twelve scout bombers at Wake as well. For the time being, MAG-21 at Ewa Mooring Mast Field was the only well from which Kimmel could draw to garner the required aircraft and crews, and doing so would nearly empty that base of aircraft. Only Bellinger's PBYs could fly to Wake and Midway on their own. The shorter-ranged fighters and scout bombers needed either to be sent via transport or flown off the two available aircraft carriers. Still, the process was under way, though with the promise of much frantic activity upcoming during December.[45]

The decisions made during October and November significantly reduced the resources—six and a half squadrons—available to Rear Admiral Bellinger. Coupled with the ongoing PBY-5 upgrades, O'ahu was down at least two to three squadrons at any given time from the critical days of October through the first week in December. On paper Bellinger had seventy-eight aircraft, but he averaged only fifty-five available over the same period. During 9–23 November 1941 that figure was down to forty-two, including machines in maintenance. With their sister units deployed elsewhere, the remaining squadrons at Pearl Harbor and Kaneohe Bay were assured of extra duty.[46]

The reinforcement of Wake and Midway also had a negative impact on the ability to mount long-distance patrols from O'ahu should they become necessary. Establishing such patrols assumed two preconditions: first, that Kimmel viewed the patrols

Land plane/carrier air group hangars and aprons along the northwest shore of Ford Island, 10 November 1941. The *Lexington* is moored to Berth F-9. The seaplane tender *Tangier* (AV 8) lies astern in F-10 with three OS2U Kingfishers on her quarterdeck. At the naval air station, approximately fifty aircraft from the *Lexington*'s air group are parked on the apron—SBDs from Scouting/Bombing 2 at center and F2A-3s of Fighting 2 to the right. The principal structures on the hangar line are, left to right: Hangar 134, Hangar 133, Building 130 (Overhaul Shop), Hangar 176, and Hangar 175.

NARA II, 80-G-279385, cropped

as essential and outweighing the risks of having no patrols; and second, that reinforcements were available to offset the inevitable wear and fatigue of the aircraft and crews. In Kimmel's mind, however, was an overarching concern to conserve his patrol capabilities for the conflict he envisioned in the central Pacific. The squadrons left behind on Oʻahu constituted a reserve that the fleet could not afford to diminish by guarding against aerial threats that Kimmel and his staff judged improbable and unlikely.[47]

Despite the warnings from Washington, neither Kimmel nor his staff expected hostilities to break out in Hawaiʻi, although submarine attacks were a possibility should hostilities commence. The principal anxiety on Oʻahu centered on sabotage, a danger that increased security could handle. No matter how close war might actually be, Kimmel viewed it as a remote possibility in Hawaiʻi.

Bellinger discontinued all security patrols during the time Special Envoy Kurusu Saburō was present in Hawaiʻi en route to Washington for meetings with Secretary of State Cordell Hull. He arrived on 12 October on Pan American Airways' Martin M-130 *China Clipper*. During the plane's stopover at Oʻahu, the American authorities waived requirements for visas, passports, inoculations, and health certificates due to the critical nature of the mission. Kurusu's arrival in the United States created a sense of complacency within the services—a feeling that Washington had control over the critical situation. Suspension of the security patrols further reinforced the sense of complacency.[48]

During late November and early December, most military leaders in Hawaiʻi remained firmly convinced that the Japanese would attack the Netherlands East Indies or Malaya in the belief that America would think it was simply not worth the trouble to intervene there. After the war, Lieutenant Commander Coe, the war plans officer for PatWing 2, said that given those circumstances and assumptions, "we believed that the Japanese would not dare to attack us." Even if Japan struck American interests, most people considered it far more likely that the Philippines would be targeted in order to secure Japan's flank. Kimmel's staff

Special Envoy Kurusu Saburō, n.d.
NARA II, 226-P-40-1092-733191

knew of no information, official or unofficial, to indicate that Japan had attained the requisite degree of development and proficiency within its naval air arm to carry out an attack on Hawaiʻi. Without such an air arm, no credible threat could exist. Additionally, the language in OpNav's 29 November 1941 message (provided to CinCPac

Pan American's Martin M-130 *China Clipper* taken by legendary photographer Tai Sing Loo, n.d.
World War II Valor in the Pacific National Monument, USAR 2186

for information only) regarding Washington's desire that "Japan commit the first overt act" diminished Kimmel's tendency to regard any threat, aside from sabotage or submarines, as likely.[49]

Although a perceived imminent threat to Oʻahu was lacking, in accordance with approved operating schedules for PatWing 2, Logan Ramsey drew up plans for "a constant daily scout" during 2–5 December as part of the wing's training regimen. In keeping with discussions by Bellinger's staff regarding probable routes of attack, it was standard practice for the aircraft on such limited patrols to search the sectors north and northwest of Oʻahu. The operating schedule called for all five

of the squadrons operating PBY-5s to participate. Because the primary purpose of the December flights was training, however, they extended no further than three hundred to four hundred miles. At no time had searches ever been conducted from Hawaiʻi or Oʻahu with a radius exceeding five hundred miles. Following the four-day period of tactical training, Ramsey set aside Saturday and Sunday for maintenance and upkeep and discontinued the training patrols "in order not to deprecate the material readiness of the planes." Hence, if the Japanese approached Oʻahu on the weekend, they would encounter no patrols north or northwest of the island.[50]

OpNav Dispatch 290110, Serial 11-928 provided to CinCPac for information, expressing the desire for Japan to "commit the first overt act."
NARA II, RG 80, CinCPac dispatches, PHLO

Antisabotage measures, however, were in place at NAS Pearl Harbor by the weekend of 6–7 December. On Thursday afternoon, 4 December, Rear Admiral Bloch called all of his commanders into a secret conference after receiving word regarding possible acts of sabotage by local Japanese. Accordingly, Capt. James M. Shoemaker, the station's commander, summoned Maj. Adolph Zuber, commanding officer of the station's Marine detachment, to his office. "Let's put on a simulated surprise sabotage attack," Shoemaker suggested, "early Saturday morning December 6." Accordingly, Zuber made the arrangements for an antisabotage drill at 0200 to involve the entire Marine detachment and a number of men from the Navy's two-hundred-man "trained seaman guard" as well. The exercise, with all hands ready to repel any acts of sabotage, "went off in apple pie order."[51]

Chapter Three

"PEARL HARBOR . . . WHERE THE HELL IS THAT?"

Young Americans who enlisted in the U.S. Navy during the 1930s did so for many reasons. Jobs were scarce in the aftermath of the Great Depression, and some wished to learn a trade in a time when higher education was out of reach for most of the population. Many enlisted simply to have three regular meals a day. Others wanted to send money home to destitute parents who had lost or were in danger of losing their livelihoods, homes, or farms. Apart from those motivations, the Navy had a romantic attraction for travel that—for all their perceived unbounded opportunities—the other services lacked. The slogan "Join the Navy and see the world!" had graced recruiting posters for decades.

The popular view of Hawai'i at the time reinforced romantic notions of a tropical paradise, and the sailors slated for reassignment there looked forward to the coming days with eager anticipation. After finishing boot camp in Newport, Rhode Island, Sea2c John Kuzma of Binghamton, New York, proceeded to Mare Island, where he learned of his final destination—Pearl Harbor. Kuzma noted with amusement that many of the younger sailors asked, "Where the hell is that?" Kuzma's knowledge of Hawai'i was not much greater than his shipmates', though, shaped largely by Hollywood films and the mental image of grass-skirted hula dancers casting leis of fragrant flowers around his neck.[1]

Taking passage with the ground echelon of VP-12 (later VP-24) on board the seaplane tender *Wright*, Sea2c Houston F. James of Brooklyn, New York, thought the prospect of the islands was "terrific" and anticipated lovely hula girls waiting for him on the pier. The reception, however, was a decided letdown. Similarly, AMM3c James L. Young Jr. boarded the O'ahu-bound oiler *Tippecanoe* (AO 21) as a passenger. The most beautiful part of the voyage came as the ship rounded Diamond Head. Young was less impressed by his new home on Ford Island, which was "just kind of a chunk of land out in the middle of the bay."[2]

The sight of O'ahu emerging over the western horizon more than fulfilled the expectations of others. Sea2c John W. Kuhn from Winnebago, Minnesota, joined the *Thornton* (AVD 11) on 8 October 1940 and was seasick the entire voyage to

Hula dancers perform for the crew of the light cruiser *Honolulu* on her first visit to the city for which she was named, 14 July 1939.
NARA II, 80-G-410161

Pearl Harbor. After graduating from radio school, he joined the PatWing 2 flag unit on 15 October 1941 and never regretted leaving the *Thornton*, which he considered—owing to her cargo of aviation gasoline—to be "a floating bomb."[3]

NAS Pearl Harbor little resembled a tropical paradise, except for "officer country" on the northeastern corner of the island with its palm trees, stately quarters, and manicured lawns. The recreation facilities for officers included a swimming pool, a clubhouse with a dance floor, and a miniscule recreation room and bar at the New BOQ (Building 78) for junior officers. A small golf course nestled among the trees was used on alternating days by enlisted men and officers. The Navy also took over the Army's older—but still attractive—duplexes and cottages on the northwest shore for married junior officers.[4]

As to the quarters for seamen and rates, the new Enlisted Barracks (Building 55) stood as the centerpiece of NAS Pearl Harbor. The barracks featured a modern galley and serving lines capable of feeding the burgeoning enlisted population. Sailors used the roof on either end of the barracks for washing and drying laundry. As for recreation, they enjoyed a large swimming pool adjacent to the barracks (with a second under construction), a tennis court, and a nearby theater. And one could always board vessels in from the West Coast to watch the latest Hollywood offerings. In addition there was a beer garden—the Blue Room—that stayed open until 2200. The station's complement could enjoy sailing and the baseball diamond and boxing ring. The men could also go into town, where there were regular efforts to provide them with a wholesome evening out. The Armory in Honolulu hosted enlisted dances, with "2,000 men, free beer, and no drunks."[5]

Housing for married petty officers posed a very real problem. Together with the ten unattached chief petty officer bungalows in the vicinity of Berth F-5, the nine four-family flats erected during 1936–37 provided housing for only forty-six families. Less senior petty officers were forced to search for more expensive housing in Pearl City, Honolulu, or Waikīkī, which posed an extreme hardship for the young families coming to Hawai'i.[6]

While most of the unmarried enlisted men from the station's complement and the attached squadrons resided in the Enlisted Barracks, some lived elsewhere on the station. Pharmacist's mates lived in a second-floor dormitory in the Dispensary (Building 76), directly above the ward and overlooking Pearl Harbor's main channel. Similarly, men assigned to the Fire Station (Building 42) had their own second-story dormitory and recreation room. Other exceptions were the forty sailors and rates who operated and maintained the station's boats and motor launches, who lived in the Boathouse (Building 44) erected over the slips. The northeasterly trade winds blowing through the open windows made life there pleasant. The Operations Building had bunk space as well to accommodate the men on duty. The sailors messed in the large barracks, with a truck shuttling them back and forth.[7]

All of the patrol squadrons based in Hawai'i flew the Consolidated Aircraft Corporation's PBY Catalina, an aircraft type in service for more than five years. Since its introduction, four subsequent variants had incorporated more powerful engines, improved crew accommodations, and a redesigned empennage and control surfaces. By early November 1941, only two of the four squadrons of PatWing 2 had upgraded to the PBY-5s, with VP-21 and VP-22 still flying PBY-3s.[8]

Three-quarters view of a PBY-5 fresh off the Consolidated Aircraft Corporation's assembly line at San Diego, 24 April 1941
NARA II, 72-AC-57D-1

Compared with the wide-open spaces of Kaneohe Bay on the windward shore, the conditions under which aviators and flight crews conducted operations at Pearl Harbor were less ideal. With Hickam and Ewa Mooring Mast Field nearby, congestion in the airspace south of Oʻahu hampered takeoffs and landings. The cramped fleet moorings and constant movement of ships in the harbor presented impediments and dangers as well.

The PBY-3 and PBY-5 variants had no landing gear and could take off and land only in the water. Eight- to ten-man beaching crews had the arduous task of attaching and detaching the beaching gear on the aircraft during launch and recovery operations. The gear consisted of two main wheel side mounts and a tail wheel steering assembly. The tires for the side mounts were filled with about 75 percent water, with just enough air to make them buoyant, although it still required two very strong men to force the wheels underwater for attachment to the hull. Attaching the tail wheel assembly required a man to swim out to the aircraft pulling the assembly behind him. With the rope around his neck, the sailor lifted the hook with a thirty-inch wand—a difficult task as the plane bobbed and weaved above. Although the work was strenuous, the men preferred it to the compartment cleaning and kitchen police duties that many young sailors found themselves performing before attaining petty officer rank.[9]

If a PBY was to remain in the water as a ready aircraft, an engineer remained on board to stand watch and to start and warm up the engines before the crew arrived by boat. Naval air stations frequently had a system of buoys in place to which such aircraft could be secured. If buoys were not available, the PBY deployed an anchor to maintain its position.

Although Bellinger's squadrons undertook no long-distance reconnaissance in the waning months of 1941, fleet operating schedules placed the squadrons in a rotation to provide security patrols covering the approaches south of Oʻahu

and the operating areas in use by the fleet. Prior to takeoff the crews received information on the location of all U.S. submarines in the vicinity, with orders to bomb any others. Generally, the ten- to twelve-hour flights began when there was enough daylight to take off safely. Depending on the size of the operating area and how many areas were to be covered, up to seven armed aircraft flew a variety of out-and-back patterns at approximately 1,500 feet to ensure that the seas were clear of submarines.

Although crews incorporated night flying into their weekly schedules, dawn patrols were "strictly a daytime business." They reflected Admiral Kimmel's concern that Japanese submarines might venture into Hawaiian waters in the event of hostilities, even if such were to break out in the Far East. Generally, U.S. submarines were authorized to operate submerged only in areas C5, C7, U1, M20, M21, and M24, which encompassed the waters off Molokaʻi, Maui, Lānaʻi, and Kahoʻolawe. Evidence of submerged submarines anywhere else was a serious matter.[10]

As a result of the Vinson Bill of 1938 and the need to prepare for future armed conflict, the Navy created new patrol squadrons in the years before World War II. "Expansion training" addressed the daunting task of securing qualified crews for each squadron. When the authorities deemed Bellinger's crews to be fully qualified, the men were subject to rotation stateside to form cadres for new squadrons being organized there. Although training flights near Oʻahu prepared PatWing 1 and PatWing 2 for war, those operations also served as expansion training and were critical for building the new patrol squadrons. Indeed, it was that mission that Kimmel and Bellinger viewed as most critical for their patrol squadrons to fulfill during 1941, and Bellinger incorporated a great deal of training into the flight schedules. Departure of experienced crews, however, was detrimental to unit cohesion and preparedness as a whole. Should

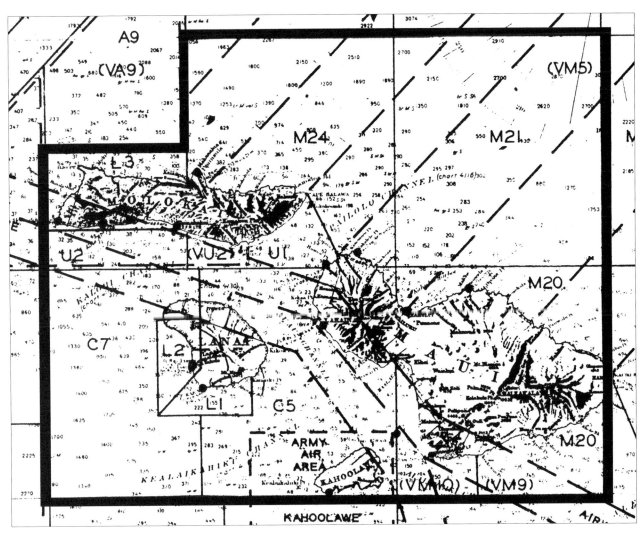

Operating Areas C5, C7, U1, M20, M21, and M24, where U.S. submarines had authorization to operate submerged
Wenger

the flow of *incoming* inexperienced aviators be disrupted, serious consequences would ensue, an issue that caused Bellinger and Ramsey much concern.[11]

In spring of 1941 Bellinger instituted a seven-day workweek, and the custom of securing for weekends came to an abrupt halt. The change affected the daily routines for those in his command, with portions of the squadrons, on a rotating basis, working seven days every week. During 5–11 November the absence of VP-14 and VP-23—then exchanging aircraft at San Diego—and VP-22's advance base operations at Midway left only four patrol squadrons on O'ahu, requiring additional duty to cover security patrols and provide ready duty crews.[12]

Operating Schedule for VP-21, Week of 5–11 November 1941

5 November	Free machine-gun practice in Operating Area VC10 (60 miles south of O'ahu)
6 November	Free machine-gun practice in Operating Area VC10
7 November	Ready duty
	Free machine-gun practice in Operating Area VC10
8 November	Dawn patrol
9 November	Ready duty
10 November	Dawn patrol
	Master horizontal bombing, qualification practice in Operation Area L1 (south of Lāna'i)
11 November	Ready duty
	High-altitude horizontal bombing in Operating Area L1
	Antisubmarine bombing in Operating Area VC10

Despite the need for a full schedule, Bellinger considered it unwise to operate planes and crews more than once every three days. RM1c James A. "Jim" Caudel of the station thought work demands prior to the war rather light for flight crews because he pulled duty every fourth day and every fourth weekend—and this taking into account the "rigorous" seven-day workweek. Among the station's company, SK3c Jacob Rogovsky considered NAS Pearl Harbor good duty with "regular working hours [and] not too frequent watches." Battle station drills—usually during daylight—comprised only a muster at the Supply Department with no additional activities.[13]

Although everyone stayed busy at NAS Pearl Harbor, the aviation squadrons were on a "tropical schedule" with shortened hours. Personnel mustered at 0700 and secured at 1200 except for the duty section (one-fourth of the squadron), which had twenty-four-hour duty. Tropical hours very closely paralleled similar practices in the Royal Air Force in the Far East and seem not to have reflected the urgency of the international situation in either location.[14]

For the men of Ford Island—particularly the aviators and aircrews—liberty policies were quite liberal. Those who received flight pay tended to have more ready cash, and there were few restrictions on leaving Ford Island while off duty. Each squadron had four duty sections, with three having liberty and one standing watch. Hence, one could go on "three in four liberty" three days out of four after working hours, having to stay on board to stand watch on the fourth day. The men also had three out of every four weekends off (unless they had flight duty), with the duty section covering the weekend chores. For those not on duty spanning a period of two days, "overnight liberty" extended from 1200 until 0700 the next morning.[15]

Sailors on liberty took the ferry to the Navy Yard and then boarded buses for Honolulu, where they found that good times could be expensive.

A man might go ashore in San Diego with only twenty-five to fifty cents in his pocket, but such was not the case in Honolulu. Men lacking money or wishing to save it could always go to the Blue Room on the base for a cheap beer. The station on Ford Island had hobby shops, a recreation center, a big swimming pool, and sports teams. On a weekend liberty, meals and a place to stay required about five dollars, so most of the men opted for a quick three- or four-hour trip into Honolulu.[16]

The sailors knew Honolulu as a "wild, wide open town"—in certain areas, at least—although the military closely monitored their decorum. Many congregated in their favorite bars on Hotel and Beretania Streets. Some went as far as Waikīkī for dinner at Trader Vic's on Ward Avenue or Lau Yee Chai's at Kalākaua and Kūhiō. The nature of the public transportation network and Oʻahu's geography made the YMCA a popular starting point. Men referred to the area around the Y and the Black Cat Café across the street as "Pick-Up Alley," the first "point option" for securing an impromptu date. For some, however, downtown Honolulu did not hold much appeal; hawkers everywhere were after their money. At the more distant nightspots in Wahiawā or Kailua the cordial locals seemed more eager to please. Waikīkī Beach was far more fun, and that was where most of the girls were, but many sailors avoided Honolulu and Waikīkī altogether when the fleet was in on the weekends because they were too crowded.[17]

Sailors were not averse to going stag with another friend who had a date. Sea1c John N. Delia's activities during liberty in Honolulu and Waikīkī mirrored those of many servicemen. His and his friends preferred to get off the bus at Hotel and Nuʻuanu Streets—five blocks *before* the YMCA. They started the evening at Bill Lederer's bar, principally because Delia's skipper, BM1c Mike Stapleton of the *YSD 19*, dated Julia Garcia, one of Lederer's barmaids. Most liberties featured visits to the beach and one or more of the many bars and restaurants, such as the Wagon Wheel on

2062 Kalākaua Avenue. After a night out, sailors often grabbed a quick breakfast at the Black Cat Café before catching a late bus back to Pearl Harbor.[18]

Liberty policy for the Marines was not as generous as the Navy's; they received liberty only every other weekend. Both sailors and Marines were forbidden to wear civilian clothing, and each man was expected to be spotless. They liked to go into town to get away from barracks food, which could be repetitive. It was also nice to be waited on rather than trudging through a mess line.[19]

Vehicles, soldiers, sailors, and Marines crowd the entrance to the YMCA on Hotel Street. The absence of wartime blackout measures applied to the vehicles' headlights dates this photo probably to 1941.
Wenger

Lobby of the YMCA on Hotel Street. Note the Oriental rug, ceramic tile wainscoting, and waxed tile floor.
Wenger

Downtown Honolulu looking north from the Aloha Tower at the foot of Fort Street, circa 1940
Weeks

Lau Yee Chai's, a well-known Chinese restaurant in Waikīkī, was a popular dining destination for many sailors, soldiers, and Marines on liberty.
Wenger

The heart of Waikīkī Beach between the Royal Hawaiian Hotel and the Moana
Hotel, circa 1941, with Club Moana just beyond the beachgoers at left
USAR 1596

Two sailors on Waikīkī Beach on the east side of Club Moana, circa 1940
Weeks

A quartet of sailors on liberty stroll past the Waikiki Tavern and adjoining arcade on a sunny afternoon. The tavern was part of the Waikiki Inn (out of the picture at left) on the shore at 2437 Kalākaua Avenue.
Wells

American soldiers, sailors, and Marines alike tended to be dismissive of Japan's military prowess and capabilities. Most of the discussion in VJ-2's squadron bull sessions centered on Germany. The fathers of many younger sailors were veterans of World War I, and many of the senior chiefs had served in the conflict as well. There was a general—and correct—perception that Germany would be no pushover in a war with America. For a multitude of reasons, however, ranging from racial prejudice to ignorance, the men had little regard for the Japanese navy. One sailor boasted that the war would be over in two months because the Imperial Japanese Navy "was made out of tin and you'd sink it all in thirty days."[20]

Others, however, had a more realistic view of worldwide events. Although some of PhM2c

Robert J. Peth's acquaintances on Ford Island felt uneasy, the holiday-like tropical routine smoothed away the rough edges of their anxiety. Others, however, sensed big trouble ahead. In discussions with friends prior to his 8 July 1940 enlistment, Sea1c John Kuzma concluded that the possibility of war was real, and that the probability of American involvement was high. That feeling never left him, the soothing Hawaiian breezes notwithstanding.[21]

The officers assigned to the station and Pat-Wing 2 held differing views as well, with those of Charlie Coe reflecting the thinking of many fellow officers. He had concluded that the Japanese were really after Southeast Asia and the Dutch East Indies. An attack on the United States would provoke a war that would interfere with that strategy. And even if the Japanese were to strike a blow against America, it would be most logical to hit the Philippines to clear Japan's flank. Given those circumstances and assumptions, Coe believed "the Japanese would not dare to attack us. . . . We on Oahu were not worried about the Japanese."[22]

As for ComPatWing 2, Pat Bellinger shared the opinions of many of his fellow officers that an aerial attack on Pearl Harbor was highly improbable, although he realized that Japan's air arm was highly experienced in actual wartime conditions. In any case, he "did not expect, as a probability, that an attack would be made on Oahu as the opening event of a Japanese–United States war." Mirroring Kimmel, he feared Japanese submarine attacks and sabotage. Kimmel never discussed with Bellinger the dispatches regarding the Konoe government and the "War Warning," even in their meetings regarding the role of the patrol squadrons in the reinforcement of Wake and Midway. The perceived remoteness of a direct aerial threat fit hand in glove with Bellinger's most immediate and pressing duty in Hawai'i—expansion training.[23]

During the weekend of 5–7 December, regulations authorized the station's commander, Capt. James M. Shoemaker, to allow 50 percent of his men to be on liberty, with ferry service and the station's boats providing transportation to the Navy Yard. Heading into the first weekend of December, the men of NAS Pearl Harbor welcomed their chance at liberty with gusto.[24]

F1c Henry de Coligny had big plans for the weekend. Before leaving he checked in with an envious Lt. William R. Kane—the station's officer of the deck—who was on duty from 0800 Saturday until 0800 on Sunday. "I just wish to God I didn't have duty tonight!" Kane lamented as he signed out de Coligny and his friend AM2c Louis J. Raiola.

Raiola's and de Coligny's destination was the residence of ACMM (PA) (NAP) Edward A. O'Donnell, also of the station, who lived east of Diamond Head at 4995 Kalaniana'ole Highway with his wife, Madeline, in a house overlooking

the ocean. Enjoying a few beers on the lanai, the sailors lingered until about 0200 before returning to the station, where they parted ways. De Coligny returned to the Boathouse, stripped down to his shorts, opened the window, and slipped into his lower-level bunk. Aided by the effects of the beer, he was soon fast asleep.[25]

John Kuzma and his friend F3c Francis M. Burke went on a double date that Saturday. Both men had civilian clothes stashed in town. Kuzma kept his civvies in a locker that he rented by the month at Battleship Mack's. Burke's girlfriend was Victoria "Vicki" Aki, a pretty Hawaiian-Chinese girl who worked as a dance instructor. Kuzma dated one of her cousins. The couples went dancing and practiced their steps—good, clean fun—and afterward stopped for a snack. The date ended at about 2230, but Kuzma walked over to the Black Cat Café for drinks before returning to the YMCA at about midnight.[26]

Earlier, on Friday, 5 December, VP-22 returned from its advance base deployment to Wake and Midway. Rather than "painting the town" after their extended absence from civilization, most of the men stayed on base. Their PBY-3s had to be secured, and all of the men needed showers and shaves. Most waited and went into town Saturday night instead because Lieutenant Commander O'Beirne had secured the squadron until 0700 on Monday. Partying was the last thing on the mind of Ens. James E. McColgan, D-V(G), USNR, who later recalled little about the tense return to O'ahu, except that it was an "eighteen-hour return flight in heavy weather." His crew landed at midnight. Absolutely exhausted, everyone hit the sack. Not waiting for Saturday night, at 1300 that afternoon AMM3c James L. Young Jr. and some friends visited Waikīkī and "had quite a few drinks." Coming back from Midway flush with cash, the men discussed staying overnight in town but decided to return to Pearl Harbor, arriving at the station at about 0100 on Sunday.[27]

Many families—including those living off base—also took advantage of the weekend. On Saturday, PhM1c Paul J. Sherrard, his wife, Alma, and their two sons, Paul Jr. and Charles, drove into Honolulu from their quarters on 124 Main Street in the naval housing near Hickam to pick up supplies for a picnic at Waikīkī and to purchase a bathing suit for Alma. Y3c Harold R. Givens from the *Arizona* (BB 39), the brother of Alma Sherrard's closest childhood friend, accompanied them. He had spent the night with the Sherrards and planned on spending Sunday with them at the beach. Alma asked him to stay overnight, but he declined, saying he had to return to his ship for a card game, but he promised to be back before lunch on Sunday. With the trip to Waikīkī in the offing, there was no partying or late-night carousing for the Sherrards—just shopping.[28]

More adventuresome Waikīkī residents RM1c Jim Caudel and his wife Dora met friends at Trader Vic's. They dined elsewhere, however, probably driven away by the crowds. Their revelry ended at about 0200 or 0300.[29]

Other men had duty on Saturday or Sunday, including Seaman 1st class Kuhn, who was to stand a six-hour watch from midnight to 0600 on both Saturday and Sunday. After coming off duty on Saturday morning he spent a few hours in Honolulu, then returned to the barracks, wrote a few letters, and went back to bed at 1800. Reporting to the Communications Center shortly before midnight, Kuhn guarded the aircraft-to-ground circuit and talked to a few planes aloft on routine night training, but "it was a slow night."[30]

In Quarters K in the senior officer housing on the north end of Ford Island on the evening of 6 December, Rear Admiral Bellinger was bedridden with influenza and had been since the previous Tuesday, having missed an important and eventful week. The schedule called for exercises off Hilo

during 2–5 December to test the capabilities of the CXAM-1 radar on board the *Curtiss* (AV 4)—Task Force 9's flagship—and to test the mettle of Bellinger's PBYs in attacking an enemy "aircraft carrier," portrayed by the *Curtiss*. Cdr. Knefler McGinnis stood in for his ailing chief. Bellinger's greatest disappointment, however, was that, for a second time, the PatWing 2 staff had postponed a special dinner that they had arranged in his honor at the Royal Hawaiian.

Logan Ramsey had acted as Bellinger's second in command, conferring daily with Bellinger at his residence and bringing in papers for the admiral's signature. Recovering from an exhausting full week of additional duties, Ramsey and his family relaxed with dinner guests at his quarters. As his friends departed, Ramsey quipped: "Well, let's hope the Japs wait until after Christmas before they start raising hell in the Pacific." He then turned in for the evening.[31]

Lt. Cdr. Knefler McGinnis at Coco Solo, Canal Zone, 12 October 1935, three days prior to his record-breaking flight of XP3Y-1 (BuNo 9459) to San Francisco
NARA II, 80-G-451369, cropped

Chapter Four

"FROM PEACE TO HELL IN A MATTER OF SECONDS"

Sunday morning began early for VP-24's AMM2c Joseph H. Strittmatter, who arose at 0300 for breakfast and reported to the hangar to prepare his standby aircraft for flight. Afterward Strittmatter stayed in the hangar to await the return of the four PBYs assigned to fly that morning and decided to lay down on a cot in his PBY-5 and go back to sleep.[1]

The dawn patrol routine called for the master-at-arms to awaken the crews at 0300. AMM1c Maurice H. Meister had the responsibility to ensure that his enlisted crewmembers were up, which took time because the men slept in the barracks by rating rather than by squadron. After breakfast, it was down to the hangar to check the planes and receive orders. Usually the aircraft were aloft by about 0500, but takeoff was later this particular morning.[2]

Preliminary orders called for four aircraft from VP-24 to search for unidentified submarines near O'ahu. After taking off at 0700, the crews received further orders to fly to the vicinity of Maui and practice visual communications with the submarine *Gudgeon* (SS 211) in Operating Area C5 off Lāhainā Roads. After the crew located the sub, the lead radiomen was to "talk" with the boat from the side blister using a blinker light.[3]

The *Gudgeon* had cleared Pier 3 at the Submarine Base three days earlier for the twelve-hour voyage to Lāhainā Roads, anchoring in Berth O-125 at 1542. On the following afternoon the submarine carried out ship-handling exercises with the *Seagull* (AM 30). On 6 December the crew worked with four groups of PBYs through the morning, forenoon, and dogwatches, beginning each scheduled evolution with a "quick dive." Sunday, 7 December, proved no day of rest. The *Gudgeon* departed Lāhainā Roads at 0740 and proceeded to her assigned operating area. At 0806 the boat's executive officer logged the approach of three planes, and the scheduled exercises began.[4]

Back on O'ahu, NAS Pearl Harbor began a new day. CRM (PA) Thomas E. Farrow had duty in the control tower atop the Operations Building (Building 84) on Ford Island that morning. Although he resided in 'Aiea, Farrow had spent the previous night in the six-bunk barracks in the northeast wing of the building's first floor, adjacent to the garage that opened onto the parking apron. Rising at 0530, he went to the chiefs' mess

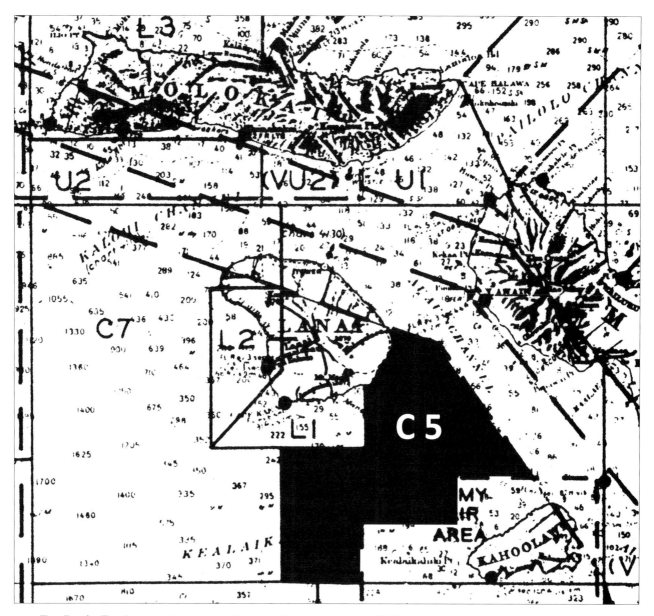

The Pacific Fleet's operating areas in the Hawaiian Islands, circa 1941.
Note the inverted color denoting Operating Area C5 southwest of Maui.
NARA, RG 38

for a leisurely breakfast with plenty of time to return to the tower by 0800.[5]

AMM3c Earnest A. Cochran's time on watch was complete, with the VJ-2 mechanic having stood duty in Hangar 177 from 0400 to 0800. Just prior to the arrival of his relief, AM1c Ralph E. "Whitey" Flora came in "loaded," and Cochran helped his boisterous buddy to a bunk in the hangar. Men not going into town often hit the sack at the hangar rather than trudge to the barracks

one-half mile away. Since Cochran planned to go into Honolulu after 0800, however, he walked to the Enlisted Barracks and went straight to his bunk on the lanai on the third deck.[6]

Sea2c Lester E. Robinson, with mess duty in the Enlisted Barracks, rose early to prepare breakfast for early risers, although many men preferred to sleep in on Sundays. Robinson intended to go down to Hangar 54 after his mess duty and meet Sea2c Glenn F. Rickard Jr., a close friend who was just coming off watch at the hangar, where they planned some ping-pong to while away the hours.[7]

In Quarters 50-B at Ford Island's CPO Quarters, CSF (PA) Albert H. Molter was busily "swabbing the deck" while his wife, Esther, four months pregnant, prepared waffle batter for breakfast. Later that day the couple planned to host some Army friends they had met at a rest camp in Kīlauea. The Molters lived in one of Ford Islands' two-story quarters with flats to accommodate four families. The other three families in Quarters 50 were those of ACM (PA) Iver Reinikka in 50-A, CQM (PA) Franklin H. Lemmon in 50-C, and CRM (PA) Allan G. MacKay in 50-D. Only MacKay and Reinikka were on watch that morning.[8]

In Pearl City, AMM1c Hubert D. "Dale" Gano was off duty at the station on Sunday morning. He and his wife, Johnie, married for only four months, had stayed in bed later than usual. Their main decision was whether to spend a lazy morning in their 54 Beryl Street cottage or go to church in Honolulu. Dale Gano preferred to be a layabout while Johnie wanted to go into town.[9]

Back on Ford Island, the officers of the station's Supply Department were to go on or off duty at 0800. Scheduled to stand the forenoon watch as supply duty officer, Lt. Jay H. Mattson, SC-V(S), arrived on Ford Island by launch at 0745 and immediately proceeded to the Storehouse, where he relieved Lt. Joseph B. Musser, SC-V(S). After checking out, Musser boarded a covered launch at Landing C together with a liberty party.[10]

Ens. "D" Arnold Singleton, A-V(S), the station's fuel officer, stood watch by the oiler *Neosho* (AO 23) at the Fuel Pier (Berth F-4). He and the men from the fuel division prepared to take "back suction on the line through which 400,000 gallons of aviation gasoline had been received during the night." Since his arrival in July 1941, the 1935 Miami of Ohio graduate had drawn on his previous experience as a terminal supervisor and assistant to the manager of Valvoline Oil Company in Edgewater, New Jersey.[11]

Lt. Leroy F. Watson, the station's communication officer, left wife Dorothy and daughter Beverly at Quarters 117 on Ford Island's northwest shore, arrived at the Administration Building at 0750, and checked his department. The supervisor on duty reported "no unusual traffic or occurrences."[12]

Captain Shoemaker arose in Quarters A on the north end of Ford Island at about 0700. His two messmen prepared a quick breakfast while he dressed for his golf date at the Oahu Golf Club with Capt. Irving H. "Hall" Mayfield, the Fourteenth Naval District intelligence officer.[13]

Although PatWing 1 had the morning's security patrols south of O'ahu, three of PatWing 2's squadrons stood prepared to lend assistance should the need arise. Their condition of readiness stood at Baker 5, which specified a minimum of 50 percent of aircraft being ready on four hours' notice. Both VP-22 and VP-23 exceeded that threshold, with almost their entire complements ready for flight within the required four-hour period.[14]

Only one of the five PBY-5s in service from VP-24 was present at the station and was in fact the ready aircraft for PatWing 2, prepared to take flight on thirty minutes' notice. The other four VP-24 PBY-5s had taken off earlier that morning to conduct training exercises with the *Gudgeon* at Lāhainā Roads. The sixth VP-24 machine was undergoing structural changes in Hangar 54.[15]

At Midway VP-21 was on a war footing, with seven PBY-3s launched at 0630. Five aircraft conducted searches 450 miles out from the island in a sector spanning 120–170 degrees to provide security for Task Force 8 returning from Wake Island and for Task Force 12 then closing on Midway. Plans called for the *Lexington* to launch eighteen SB2U-3s from VMSB-231. Two of the seven PBYs in the air were to rendezvous with the carrier, patrol during launch, and escort VMSB-231 to the atoll. In addition, VP-21 retained its four remaining PBYs, each armed with two 500-pound bombs, as a ready strike force on ten minutes' notice.[16]

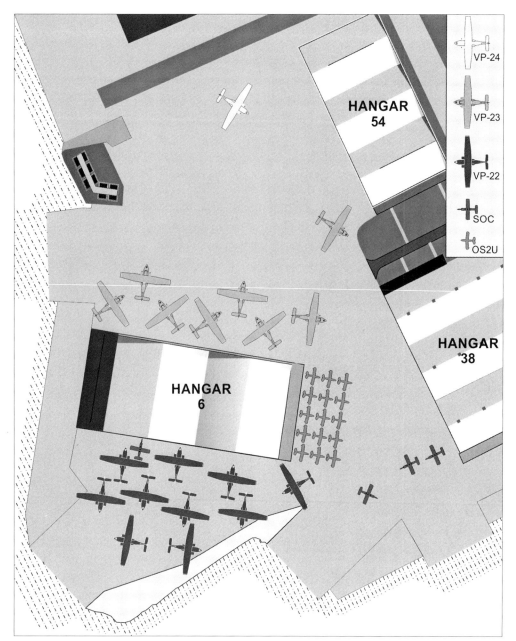

HANGAR
54

VP-24

VP-23

VP-22

SOC

OS2U

HANGAR
38

HANGAR
6

The seaplane hangars at NAS Pearl Harbor, showing the approximate locations of aircraft on 7 December 1941. Prewar aerial photographs indicate that the station arranged OS2Us and SOCs in columns extending from the east side of Hangar 6. There were approximately three PBYs in Hangar 6 and five aircraft jammed into Hangar 54.
Di Virgilio

As the yellow light of a serene dawn spilled peacefully over the buildings on Ford Island, trouble lay, quite literally, just over the northern horizon. With the acquiescence of Emperor Hirohito, Japan's military government had decided to wage war with the United States, Great Britain, and the Netherlands. To ensure America's noninterference with Japan's plans for conquest, the Imperial Japanese Navy (IJN) abandoned the core of its long-held naval strategy. Rather than lying back to await an all-out battle with the Americans in Japan's home waters, the IJN was to go on the offensive and eliminate at the outset the potential of American naval intervention during the conquest of the "Southern Area." To that end, a powerful force of six aircraft carriers supported by battleships, cruisers, destroyers, and submarines had advanced from the Kuriles across the stormy northern Pacific and then steamed south to within two hundred miles of the Hawaiian Islands with the intent of immobilizing the Pacific Fleet.

NAS Pearl Harbor viewed from the southwest at an altitude of 2,800 feet on 10 October 1941. The *Enterprise* lies in Berth F-2 at right on Ford Island's southeast shore. The hangars of the seaplane base are at lower right, and the hangars and maintenance facilities supporting the carrier air groups are at left. NARA II, 80-G-279375, cropped

Under the command of Vice Adm. Nagumo Chūichi, *Kidō Butai*, the Carrier Striking Force, launched a massive initial strike of 183 aircraft starting at 0555 on 7 December 1941, led by Cdr. Fuchida Mitsuo. Almost half of that force—forty torpedo bombers and forty-nine horizontal bombers—had as its objective the American battleships and aircraft carriers. A force of forty-three fighters was to provide cover, strafing Oʻahu's airfields if circumstances permitted.

The remaining fifty-one dive-bombers were to attack American air power at Wheeler and Hickam Fields and NAS Pearl Harbor. Responsibility for

attacking those targets rested on Lt. Cdr. Takahashi Kakuichi, who exercised overall command of the dive-bomber force from the aircraft carriers *Shōkaku* and *Zuikaku*, composed as follows:

- *Zuikaku* dive-bomber group—Lt. Sakamoto Akira, twenty-five aircraft; target: Wheeler Field, Army fighter base
- *Shōkaku* dive-bomber group—Lt. Cdr. Takahashi Kakuichi, twenty-six aircraft; target: Hickam Field Army bomber base and NAS Pearl Harbor Navy patrol bomber base

Hickam Field and NAS Pearl Harbor were top priorities to ensure the safety of the Japanese carriers north of O'ahu. Two of Takahashi's subordinate nine-plane divisions, or *chūtais*, were to bomb Hickam while the nine lead aircraft under his direct command attacked NAS Pearl Harbor.

After arriving at a position approximately five miles north-northeast of Kahuku Point shortly before 0740, the inbound strike on O'ahu awaited Fuchida's order to deploy.[17] Before giving that order Fuchida had to know whether a surprise attack was possible, with the answer driving the deployment north of the island. He had little time to think, because cloud cover north of O'ahu delayed visual acquisition of the island until the last moment, but empty skies indicated that surprise had been achieved. Satisfied, Fuchida instructed his radioman, PO1c Mizuki Tokunobu, to tap out the general deployment order, the first radio message to come from the aircraft in the inbound attack wave:

··−·· ·−−· −−− "ト-ツ-レ" (*to-tsu-re*),

"Assume preliminary charge formation."[18]

To reinforce the order visually and indicate his conclusion that surprise had been achieved, Fuchida pulled back the center canopy of his Nakajima Type 97 to fire a single Black Dragon signal flare. On that signal Lieutenant Commander Murata's torpedo bombers were to traverse the Ko'olau Range and descend into the harbor area first, followed by the dive-bombers striking the airfields. Fuchida pointed the flare pistol into the air at 0740 and squeezed the trigger.[19]

To Fuchida's left, Takahashi's southbound formation of fifty-one Type 99 carrier bombers deployed, setting up attacks on three of O'ahu's largest airfields. In advance of actual landfall over the island, Takahashi led his two groups into a sharp, climbing turn to starboard, passed over the

Page of a codebook retrieved from Japanese aircraft wreckage after the attacks on O'ahu. In the box at upper right is the code word *to-tsu-re* for the command "Assume preliminary charge formation."
NARA, RG 80, via Dr. Mulligan

strike force, and ascended to a standby altitude of four thousand meters. Takahashi was to coordinate the approach of the *Shōkaku*'s bombers so that their attacks on Hickam Field and NAS Pearl Harbor commenced *after* Fuchida's horizontal bombers struck Battleship Row. In contrast, Lt. Sakamoto Akira's group from the *Zuikaku* was free to attack the American fighter base at Wheeler as soon as Murata's forty torpedo bombers flew past it.[20]

The original deployment plan dictated that after climbing to their standby position the dive-bomber units were to advance straight into their respective target areas from a position about twenty miles northeast of (or upwind from) the airfields. The late visual acquisition of the island, however, created problems north of Oʻahu. At the time Fuchida ordered the deployment, not only was Takahashi already within the area specified from which to commence his final approach, but his ascent to the standby altitude was to have occurred much farther north of Oʻahu. Now, the approach from the northeast forced an impromptu flight across the island, an improvisation that posed an additional risk of alerting the Americans, all brought on by the cloud cover hiding Oʻahu from the north.[21]

Until that point, the launch, flight, and approach had gone off without a major hitch, excluding the proximity of Fuchida's deployment to Oʻahu. Initially, all seemed well, with Murata (actually in a moment of indecision) leading his torpedo group south toward the harbor and Takahashi banking outside to the west, opening the distance between his group and the airfields, thereby allowing Murata's torpedo bombers room to strike first.

As the entire strike force was flying over the slopes of the Koʻolau Range, the carefully laid plans unraveled before Fuchida's eyes. With the new course set for the level bombers, he looked toward Pearl Harbor hoping to see Murata charging south. Instead, however, the torpedo group still flew one thousand meters below him, having turned unexpectedly to starboard after crossing the coastline,

paralleling Fuchida's new course set for the horizontal bombers. Surprise or no surprise, the torpedo units had orders to head south down the valley. Why was Murata flying south-southwest instead of south? Could he have missed seeing the signal flare to attack?

Fuchida quickly decided to fire a second flare to alert the torpedo units below and to port to proceed with their deployment. The two-second interval for the two-flare "Force!" (no surprise) signal had long since passed, so surely no one would misinterpret the repeated signal to Murata. Thus, at about 0742 Fuchida fired a second flare toward the harbor, *directly at Murata*, who had already passed over the northwest extremity of the Koʻolau Range near Kahuku Point.

To Fuchida, the second flare appeared to correct, in part, Murata's inexplicable hesitation over northern Oʻahu. The flare, however, also elicited an unintended response from the dive-bombers. The second Black Dragon probably caught the eye of Takahashi's observer, Lt. (jg) Koizumi Seizō, who brought it to his chief's attention. Far above Fuchida and to the right, Takahashi concluded that Fuchida was signaling "Force!" Without voice communication, too far away for hand signals, and believing himself to be acting under orders to strike first, Takahashi deployed his units *straight at the airfields*. With throttles wide open, the Type 99s abandoned their standby position to starboard and instead shaped a course southeast toward Wheeler Field. Looking up at the dive-bombers crossing above him, Fuchida saw that the carefully choreographed deployment had fallen apart. The torpedo planes and Takahashi's own division of dive-bombers were set to blunder into the harbor at almost the same instant.[22] Owing to the various delays, Takahashi surely felt one step behind the game, pushing forward all the harder because it would now take several minutes for the dive-bombers to catch up with the lead elements of the developing torpedo attack.[23]

Thus, while Fuchida fumed below, at approximately 0743 Takahashi's force raced southeast. Two miles northwest of Wheeler, at approximately 0745, Takahashi rocked his wings to signal Lieutenant Sakamoto to break away and attack the Army field that lay practically dead ahead. While Takahashi held steady in his rapid approach route toward ʻAiea Heights northeast of Pearl Harbor, Sakamoto's twenty-five dive-bombers following astern banked away in a gliding turn to port, heading on a divergent course that cleared the *Shōkaku* contingent ahead and to the right.[24]

Meanwhile, Takahashi's carrier bombers from the *Shōkaku* stood down the wide valley separating the Waiʻanae and Koʻolau mountain ranges, pressing ahead on a southeasterly course until just short of Red Hill, northeast of Hickam. At about 0750 Takahashi's radioman/observer, Lieutenant (jg) Koizumi, transmitted the attack order for all dive-bombers of the first wave. After Koizumi sent the order, Takahashi again wagged his wings to release the two trailing divisions of dive-bombers under Lt. Yamaguchi Masao and Lt. Fujita Hisayoshi to fly farther downrange for the attacks

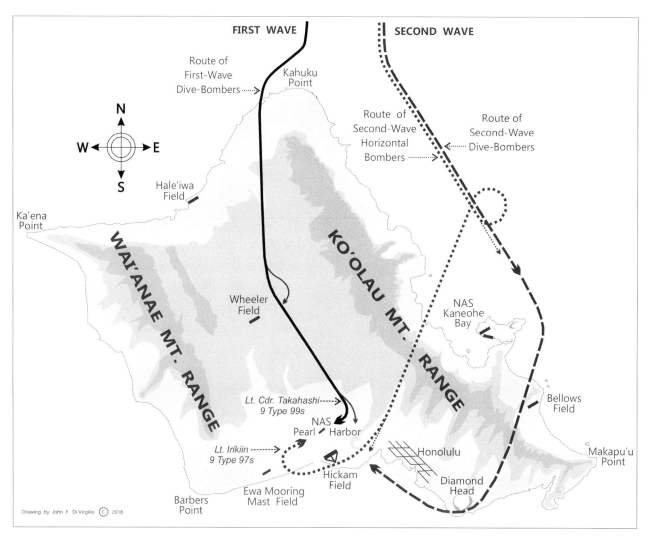

Deployment of the first-wave dive-bombing units from the *Shōkaku* and *Zuikaku* under the command of Lieutenant Commander Takahashi and the second-wave horizontal bombers under the command of Lieutenant Commander Shimazaki. Note the approach of the *Zuikaku* unit to Wheeler Field, with the *Shōkaku* unit passing to the southeast toward a position where the Hickam Field and Ford Island attack units separated.
Di Virgilio

on Hickam Field. Having already traversed the 'Aiea sugarcane fields north of Pearl Harbor, the remaining bombers under Takahashi approached the Āliamanu Crater, where they turned hard to starboard, now with the east-northeasterly wind at their backs. Takahashi and his nine bombers set up a textbook upwind approach to their target—the seaplane hangars and PBYs on the southern tip of Ford Island.[25]

Meanwhile, from his vantage point flying top cover with the *Kaga*'s fighters over the harbor, Lieutenant Shiga felt that something had gone haywire with the deployment. "Wrong! The attack sequence [is] wrong!" What was Takahashi doing plummeting into the airfields so early? For a fleeting moment Shiga thought the situation had changed to a *kyōshū*, or "nonsurprise" attack. In near panic he scanned the sky for American interceptors but saw none. The entire area was about to transition "from peace to hell in a matter of seconds."[26]

Chapter Five

"AIR RAID PEARL HARBOR X THIS IS NO DRILL"

At about 0730 Lt. Richard R. "Dick" Ballinger—PatWing 2's communications officer and staff duty officer—picked up his telephone and dialed 661. The call awakened Logan Ramsey at his residence on the northeast end of Ford Island. Ballinger related that he received a message from 14-P-1 (PBY flown by Ens. William P. Tanner), then patrolling over the restricted area south of O'ahu. Transmitted at 0715, the message stated that the aircraft had bombed and sunk a submerged submarine one mile off the Pearl Harbor entrance channel. While shaking off the effects of being roused suddenly from slumber, in the back of Ramsey's mind lay the possibility that the PBY might inadvertently have transmitted "a drill message of some variety." He asked Ballinger if he had authenticated the message. "No," Ballinger replied, "it was in plain English."[1] Ramsey ordered Ballinger to request an authentication of the message at once. Neither man was aware that 14-P-1 had sent a coded message earlier at 0642, or that fifty-four minutes had elapsed since the initial notification from the plane. "All right," Ramsey said. "I'll be down immediately!"[2]

At 0735 Ramsey telephoned Cdr. Vincent R. Murphy, CinCPac staff duty officer, who—after several frustrating and unsuccessful attempts to contact Rear Admiral Bloch regarding a similar report from the destroyer *Ward* (DD 139)—arrived at his office just in time to hear his telephone ringing. Ramsey relayed the content of the PBY's transmission, also saying that he had requested verification. "That's funny," Murphy replied. "We got the same sort of message from one of the destroyers on the inshore patrol." After Murphy explained that he had been unable to obtain further details, Ramsey said: "Well, you had better get going, and I'll be down at my Operations Center soon."[3]

Ramsey threw on an aloha shirt and slacks, hopped into his 1939 Oldsmobile, and began the short drive to the north parking lot of the Administration Building. Although at the time he did not think the message referred to an enemy presence, the bombing of any target so close to the entrance channel was a serious matter. Should Lieutenant Ballinger authenticate the message from 14-P-1, the incident certainly justified changing the existing patrols.

Lt. (jg) Richard R. "Dick" Ballinger, personnel officer for VP-4, Fleet Air Base, Pearl Harbor, 1 August 1934
NPRC, St. Louis

Lt. Cdr. Logan C. Ramsey, 24 October 1934, while commanding VS-10S on board the *Chicago*
NPRC, St. Louis

PBY-5 14-P-1 from VP-14, 13 October 1941, believed incorrectly for many years to be the aircraft Ens. William P. Tanner was flying during the encounter with the Japanese midget submarine. However, the squadron exchanged its early-production PBY-5s for new aircraft in San Diego and returned to NAS Kaneohe Bay on 23 November.
NARA II, 80-G-279382, cropped

Radio log from Ensign Tanner's aircraft and text of the radio message he sent to PatWing 1 Headquarters at 0642. ODTH was the code word that referred to the submarine attacks, with the three repetitions implying a degree of urgency; 114A was the call sign for Tanner's aircraft, with 114B and 114C denoting aircraft 14-P-2 and 14-P-3 on the message's distribution.
Ramsey Collection, HAD, NHHC

```
7 DEC. '41                14-P-1              ENS TANNER
                                              MOORE-MCCLINTOCK

1645   OVER THE SIDE
       PUT-PUT TIME  20 MIN.

       7Y9S 8Y9S V 114C AR
       114A 14A V 114C AR
       V 114A K         S IMI S5 S IMI S5
1700   8Y9S 8Y9S V 114A AR
       114C V 114A ZCA 8Y9S /K
       114A 114B 114C V 8Y9S AR     V A K
       8Y9S V 114A AR
       V 114A OUT K
       V 114A R / ZCA 114B 114C L/ K
       ODTH ODTH ODTH ODTH V 114A 114A AR     (SANK SUB)
       114B 114B 114C 114C V 8Y9S AR
       8Y9 S V 114C K
       V 8Y9S OUT IMI K        8Y9S V 114C OUT /K  V 8Y9S R
1725   8N  8NML 8NOP V 124A 124A AS
```

Cdr. Vincent R. Murphy, circa January 1940, while he was the war plans officer on the staff of Adm. James O. Richardson, CinCUS
NARA, St. Louis

Ramsey parked his car and hurried up to his office on the second floor in the north corner of the building, directly across from Rear Adm. Patrick Bellinger's office, and asked for the text of the message from 14-P-1. After reading it he judged it to be "apparently authentic."[4]

Although he decided to await authentication before taking further action, Ramsey left his office and strode to the wing plotting and chart room several doors down on the left and began work on a modified search plan at about 0752. The new plan needed to take into account not only the existing morning security patrols but also the four aircraft from VP-24 then engaged in "inter-type tactics" with the *Gudgeon* seventy miles east-southeast of

The General Facilities Building (Building 661) at Pearl Harbor's Submarine Base, 13 October 1941, looking northwest. Admiral Kimmel's headquarters and the offices of his staff—including Commander Murphy—were on the second floor.
NARA II, 80-G-451125, cropped

The Administration Building (Building 77) seen from the station's water tower on the afternoon of 8 December 1941. The office of Capt. James M. Shoemaker (CO, NAS Pearl Harbor) was on the first floor in the leftmost corner of the Administration Building, with Rear Admiral Bellinger's office directly above on the second floor. The wing plotting and chart room from which Ramsey and Ballinger heard Lieutenant Commander Takahashi's Type 99 dive toward Hangar 6 was two compartments to the right. NARA II, 80-G-32501, cropped

O'ahu in Operating Area C5. Ramsey based the search area on extensive discussions with the staff that took into account "prevailing wind conditions and the presence of outlying islands and other factors." The best estimate indicated that the northwest sector would be the most likely avenue of approach by the Japanese, so Ramsey drafted an order for the PBYs to conduct a search northwest of O'ahu in a pie-shaped, 90-degree sector from 270 to 0 degrees.[5]

After writing up the order, Ramsey descended the stairs, went to the radio room at the end of the hall, and handed it to one of the radiomen, instructing him to code the message and stand by to transmit it. There was still no certainty that the message would be necessary, because Ramsey was still awaiting confirmation of the earlier dispatch from 14-P-1. He stayed in the radio room briefly before returning upstairs.[6]

In the OOD office at the north entrance of the Administration Building, Lt. Frank "Eric" Erickson, USCG—aviator on board the *Taney* (Coast Guard Cutter No. 68)—awaited the arrival of his 0800 relief and thought of the day's activities that he had planned with his family at Waikīkī. At about 0753 the Marine color guard posted for Colors. Erickson stepped back into the OOD office on the east side of the lobby and doubled-checked that his assistant OOD stood ready to play the "Colors" recording over the loudspeaker system.[7]

Sea2c Glennon J. Ryan had mustered with about one hundred of his shipmates at 0745 in front of the Administration Building's northeast entrance, having drawn maintenance and cleanup duty in one of the chief petty officer quarters. Ryan and the other men waited for the Marines standing nearby to raise the Stars and Stripes, then began answering the roll call at 0755.[8]

The Administration Building on Ford Island (at center left, just beyond the *Enterprise*'s island) looking northwest down the harbor's Southeast Loch, 13 October 1941. The Enlisted Barracks is at upper center, and the Dispensary is at right. At the center of the area bounded by these three buildings is the flagpole where the Marine color guard prepared to hoist the Stars and Stripes on the morning of 7 December.
NARA II, 80-G-451122, cropped

Ens. Frank A. Erickson, USCG, circa 1935
NPRC, St. Louis

Meanwhile, the dive-bombers under Lieutenant Commander Takahashi—having already traversed the 'Aiea plantation sugar fields north of Pearl Harbor—turned hard to starboard upon approaching the Āliamanu Crater.[9] Holding fast at four thousand meters, Takahashi's new course cut a path across Pearl Harbor from the northeast. Banking right, the dive-bomber commander and the crews who followed beheld the sunlit panorama of Pearl Harbor and the seaplane facilities on the southern tip of Ford Island. The American fleet lay sleeping in the morning light, and enemy interceptors were nowhere to be seen; the sky was completely clear of antiaircraft fire. The Japanese had achieved total tactical surprise.[10]

Takahashi led his column west by southwest over the east channel, paralleling the southeast

Administration Building - NASPH Northwest Wing

ComPatWing 2 | Flag Lieutenant | Wing Plot & Chart Room

Main Corridor

Wing Operations | Stairwell | Secretary's Office

Wing Gunnery

Auditorium

Base Files

Vault

Radio Files

Base Conference & Coding Room

Radio Officer

Radio Department

1st Floor

2nd Floor

Floor plan of the Administration Building's second floor and the first floor's west wing locating various features that figured prominently in the events of 7 December 1941
NARA II, RG 71I

shore of Ford Island, and then banked again to starboard over the seaplane hangars, keeping the target area visible over his right shoulder. After the nine Type 99s circled clockwise toward Pearl City Peninsula and the western edge of the sugarcane fields of 'Aiea, the planes began their dives one after the other. The *kanbaku*s dove in three-plane sections, with each succeeding aircraft circling slightly further east before pushing over into the target area.[11]

Takahashi plummeted in a steep 55-degree dive toward the seaplane hangars, his two wingmen

trailing astern in echelon left. Following at close intervals, the two trailing sections under Lt. Hira Kunikiyo aimed for targets slightly to the northeast, up the rungs of the "stepladder" to be set in place by their chief's bomb impact. While steadying his aircraft, Takahashi reached forward with his left hand and pushed a long, thin metal rod through a hole in the windscreen to remove the protective wind cap that covered the tubular Navy Type 95 bombsight mounted through the Plexiglas. He leaned forward, peered into the gridlined aiming lens, and moved his left hand to the

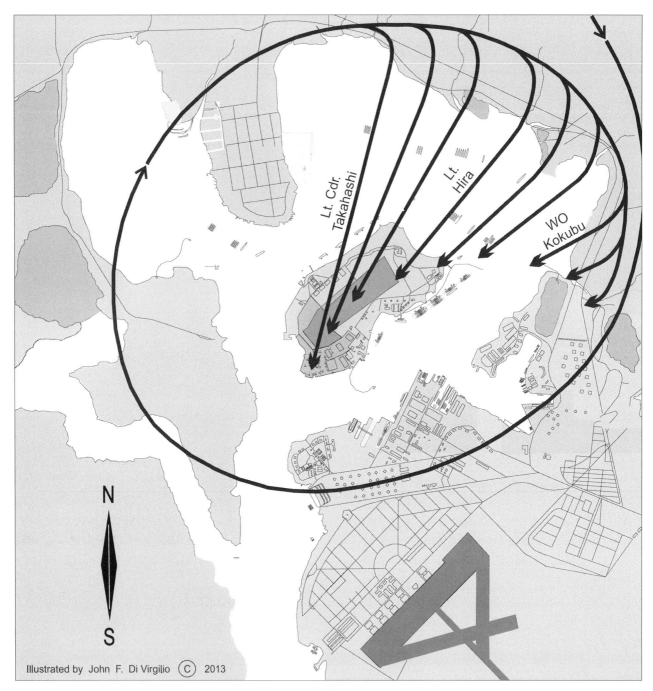

Lt. Cdr. Takahashi

Lt. Hira

WO Kokubu

N

S

Illustrated by John F. Di Virgilio ©ⓒ 2013

The deployment of the *Shōkaku* dive-bomber unit over Pearl Harbor. The nine aircraft under Takahashi's command circled the harbor in a clockwise spiral and set up their runs from the northeast.
Di Virgilio

bomb release lever. From the rear seat, Lieutenant (jg) Koizumi monitored the bomber's steadily decreasing altitude, calling out each two-hundred-meter interval through the voice tube. At six hundred meters—just prior to release—Koizumi yelled, "*Yoi!*" (Ready!), and then at four hundred meters, "*Te!*" (Release!).[12] The Type 99 jolted as the bomb release cradle arm swung downward, throwing the 250-kg Type 98 high-explosive land bomb—fused for extra penetration with a 0.1-second delay—from the carrier bomber's underside.[13]

Navy Type 95 bombsight mounted on an Aichi Type 99 carrier bomber recovered from the water after the attack on Pearl Harbor. Note the position of the protective lens cover, draw bar, and handle (just visible at right center inside the windscreen). The handle was at the rear end of the draw bar that protruded into the cockpit through a hole in the center pane of the windscreen. NARA II, 80-G-33017, cropped

The gathering engine noise was so in keeping with the norm near the base that few individuals in the harbor noted the arrival of Japanese aircraft to the north. Moreover, the *Enterprise* and her air group had been absent since 28 November, and although few at Pearl Harbor were privy to her secret mission to Wake Island, the air group's arrival during the weekend would not have been unexpected. It is thus not surprising that, in all the deck logs, action reports, and war diaries compiled subsequent to the Japanese air raid, only one individual noted Takahashi's eastward passage north of the harbor.[14] From the destroyer *Allen* (DD 66) in Berth X-5 northeast of Battleship Row, BM2c (F-4-C) Elliot R. Milliken noticed twenty to twenty-five aircraft circling off to the north but, "in view of frequent Air Attack Drills," attached "no importance . . . to their presence." Only after Takahashi's bombers turned southwest did observers take notice in appreciable numbers. The war diary for NAS Pearl Harbor noted that at 0750,

aircraft approached the station from the direction of Merry Point and Hickam Field, possibly observing the clockwise spiral of the planes over the harbor. Northwest of Ford Island, signalmen on board the *Zane* (DMS 14) moored in Berth D-7 witnessed aircraft making a "long gliding approach from Northward." On board the *St. Louis* (CL 49), moored portside to the *Honolulu* in Berth B-17 in the Repair Basin, Gun Wilfred G. Wallace, junior officer of the watch, "observed a large number of dark colored planes heading in the direction of Ford Island from Aiea." As Takahashi's unit passed through the layer of broken clouds and descended on the station, observers on board the *Pennsylvania* (BB 38) in Dry Dock Number One thought they saw the nine aircraft plummeting in single file through the clouds directly over Ford Island.[15]

At least two astute observers recognized the aircraft as Japanese just prior to the bombing. On board the light cruiser *Helena* (CL 50), SM1c

CBM (AA) Elliot R. Milliken, circa August 1943
Doolittle

Charles A. Flood was ready to go below after chatting with shipmates on the signal bridge when he heard someone comment about the planes high over Ford Island—not at all usual for a Sunday morning. "I picked up a pair of binoculars," he later wrote, "and looked them over." Although he could see no markings at that altitude, something in their approach struck him as unusual but familiar. In early 1932 Flood had served in a bluejacket landing force during the Sino-Japanese hostilities at Shanghai, China, and remembered the Japanese "bombing technique, which was a form of glide-bombing. The planes over Ford Island were approaching in the same manner." Flood quickly bellowed down to the men on the main deck: "Japanese planes bombing Ford Island!" His shouting attracted the attention of Ens. William W. Jones, the officer of the deck. In a display of "initiative and prompt action," Jones instantly passed the word: "All hands to General Quarters—break out service ammunition."

Ens. Henry D. Davison on board the *Arizona* had just sent a messenger to deliver the 0800 reports to Capt. Franklin Van Valkenburgh when dive-bombers passing directly overhead attracted his attention. Putting a spyglass on the aircraft, Davison saw red dots on the wings, though he still entertained second thoughts regarding the machines' provenance until he saw the bombs falling.[16]

Ramsey, now in Wing Plot, glanced out the window at the color guard moving into place in front of the Administration Building. Just then, aircraft noise distracted him, leading him to conclude that a "flat-hatting" aviator was buzzing the station. Ramsey crossed the corridor to the window to the left of the stairway and saw a plane zooming away, pulling out of its dive, low over the seaplane hangars to the south. Although he strained to determine the offending machine's side number—thinking that the pilot had broken any number of the station's flight restrictions—he was a moment too late. The aircraft sped into the distance too quickly to allow identification. Calling out to Lieutenant Ballinger, whose window afforded a better vantage point, Ramsey inquired tartly, "Dick, did you get his number?" Ballinger missed the number

Lt. (jg) Charles A. Flood, circa 1944
Espinoza

Midn. William W. Jones, circa 1940
Lucky Bag, 1941

Midn. Henry D. Davison, circa March 1939
NPRC, St. Louis

too but said, "No, but I think it was a squadron commander's aircraft because I saw a band of red on it." The aircraft—emblazoned with Takahashi's red *hikōtaichō* command stripes—pulled out of its dive, and an explosion and red flash in the distance prompted Ramsey to wonder whether blasting was under way somewhere in the harbor or perhaps the reckless pilot had crashed. The explosion of a second bomb and the appearance of more aircraft left no doubt in Ramsey's mind. "Never mind!" he shouted at Ballinger. "It's a Jap!"[17]

Ramsey hurried across the hall and dialed 663 to reach Rear Admiral Bellinger's private phone. Bellinger was still in bed, but he had heard the noise of an aircraft that sounded as if it were in a dive and then the thud of a bomb. In a "very brief" conversation, Ramsey informed his chief that planes were bombing the hangars. Bellinger responded with the incredulous retort, "You wouldn't kid about a thing like that?" Assured that Ramsey was not joking, Bellinger said, "Well, let's get going. I'll be right down."[18]

Ramsey threw down the phone, ran across the hall to the communications room, and raised RM2c David T. Montgomery of the ComPatWing 2 flag

unit on the voice tube. Perhaps remembering Rear Admiral Bloch's alert messages beginning with the word "DRILL" that initiated all bimonthly exercises of the Naval Base Defense Air Force, Ramsey instructed Montgomery to "broadcast on all wavelengths and over all means of communication," in plain English, "AIR RAID PEARL HARBOR X THIS IS NO DRILL." Ramsey then scurried back to Wing Plot to modify the search plan and messages to the two groups of PBYs then on patrol. The time was 0758.[19]

Even as explosions rocked the foot of Ford Island, Gun Wilfred G. Wallace on board the *St. Louis* continued to watch the events off to the west. He experienced the curious phenomenon of "acoustic shadows" experienced so frequently during artillery bombardments of the American Civil War. Planes dropped their deadly missiles, "which caused flame but no sound."[20]

Takahashi's bomb—the first to fall into Pearl Harbor—detonated at the water's edge along the southeastern portion of Ramp 4, sending an immense column of water, mud, and concrete shards hurtling skyward and partially disabling the ramp when the explosion upended a slab of

The southwest face of the Administration Building looking east, 11 August 1941. The radio room from which the "AIR RAID PEARL HARBOR" message was sent was on the first floor at far left.
NARA II, 71-CA-152C-14625

RM1c David T. Montgomery, circa February 1942
Sturmon

concrete. Takahashi's two wingmen—PO1c Shinohara Kazuo and PO2c Fukuhara Jun—targeted VP-22's PBY-3s on the apron, scoring solid hits among the aircraft south of Hangar 6. Next in line, and leading the six aircraft of the 3rd Chūtai, Lieutenant Hira, the squadron's junior division officer, shifted his aim farther northeast and targeted Hangar 6, followed by his two wingmen, PO2c Nakadokoro Shūhei and Sea1c Harashima Masayoshi. Although he reported that his section scored three direct hits on the hangar, Hira in fact overshot; his bomb landed midway between the building and the shore. The bombs his wingmen dropped landed close aboard the eastern face of the hangar, one of them opening a crater twenty feet across and seven feet deep. The other bomb struck the small-arms magazine on the northeast corner of Hangar 6 and broke apart, igniting the hangar itself along with the contents of the offices

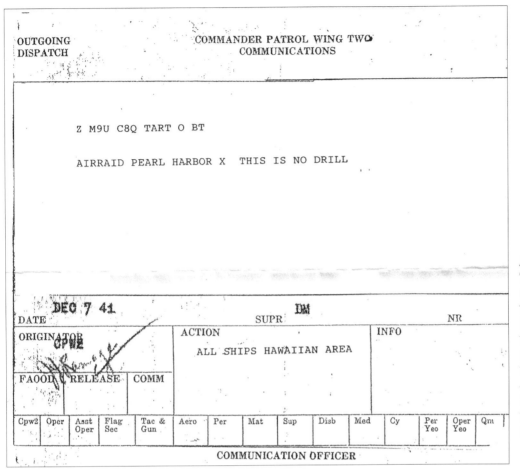

OUTGOING
DISPATCH

COMMANDER PATROL WING TWO
COMMUNICATIONS

Z M9U C8Q TART O BT

AIRRAID PEARL HARBOR X   THIS IS NO DRILL

DEC 7 41

DATE   SUPR   IM   NR

ORIGINATOR
CPW2

ACTION
ALL SHIPS HAWAIIAN AREA

INFO

FAOOD RELEASE   COMM

Cpw2	Oper	Asst Oper	Flag Sec	Tac & Gun	Aero	Per	Mat	Sup	Disb	Med	Cy	Per Yeo	Oper Yeo	Qm

COMMUNICATION OFFICER

A typed draft of the "Air Raid Pearl Harbor" message as preserved by then-RM2c Montgomery. Note the initials showing that he was the radio room supervisor at the time, and that Ens. John J. Ramage authorized ComPatWing 2 as the originator.
Burdette

in the lean-to along the building's east face. The bomb failed to detonate "but burst asunder" from the impact, scattering its explosive charge of picric acid—"a bright yellow granular powder"—on aircraft and lockers inside the hangar. Flying splinters and concrete shards rained down among the buildings and nearby aircraft, puncturing and igniting the fuel cells of the planes on the apron and elsewhere. Among them was a new Dutch PBY-5 in the hangar that was to be flown to Java after reinstrumentation but was "pretty well demolished" by the debris. Within moments the tip of Ford Island erupted in flames, as did the northeast corner of Hangar 6.[21]

The tactical orders for Takahashi's dive-bomber crews directed them to fire their machine guns as soon as they released their bombs so as to "thoroughly destroy the enemy and maximize damage," and then to clear the area to "avoid being a

hindrance to [the fighters]." Hence, it might have been the machine-gun fire that first alerted some of the men on the ground, particularly those at the station. The chatter of both fixed and flexible 7.7-mm machine guns blended with the din of exploding bombs while the dive-bombers headed straight away from the station at full throttle. The pilots attempted no evasive maneuvers aside from disrupting the defenders' aim by blending into the ground cover at low altitude.[22]

Behind Lieutenant Hira's trio of bombers, meanwhile, with a towering column of smoke already obscuring the target area, the trailing section under WO Kokubu Toyomi entered the fray in echelon left. Conforming to the stepladder tactics, Kokubu's pilot, PO2c Suzuki Toshio, shifted to the northeast, targeting either other hangars or the OS2Us and other aircraft parked close by. His bomb burst among aircraft near the west corner of Hangar 38, carrying away a substantial portion of that structure's side window lights. A great shower of fragments and debris rained on VP-24's ready airplane nearby, which "suffered a severed wing spar from a large flying missile." Nearby patrol and scout planes went up in flames as well.[23]

Kokubu's first wingman, PO3c Kitamura Fusao, released a bomb that failed to detonate. The missile penetrated the roof of Hangar 38, broke apart, and imbedded itself into the concrete floor of the Staff Repair Shop in the building's west corner. Except for the impact holes in roof and floor and the yellowish powdered explosive scattered about the hangar, the bomb did little damage.[24]

At the end of Takahashi's string of nine carrier bombers, Sea1c Seki Masao concluded the bombing attack. On the ground at that moment, after taking a few steps outside Hangar 54 to investigate the detonations at Hangar 6, Sea2c James S. Layman looked up and saw Seki's carrier bomber heading his way over the water tower. Because the

markings on the plane left "no doubt as to the nationality," Layman immediately turned to run away from Hangar 6. At that instant, Seki released his bomb. Layman quickened his pace, noting later that his "strides took on greater proportions." Although Seki claimed he dropped his bomb among the aircraft close by Hangar 6, it actually fell far short of that objective and detonated in the street immediately south of the old Assembly and Repair Building No. 2 (Building 2). The explosion showered the fleeing sailors with concrete shards and cinders, opened up a large crater, and damaged OS2Us and SOCs parked between Hangar 38 and the Engine and Aircraft Overhaul Shop (Building 39). According to Sea1c Houston James, there was a loud thud at impact but no audible explosion, and the ground lifted up in front of him. Closer to the impact, the force of the partial detonation threw a group of sailors against the exterior of the Assembly and Repair Building, injuring one of them.[25]

The aerial assault on Pearl Harbor begins. Almost simultaneously, torpedo bombers from the *Sōryū* strike the *Utah* (AG 16) at far left and the light cruiser *Helena* at center right along 1010 Pier while the detonations of Takahashi's bombs send up a plume of smoke from the PBY-3s on the apron in front of Hangar 6. The destroyer *Helm* (DD 388) at far right turns to starboard around Waipi'o Peninsula toward the deperming buoys in West Loch.

BKS, Nagai Collection

The column of smoke rising from the foot of Ford Island dissipates in the humid morning air. No torpedoes have yet hit the battleships. This image is from motion picture footage taken from one of the *Kaga*'s torpedo bombers as that unit advanced, left to right, toward the entrance channel and Hickam Field.
NARA II, Motion Picture Reel 242.290

A torpedo bomber from the *Hiryū* at upper right banks hard in a wrenching port turn near the southern tip of Ford Island after launching a torpedo against the *Helena*. Below and to the right, shadows cast by smoke from explosions and fires completely hide Hangar 6 from view. Only two PBYs are visible outside the southwest doors of Hangar 54 at lower center. This photograph is the highest-quality image to have survived the war that documents this early phase of the attacks.
NARA II, 80-G-30554, cropped

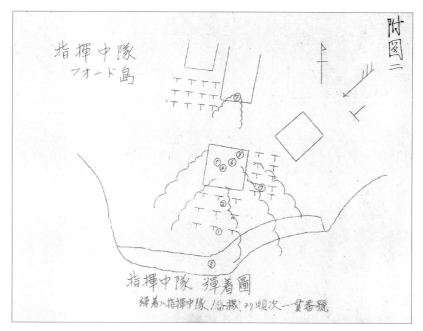

The Japanese interpretation of results of their dive-bombing attack as presented in the action report of the aircraft carrier *Shōkaku*. Although the placement of the aircraft around Hangar 6 at center is approximately correct, the array of hits allegedly scored on Hangar 6 is fanciful at best, as are the imaginary fires belching forth from a second building, supposedly Hangar 54.
BKS, *Shōkaku* action report

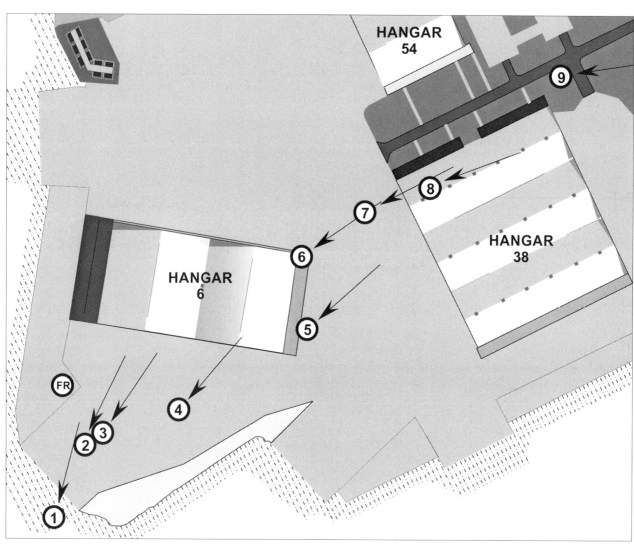

Reconstruction of the actual bomb impacts on the southern end of Ford Island using contemporary photography, the annotated map that accompanied Captain Shoemaker's damage report, and on-the-spot exploration of the paved area by Jeff Dodge of NAVFAC and authors Di Virgilio and Wenger. "FR" at left represents a "false report" of a crater in Shoemaker's report.
Di Virgilio

Debris covers the roof of Hangar 38 at far right following the Japanese dive-bombing attacks. Note the missing skylights on the hangar's west corner, almost certainly carried away by the blast deflected upward from a bomb detonation just beyond the hangar or by partial detonation of the bomb that passed through the roof near the hangar's west corner. View from the water tower, 8 December, looking southwest.
NARA II, 80-G-32504, cropped

Vertical view of the vicinity of Hangar 38, 10 December 1941. One of the more obscure details in this heavily cropped photograph is the impact site of Sea1c Seki Masao's bomb that hit just south of Building 2 at center right. The explosion and the resulting crater obliterated the curbing on the east side of the thorough-fare—the only road leading south to the hangars. Crews filled the crater almost as soon as the aircraft of the first wave departed, and the temporary dirt patch is plainly evident three days later. Building 3 was removed in late September, leaving behind only its concrete pad (top center) to the right of Hangar 54.
NARA II, 80-G-387569, cropped

Lt. Takahashi Kakuichi, circa late 1930s. During this period Takahashi served on board carriers *Kaga* and *Sōryū* and with the Ōmura, Usa, and 12th Air Groups.
Goldstein

Lt. (jg) Koizumi Seizō, Takahashi's observer/radioman, circa late 1930s
Kamada

Lieutenant Shiga, commanding the *Kaga*'s fighters directly overhead, saw Takahashi's bomb explode in a white flash in the shallow water off the southernmost seaplane ramp. A scarlet fireball erupted, followed by a plume of smoke that climbed to the southwest and was carried away by the prevailing winds. The methodical pounding administered by the *Shōkaku* bombers impressed Shiga: "Flash after flash. Being the best bombers, they had been trained to hit moving targets, so they didn't miss these stationary targets at all. In a matter of a few seconds, the calm in the harbor was shattered."[26]

After the bombing concluded, Takahashi led his unit in a wide circuit out to starboard, circled over the harbor to the west, and set up strafing runs against Ford Island from the northwest, likely drawn by the chrome yellow wings of unscathed utility aircraft on either side of the island. Speeding east across Ford Island's runway, Takahashi opened fire on the J2Fs as Lieutenant Hira did the same on the larger JRS-1s of VJ-1, though inflicting little damage. The other seven pilots targeted VJ-2's parking apron fronting Hangar 177 on the opposite shore. PO2c Nakadokoro and PO3c Kitamura swung out even wider to port, making

Lt. Hira Kunikiyo, commander, 3rd *Chūtai*, *Shōkaku* dive-bombing unit
Maru

WO Kokubu Toyomi, section leader, 3rd *Chūtai*, *Shōkaku* dive-bombing unit
Maru

Lt. Shiga Yoshio, commander, *Kaga* fighter unit, before the war
Prange

First-Wave Attack on NAS Pearl Harbor
Lt. Cdr. Takahashi Kakuichi
Shōkaku Dive-Bombing Unit

	Pilot	Observer/Radioman/Rear Gunner
Command	Lt. Cdr. Takahashi Kakuichi	Lt. (jg) Koizumi Seizō
Shōtai	PO1c Shinohara Kazuo	PO1c Koitabashi Hiroshi
	PO2c Fukuhara Jun	PO2c Mototoshi Jirō
	3rd *Chūtai*	
27th *Shōtai*	Lt. Hira Kunikiyo	PO1c Chō Mitsuo
	PO2c Nakadokoro Shūhei	PO3c Ōura Minpei
	Sea1c Harashima Masayoshi	Sea1c Yoshinaga Shirō
28th *Shōtai*	PO2c Suzuki Toshio	WO Kokubu Toyomi
	PO3c Kitamura Fusao	PO2c Tomigashi Katsusuke
	Sea1c Seki Masao	Sea1c Yamanouchi Hiroshi

their runs almost from the north to strafe the old PBY-1s and about ten of the smaller J2Fs on the apron. Each dive-bomber pilot brought two of the aircraft under fire and later claimed to have set three of them ablaze.[27]

Takahashi and his unit sped south at low altitude, zoomed clear of antiaircraft fire, veered right, and pulled up east of Ewa Mooring Mast Field—the location from which they were to fly to the rendezvous area off Ka'ena Point west of O'ahu. Takahashi was confident that his group's well-disciplined effort and rigid adherence to the step-ladder tactics had yielded significant results. He estimated that the concerted dive-bombing attack set two hangars afire, with flames destroying one and setting Hangar 38 ablaze as well. In addition, he claimed twenty PBYs and other aircraft nearby "exploded in flames." Takahashi loitered in the general area south of Pearl Harbor, orbiting at 1,000–1,500 meters in order to confirm the results and photograph the destruction.[28]

An unintended result of Takahashi's premature assault was the smoke plume rising from Hangar 6 and vicinity. Although it did not hinder the *Sōryū*'s torpedo group that attacked the fleet moorings northwest of Ford Island just as Takahashi pushed over, the incoming *Hiryū* group and the more distant formations from the *Akagi* and *Kaga* found

a wall of smoke boiling up from the naval air station blocking their line of sight. Hence, from the standpoint of the torpedomen, the dive-bombing attack on Ford Island did more harm than good and justified Fuchida's well-founded fears regarding Takahashi's potential interference with the torpedo and horizontal bombing attacks.[29]

At the conclusion of Takahashi's attacks, several Japanese carrier fighters under Lt. Ibusuki Masanobu of the *Akagi* fighter unit approached the station from the direction of Hickam Field and sprayed the seaplane base with machine-gun fire. They strafed along an axis running southeast to northwest in order to acquire targets under the billowing smoke. Extending that axis to the northwest would have brought them directly over the seaplane base at NAS Pearl Harbor. Lieutenant Ibusuki claimed to have approached the station in that manner and fired "at several flying boats at islands [sic] edge," but then quickly reversed course and returned to the center of action at Hickam Field, the fighters' primary objective.[30]

In the Administration Building, meanwhile, Logan Ramsey made final adjustments to the search plan intended to uncover the location of the Japanese fleet. The staff had concluded previously that any inbound air strike was likely to come generally from the north, reasoning that the

At left center, five of VJ-1's ten JRS-1s lie on the apron north of Hangar 37, with three J2F Ducks parked out to the right at the time Takahashi's dive-bombers were strafing. The battleship *California* (BB 44) is in the background with two OS2U-3 Kingfishers perched atop Turret 3. Cropped from a much larger photograph.
Pederson, cropped

At center, a pair of PBY-1s and approximately ten J2F Ducks huddle together on VJ-2's parking apron in front of Hangar 177 at the southern end of the hangar line on the northwest side of Ford Island. Note Hangars 133 and 134 at upper left. Cropped from a much larger photograph.
Pederson, cropped

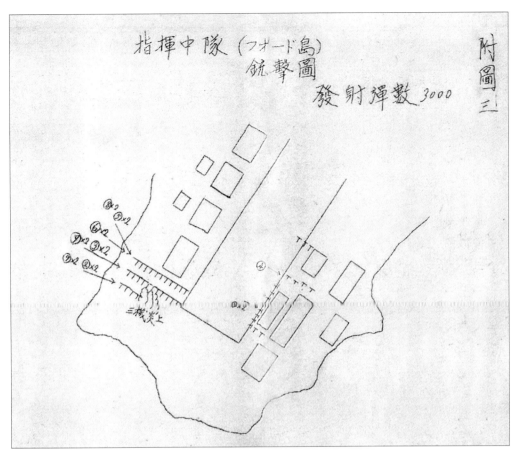

指揮中隊（フォード島）
銃撃圖
發射彈數 3000

附圖三

Strafing attacks on the utility aircraft of VJ-1 and VJ-2 by Takahashi's dive-bombers that occurred shortly after the bombing near Hangar 6
BKS, *Shōkaku* detailed action report

Lt. Cdr. Ibusuki Masanobu while serving with the Yokosuka Air Group, circa 1945
Prange

Japanese would use the northeasterly tailwinds to compensate for the heavy bomb loads. No information regarding the enemy's direction of approach was available, though, hence Ramsey's decision to implement a 360-degree search plan.[31]

Ramsey's plan called for eighteen PBYs from PatWing 1 to scour the sea west of Oʻahu, with six aircraft from each squadron covering a 60-degree, wedge-shaped area. To the east, six planes from VP-24 were to search a 60-degree sector east of north. Army bombers from Hickam Field, the Base Force's utility squadrons, and battleship/cruiser floatplanes were to explore the less critical sectors to the east and southeast. Ramsey took immediate advantage of the four aircraft from VP-24 exercising with the *Gudgeon*, and also of the three VP-14 craft patrolling the operating areas south of Oʻahu. Further, he assigned VP-23 "to plug holes" in the search pattern, with the balance of the squadron forming a strike force reinforced by VP-22.[32]

Modified 0800 Search Plan
for 7 December 1941
Cdr. Logan C. Ramsey,
Operations Officer, PatWing 2

Resources	Search Sector and Orders
VP-14, 6 PBY-5s	300–000 degrees
VP-11, 6 PBY-5s	240–300 degrees
VP-12, 6 PBY-5s	180–240 degrees
VP-24, 6 PBY-5s	000–060 degrees
VJ/VO/VCS/Army	060–180 degrees
VP-23, 12 PBY-5s	Form strike group and assist with search
VP-22, 12 PBY-3s	Form strike group

Having paused briefly to watch the first torpedo attack on the *California*, Ramsey remembered that he had not yet transmitted his search plan to the seven planes in the air and to the squadrons on the ground. Owing to the urgent circumstances, he dispensed with coding the dispatch and ordered it sent in plain English along with the instruction that all craft change frequency to 4040

kilocycles. The search plan went out by radio at 0759 and was "received by planes in air at 0805." Unfortunately, in the confusion of the moment, either Ramsey neglected to insert instructions for VP-24 or the radioman on duty omitted the message line. Hence, only the units from PatWing 1 received the transmission. The four PBYs over Operating Area C5 finally got word of the attack on O'ahu at about 0815 but received no instructions to change their frequency or position. The net result of the communications mix-ups was a nearly hour-long delay in the redeployment of VP-24 back toward O'ahu and points west.[33]

Apart from the oversight regarding VP-24, the obvious flaw of Ramsey's search plan was that by 0800 the attacks on O'ahu's airfields had rendered it superfluous. Unknown to the staff of PatWing 2, fighters from the *Shōkaku* and the *Zuikaku* had paralyzed Kaneohe Bay, damaging or destroying perhaps half of the station's aircraft with machine-gun fire and rendering the airworthiness of many

Commander Ramsey's order regarding the aerial search for the Japanese attack force. Note the rather heavy reliance on VP-11 and VP-12, which had taken heavy losses at Kaneohe by 0800. In that order Ramsey also notified the aircraft to change their radio frequency to 4040 kilocycles. Ramsey Collection, HAD, NHHC

other PBYs questionable. Burning wreckage hemmed in the few undamaged aircraft. Confusion and disorganization hampered effective action by preventing the assembly of plane crews. Thus, the strafing attacks on the island's windward shore by only eleven fighters had shredded half of Ramsey's search plan before he could implement it.

The situation at Hickam Field was little better. True, the dive-bombing attack by the seventeen carrier bombers from the *Shōkaku* under Lieutenant Yamaguchi had targeted the hangars rather than the flight line, damaging or destroying only aircraft undergoing maintenance. The dive-bombers, however—augmented by the *Akagi*'s nine Mitsubishi Type 0 carrier fighters under Lt. Cdr. Itaya Shigeru—followed with a strafing attack on the field that destroyed or disabled most of the B-17Ds and B-18s that Ramsey counted on to search the sectors to the east and south.

Even at NAS Pearl Harbor, Ramsey seemed unaware of the destruction on the ramps and aprons surrounding Hangar 6 at the southern tip of Ford Island. Here, the "strike group" earmarked to land a blow against the Japanese fleet was out of action with the exception of several PBY-5s from VP-23 undergoing maintenance in Hangar 54. In addition, bombing and strafing attacks had wrecked a substantial number of floatplanes from the cruisers and battleships. As at Kaneohe, the wreckage on the debris-strewn aprons fouled access to the seaplane ramps and bottled up many surviving aircraft.

Meanwhile, in the opening moments of the attack, the men mustered in front of the Administration Building shortly before 0800 heard "the drone of aircraft in the distance, getting closer all the time," and saw a plane diving over Ford Island and buzzing the station. Sea2c Ryan observed correctly that the aircraft was in a shallow dive, not the steep angle associated with U.S. Navy aircraft. Suddenly a bomb detached from the plane, almost as if it were thrown out, and fell into the water off

the foot of Ford Island with a tremendous splash. Another bomb struck the PBYs on the seaplane ramp immediately afterward.[34]

Perceiving grave danger to the mustered men, Lt. (jg) Lloyd B. Osborne, A-V(G)—the junior OOD—ordered the men into the Administration Building. ChPayClk Clifford B. Pischner, the station's assistant disbursing officer, rushed to the small boat landing and cleared sailors from that location as well. Lt. William R. Kane, the station's OOD, had just passed through the north entrance to investigate the heavy explosions when he encountered sailors shouting, "Those are Jap airplanes and they are bombing us!" He ran inside and sounded General Quarters on the air horn because the "seaplane tower" was unmanned and the air raid siren there could not be used. Sea2c Victor Kamont recalled the scene as "utter chaos in mind if not in body."[35]

In Quarters A at the north end of Ford Island, Captain Shoemaker was donning his golfing togs when he heard "the boom booming and bang banging outside and the roar of planes." Wondering "what in the hell was going on," Shoemaker rushed to the telephone and called his headquarters in the

Cdr. William R. Kane, circa September 1946
NPRC, St. Louis

Administration Building. When Lieutenant Erickson answered the phone Shoemaker inquired: "What the Hell kind of drills are you pulling down there?" The Coast Guard aviator confirmed that a Japanese attack was under way, and Shoemaker ordered, "Sound General Quarters." Shoemaker shucked his golf clothing for the tropical uniform of the time—shorts, short-sleeve shirt, and tropical helmet. After telling his family to remain in their quarters, he went outside and got into in his black Model A Ford sedan. Then, having second thoughts regarding his family's safety, he went back inside and instructed his family to go to Bellinger's bomb shelter immediately.[36]

The three-man Marine color guard stood at attention at the flagpole in front of the Administration Building during the strafing and bombing, awaiting the orders of the OOD. Ultimately, Pfc. Frank Dudovick, Pfc. James D. Young (acting corporal), and Pvt. Paul O. Zeller, USMCR, did not wait for Colors to play on the loudspeaker system. "The flag went right up" with the same smartness and precision that marked their participation in that ceremony in peacetime, although the trio raised the flag to the tune of General Quarters.[37]

Among VP-23's standby crew in Hangar 54, AMM1c (NAP) Gale C. Burkey peered through the open hangar door and got his first glimpse of the Pacific War that would engulf his life and those of so many other men. As bombs arched down and exploded, he made a decision that probably saved his life—he opted not to venture outside or to offer assistance at Hangar 6 because it seemed too obvious a target. While scurrying for protection elsewhere, Burkey noted with dismay that American aircraft were nowhere to be seen and, further, that he could hear no return fire. The opening Japanese blows seemed totally unopposed.[38]

At first, the men in and near Hangar 54 were at a total loss at what to do, having no orders, guidance, or direction. Then someone remembered that engineers had dug a five-foot-deep trench for a pipeline about fifty yards from the hangar, and all of the men ran to the safety of the ditch. Emotions there ran the gamut. All the men were frightened, although some seemed more collected than others. A burly aviation machinist's mate broke down and wept uncontrollably.[39]

At Hangar 37, home to VJ-1 a quarter mile northeast of the action near Hangar 6, RM2c Harry R. Mead assumed that the commotion was a mock air raid. He stepped outside the radio shack to watch the diving planes and saw something black detach itself from one of the aircraft that he

Pvt. Frank Dudovick, USMC,
16 November 1940

NARA, St. Louis

Pvt. James D. Young, USMC,
3 April 1940

NARA, St. Louis

Pvt. Paul O. Zeller, USMCR,
16 November 1940

NARA, St. Louis

assumed to be part of its cowling until there was a tremendous explosion, followed by another. One of the squadron's chief petty officers who had seen service in China recognized the Japanese markings on the planes. Mead turned to immediately and began monitoring the air raid frequency. Messages came over the circuit in short order.[40]

As CRM Thomas Farrow walked toward the Operations Building after breakfast with his buddy ACMM (PA) Ray Crocker, they heard the sound of aircraft engines and looked up at "three flight levels of planes coming in from the northeast." Farrow declared years later, "I don't know what I thought" as the explosions began; "we were just paralyzed with the sight." Farrow and Crocker took cover in an excavated ditch east of the building but ultimately gained their objective, where Farrow reported to Central Control in the building's lower level.[41]

Back at the dock, a covered launch carrying a liberty party had just cleared Landing A when the lead aircraft diving over the station dropped what appeared to be a helium cylinder over Hangar 6. A column of smoke and flames arose, and the

boatswain put about immediately and returned to the dock. There the men received instructions "to crowd close against the landing bulkhead to escape machine gun bullets which were then pattering by." Lieutenant Musser left the landing and ran back to the General Storehouse, where he commenced working with the duty section there.[42]

Of the doctors who reported in early to the Dispensary, none experienced more difficulty getting there than dentist Lt. Elmer E. Schuessler, DC-V(S). Arriving late at Landing C near the Naval Hospital at 0750, he had to wait for the 0800 officers' motorboat. While he was waiting he telephoned the Dispensary to notify the officer he was to relieve of his tardiness. At about 0755 Schuessler heard the roar of an aircraft engine, and a plane passed over the water in front of him at fifty feet altitude with a *hinomaru* and large torpedo in plain view—probably the aircraft of Lt. Nagai Tsutomu of the *Sōryū* torpedo group charging toward the light cruiser *Helena*. Seconds later there was an explosion, and aircraft at the seaplane base across the channel erupted into flames. Schuessler and another officer at the landing attempted to

Ens. Gale C. Burkey, circa May 1942
NPRC, St. Louis

RadElec Thomas E. Farrow, circa December 1943
NARA, St. Louis

View of the Operations Building, 10 December 1941. Note the utility excavations at bottom into which Farrow and Crocker jumped when Lt. Hira Kunikiyo of the *Shōkaku* dive-bomber group strafed VJ-1's parking apron.
NARA II, 80-G-32483, cropped

man the saluting battery nearby, obviously without success. The sound of machine-gun bullets hitting the landing's garage sent the two men scurrying for cover.[43]

When a motorboat finally arrived, Schuessler was last to board, and the craft departed amid a hail of gunfire. The excited coxswain opened the boat's throttle so quickly that Schuessler toppled over and sustained severe bruising on his left thigh. When the boat docked at Ford Island he disembarked and hobbled painfully toward the Dispensary.[44]

PhM1c Paul J. Sherrard and his family arose at their quarters in the Navy housing north of Hickam Field at 124 Main Street hoping for an early breakfast and a timely departure for Waikīkī. When Alma Sherrard commented on the airplane noise outside, her husband retorted that the Navy did not fly on Sundays. "Well, they're flying today," she answered. Alma walked outside and noted calmly that the aircraft several hundred feet above were marked with red balls, to which her husband responded, "Hell, this is war!" Sherrard dressed hurriedly, forgetting one sock in his haste.[45]

View of Landing C looking southwest down the channel, circa 1940
NARA II, 71-CA-164B-1

Lt. Richard B. Black, D-V(S)—the officer in charge of the Intelligence Field Unit at NAS Pearl Harbor—was with his family in their bungalow on Kirkbridge Avenue on Pearl City's windward waterfront when distant explosions shook the windows of the house. Moments later, a Japanese aircraft—a Type 97 from the *Sōryū*—roared over the house from the west, turned south over the fishpond east of the house, and machine-gunned a fisherman on the breakwater. As the gunfire increased, fragments and splinters fell into Black's yard.[46]

In his Honolulu apartment at 1330-A Heulu Avenue, Ens. John P. Edwards, A-V(N), rose early because he was VJ-1's duty officer for 7–8 December. Rather than following his usual routine—an early drive to Pearl Harbor and a leisurely breakfast at Ship Services (Building 17)—he had arranged to meet his sister Betty at her cottage near the Halekulani Hotel. She was to drive Edwards to Pearl Harbor and keep the car for the rest of the weekend. All appeared normal until the pair reached Hickam Field and saw antiaircraft fire, which Edwards dismissed as target practice. Arriving at the Navy Yard gate, however, they encountered Marine sentries with pistols drawn taking potshots

at the Japanese planes above. Realizing the true nature of the situation, Edwards instructed his sister to return immediately to Waikīkī and jumped out of the car.[47]

Shortly before 0800, Lt. Frederick Volbeda (ChC), the chaplain for NAS Pearl Harbor, was en route to deliver the morning sermon, having left his wife, Katherine, and three daughters at their 2255 Mahalo Street home in north Honolulu. The "first intimation of irregularity" occurred as Volbeda crossed King Street near Fort Shafter and saw many aircraft over Pearl Harbor. While crossing the intersection he heard a dull explosion that was followed by billows of smoke to the west. His thought was that saboteurs had set fire to the fuel tanks in the Navy Yard and "planes were bombing the fire to get it under control." When he passed Dillingham Road, the fires at Hickam came into view, as did the results of the bombing in the harbor. Volbeda pressed his accelerator and drove toward the Navy Yard's main gate, where Ensign Edwards and one of VJ-1's ordnancemen hailed him for a ride. The pair jumped in, and Volbeda made straight for Landing C at the Naval Hospital, hoping to board a boat headed for Ford Island.[48]

Marine sentries stop two outbound vehicles attempting to pass through the Pearl Harbor Navy Yard's main gate, circa late 1930s. The YMCA building is visible in the background at far right, with South Avenue passing out of the photo at left toward the Marine Corps Reservation and the Lower Tank Farm.
NPS, USAR 2261

Lt. Frederick Volbeda at the time of his transfer from the seaplane tender *Wright* to NAS Pearl Harbor, circa June 1940
NPRC, St. Louis

Back in Honolulu, the chaos erupting in Pearl Harbor far to the west failed initially to arouse some of the officers and senior NCOs living there. At their apartment on 336 Seaside Avenue in Waikīkī, only the distant wail of air raid sirens awakened VJ-1 roommates Lt. (jg) Gordon E. Bolser, A-V(N), and Lt. (jg) James W. "Jimmy" Robb, A-V(N), to the reality of the Japanese attack. Dressing hurriedly and piling into Bolser's automobile, the pair headed west on Kalākaua Avenue to Kau Kau Corner but encountered a traffic jam on the Kamehameha Highway leading to Pearl Harbor. Japanese aircraft strafed the thoroughfare intermittently and with complete impunity. Recognizing his vulnerability, Bolser drove on the road's shoulder, beneath the palms arching over the roadway.[49]

North of the harbor in Pearl City, a greatly alarmed Lieutenant Black loaded his wife, Aviza, and eleven-year-old son, Douglas, into his car and left for the Navy Yard at about 0800. En route to the Navy Yard gate the family witnessed twin horrors through the car's right-side windows—the *Arizona* blowing up and the *Oklahoma* (BB 37) capsizing. At the gate, Black instructed his wife to proceed to Washington Place (the location of the governor's mansion on Beretania Street) and caught a ride with another officer to Landing C at the Naval Hospital.[50]

Buglers blowing General Quarters were clearly audible inside the four-family flats on Ford Island. In Building 50, CSM Molter noticed that his upstairs neighbor, CQM Lemmon, bolted for the Administration Building as soon as General Quarters sounded. From 50-B, the other upstairs flat, Augusta MacKay—wife of CRM MacKay, then on watch in the Administration Building's radio room—screamed downstairs to Molter, "For God's Sake, Al, look down toward the hangars!" Molter saw part of the hangar roof flying through the air and a plane pulling out of its dive. Even when he saw the Japanese insignia Molter didn't make the connection—"no more than you would expect the next man you see to take a full swing at you without warning. I said, 'Sunday morning, what a hell of a time for an air raid drill.'" Esther Molter then cried out, "Al, there's a battleship tipping over!" Molter ran to the back window and watched the *Oklahoma* heel over and begin to capsize, "almost without a splash, slowly and stately, just as if she were tired and wanted to rest."[51]

Molter ordered Esther, his son, Richard, and the other women and children down into the cellar. His wife asked, "It isn't real, is it?" Molter replied, "I don't know, but if it isn't, it's the best damn imitation I ever saw." At the doorway of the basement he remembered that one of the station's reserve fuel tanks—No. 61—stood a short distance to the northeast and knew that he would

have to get his family and the others away from the basement and that possible danger quickly if the tank should rupture.[52]

When the raid started, Sea2c George W. Edmondson was on duty as a cook in the Enlisted Barracks' mess hall, where the men "were just finishing up the cleaning detail from breakfast."

CRM Allan G. MacKay, his wife, Augusta, and their son, Allan Jr., circa 1941
MacKay

Carp Albert H. Molter, circa September 1942
NPRC, St. Louis

Several of them watched the attack through the window, many thinking that it was a practice air raid by the Army Air Force. The cooks realized the raid was not a drill about ten minutes later when they saw a plane go down in flames in the Navy Yard. Almost simultaneously, CQM Lemmon, the station's chief master-at-arms, ran into the hall bellowing that the harbor was under attack by the Japanese. The men received orders to get on the floor and stay there, although some could not resist going to the windows to watch. Others, like SK3c Rogovsky, now realizing now that an air raid was in progress, crawled under a mess table for protection. While waiting for the raid to end he and SK3c Edwin R. Bishop remained underneath the table eating raisins.[53]

On the upper floor of the Enlisted Barracks, Sea1c John W. Kuhn of PatWing 2's flag unit was still half asleep when he heard aircraft noise and someone saying, "That guy came down awful low today, didn't he?" At the sound of an explosion someone else said, "Well, now look, they're setting off charges out there to make this sound real!" Then a third sailor exclaimed, "There goes one of them planes, and they've got red balls on the wings." Kuhn jumped out of bed as the concussion from the bombs shook the building. Amid the tremendous commotion erupting in the barracks he and the others dressed and raced outside, apparently soon enough to avoid the Marines who subsequently blocked all the exits.[54]

Loud talking and what sounded like a sledgehammer blow to the roof awoke AMM3c James L. Young Jr. of VP-22. Someone ran through the barracks yelling that the station was under attack. The VP-22 men, still groggy after their flight from Midway, were disbelieving. "What in the hell is wrong with you?" someone said. And, "This guy's flipped his wig!" The bearer of the news responded, "Get your goddamned heads down!" just as bullets struck the lanai between the bunks. That convinced most of the men, and the loudspeaker system

added authority. The sailors near Young were startled and frightened, one so much so that he urinated on the barracks floor.[55]

Shortly thereafter Young and the others received instructions to report to their squadrons. The men dressed quickly as the rear gunners in Takahashi's Type 99s strafed the area and, cursing, descended the congested stairways to the mess hall. Their efforts to report to their duty stations came to a halt at the doorway, where Lemmon stood rock solid, blocking the exit with his stocky five-foot, ten-inch frame and refusing all pleas to be let outside. Rising above the cacophony were the screams of a hysterical young woman who worked in the mess hall. At first Lemmon tried to calm her, but he soon lost patience. "I told you to shut up! This is no time for hysterics!" Finally, he slapped the woman, and she calmed down.[56]

The men who had been on the top floor were the last to arrive in the barracks lobby—a comforting place because "you had concrete walls all around you." With men streaming in and Lemmon blocking the exit, the lobby was "jam packed with nervous sailors." Showing great presence of mind, Lemmon had smashed out the glass in the windows and six front doors to prevent bomb concussions from showering the lobby's occupants with glass.[57]

At Quarters K on the north end of Ford Island, Rear Admiral Bellinger hurried to depart for the Administration Building, although his first concern was to move his family to safety. His residence sat atop the abandoned casemated Battery Adair that the Navy had designated as an air raid shelter for dependents in the Senior Officer Quarters.[58]

At Quarters J, close by the Bellingers, Charlie Coe was still in bed at about 0745 trying to summon enough gumption to set about his customary Sunday routine of starting a batch of pancakes in the kitchen with the eager assistance of his five-year-old son, Chuck. When he heard the noise of a dive-bomber over Ford Island and an explosion on the southern end of the island, Coe needed no visual verification. He knew almost at once what was happening and shouted to his wife, "Get up, the war is on!" Curiously, his initial reaction to the attack was not fear but rather deep anger. "Those damn sons of bitches!" he muttered under his breath. Coe later recalled, "I did not have time to be scared, there was simply too much to do."[59]

The Coes threw on slippers and bathrobes and dressed their children. Chuck seemed highly amused by the proceedings in the harbor. The sound of the aircraft and bombs and the Fourth-of-July-like fireworks stimulated the excitable youngster, who dashed out the door. Coe chased the boy around the yard for what was almost surely only a few seconds but seemed much longer. Finally getting a firm hold on his son, he rushed his family north to the air raid shelter in the basement of the Bellingers' residence approximately two hundred feet away. Coe kissed his wife goodbye and turned to depart, thinking that he would never see his family again.[60]

At 0755 the sound of small-arms fire outside the bedroom window at Quarters T, just off the battleship *Tennessee* (BB 34)'s starboard quarter, alarmed Maj. Adolph Zuber, CO of the station's

Marine detachment. Running to his front window, he saw a low-flying plane making an attack run on the *West Virginia* (BB 48); an "explosion followed almost immediately." At that juncture a 5-inch/25-caliber antiaircraft battery on Battleship Row opened fire. Zuber sent his wife and two daughters to the air raid shelter at Quarters K, then telephoned the sergeant of the guard at the Enlisted Barracks and passed the order "to have all automatic weapons sent to the roof . . . to engage the enemy planes."[61]

With VP-21 under Lt. Cdr. George T. Mundorff Jr. at Midway Island and Lt. Cdr. John P. Fitzsimmons away leading VP-24's exercises, only two of Bellinger's squadron commanders Frank O'Beirne (VP-22) and Massie Hughes (VP-23)— were on Ford Island at the time of the attack. At Quarters P in the senior officer housing on the north end of Ford Island, Hughes pulled his uniform on over his pajamas and set off for the Administration Building to pick up instructions and orders from PatWing 2 headquarters.[62]

At Quarters 112-A in the Junior Officer Quarters on Ford Island's northern shore, explosions awakened Seattle, Washington, native 1st Lt. Daniel P. Closser, the executive officer of the station's

Lt. Charles F. Coe, 15 July 1934, after his transfer to the Bureau of Aeronautics
NPRC, St. Louis

Maj. Adolph Zuber, circa November 1940, shortly after taking command of NAS Pearl Harbor's Marine detachment
NARA, St. Louis

Marine detachment. He looked through the front window of his duplex directly across from Berth F-12 just in time to see a torpedo strike the light cruiser *Raleigh* (CL 7), which "seemed to shake violently." Realizing instantly that an attack was under way, Closser instructed his family and the maid to take cover under the house. Helen Closser objected. It was "nasty" under the house, she said, and there were cockroaches to boot. Further, Mrs. Closser had donned a beautiful Hawaiian dress for Mass and was not about to ruin it. Lieutenant Closser relented and packed his wife, the maid, and thirteen-month-old Daniel Jr. into the family car and drove four hundred yards east to the New Bachelor Officer Quarters (Building 78), the designated air raid shelter for the junior officers' families.[63]

Lt. (jg) Jaroud B. Smith Jr. (MC) got up early to go on duty at the Dispensary, leaving his wife behind at Quarters 113-A while he drove along the south shore of Ford Island. Upon reaching the station's garage at about 0755 he heard a loud

explosion. Looking left from his car window he saw aircraft with red circles on the wings coming from the direction of the battleships at one hundred feet altitude. Recognizing the planes as Japanese, Smith pressed on south to the Dispensary, seeing what he thought were several dive-bombers attacking the station from the direction of the Navy Yard.[64]

Lt. Magruder H. Tuttle, the station's gunnery officer, was to relieve Lieutenant Kane, then on duty as OOD at the Administration Building. As he was preparing to leave his wife, Dorothy Mae, and one-year-old son, Harry, at Quarters 115, Tuttle heard a large explosion, rushed to the back door, and saw flames rising from the vicinity of Hangar 6. His first thought was that a depth charge accident had occurred. Going inside, he telephoned the ordnance crews to remove all explosives from the vicinity of the squadrons. At that instant an aircraft passed on a southerly course across Ford Island with "the unmistakeable [*sic*] Japanese emblem on the plane."[65]

Quarters 112-A/B on the north shore of Ford Island, 28 October 1928, shown as Quarters 24 at Luke Field. Daniel and Helen Closser occupied Unit A at left, and Lt. (jg) Kenneth Lovell and wife Judith occupied Unit B at right.
NARA II, RG 77

Tuttle gathered up his wife and young son and went next door to Quarters 114 to pick up Lieutenant Kane's family—wife Madeline and children William and Judith. At that moment a Japanese aircraft burst into flames over the dry dock channel, but the elevated runway in the center of the island prevented him from seeing whether the aircraft fell. In the other direction the torpedoed *Utah* was listing badly to port as her crew clambered over the starboard rail and onto her hull.[66]

Having duty that morning, VJ-1's Ens. Wesley H. "Wes" Ruth, A-V(N), was up early to make the short trek from his first-floor suite to the wardroom in the New BOQ. Increasing aircraft engine noise high over the harbor distracted him from his breakfast. Ruth walked to the windows expecting to see yet "another mock attack that we frequently had on the weekends." When the bombs began to drop, however, Ruth hurried back to his suite, retrieved his cover, and hastened out to the lobby. Passing several panic-stricken families arriving from the officers' quarters on the north side of Ford Island, he ran to his yellow Pontiac convertible and sped along the road leading southeast and then southwest, parallel to Battleship Row.[67]

Unlike Ensign Ruth, Lt. James B. Ogden of VP-23 was not scheduled for duty, but he was up early at the BOQ to get a jump on the weekend. He heard aircraft noise as he left the shower and thought that some "doggone Army aviators didn't know enough to stay in bed on Sunday morning." The smoke roiling up from the vicinity of a trash dump near the foot of Ford Island seemed strange for a Sunday morning. Off to the southwest, an aircraft—he thought a Douglas TBD—droned in toward the harbor from the direction of the Ewa Mooring Mast Field, which was even more peculiar. "Good God," Ogden thought, "that guy's going against the course rules." Then a plane approaching from the vicinity of Pearl City dropped a torpedo, pulled up over the ships in the berths north of Ford Island, and banked south,

displaying the *hinomarus* on the wings. An explosion alongside the *Utah* spurred Ogden into action. He pulled on some clothing and bounded down the stairway to the lobby, where women and children from the adjacent married officer housing had gathered and were "piling into the basement." Ogden caught a ride to the PBY parking aprons near Hangar 54 at the southern tip of Ford Island, arriving at about 0820.[68]

Ens. James E. McColgan, D-V(G), VP-22's assistant personnel officer—and probably one of the few men of his squadron up for breakfast—heard an explosion, looked out, and saw columns of smoke rising from the south end of Ford Island. His first thought was that the magazine in VP-22's hangar (Hanger 6) had blown up. Running to his car, he saw an *Omaha*-class cruiser under attack and firing at the incoming aircraft. McColgan realized the attack was real when the airplane—complete with *hinomarus* on the underside—strafed the BOQ and bullets struck the ground all around him. McColgan raced for Quarters 105 next door, where the squadron's executive officer, Lt. Doyle G. Donaho, lived. Donaho told McColgan to go back to the BOQ, "break out the officers," and have them muster at Hangar 6. To McColgan's surprise, some of the men were so exhausted from the rigors of the recently completed advanced deployment to Wake and Midway that he had to shake them awake.[69]

A number of the officers reported later that the "general alarm whistle" (presumably the air horn that Lieutenant Kane in the Administration Building sounded) was not enough to wake them and was in fact inaudible, being on the opposite extreme of Ford Island. Only the general din and gunfire nearby awakened the men.[70]

In the General Storehouse (Building 75), Lt. Jay H. Mattson, SC-V(S), heard "a loud report" a considerable distance away followed seconds later by a "terrific explosion, which shook the building violently"; apparently this was the bomb explosion in the water off the seaplane ramp and the subsequent first detonation on the apron. Through the upper-floor windows he saw smoke and debris flying skyward from Hangar 6. Mattson called out, "Explosion or air raid!" and descended the stairwell to the ground floor, accompanied by two assistant duty supply officers.[71]

At the Boathouse, Sea1c John N. Delia dressed quickly and reported to the *YSD 19*, where he took the initiative and started the blowers that had to run for five minutes before starting the seaplane wrecking derrick's diesel engines. While waiting on the blowers, he opened the starboard hatch of the engine room and saw a torpedo plane bear down on the *California* and drop a torpedo—which for a moment seemed to be headed straight for the yardcraft. Delia had a perfect view of the battleship's port quarter and watched the "fish"

strike her stern. Shaken, the young sailor made straight for the bilges, where a pint of whiskey was secreted, and took a deep draft to settle himself down. With no one else on board, he shut down the blowers. Even the skipper, BM1c Stapleton, was absent, being ashore with his girlfriend.[72]

Having reached Landing C across the channel with Chaplain Volbeda, Ensign Edwards of VJ-1 spied a coxswain circling offshore in a motorboat from the *Vestal* (AR 4). Edwards ordered him to the landing, and he, Volbeda, and Lieutenant Black boarded and told him to make for Ford Island just as Commander Fuchida's flights of horizontal bombers passed overhead, parallel with the southeast shore of Ford Island. The coxswain took the shortest route possible, stopped at a seaplane ramp, and deposited his passengers on the shore.[73]

General Storehouse (Building 75) seen from the station's water tower looking east, 8 December 1941
NARA II, 80-G-32501, cropped

Edwards set out for Hangar 37 and found the men in a state of near panic. The young ensign did his best to take charge, but order returned only with the arrival of Lt. Cdr. Thomas G. Richards, VJ-1's commanding officer. Lieutenant Black rushed to the Administration Building, drew a rifle and ammunition, and opened fire from the building's north steps. Volbeda rushed to his post at the Administration Building, where he remained throughout the attack along with stunned officers and men "too surprised to fully realize the implications of the attack."[74]

Lt. Cdr. James W. Baldwin, D-V(S), the station's first lieutenant, noted fires at Hickam while passing by. When he and his wife, Carolyn, arrived at the Navy Yard's gate, the Marine guards told him that an air raid was in progress and he should park to the right of the gate. When he saw tracers and antiaircraft bursts, Baldwin told Carolyn to return to their residence at the Moana Hotel in Waikīkī. Baldwin set off at a run for the Merry Point ferry slip, where he found about one hundred men congregated.[75]

Baldwin ordered them to scatter just as a Nakajima Type 97 attack plane roared past, the rear gunner strafing the men below. Sailors and civilian workers crowded onto the ferry—either the *Manuwai* (YFB 16) or the *Nihoa* (YFB 17). Carp Clyde L. Ernst, the station's assistant first lieutenant, arrived and helped get the vessel under way. With BM1c John F. Desmond at the wheel, the ferry chugged down the Southeast Loch toward Ford Island while bombers overhead launched torpedoes against the battleships.[76]

Lt. Cdr. Thomas G. Richards, 21 March 1941
NPRC, St. Louis

Carp Clyde L. Ernst, circa late 1939
NPRC, St. Louis

Lt. Cdr. James W. Baldwin, circa May 1939
NPRC, St. Louis

Bosn John F. Desmond, circa September 1943
NPRC, St. Louis

More torpedo bombers appeared aft above the ferry's wake, flying directly toward the stricken battleships. Antiaircraft fire hit three of the aircraft immediately, with Lt. Suzuki Mitsumori's plane from the *Kaga* exploding in midair. Another of the *Kaga*'s Type 97s fell into the channel east of Ford Island, and still another disappeared beyond it. A rear gunner opened fire on the ferry, and Baldwin ordered all hands to hit the deck just as the burst of machine-gun fire penetrated the starboard side of the craft, passing over the prone passengers. The crew quickly hosed down the decks to prevent fires in case hot bomb splinters hit the ferry.[77]

At about 0815, Lt. (jg) Rodney T. West, MC-V(S), was at his residence on 2715 Mānoa Road, north of Waikīkī, with his wife, Mary Ann, and their two children. While he was preparing to go downtown to his private practice his father telephoned. "Rod, turn on your radio and listen to what's going on. I'll talk to you later."[78]

West tuned into KGMB and heard the familiar voice of announcer Webley "Web" Edwards instructing all military personnel to report immediately to their duty stations, shouting for emphasis, "We are being attacked! This is the real McCoy!" West "knew that it was the real thing." He put on his uniform and bid a sad good-bye to his wife and children, then gathered several other men and made his way toward Pearl Harbor, turning right into the traffic jam on Beretania Street.[79]

Immense columns of heavy smoke rose on the horizon. Moving over to King Street, West passed two checkpoints past which no Japanese were allowed. West of Honolulu they encountered one last check at which two armed guards looked in the trunk and then sent them on their way.[80]

Back at Pearl Harbor, the men of Ford Island responded quickly to the Japanese onslaught. The reaction of Sea1c George M. Hemingway was typical. Although afraid, he was also angry and frustrated at not being able to respond and inflict on the Japanese a measure of retribution commensurate with the destruction in clear view at Pearl Harbor. Although initially everyone was "confused, shocked and frightened," the worst of the fear was momentary. The men were soon too busy to think. Most engaged in activities they thought correct at the moment—taking cover or salvaging machine guns from the damaged aircraft, setting them up, and firing back at the Japanese. Many of the younger sailors acted in total disregard of the danger in their efforts to mount a defense of their base.[81]

Chapter Six

"WE ARE NOW IN
A STATE OF WAR"

At the Enlisted Barracks, finally realizing that the men needed to report to their duty stations, Master-at-Arms Lemmon bellowed, "Everybody get out and get to your squadron!" AMM3c Earnest A. Cochran was determined to report to VJ-2, but the Marine guards refused to let the men pass. Seeing a flatbed truck headed toward the other side of the island, Cochran and several other sailors pushed through the crowd and hopped in.[1]

After that Chief Lemmon allowed ten or so men to leave the building at a time, depending on the intervals between strafing aircraft. The *California* appeared to be preparing her antiaircraft batteries for action when a torpedo detonation jarred her severely and caused one of the 3-inch/50-caliber mounts to discharge, with the shell grazing the corner of the barracks. Sea1c George M. Hemingway and the other men took advantage of the excitement to break past the guards and scramble to their duty stations.[2]

Upon arriving at the barracks, detachment commander Major Zuber directed his leathernecks to break out all ammunition and sent word to the Armory—three hundred yards to the southeast—to deliver additional ammunition and automatic weapons. There were problems securing additional ammunition, however, because no one could find the person who had the keys to the sheds where the extra ammunition was stored. Cpl. Lawrence J. Keith, the outgoing sergeant of the guard, used his .45 to blow off the locks one after another. He was later fined a dollar for the destruction of each lock but then was awarded two cartons of cigarettes for each lock as a reward for his initiative.[3]

With Hangar 6 ablaze, the squadron duty officer instructed sailors to remove what equipment they could as quickly as possible, including a gasoline truck, an oil truck, a 1,500-gallon waste oil bowser, and about 20,000 rounds of belted ammunition. The explosions had sprung the hangar doors, so Sea1c George M. Hemingway and his VP-22 shipmate Sea1c Jack Sparks used ramp tractors and cables to open them so they could drive the trucks to safety. Despite the exploding ammunition, Sparks and Hemingway retrieved parachutes from the hangar's loft as well. Sailors with hoses played water on the ammunition until the station lost water pressure.[4]

Other men received instructions to go out to the aprons and man machine guns in the surviving aircraft or pull the PBYs away from the fires. Tractor driver Sea2c Robert C. Vajdak of VP-24 helped tow planes clear of Hangar 6 and away from other burning aircraft. Lieutenant Commander Fitzsimmons later praised Vajdak's "fearless manner," saying he "was in the midst of a most effective straffing [*sic*] attack, but would not be driven from his post of duty."[5]

AOM1c Theodore W. Croft was standing in one of the doorways at Hangar 6 when the *Shōkaku*'s dive-bombers strafed the area. Bullets struck him in the right arm, abdomen, and near his spleen, inflicting life-threatening injuries. The first ambulance to venture forth from the Dispensary transported Croft from the hangar to the Dispensary at about 0815.[6]

Near Hangar 54, the scarcity of proper mountings forced RM1c Perry B. F. Spanfelner to fire a fixed-mount gun like a free gun, reportedly balancing the Browning on a PBY's horizontal stabilizer to steady it. Vajdak picked up a .50-caliber machine gun and fired it as he cradled it in his arms. RM3c Glenn E. Pennock of VP-23 manned a .30-caliber machine gun only to find that its sight was missing. Undeterred, he opened fire and used the tracers to bore in on his targets.[7]

During a brief lull in the attacks, Strittmatter and others left the cover of the trench near Hangar 54 and ran to their ready aircraft, 24-P-3 (BuNo 2413), which had a severed wing spar and damage to the supporting structure for the wing. The men unshipped the machine guns and awaited the attackers' return. They did not have to wait long. Japanese aircraft—either the *Shōkaku* dive-bombers or Lieutenant Ibusuki's *Akagi* fighters—strafed the PBY, setting the wing afire. Seeing the aircraft in grave jeopardy, four other sailors in the waterline trench—ACMM (PA) Leif I. Larson, ACMM (AA) Albert P. Ferguson, and Sea2c Joseph A. Howard from VP-24 and AMM3c James M. Nelson from the station's complement—dodged gunfire and ran to the stricken aircraft, which was laden with high-octane fuel. One of the chiefs mounted the wing and extinguished the fires with a carbon dioxide bottle. Their actions saved the plane, which otherwise surely would have been lost. Similarly, near Hangar 38, Sea2c Roy R. Bratton, Sea2c Frank S. Evans, and Sea1c Burt L. Swisher drew water from the harbor to save three OS2Us and SOCs burning on the shore.[8]

Pvt. Lawrence J. Keith,
USMC, 27 March 1940
NARA, St. Louis

RM2c Perry B. F. Spanfelner,
6 August 1941
NARA, St. Louis

AS Charles J. Vajdak,
1 October 1941
NARA, St. Louis

Lt. Cdr. Leif I. Larson,
circa November 1951
NPRC, St. Louis

Sea2c Burt L. Swisher,
circa 1941
NARA, St. Louis

Ens. Daniel S. Hamway,
A-V(S), 29 October 1941
NPRC, St. Louis

Confusion reigned as well at VJ-1's Hangar 37 to the northeast. The squadron's OOD herded all "unnecessary personnel into the Operations Building [Building 84]." RM2c Harry R. Mead and VJ-1's other communication watchstander dutifully followed the other men inside but shortly thereafter received orders to return to the base radio station.[9]

Ens. Daniel S. Hamway had arrived at Operations from the BOQ but found no arms in the building. Undeterred, Hamway commandeered a truck and, with CAerog (AA) John Van Domelen of VP-23, drove to the Storehouse and obtained a .30-caliber machine gun, two BARs, and ten Springfields that were later augmented by three Lewis machine guns and three .50 Brownings. After distributing the weapons among the men at Operations, Hamway took the truck and driver back to the Storehouse and then helped distribute blankets and towels at the Dispensary. Lieutenant Erickson—relieved as OOD by Lieutenant Tuttle—proceeded from the Administration Building to Hangar 37 and the Operations Building, where he assumed command of the land plane control tower and of Hamway's impromptu antiaircraft battery being set up on the roof.[10]

Aerographer John Van Domelen, circa July 1943 while assigned to the Pearl Harbor Navy Yard
NPRC, St. Louis

Back in the ditch near Hangar 54, AMM3c Earnest A. Cochran and two shipmates took cover from the Japanese machine guns in a steel junction box until there was a lull in the strafing. As soon as they could they bolted from the ditch and rejoined their VJ-2 shipmates across the field. Although Hangar 177 was unharmed, none of VJ-2's aircraft was flyable after the *Shōkaku*'s dive-bombers strafed them with incendiary bullets that burned the wing fabric. The hump at the center of Ford

Island's landing field and the smoke on the south side made it difficult for the men to discern what was occurring there. Although petty officers barked orders, there were no officers to provide unified direction. On their own initiative, men seeking cover in the hangar broke out .30-caliber rifles and .45s. Some attempted to mount .30-caliber machine guns in the J2Fs.[11]

One senior petty officer—AMM1c Ralph E. Flora—rallied the men and took charge, even assigning tasks to the chiefs. His resourcefulness was all the more ironic because he was the inebriated sailor whom AMM3c Cochran had helped into a bunk near the end of his watch. Another man who impressed Cochran was AMM3c Ralph B. "Brigham" Young, who had enlisted in Salt Lake City, Utah. When Cochran arrived, he found Young in the rear cockpit of a Grumman J2F amphibian returning fire against the Japanese with its .30-caliber Browning. Young refused to leave the cockpit until the attack was over, even though bullets holed the plane in many places.[12]

AMM1c Ralph B. Young, circa 1941
Young

VJ-2's parking apron in front of Hangar 177 (out of view at left). A J2F-4 from the squadron, 2-J-22 (BuNo 1641), sits in the foreground with one of the unit's two PBY-1s immediately behind.
NARA II, 80-G-32670

After fragments and splinters pierced the walls of CRM (PA) Andrew J. Giemont's upstairs flat in Quarters 49-D, he sent his wife, Minnie, and son, Jack, to the basement for safety as he left for the Administration Building. When strafing aircraft set his automobile afire, he commandeered another and drove "without regard [for] his personal safety to the Patrol Wing TWO Communication Office" where his "cool manner and excellent leadership" maintained good order in one of the most critical locations on the station.[13]

Ens. William A. Keutgen, A-V(S), and other officers who made it to the Administration Building received an issue of pistols from the Armory, but the supply was soon exhausted. Some of the officers handed their .45s to sailors. The haphazard manner in which the arms were handed out left men with legitimate needs wanting while others received weapons to no good purpose. Keutgen armed a detail to guard a radio transmitter by reassigning four rifles to the radio room guards.[14]

RM3c Raymond D. Strong and other sailors encountered flying fragments and bullets when they entered the radio room and were forced to leave, although they returned in short order. CRM (PA) Allan G. MacKay instructed Strong to guard a circuit to one of the outlying islands and put three or four radiomen on each circuit in order to clear message traffic quickly. Transcribed messages went to Chief MacKay or to the first available officer. RM2c James C. Lagerman guarded the circuit with the three aircraft from VP-14. Maintaining communication with the seven PBYs airborne from VP-14 and VP-24 was the radiomen's most critical task. Their shipmates with 1903 Springfields posted outside the radio room attested to the importance of their work. Their orders, as directed by Chief MacKay, were "to shoot any god damned slant-eyed bastards who try to get [in]."[15]

Over Operating Area C5 southwest of Maui, VP-24's PBYs finally received late word of the attack. At 0815 a radioman brought AMM1c Meister a plain-language message that "hostilities with Japan commenced with air raid on Pearl X." Meister passed the message to another radioman in a waist blister, who relayed the text to the *Gudgeon* via blinker. The submarine crash-dived immediately—no response, no acknowledgment.[16]

After several failed attempts, a VP-24 radiomen contacted Pearl Harbor, inquiring whether a drill was under way. "No! Hell, no!" was the reply. "Get off the air!" After "milling around for

RM3c Raymond D. Strong,
circa 1941
NARA, St. Louis

ATC James C. Lagerman,
circa December 1951
NPRC, St. Louis

CHRONOLOGICAL RECORD OF EVENTS

Submarine Base, Pearl Harbor   DATE 7 Dec. 1941

DUTY
OFFICER   WATCH

DUTY
YEOMAN

TIME OF OCCURRENCE		REMARKS
Sent	**Rec'd**	
1842	Outgoing	Hostilities with Japan commenced with air rail on Pearl.
	1842	COMSECTOR FOUR: Prepare to get underway.

CinCPac's radio message regarding the attack on Pearl Harbor sent at 0812 (1842 GCT) and intercepted by the PBYs operating with the *Gudgeon* off the coast of Maui
NARA II, RG 80

View off the *Gudgeon*'s port quarter, 7 July 1941, near Mare Island, Calif.
Navsource

three or four lifetimes," the PBYs finally received instructions: fly to Barbers Point and search for the Japanese. Not well equipped for action, the planes carried only a few bombs and depth charges along with machine-gun ammunition in thirteen-round strips for target practice.[17]

P3c John W. Burton's section had worked all night in the Fleet Air Photographic Laboratory (Building 20) west of the Storehouse. Just as he left the building, bombs struck in the vicinity of Hangar 6. Initially Burton thought that something had exploded in the hangar, but seeing the Japanese markings on the aircraft pulling away from the scene, he backtracked toward the lab to retrieve "patrol cameras" to photograph the damage. Since the bombs "were generally covering quite an area," though, he thought better of it.[18]

Twelve other photographers from VJ-1 who had just finished breakfast had quite different ideas. After seeing the diving aircraft and hearing explosions they hastened to the Fleet Air Photographic Laboratory to prepare the film and cameras. The first men to arrive had to kick in the door to gain access. Fortunately, some cameras lay ready, having been prepared to record a Monday exercise. More men arrived and prepared film, cutting sheet stock into four-by-five-inch pieces. The men also readied several aerial cameras. When he arrived at Building 20 at about 0815, CP (PA) Earl Sever discovered that six to eight photographers had already departed to record the events outside.[19]

In the General Storehouse, the trio of Lieutenant Mattson, Ens. Raymond S. Cope, SC-V(G), and Ens. Rolland A. Helsel, SC-V(P), retreated hastily to the storage vault shortly after the raid began as bomb explosions and gunfire grew louder. They drew fire extinguishers from stock and charged and prepared them for distribution. Other men came in soon afterward, and some assisted with the extinguishers while others reported to the ordnance storeroom and cleaned weapons. The cleaning and issuing of firearms and firefighting equipment continued for about an hour, with a number of women—presumably wives from the chief petty officer housing—lending assistance. Lt. Joseph B. Musser and some others assembled fire extinguishers from crates slated for delivery to the outer islands, and two of the women prepared the Foamite mixture needed to charge them.[20]

The ordnance section under AOM2c Raymond L. Kelly "did splendid work assembling machine guns and rifles, and instructing in their use." Old peacetime practices and habits sometimes died hard, though. When VJ-1's CO, Lieutenant Commander Richards, ordered the men to draw weapons, one of the storekeepers in NAS Main Supply refused to issue them because the men did not present a standard BuSandA 307 Stub Requisition.[21]

Lt. Jay A. Mattson, SC-V(S), circa July 1941
NPRC, St. Louis

Ens. Raymond W. Cope, SC-V(G), circa September 1940
NPRC, St. Louis

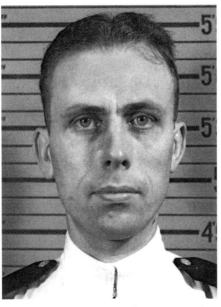

Ens. Roland A. Helsel, SC-V(P), circa late 1941
NPRC, St. Louis

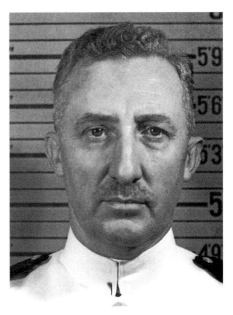

Lt. Joseph B. Musser, SC-V(P), circa 1941
NARA, St. Louis

By the time Lt. Walter F. Arnold, MC-V(S)—the first physician to arrive—and his driver, PhM2c Kurt O. Flechel, got to the Dispensary, they found the mood there surprisingly calm. The pharmacist's mates were preparing medications and dressings for the anticipated flood of casualties. Other doctors arrived shortly thereafter, with Lt. (jg) Jaroud Smith coming on board first, although by a circuitous route. Upon reaching the Dispensary, he received word that Hangar 6 was ablaze and immediately set off in an ambulance for the hangar, stopping on the apron to pick up a sailor with a lacerated forehead. At about 0805 Smith returned to the Dispensary with the first casualty of the day.[22]

When PhM2c Robert J. Peth in the Dispensary received word of seven casualties near Hangar 6, he and another pharmacist's mate took an ambulance to the hanger, leaving PhM2c Chester L. Morris to man the line. The ambulance driver narrowly missed the bomb crater near Building 2 but returned safely with his charges to the Dispensary, where Peth and his shipmate unloaded the wounded.[23]

Arriving at the Boathouse, Lieutenant Commander Baldwin ordered all craft to conduct rescue operations. CBM (AA) Clarence W. Fisher assigned boats, and soon all of the craft were out picking up sailors from the water. The boat crews rescued hundreds of sailors during the morning and landed them ashore at the small boat landing (Landing A). Baldwin marveled at the bravery of the boat crews, who "behaved splendidly under . . . heavy machine gun fire, and much falling splinters, seemingly ignoring altogether either the presence of enemy planes, or their fire." Bullets struck several of the boats, sinking one; sailors in other damaged craft plugged holes with pieces of pencils.[24]

Captain Shoemaker encountered no one during the short trip from his quarters to the southeast end of Ford Island. When he arrived at the seaplane ramps, he found Hangar 6 and the aircraft around it "burning like a forest fire" with "scarcely a single plane left on the apron undamaged." Great clouds of black smoke churned out of the northeast corner of the building. Shoemaker ordered a petty officer and some enlisted men taking cover nearby to "pull the good planes away from the fire." Ens. James McColgan of VP-22 used a "mule" (ramp tractor) to remove the aircraft from the line of fire.[25]

Lt. Walter F. Arnold, MC-V(S), 28 March 1941
NPRC, St. Louis

Lt. Jaroud B. Smith Jr., (MC), 18 September 1939, while a physician at the U.S. Naval Hospital, Charleston, S.C.
NPRC, St. Louis

Midn. James E. McColgan at the USNR Midshipmen's School *Prairie State* (IX 15) in New York, N.Y., circa late 1940
NPRC, St. Louis

While the men were moving the aircraft to safety the *Arizona* blew up. Apart from the dreadful concussion and noise, what struck Shoemaker about the battleship's demise was the "awful hissing and swishing sound, as though the whole business came right out of the bowels of the [ship]." The sinking *Arizona* came to rest on the water line that passed through her berth and served the rest of the station. At that juncture Lt. Robert C. Winters of VP-23 arrived, and Shoemaker ordered him to clear all sailors from the trench near Hangar 54. The two officers and others moved undamaged OS2Us from alongside Hangar 38. The sailors also moved a PBY-5 "leaking gasoline at a high rate" to Ramp 2 along the channel near Hangar 38 so the fuel could drain into the water.[26]

As Charlie Coe was bidding his family farewell at the Quarters K "dungeon" Rear Admiral Bellinger bounded down the stairs fumbling furiously with the zipper on his pants. "Come on Charlie," he said; "let's get down to headquarters!" Still clad in pajamas, robe, and slippers, Coe responded, "Admiral, at least let me get my pants on. I'll drive down in my own car."[27]

Finally conquering his balky zipper, Bellinger looked out a window and saw aircraft passing at a low altitude to the southwest. Suddenly "there was a tremendous explosion that shook the house to its foundations." Later, when he learned that the exploding *Arizona* was responsible for the shock wave, Bellinger thought of Rear Adm. Isaac C. Kidd, ComBatDiv 1, who had perished on board his flagship. When BatDiv 1 was in port, Kidd was fond of disembarking early in the morning before Colors for a brisk walk on Ford Island

Capt. James M. Shoemaker, NAS Norfolk, 19 July 1943
NARA II, 80-G-42676, cropped

A PBY from VP-23 lies at water's edge near Ramp 2 at the south corner of Hangar 38, most probably to allow its fuel tanks to drain into the water rather than onto the pavement. The damaged aircraft remained in that location for at least three days.
NARA II, 80-G-32714, cropped

to start the day. The morning of 7 December was no exception; the admiral got in his constitutional and returned to the ship before the attack started. "This was his last walk," Bellinger later observed poignantly. Jumping into his car, Bellinger drove south "like a bat out of hell."[28]

Lieutenant Commander Coe was running "pell-mell" to Quarters J to grab a pair of pants when the *Arizona* blew up. At first Coe felt only the concussion, "a terrible strange movement of the air," followed a split second later by the sound of the magazines exploding. "It just took my breath," he related later.

> There was a sudden pressure wave or massive air movement, like a 16-inch salvo going off a few feet away. First the terrible concussion and then the deafening roar of the detonation which followed. In just a moment, I saw all kinds of debris on the lawn in front of my quarters on the waterside. This consisted of thin plating and superstructure parts of the *Arizona* which littered the lawn. A piece of armor, a piece of shattered steel, that is, about the size of a brick came right through two layers of wood of my garage and lodged on the bumper of my car.[29]

Recovering from the shock, Coe ran to the house, pulled on a shirt and trousers over his pajamas, and slipped shoes on his bare feet. Jumping into his car, he raced "hells bells" for the Administration Building.[30]

The concussion from the *Arizona*'s exploding magazines shook the Administration Building with tremendous force, creating an illusion for the occupants of the concrete floor rippling like a wave. The concussion made Sea2c Ryan feel as if he was being squeezed from all directions and then let go. The unanimous reaction of the sailors was to stay right where they were.[31]

Ensign Ruth of VJ-1 was driving southeast at the midpoint of Battleship Row when the *Arizona* blew up. Debris and unexploded cordite pellets began "dropping all around, just like snow," even into Ruth's convertible. Frightened that he might be strafed, he continued at high speed until he reached Hangar 37 at the southeast side of the station's landing field. Taking advantage of the trees along the hangar's south face for cover, he parked and rushed in to await orders. Not seeing Ensign Edwards, who had arrived at about the same time, Ruth thought himself the only officer present.[32]

The *Arizona*'s demise also put an end to effective firefighting efforts. Lieutenant Kane dispatched a fire truck to Hangar 6 but received word that water pressure was failing because the twelve-inch water main from Kūāhua Island to Ford Island had been severed—crushed by the sinking *Arizona*. ChMach Joseph A. Sanders—an assistant to Lt. Thomas L. Davey, the station's public works officer—arrived at the Boiler House and found "the boiler secured and no pressure on the water main." In addition, damage to the temporary six-inch line in the vicinity of 1010 Pier where it crossed to Ford Island had cut off the external water supply to NAS Pearl Harbor completely.[33]

En route to the Administration Building, Rear Admiral Bellinger glimpsed torpedo planes pulling up over Battleship Row at about 150 feet. Japanese horizontal bombers were high above the harbor at this point, above a broken cloud deck that was perfect for the bombers but "not so good for the antiaircraft fire."[34]

The sight of the other battleships under attack added to Charlie Coe's shock at the demise of the *Arizona*: "The *Oklahoma* was to me a sight beyond all belief. It was in fact the most awful thing I had ever seen. To watch this big battleship capsize and to see only her bottom sticking up out of the water like the back of a turtle and to realize that U.S. officers and men were still in there—well, I just couldn't believe it. It made me realize as nothing else that war had come to Hawaii."[35]

The south corner of Hangar 37 and the trees under which Ens. Ruth parked his 1939 Oldsmobile

NARA II, 71-CA-153B-13599

The Boiler Plant (Building 40) looking northwest from Landing A, 2 October 1941. Note the Fire Station (Building 42) with the radio transmitter room and antenna mast atop the tower.

NARA II, 71-CA-154A-14629

ChMach Joseph A. Sanders,
circa January 1942
NPRC, St. Louis

BM1c John N.
Delia while
stationed at
NAS Hilo,
circa 1944
Delia

Among those conducting rescues in the harbor, Sea1c Delia's crew went straight for the sailors bobbing up and down in the water. With so many men to pick up, the crew had to be selective. Anyone still alive—or who appeared able to survive—came on board; the obviously dead were abandoned for the time being. The crew filled the boat on each of three trips. Apart from applying compresses made from their shirts, there was little the boat crews could do for the injured men.[36]

Casualties came to the Dispensary from many locations. Ens. Guy R. Nance, E-V(P), the station's transportation officer, conveyed wounded survivors from the *Utah* and other battleships to the Dispensary via truck and then collected casualties from the BOQ. For about twenty minutes after the *Arizona* disaster, many sailors came ashore near the Chief Petty Officer Quarters in the vicinity of Berth F-4 and also near the Senior Officer Quarters.[37]

Doctors continued to report to the Dispensary. While driving south from Quarters E, Lt. Cecil D. Riggs (MC) rounded the corner at the Old BOQ and saw the red car of the station's fire marshal—ACMM (AA) Shirley H. Brown—hit by bursts of machine-gun fire from a passing torpedo bomber.

Guy R. Nance,
circa September
1940 while
employed at
the U.S. Rubber
Company
NPRC, St. Louis

When he reached the Dispensary, Riggs found that he was the senior physician on duty because Cdr. Louis Iverson (MC), the station's chief medical officer, was still absent.[38]

Guards waylaid Lt. Cdr. George W. Dickinson (MC) near the hospital landing. A flight surgeon since August, the thirty-nine-year-old Arkansas native was to have sailed the following day for Wake Island. He and his wife, Lillian, had stayed overnight in Quarters 364 near the Pearl Harbor Naval Hospital with their friend Lt. Oran W.

Chenault (MC). A loud explosion awoke him shortly "before 0800," he later wrote, and he saw "large billows of smoke and flame" issuing from Hangar 6. Dickinson saw "the emblem of the rising sun" on the wings of a plane overhead. Having served in China with the Fourth Marines at the time of the Japanese assault on Shanghai in August 1937, he comprehended instantly the identity of the attacking aircraft. Heading for Landing C, he reached the corner of Capt. Reynolds Hayden's residence near the hospital, where a Marine sentry, seeing Dickinson's civilian attire, prevented him from going further. Dickinson sprinted to take cover at the hospital.[39]

At the Dispensary on Ford Island, Lieutenant Riggs found Lieutenant Arnold and Lieutenant (jg) Smith already at work tending to casualties and preparing for more arrivals. The doctors stripped the wounded of their clothing and administered morphine while corpsmen covered and tagged the men. To avoid confusion over who had been given morphine, corpsmen painted a large M on the patients' foreheads with Mercurochrome. With the resources of the Dispensary stretched to the breaking point, Riggs set a division of labor that of necessity included dentists. Burn cases and other severe injuries came under the care of Lt. Rush L. Canon (DC) on the second floor. Riggs directed Arnold to care for wounded in the outpatient department and put Smith in charge of patients in the first-floor ward. In the months before the attack Riggs had trained his men in every manner of skill, and it was gratifying to see tangible results.[40]

AOM1c Croft, wounded in the doorway to Hangar 6 during one of the strafing attacks, was in severe shock from internal hemorrhaging. The staff administered morphine and delivered saline and glucose intravenously, but it was not enough to save him; he died at 0835. Croft was the sole fatality from the station and its attached squadrons. He left behind a wife, Louise, and stepsons Donald A. "Don" and Gerard T. "Jerry" Morton Jr. Ironically, his stepsons were fishing at Pearl City when the attacks began across the water on Ford Island, where Croft now lay dead.[41]

Early in the attack, a very dangerous situation developed at Ford Island's Fuel Pier. The oiler Neosho had arrived there on the morning of 6 December with a cargo of oil and gasoline taken on board from the Standard Oil docks in Los Angeles, California. After tying up to the wharf at Hickam Field, she discharged approximately 400,000 gallons of

ACMM (AA) Shirley H. Brown, circa June 1941
NPRC, St. Louis

Lt. Cecil D. Riggs, (MC), circa January 1940, at NAS Pensacola
NPRC, St. Louis

Lt. George W. Dickinson, (MC), 14 January 1942
Sherrard

Lt. Rush L. Canon, (DC), 14 January 1942
Sherrard

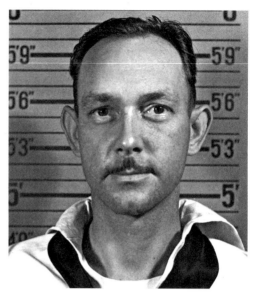

AOM1c Theodore W. Croft, circa 1941
NARA, St. Louis

aviation fuel. That evening she moored to the Fuel Pier (Berth F-4) at Ford Island at 2140 and commenced discharging her remaining cargo of gasoline. With that transfer complete at 0750 on 7 December, the crew on the Fuel Pier prepared "to take back suction on the line" through which they had transferred the gasoline during the night.[42]

When the attack began, men secured the pumps and valves between the *Neosho* and the tanks on Ford Island, and gasoline truck drivers received orders to disperse their vehicles. The station's fuel officer, Ensign Singleton, directed "the uncoupling of all lines, thereby reestablishing the security of the station gasoline fuel system and enabling *Neosho* to leave [her] dangerous berth." The dock crew—including "Oil King" CMM (PA) Alfred L. Hansen and AMM2c Albert C. Thatcher—used fire axes to cut the lines securing the oiler to the pier. Singleton and Thatcher took cover until the worst of the strafing had passed, then proceeded to the Gasoline Pump House (Building 33) to start the saltwater pumps that supplied sprinklers atop the aboveground reserve gasoline tanks. Cdr. Charles J. Harter (SC), the station's supply officer, provided transportation to the tanks, where Singleton "opened valves on the sprinkler system, and turned on the pumps."[43]

Looking northeast, opposite the battleships *Maryland* (BB 46) and *Oklahoma* in Berth F-5, Harter noticed a grass fire near Tank 63 in the vicinity of Berths F-5 and F-6. It appeared to him that the sprinkler system "would not bring sufficient water to bear," so Harter drove quickly to the Fire Station (Building 42) and asked the men there to help Singleton's fuel division extinguish the fire. Since the system had just received 400,000 gallons of gasoline, Harter set plans in place to empty the fuel tanks into their surrounding berms if necessary.[44]

Meanwhile, four tanker trucks—likely those dispersed previously—sat parked perilously close to the blazing *Arizona*. A grass fire underneath one of the vehicles endangered the entire area near the Senior Officer Quarters, and drivers moved the trucks far away from the stricken battleships. Ensign Singleton returned to the Gasoline Pump House "to stand by for contingencies." Lieutenant (jg) Osborne ordered him to proceed to the mess hall in the Enlisted Barracks to relay orders from Cdr. Harry F. Carlson, the station's executive officer.[45] Subsequently, Captain Shoemaker praised Singleton for his "ability for quick thinking in any emergency." For their resourcefulness and bravery under fire, Singleton, Hansen, and Thatcher received the Navy Cross.[46]

The *Neosho* lies moored at Berth F-4 at about 0800 on 7 December, just as the station's fuel division took steps to secure the fuel system and get the ship under way from the Fuel Pier.
Matsumura, cropped

The pipelines on the Fuel Pier (seen here 9 February 1925) conducted aviation gasoline and motor fuel to the aboveground storage tanks.
NARA II, 71-CA-154F-5312

Capt. Charles J. Harter, (SC), 4 May 1942, shortly before he was reassigned from Hawai'i to Mare Island Navy Yard
NARA II, 80-G-63416

Ens. "D" Arnold Singleton, A-V(S), circa July 1941
NPRC, St. Louis

Ens. Lester D. Satchell, SC-V(G), circa July 1941
NPRC, St. Louis

Within minutes of the sound of the bombs exploding, trucks and private vehicles arrived at the New BOQ with women and children from the Married Officer Quarters along the northwest shore of Ford Island. Ens. Lester D. Satchell, SC-V(G), and his wife, Alice, gathered several of the families and drove them to shelter. Ens. Robert W. Reed, SC-V(P), helped them herd the dependents into the west wing of the BOQ's first floor. First Lieutenant Closser and his family arrived from Quarters 111 as well. While Helen Closser ran upstairs and placed Daniel Jr. in a bathtub, her husband remained downstairs amid "children and semi-hysterical women." Dismayed by the disorder, he brandished his .45, "took the floor and quieted the people milling around in the lobby." Then he issued strict instructions "to sit in the hall against the walls."[47]

Survivors from the *Utah* followed on the heels of the dependents. Cdr. Solomon S. Isquith, the senior officer on board, ordered all those who came ashore to take cover in a six-foot-deep trench excavated for an unfinished public works project that extended south from Quarters 112A/B to Quarters 120A/B. Seeing that HA1c Jean W.

Kerns had brought a first-aid kit ashore, Isquith went to Quarters 118 (assigned to Lieutenant Church, the assistant public works officer at NAS Pearl Harbor) to set up a first-aid station there. As the intensity of the first Japanese attacks waned, Ens. James W. Cronenberg, A-V(S), drove a truck to the vicinity of Berth F-11, where the *Utah* lay capsized, and distributed blankets to the shivering, wet survivors in the trench along the shore, then transported them to the BOQ.[48]

Water- and oil-soaked sailors from Battleship Row also crossed the threshold of the BOQ. After reporting to the Administration Building, Ens. William G. Boynton, A-V(S), secured a light truck and brought in sailors who had abandoned the stricken battleships. Those refugees soon filled the balance of the first floor, which had a first-aid station set up at the entrance. The sailors, in "all stages of dishevelment," were issued clothing appropriated from the officers' rooms upstairs. Among the scavengers was Ens. Daniel S. Hamway, A-V(S), who joined in ransacking his shipmates' rooms for towels and blankets for the wet survivors from the *West Virginia* and *Arizona* flooding the building.[49]

Aerial view of the northwest shore of Ford Island, 10 December 1941. Note the utility trench excavated next to the Junior Officer Quarters where survivors from the *Utah*—seen capsized at lower right—took refuge in large numbers. The torpedoed light cruiser *Raleigh* lies to the left, with the destroyer tender *Whitney* (AD 4) providing services alongside, having moored to the stricken cruiser at 1500 on 9 December.
NARA II, 80-G-387581, cropped

Quarters 118 on the north shore of Ford Island, shown on 28 October 1928 as Quarters 36 at Luke Field. On 7 December 1941, Lt. William C. G. Church, wife Anna, and two young sons occupied the unit.
NARA II, RG 77

Ens. James W. Cronenberg, A-V(S),
31 October 1941
NPRC, St. Louis

Ens. William G. Boynton, A-V(S),
29 October 1941
NPRC, St. Louis

When matters threatened to get out of hand, 1st Lieutenant Closser got on top of a desk in the lobby and ordered the occupants to sit tight. Some of the women present at the BOQ were a calming influence; they stayed on duty for two days and nights and "offered no end of comfort to the officers and men survivors with no thought of their personal comfort."[50]

On the other end of Ford Island, Bellinger arrived at the Administration Building about fifteen minutes into the attack and joined his staff in their determined efforts to find the Japanese carriers. Ramsey had radioed the seven airborne PBYs to search sectors north and northwest (VP-14) and northeast (VP-24), hoping that VP-11 and VP-12 could follow shortly. Coe attempted to "contact the Army Air and find out where the hell the Japanese planes were coming from" but could not get through. When communications went out temporarily at the station during the bombing, Bellinger contacted his squadron commanders personally on foot to determine aircraft availability and to issue instructions. Ramsey eventually established a telephone connection with Kaneohe to relay instructions directly to PatWing 1.[51]

The flood of casualties coming into the Dispensary was overwhelming the staff. As Lieutenant Schuessler limped in on his badly bruised left leg, a Marine standing in the doorway to the Enlisted Barracks hailed him, pleading for help with the casualties that had just arrived in the mess hall. Schuessler located Lieutenant Riggs and informed him of the situation, and Riggs ordered him to the barracks with PhM1c Verne Crawford to set up a first-aid station. Schuessler administered first aid to the four wounded four sailors he found in the mess hall, but more casualties filled the space quickly, and he requested mattresses and blankets for them. Schuessler depended heavily on Crawford—a World War I veteran of the Medical Service—who risked his life racing to and from the Dispensary to replenish supplies as well as treating the wounded.[52]

Anticipating the necessity to evacuate the crowded Dispensary, Lieutenant Riggs directed CPhM (PA) Eugene Griffith to secure additional bed space in the barracks. Eventually, the medical staff set up an emergency first-aid station in the BOQ as well. The Supply Department distributed a vast quantity of blankets, sheets, and cots to

Lt. Elmer W. Schuessler, DC-V(S),
14 January 1942
Sherrard

PhM1c Verne G. Crawford,
14 January 1942
Sherrard

the first-aid stations. Riggs placed Lt. Carl H. B. Morrison—just detached from the *Lexington*—in charge of securing the required blankets and mattresses.[53]

As casualties arrived in the mess hall on stretchers, sailors ran upstairs, stripped sheets and blankets from second-floor bunks, and placed the blankets over the men to keep them warm. Schuessler and Crawford distributed morphine syringes to volunteers who administered the pain-killing injections and attempted to wipe the fuel oil from the injured. The oil was a heavy, thick substance that could not be wiped away easily. To minimize the danger flying glass posed to the incoming casualties, Master-at-Arms Lemmon continued his spree of breaking out windows on the first floor, now using a golf club.[54]

Due to the emergency the medical staff maintained no comprehensive records of the men treated outside the Dispensary, but the war diarist for NAS Pearl Harbor estimated that approximately two hundred men received treatment in the Enlisted Barracks and New BOQ. That number included neither the sailors in Hangar 37 nor the large number of men in shock wandering aimlessly about the

station. When CRM Thomas Farrow came out of the Operations Building he found dazed men, some burned, some covered with oil. He went to Hangar 37 nearby and called in pharmacist's mates to set up a first-aid station and provide treatment, then went back out and gathered the wandering sailors and led them to the safe haven of the hangar.[55]

The Assembly and Repair Department began assessing the station's material casualties even before the first wave of attackers departed. At about 0815, Ens. Henry J. Bultman Jr., A-V(S), received orders to inspect the Engine and Overhaul Shop and Final Assembly Shop for damage. Finding no major problems, he detailed a party to fill the bomb crater in the street at the south end of Building 2. Although bomb splinters had damaged several floatplanes, he was more concerned that the crater blocked access to the hangars via the only major thoroughfare leading south. Bultman next used the A&R men to move surviving aircraft further away from Hangar 6, which was still burning fiercely.[56]

As more officers and men converged on the seaplane hangars, Captain Shoemaker decided his presence was unnecessary and left to conduct a firsthand inspection tour of the station. With the attacks of the first wave tapering off, Shoemaker hopped into his Model A Ford and drove northeast toward the officer quarters on that end of Ford Island.[57]

Japanese estimates of the damage done to Ford Island overstated the real damage inflicted, which was bad enough. The exuberant bomber crews claimed twenty-three PBYs destroyed—an inflated number attributable to poor visibility—and exaggerated the number of PBYs present on Ford Island, claiming one hundred, almost four times the actual number. The actual damage done was great. Despite one near miss in the water and two duds, Takahashi's group destroyed six VP-22 PBY-3s outright and damaged or disabled the rest. VP-23 fared similarly with perhaps half of its

Ens. Henry J. Bultman Jr., A-V(S), circa October 1941
NPRC, St. Louis

An unknown individual (possibly Capt. James M. Shoemaker) in short-sleeved shirt and tropical helmet stands in front of the main entrance to the Administration Building gazing north over the Dispensary late in the first-wave attack. If the man is indeed Shoemaker, he is about to depart on his inspection tour of the station.
NARA II, 80-G-32463

Lt. (jg) Frank O'Beirne at NAS
Pensacola, 15 March 1935
NPRC, St. Louis

Lt. (jg) Doyle G. Donaho at NAS
Pensacola, 15 July 1934
NPRC, St. Louis

PBY-5s lost in the fires near Hangars 6 and 54. The four PBY-5s of VP-24 east of O'ahu escaped damage, but the squadron's ready aircraft was badly damaged. The planes undergoing maintenance in Hangar 54 were intact. The aircraft of the Base Force Utility Wing fared badly—by 0830 VJ-2 had no flyable aircraft.[58]

Hangar 6 suffered significant structural loss, with 40 percent of its wooden portion burned. Fires ignited by the bomb explosion east of the hangar caused severe damage to the northeast corner of the building, although the hangar's steel framework was intact. Hangar 38 sustained superficial damage from the near miss and the dud that crashed through the roof. Far more serious was the water main the *Arizona* had crushed, which meant that fires would continue burning because there was no water to put them out.

When the raid slackened, Frank O'Beirne, VP-22's commander, and his executive officer, Lieutenant Donaho, solicited volunteers to get planes up to search for the Japanese fleet. They wanted mechanics, ordnancemen, and pilots—everyone necessary to get the planes in the air. The officers' tone was grim, and their admonishment made a lasting impression on AMM3c James L. Young. "We are now in a state of war, and you will be treated as such, period."[59]

Chapter Seven

"WELL, THERE'S NOTHING LEFT, SO I GUESS IT'S GOING TO BE EVERY MAN FOR HIMSELF"

When the skies over Pearl Harbor finally cleared of enemy planes shortly before 0830, the exigencies of the moment allowed little time for contemplation of the future. There was wreckage to clear, bomb craters to fill, fires to extinguish, and casualties to treat.

As Captain Shoemaker drove northeast on the first leg of his inspection tour, he encountered a great quantity of debris from the *Arizona*. Fragments littered the entire northeast corner of the island—"parts of the battleship's mast, bridge railings, armor plate, and sheet metal." Appalled at the conditions close to his quarters, he later said that "the place was a mess; it looked like a junk yard." After retrieving his pistol from Quarters A, he drove hurriedly toward the northwest shore of the island.[1]

Meanwhile at the seaplane base, sailors from the Assembly and Repair Department hove to, clearing the aprons between Hangars 6 and 38. Debris strewn over a wide area hindered movement of undamaged planes and vehicles and blocked access to Ramps 2 and 3 at the south end of the aprons separating the hangars. The floatplanes

that had been moved to prevent their destruction also obstructed the ramps. With the initial shock having passed, sailors broke out spare machine guns and mounted them in several OS2U-3s parked near Hangar 54 and Hangar 38.[2]

The bomb craters and incinerated planes near the hangars did little to inspire confidence or optimism. Across the landing field at Hangar 177, Lt. Cdr. William B. Whaley made a morose admission in an unguarded moment. Noting that VJ-2 had no flyable aircraft, he declared, "Well, there's nothing left, so I guess it's going to be every man for himself," a sad acknowledgment that his command had no resources on which to draw.[3]

Back in the Administration Building, Bellinger's staff was desperate to determine the location of the Japanese. Halsey's Task Force 8, though ready to "go roaring after the Japanese," required information if it was to strike a blow. Ideally, intelligence on such a distant force would come from Bellinger's PBYs. With few aircraft available and the aprons obstructed by debris, it would require a herculean effort just to get planes into the water. Commander Ramsey ordered VP-23's four intact

The vicinity of Hangar 6 at the foot of Ford Island during the lull between attack waves appears much like what Captain Shoemaker and Rear Admiral Bellinger saw when they surveyed the conditions at the southern end of the island. The roof of Hangar 6 is ablaze, and fires are still burning in the interior. At bottom right and center lies the wreckage of VP-23's PBYs, earlier lined up against the rear doors of Hangar 6. On the other side of the structure are three apparently intact PBYs from VP-22. Numerous OS2U-3s from the battleships (with a solitary SOC) sit on the apron separating Hangar 6 and Hangar 38.
NARA II, 80-G-32634/32663 collage

Assisted by about a dozen sailors, a ramp tractor driver tows an OS2U-3 from VO-1 away from the shoreline between Hangar 6 and Hangar 38, with the corner of Hangar 6 just out of the photo at right. Note the crater at center resulting from the bomb dropped by WO Kokubu Toyomi.
NARA II, 80-G-32472, cropped

Lt. Cdr. William B. Whaley,
CO of VJ-2, circa 1941
NPRC, St. Louis

planes to supplant VP-24's searches to the west and southwest, though with gaping holes in the patterns and fewer than half the necessary planes. Beset by disrupted communications and disabled or hemmed-in aircraft, a frustrated Charlie Coe later observed, "We were simply not in a position to retaliate."[4]

At midmorning Cdr. John L. Murphy—commander of the Base Force Utility Wing—offered his planes and crews. Reluctantly, Bellinger pressed Murphy's short-winded and nearly defenseless amphibians into service. They were an odd assortment of five Sikorsky JRS-1s and three Grumman J2F Ducks, all from Tom Richards' VJ-1. No planes were available from VJ-2; strafing dive-bombers had disabled all the squadron's aircraft. In addition, Logan Ramsey lined up six OS2Us and SOCs from the battleships and cruisers that had weathered the early-morning storm of bombs and machine-gun fire, and later, SBDs from the *Enterprise*.[5]

Hopeful that the damage at Kaneohe was not as bad as what he was seeing at Pearl Harbor, Ramsey, "with some difficulty," established telephone contact and received the disheartening news that *only two aircraft* were operational. Consulting his original search plan, he selected a sector of 280–300 degrees and directed Kaneohe to launch as soon as possible. Ten planes—VP-14's three, the four from VP-24, the solitary aircraft at Pearl Harbor, and the pair at Kaneohe—were a paltry force to prosecute a war, but the Japanese had to be found. At least orders had gone out for the PBYs to cover, albeit thinly, critical sectors to the north and northwest. Bellinger acknowledged later that there was only "a forlorn hope" of success.[6]

Frustrated by the communications blackout during the first wave and his inability to obtain firsthand information from his squadron commanders, an exasperated Pat Bellinger left the Administration Building and headed for the hangars to look things over in person. What he beheld was depressing; "the area was pretty well cluttered up with debris, planes and various parts." He concluded that there seemed to be little concerted effort under way to clear the seaplane base and restore order, so he directed the cleanup himself.[7]

Earlier that morning, as the *Enterprise* and Task Force 8 returned from Wake Island, the carrier had sent out a routine search ahead of the force, launching eighteen SBDs at 0618. The group—commanded by Lt. Cdr. Howard L. Young, CEAG—fanned out in nine two-plane elements in a pattern northeast to southeast of Halsey's force. At the 150-mile mark each pilot turned toward O'ahu, heading for a landing at NAS Pearl Harbor.

Among the first aviators from the *Enterprise* to encounter the Japanese during the inbound leg of their flight were Young and Ens. Perry L. Teaff, A-V(N), his wingman. Surprised by the Japanese fighter that fired on their planes from astern, the two American pilots nevertheless successfully evaded their attacker. The frantic action took both SBDs down to low altitude over a cane field north of Pearl City Peninsula. After circling for a short time, Young realized that even though they had lost their pursuer, they could not hope to evade the friendly

One of only two PBYs deemed airworthy at the conclusion of the first wave of attacks at NAS Kaneohe Bay lies on the water in the far background just minutes before the arrival of the second attack wave.
NARA II, 80-G-77605, cropped

antiaircraft fire being directed their way. Knowing also that they had insufficient fuel to return to the *Enterprise*, Young elected to try a harrowing landing at Ford Island. The two pilots came in low, hoping to attract as little attention as possible.[8]

When the *Enterprise* SBDs appeared, the men at the naval air station immediately mistook them for returning Japanese. Even Bellinger stood frozen for a moment on the apron. One of the men shouted, "Get in the corner of the hangar, Admiral!" Bellinger was on his way when the thought came to him, "This is a hell of a thing for me to be doing."[9]

The defenders, though taken by surprise by Young's and Teaff's "attack," sprang into action quickly. Massie Hughes, VP-23's skipper at the time, was making preparations to take off when Young and Teaff attempted to land about 0830. Seeing his men open fire on the slow-moving Dauntlesses, he purportedly threw rocks at the gunners to make them stop. Luckily for the two desperate pilots, the fire was not very accurate, and Young "by the Grace of God landed intact." In the second plane, Ensign Teaff had seen enough and pulled up and away from the station before trying a second attempt, braving a maelstrom of metal both coming and going.[10]

The SBD-2 (BuNo 2162) assigned to CEAG Lt. Cdr. Howard L. Young on the morning of 7 December
NARA II, 80-G-279380, cropped

Captain Shoemaker had just transported a wounded survivor from the *Utah* to the aid station at Quarters 118 when he saw two planes approaching the Luke Field side of the station from the southwest. The first landed, and the second plane, which appeared to be chasing it, turned away. Shoemaker hurried toward the first plane, and to his surprise out jumped Brig Young, commander of the *Enterprise* air group, and Lt. Cdr. Bromfield "Brom" Nichol, Vice Admiral Halsey's flag secretary. Fired at by friend and foe alike, the two officers cried out, "What the hell goes on here?" When Young and Nichol insisted on reporting to Admiral Kimmel's headquarters right away, Shoemaker drove them across the field to Landing A and "shoved them off for the Submarine Base in a NAS boat."[11]

Suddenly, gunners again opened fire from both sides of the field as Ensign Teaff made his second attempt to land. He managed to get down safely, though with hits in the fuselage and several critical hits in the engine and hydraulic system.[12]

Lt. Cdr. Bromfield B. Nichol observes flight operations on board the *Enterprise*, 29 July 1941.
NARA II, 80-G-21056G, cropped

Lt. Cdr. Hallsted L. Hopping of VS-6 enjoys a Lucky Lager and a smoke while talking shop with Lt. Cdr. Howard L. Young during a VS-6 picnic, circa October 1941.
Coslett, via Cressman

An SBD scout bomber from the *Enterprise* is parked on the apron separating Hangar 6 and Hangar 54 in this cropped image taken from the water tower on Ford Island at approximately 0830, prior to the takeoff of the first PBY searchers. According to Captain Shoemaker's account, Young and Nichol left their aircraft near the land plane hangars on the northwest side of the landing field, which indicates that the aircraft is 6-S-2 (BuNo 2175), the mount of Ensign Teaff and RM3c Jinks. NARA II, 80-G-32449, cropped

At about 0830, 23-P-4 (BuNo 2447) sat in Hangar 54 ready for flight. After crews rolled the aircraft far enough out of the west doors to allow the northeasterly trades to carry away the engine exhaust, the PBY's two engines sputtered to life.[13]

Earlier, Massie Hughes had rushed to the hangar from Quarters P and found 23-P-4 ready to go. He dashed to the Administration Building for orders. In Ramsey's original plan, VP-23 was to "plug holes" and serve as a strike group while VP-11 was responsible for a 15-degree wedge-shaped pattern due west from O'ahu. Since VP-11 had no operational aircraft, Ramsey reassigned that sector to Hughes.[14]

Lt. James B. Ogden, VP-23's gunnery officer, was waiting at Hangar 54 when Hughes returned. "Come on, Jimmy," Hughes said. "Pick yourself a crew." Ogden selected AMM1c (NAP) Theodore S. "Swede" Thueson for the third pilot and made a beeline for the squadron's best shots to man the Brownings.[15]

Men cleared debris from a path alongside Hangars 54 and 38 to the seaplane ramp. RM3c Francis Shacklett, a member of the beaching crew,

wondered whether the plane descending Ramp 2 would ever been seen again. With "no thought of wind direction, channel or warmup," Ogden opened the throttles and taxied around the south end of Ford Island to the Middle Loch for take-off. After his final turn he weaved his way around the heavy timbers that had slipped off the *Utah*'s deck when she capsized and "made a mental note that this would be something to bear in mind on our return—when and if."[16]

Ens. Perry L. Teaff of VS-6, 24 January 1942 NARA II, 80-G-464484, cropped

A photographer on Ford Island's water tower exposes a four-by-five-inch negative just as the crew warms up the engines of 23-P-4 (lower left) after rolling it out of Hangar 54. PBY debris smolders adjacent to the north side of Hangar 6 in the background while at left sailors assist a ramp tractor driver in moving a fire-damaged OS2U. Note that the fabric has burned away from the Kingfisher's vertical stabilizer. At right, a similarly damaged PBY-5, 23-P-11 (BuNo 2454), sits on the apron facing south outside Hangar 54.

NARA II, 80-G-32449, cropped

The timbers intended as protection for the *Utah*'s deck float in the north channel after slipping off the ship as she capsized. The hazard they posed to taxiing seaplanes is obvious.

NARA II, RG38

Massie Hughes, from Charlottesville, Virginia, had graduated from the Naval Academy with the class of 1923. He entered flight training at NAS Pensacola in May 1930 and joined the aviation unit of the heavy cruiser *Chicago* in March 1931. Carrier duty with bombing squadrons followed. Hughes was promoted to lieutenant commander on 23 June 1938, and on 8 August 1940 assumed command of VP-23. Someone who knew Hughes quite well declared, "This officer is a fighting man."[17]

Lt. James R. Ogden, a native of Knoxville, Tennessee, graduated with the Naval Academy class of 1933. Service in the *Chicago* followed graduation, as did an appointment to NAS Pensacola for flight training in July 1935. His first billet as a naval aviator was the *Northampton*. In May 1938 Ogden transitioned into patrol aviation, bringing to VP-23 broad experience.[18]

AMM1c (NAP) Theodore S. Thueson was a native of the Hudson River town of Newburgh, New York. After enlisting on 23 April 1934, he advanced to the rating of aviation machinist's mate third class, serving for one and a half years with the aviation unit in the *Raleigh* before receiving a recommendation to undergo flight training. Thueson won his wings on 9 April 1940 and transferred to VP-23 in July.[19]

As the patrol aircraft were preparing to take off, survivors from the *Oklahoma* struggled ashore, evading the oil fires by heading for a narrow strip of beach close to the Fuel Pier. Along with several other men, CSF Molter waded out and helped them ashore. Someone established a first-aid station in the two downstairs flats of Quarters 50—Molter's residence and that of ACM Iver Reinikka. Molter, who was the field commissioner for the station's Boy Scout troop, remembered the very complete first-aid kit in the scout hut situated on the other side of the tennis courts. He used a fire ax to break the padlock securing the door, found the first-aid supplies along with a large stockpile of fruit juice and canned fruit, and told the men to help themselves.[20]

Next Molter raided the CPO Quarters for sheets, towels, blankets, and clothing. He later recalled that one officer received "an enlisted white jumper" while one of the enlisted men received "a pair of officers white trousers, a regulation enlisted undershirt, a rear admiral of the line's swallow tail dress uniform coat [presumably Rear Admiral Bellinger's] and a full dress 'fore and aft' hat. Uniforms meant nothing."[21]

Lt. Francis M. Hughes,
circa mid-1930s
NPRC, St. Louis

Ens. James R. Ogden,
9 September 1934
NPRC, St. Louis

AMM3c Theodore S. Thueson,
circa 31 May 1939, beginning
flight training at NAS Pensacola
NPRC, St. Louis

Distribution of arms, machine guns, and ammunition continued through the lull, although ordnance was very much outside the area of expertise for many who engaged in that activity. Typical was CRM Thomas E. Farrow, who helped to break out machine guns for the defense of the Operations Building. After a break in the attack, Sea2c Layman of VP-23 went to the ordnance shack and assisted with belting .50-caliber ammunition for the guns in the waist blisters of aircraft that were still intact. The seaman on watch refused to issue ammunition without the chit customarily required for authorization, but "needless to say, his protest didn't delay operations."[22]

Meanwhile, sensing a break in the action, curious sailors in the Enlisted Barracks moved to the lobby to look outside. Lieutenant (jg) Osborne received instructions from Lieutenant Kane at about 0830 to proceed to the Enlisted Barracks and "take charge." Finding a great many sailors in the southwest lobby "standing in a disorderly fashion," Osborne ordered them into the mess hall to await further instructions. Ensign Singleton—who had performed so courageously while securing the Fuel Pier—kept the men quiet and away from the windows. To assist Dr. Schuessler and his pharmacist's mates, Osborne set up a ping-pong table as a staging area for medical equipment.[23]

Lt. (jg) Lloyd B. Osborne, final assembly officer at the station's Assembly and Repair Department, circa July 1941
NPRC, St. Louis

The men along the north shore of Ford Island took heart upon seeing vessels moving in the harbor—seven of them were under way by 0900. The first to move was the *Monaghan* (DD 354). For Ensign McColgan of VP-22, the sight of the destroyer standing down the north channel after backing out of Berth X-14 at 0827 was one of the most memorable events of the raid. As improbable as the *Monaghan*'s sortie seemed, on she charged, "boiling around the island, heading to sea, and throwing depth charges as she came." McColgan thought the crew "had gone nuts" until he later heard that the destroyer sank a Japanese midget submarine.[24]

The *Monaghan* off Mare Island, 17 February 1942
NARA II, 19-N-28344

After Young and Nichol embarked from Landing A, Captain Shoemaker attempted to address "the rush of refugees" and badly injured men on the dock and organized the rush of well-meaning sailors intent on delivering the casualties to the Dispensary. At that point Shoemaker recognized the dire situation at the Fuel Pier. Although the *Neosho* had cleared the dock, oil fires from the battleships had set the northeast end of the dock and two dolphins ablaze. The Fire Department emptied the entire Foamite contents from a chemical truck, but their efforts to quench the fires proved unsuccessful. Shoemaker commandeered a boat, organized a bucket brigade, and put an ensign from the *Oklahoma* in charge of the operation. They soon extinguished the fires.[25]

With the Fuel Pier secured, Shoemaker finally allowed himself to check on his wife and children in the air raid shelter at Quarters K. When he arrived at Rear Admiral Bellinger's residence, Shoemaker found his family safe and the situation well in hand. Just after Shoemaker left Quarters K, however, the Japanese reappeared overhead and began a sustained dive-bombing attack, serving notice that the battle was not yet over.[26]

Earlier that morning, as Shoemaker drove to the western shore of Ford Island, he found himself oddly philosophical, as if it seemed almost too late for anger. The realization struck him squarely that "this is the beginning of the Pacific War with Japan."[27]

The oiler *Neosho* clears the Fuel Pier (Berth F-4, visible at far left) at about 0845. Photo taken from the water tower on Ford Island looking over and past the *California*. The smoke hanging over the *California* amidships is probably from the fires—by then extinguished—on the dolphins and east portion of the pier.
NARA II, 80-G-32588, cropped

Chapter Eight

"GET YOUR ASS IN THE PLANE AND PRE-FLIGHT IT!"

Shortly after the departure of the first wave of attackers an inbound second-wave strike unit of 163 Japanese bombers and fighters approached Oʻahu from the northeast. Lt. Cdr. Shimazaki Shigekazu ordered the preliminary deployment at 0843, and the formation's components separated. A force of thirty-five fighters under Lt. Shindō Saburō took station at various points over Oʻahu to ensure the safety of the bombers then preparing to attack Pearl Harbor and the island's airfields while seventy-eight Aichi Type 99 D3A1s under Lt. Cdr. Egusa Takashige continued south and then turned west toward a point south of Hickam Field, where they deployed. Twenty-seven Nakajima Type 97s from the *Zuikaku* under Shimazaki—half of the horizontal bombing force—headed southwest toward Hickam. Of the other twenty-seven bombers from the *Shōkaku* under Lt. Ichihara Tatsuo, eighteen deployed for attacks on Kaneohe. The remaining nine under Lt. Irikiin Yoshiaki followed Shimazaki's larger force toward Pearl Harbor with the objective of renewing the attacks on Ford Island's hangars.

As the second wave converged on Pearl Harbor, American officers and men struggled to report to their ships and facilities. Delays stemmed not only from the congestion on Oʻahu's roads but also the distance of their residences from the harbor. Having dressed hurriedly, PhM1c Paul J. Sherrard hitched a ride to Landing A rather than endanger his wife by having her drive him. Before parting with Alma, Sherrard instructed her to "go in the closet and lock the door, and not to answer the door unless they were military." Along with several other men he hopped into a passing truck driven by Lt. (jg) Harry P. Muller, C-V(S), the assistant communications officer for the Fourteenth Naval District, who was nearing the end of a long drive from Mokulēʻia Beach to the District Communication Office at Wailupe. Delayed by heavy traffic, Sherrard arrived at Landing A just as the Japanese second wave appeared and the *Nevada* (BB 36) stood down the channel in her attempt to sortie from the harbor.[1]

Although the dramatic view of the *Nevada*'s sortie was not readily visible from Landing C near

Lt. Cdr. Shimazaki Shigekazu,
commander of the *Zuikaku*
air group, circa early 1942
Chihaya

Lt. Cdr. Egusa Takashige,
possibly in 1944 as *hikōtaichō*
of the 521st *Kōkūtai*
Mrs. Egusa

PhM1c Paul J. Sherrard,
14 January 1942
Sherrard

Harry P. Muller,
circa 6 March 1939,
at the time of his
application for a
commission in
the USNR
NPRC, St. Louis

the Naval Hospital, officers and men on Ford Island saw the events as they unfolded from various vantage points. Lt. Cdr. James Baldwin witnessed the attacks that occurred just as the battleship passed 1010 Pier: "A Japanese bomber dropped out of a cloud, dived and dropped a bomb directly upon the forecastle. . . . Thereafter 18 bombers, spaced 700 yards apart, dropped out of the same large and low cloud and it appeared that about all of them succeeded in hitting the *Nevada*." The destroyer *Shaw* (DD 373) in Floating Dry Dock No. 2 (YFD 2) fired her machine guns and, combined with fire from the *Nevada*, struck four of the bombers, apparently setting their engines afire.[2]

For AM1c Thomas S. Malmin, the battleship's sortie was "a beautiful and inspiring sight":

The battleship *Nevada* was in the harbor, moving slowly toward the channel, and was almost engulfed by thick black smoke. Through a clearing in the smoke, I could see our Stars and Stripes momentarily in the sun, against a bright blue sky. It was only for a few brief seconds, but long enough to give anyone a lift had they glanced in that direction. I remembered later, it was under somewhat similar circumstances that "The Star Spangled Banner" was conceived and written. I felt the thrill of feeling and living the same experiences, the same pride that was his, and could understand better Francis Scott Key's words.[3]

The events were no less dramatic seen from inside the Administration Building. The *Nevada* came into Rear Admiral Bellinger's view through the windows of his second-floor office while he was on the phone with Brig. Gen. Jacob Rudolph at Hickam Field requesting more aircraft. As the *Kaga*'s dive-bombers swarmed down on the ship, the vessel seemed to stagger in mid-channel, with flames shooting up alongside her. Bellinger exclaimed, "Hold the wire a minute, General, I think there is going to be one hell of an explosion." Bellinger continued speaking with the general as the *Nevada* disappeared around the corner, though he was unable to secure more aircraft from him. Rudolph replied to all entreaties for planes with an irritating, "Okey-dokey," a superfluous response that Bellinger remembered for the rest of his days.[4]

The drama in the channel caught up with the men boarding boats at Landing C. The craft in which Lt. (jg) Kenneth L. Longeway (DC) was a passenger stopped at the end of the dredge line that extended from the southeast shore of Ford Island, and the men disembarked and walked the line up onto land. Lt. Jackson D. Arnold's boat veered to starboard to avoid colliding with the *Nevada* and passed aft. After rounding the battleship's stern, the wide-eyed coxswain grounded the

Brig. Gen. Jacob Rudolph, commanding general, 18th Bombardment Wing, circa 1941
Knight

boat on Ramp 2, discharging the occupants at the southern corner of Hangar 38. Arnold disembarked, hurried to the Administration Building, drew a .45 from the armory, and organized squads from the Seaman Guard to fire back at the attackers.[5]

The *Nevada* (far right) stands down the channel, as seen from the front steps of the Administration Building overlooking the north parking lot just before 0900. Rear Admiral Bellinger would have had a similar view from his office windows. Note the oiler *Neosho* in the distance at far center, having backed out of Berth F-4 prior to the *Nevada*'s sortie. The *California* is at left in Berth F-3.
NARA II, 80-G-32635

A station photographer behind the northwest wing of the Administration Building documents the unfolding attack on the *Nevada* just as the battleship passes on the opposite side of the building at about 0900. The three Type 99 carrier bombers shown here are attacking from two angles, with 200–300 meters separating the two aircraft in line. The fact that the aircraft at lower left has just released its bomb is not so readily apparent.
NARA II, 80-G-32571, with inset

View looking northeast along the pilings of Berth F-1 toward the rear entrance and the southeast wing of the Administration Building. The small seaplane tender *Avocet* (AVP 4) is moored in Berth F-1½ in this, one of the finest photographic studies of a fighting ship from 7 December 1941. Note the vessel's identification number in white on the bow and her Measure 1 camouflage—5-D dark gray with 5-L light gray above the line of the funnel. On the right corner of the building (see inset) a Navy photographer in whites is visible working with a large-format camera. It was very likely this sailor who documented the *Nevada*'s sortie and the subsequent explosion of the *Shaw* from the roof of the building, atop PatWing 2's photographic offices.
NARA II, 80-G-32669, with inset

The *Nevada*—heavily afire on her boat deck, forward superstructure, and forecastle—prepares to run aground on Hospital Point after her sortie; photographed from the roof of the Administration Building, looking over the *Avocet*. Note the tender's pair of 3-inch/50-caliber antiaircraft mounts forward and the Lewis machine gun mounted atop her pilothouse.
NARA II, 80-G-32583

A collage of two photos taken on the afternoon of 8 December showing the dredge pipeline used as a drop-off point during trips to Ford Island from Landing C. The walk from the head of the line to Landing A (or to the Administration Building) was a long distance to cross in the open during the strafing attacks. The destroyer *McCall* (DD 400) stands up the main channel at center following her return from the mission of reinforcing Wake Island, in which she was part of the screen for Task Force 8.
NARA II, 80-G-32502/32503 collage, cropped

"Dodging other rapidly moving vehicles," Lt. (jg) Rodney T. West reached Landing C near the Naval Hospital and parked. VJ-1 aviators Gordon Bolser and Jimmy Robb arrived almost simultaneously after their nerve-wracking drive from Waikīkī. Bolser's car lurched to a stop on the packed coral of the parking lot just as West raced on foot toward the landing. The doctor was a moment too late, however, because the whaleboat had just pulled away, eventually to "dock" at Ramp 5, around the southeast corner of Ford Island.[6]

Having returned to Pearl Harbor via taxi, Sea1c John Kuzma ran west through the Navy Yard and assisted briefly with fighting the intense fires on the destroyers *Cassin* (DD 372) and *Downes* (DD 375). While hurrying on toward Landing C he heard that the destroyer *Shaw* in the *YFD 2* required assistance and ran toward the destroyer's bow, where a gangplank led up to the 18,000-ton floating dry dock.[7]

As Kuzma drew nearer to the stricken *Shaw*, fires detonated her forward magazines. The force of the explosion blew him into the air, and an experience from his childhood flashed into his mind. He and another boy were sailing through the air into a swimming pool. Instead of water, though, Kuzma landed headfirst on the hard ground. When he regained consciousness he wiped away the blood that was running from his nose into his eyes and struggled to his hands and knees. He stood—dizzy and unsteady—but nonetheless assisted another wounded sailor, guiding him toward Hospital Point.[8]

At Landing C, Bolser and Robb had just opened their car doors when the *Shaw* blew up in a "big flash and an earth-shaking explosion." Seconds later, debris and body parts rained down on the parking lot. Bolser and Robb bypassed the steps altogether and jumped from the lot to the landing just as a motor whaleboat arrived with a casualty on board. The pair lifted the wounded sailor and placed him into an ambulance that had just driven up from the Naval Hospital.[9]

The *Shaw*'s forward magazines erupt as a huge fireball rolls forward out of the floating dry dock. Just beyond the *Avocet* is the garbage lighter *YG 21*, under the command of CQM (PA) James J. Reams, preparing to land a three-man firefighting party from MTBron 1 and the Receiving Barracks.
NARA II, 80-G-32587

In one of the most iconic combat photographs of World War II, the blast from the explosion of the *Shaw*'s forward magazine ejects debris and unexploded 5-inch shells in all directions. Note the silhouetted main battery of the *Nevada* at far right. Just below her forward turrets is a motor whaleboat en route to Landing C.
NARA II, 80-G-16871

The *Shaw*'s explosion catches the attention of several sailors, causing one to crouch low as the blast and sound waves are heard and felt one-third of a mile away. The timing of this photograph is almost identical with that of the above image. Seconds later, the Navy photographer took the frequently published photo 80-G-19948. To the authors' knowledge this photo has never before been published, perhaps because there is no print or reference mount card at the National Archives. Only a negative exists.
NARA II, 80-G-32658

For the men at the station, the *Shaw*'s explosion seemed like a fireworks explosion. Sea1c Edward P. Waszkiewicz stood mesmerized while one of the *Shaw*'s 5-inch shells arched over toward a nearby fire truck. He ducked behind the vehicle and heard the projectile bounce off the concrete into one of the hangars, sounding like a huge bowling ball.[10]

Back at the Hospital Landing, a coxswain shouted, "If you're going to Ford Island, get aboard!" and Lieutenant (jg) West complied. Avoiding the oil fires, the boat passed outboard of the *California* and almost up to the capsized *Oklahoma*, "a sad and ugly sight." Then the coxswain turned toward Ford Island and reversed course to Landing A, where the passengers disembarked "with much relief at being alive." Another coxswain delayed his departure from Landing C until Robb and Bolser returned from the ambulance. The boat sped across the channel and beached on one of the seaplane ramps. The two aviators waded ashore and ran north through the maze of buildings toward Hangar 37. Sea1c Kuzma, his face bloody, boarded yet another motor launch bound for the station. As he surveyed the damage in the harbor for the first time, Kuzma's thoughts turned to his friends at the Fire Station, wondering whether any of them could still be alive.[11]

As the attacks intensified, the demand for ordnance quickly outstripped the supply. Vehicles crossed to the north side of Ford Island in search of ammunition, heading toward Small Arms Magazine No. 1 (Building 168) and Small Arms Magazine No. 2 (Building 169), located behind Hangars 133 and 134 on the old Luke Field side of the station. Each squadron sent groups of men across the field to draw weapons and ammunition. Sea2c Virgle A. Wilkerson and men from VP-23 transferred seventy-five boxes to their truck. VP-22, however, had little luck fulfilling their need for arms. By the time Sea1c George Hemingway got there with a squadronmate, little was available in the magazines. "We picked up what they had left,

which wasn't much," just a few Springfields and five boxes of ammunition.[12]

Men in vehicles assigned to the Supply Department also drew ammunition from the station's magazines and returned to the vicinity of the Administration Building, where they issued ammunition to sailors who had rifles but no cartridges. Then the trucks lumbered to the Storehouse and unloaded the balance of their cargo. AOM3c Maynard F. Gannon and AOM2c Raymond L. Kelly issued an immense quantity of arms and ammunition while women from the CPO quarters who had sought refuge at the loading platform of the Storehouse assisted with cleaning the weapons. Commander Harter used the newly cleaned and acquired arms and ammunition to place machine-gun batteries nearby and detailed a lieutenant to place fire extinguishers and buckets of sand on the roofs of the General Storehouses and Annex (Buildings 26, 26-A, and 75).[13]

In the station's Photography Lab, by 0900 CP (PA) Earl Sever was "directing the efforts of the other naval photographers who had arrived," including preparing and loading still and motion picture film, mixing chemicals, and setting up equipment

AOM3c Raymond L. Kelly circa 1941
NARA, St. Louis

A sailor clad in dungarees, work shirt, and steel helmet walks through the grass (apparently barefoot) armed with a bolt-action Springfield and an ammunition bandolier while an officer and a chief converse on the steps of the east entrance to the Administration Building.
NARA II, 80-G-32776, cropped

to develop negatives and prints when the photographers returned. P3c John W. Burton was developing the first film returned to the lab in a darkroom that seemed to be rocking from the force of the new attack.[14]

The photographers set out afoot and in boats and documented the return of the Japanese while facing friendly fire, fragments, and splinters. Captain Shoemaker later commended P1c Leroy E. Bartels for his "extraordinary initiative and disregard of personal safety" as he photographed the attacks on NAS Pearl Harbor despite the dangers presented by the bombing and strafing. Armed with a 35-mm Mitchell motion picture camera, P1c Will R. Sutherland boarded a boat and recorded diving aircraft, the *Nevada* firing her antiaircraft battery during her sortie, and the explosion of the *Shaw*.[15]

As the Japanese dive-bombers deployed over the harbor, the American naval aviators watched them with deep professional interest. Captain Shoemaker noted that rather than the steep dive American aviators employed, the Japanese used a "gentle glide" that was "about 30 degrees below horizontal." After dropping their bombs, the aircraft simply pulled level and "weaved their way

Carp Earl Sever, circa 1942
NARA, St. Louis

P1c Leroy E. Bartels, circa 1939
NARA, St. Louis

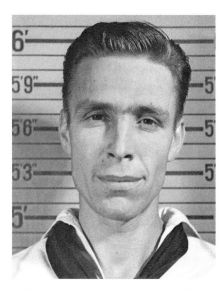

P1c Will R. Sutherland, circa 1939
NARA, St. Louis

out." The slow diving speed of the Type 99s impressed Lt. Samuel M. Randall, formerly of VB-6. Similarly, the "nonchalance of the enemy . . . in the face of the heavy anti-aircraft fire of all description" amazed Cdr. Harry F. Carlson, the station's executive officer.[16]

During the dive-bombing attacks the ships threw skyward a tremendous volume of antiaircraft fire, and it seemed to RM3c Kenneth P. Anderson of VP-24 that metal fragments, splinters, and spent bullets rained from the sky. His shipmate Sea2c Houston F. James was disappointed with the ineffectiveness of the ships' 3- and 5-inch batteries, but the rifle and pistol fire seemed worse than nothing. Cpl. Lawrence Keith of the station's Marine detachment expended all of the ammunition in his bandolier but felt frustrated and helpless at having only a rifle to fire at the attacking planes, likening it to "throwing peanuts at them."[17]

The machine-gun fire seemed far more effective—particularly against the dive-bombers—after crews at the station took the opportunity to reposition their weapons during the lull. Moreover, the Supply Department was very successful in distributing arms and ammunition. These factors substantially increased the odds of damaging or destroying enemy planes.[18]

The dive-bombing continued, however, despite the increasingly effective American opposition and inflicted material casualties apart from units of the fleet. A bomb struck the floating dry dock and parted the 2,300-volt service cable to Ford Island at approximately 0910 or 0915. The resulting loss of electrical power in the Administration Building disrupted the newly reestablished telephone service along with radio and page-printer communications. In the first-floor radio room, CRM Andrew Giemont shifted his men over to PatWing 2's auxiliary emergency equipment and continued to monitor regular operating frequencies. To provide further backup he sent a messenger to the Utility Wing's radio shack and asked them to monitor the frequencies of the Naval Base Defense Air Force—by now activated by the emergency.[19]

The Utility Wing's radio station had no power, so CRM (PA) Frank R. DeAugustine of VJ-1 ran onto the parking apron near Hangar 37, boarded a Sikorsky JRS-1 amphibian, and used the onboard battery to put the aircraft's radio into service. Even after crews restored power he guarded the appropriate frequencies and set radio watches in several damaged aircraft. VJ-1 also maintained communication with NAS Maui and with the planes on patrol later in the day. With the "highest degree of efficiency," DeAugustine facilitated the ongoing search missions and relieved a substantial portion of the communications load on PatWing 2.[20]

Back at the Administration Building, Giemont was checking the emergency equipment just prior to the power failure and discovered that gunfire had shot away the antenna. Immediately the forty-one-year-old chief "directed his material man as to its proper restoration." The latter—probably RM3c Harry L. Hansen, assisted by RM2c Arthur J. Balfour—mounted the roof of the Administration Building, "reinstalled" the antenna, and effected repairs despite fire from friend and foe alike.[21]

The power interruption to Ford Island proved short-lived. Within fifteen minutes, maintenance crews arranged "to take 2,300 volt service by transforming the 11,000-volt feeder line." With power restored, the TBR-2 transmitter went back on line at 0920. Sailors set up another radio set in the direction-finder station on the northwest side of the island at 0925.[22]

At about 0900, horizontal bombers appeared southwest of Pearl Harbor, approaching from the southwest, visible between breaks in the clouds and smoke at about eight thousand feet. Having followed Shimazaki's twenty-seven aircraft bound for Hickam Field from the vicinity of Honolulu, Lt. Irikiin Yoshiaki led his *chūtai* of nine Type 97s from the *Shōkaku* into a broad turn to starboard to the southwest, following the route of Egusa's dive-bombers along the coast. Spotting the target area to the north, Irikiin crossed south of the Pearl Harbor entrance channel, banked again to starboard—almost reversing his course—and leveled

Hangar 37 and its surrounding aprons seen from the landing field on Ford Island, 5 November 1941, looking south, where CRM DeAugustine rushed to put aircraft radios into operation in the wake of the station's power failure. Note JRS-1 1-J-6 (BuNo 1057) at right; another like aircraft is tucked behind the corner of the hangar.
NARA II, 71-CA-153E-14822, cropped

Lt. (jg) Frank R. DeAugustine, circa 1944
NPRC, St. Louis

Starboard-side radio compartment on a Sikorsky JRS-1. The door leading to the flight deck opened on the left.
NARA II, 72-AC-35B-6349

out at 0905 on a northeasterly heading that intersected the coastline three to four miles west of the entrance channel. For reasons unknown, Irikiin remained in place to command the drop rather than signaling his number-two aircraft to rotate into the lead slot.

Irikiin's division carried a mixed load of bombs. Although one machine (possibly Irikiin's lead plane) carried two No. 25 (250-kg) Type 98 land bombs, the other eight *kankōs* shipped a single No. 25 bomb suspended behind the port wheel well and an additional six No. 6 (60-kg) Type 99 ordinary bombs suspended in pairs from crutches mounted just right of the aircraft's centerline.[23]

Because of the dive-bombing attacks unfolding in the harbor, relatively few observers noticed the approach of the *Shōkaku*'s horizontal bombers. Irikiin's deployment placed his unit about six miles west-southwest of his designated target: the seaplane hangars at the southern tip of Ford Island. Thick smoke boiling skyward from Hangar 6 and Battleship Row obscured the objective, however,

Lt. Irikiin Yoshiaki, commander, 3rd Chūtai, *Shōkaku* horizontal bombing unit
Maru

WO Kawashima Heisaburō, would-be expert bombardier, 3rd Chūtai, *Shōkaku* horizontal bombing unit
Maru

Pearl Harbor seen from the southeast as a Type 97 attack bomber from the *Shōkaku* banks to starboard and crosses to the southwest, heading out to sea and circumventing Hickam Field, which is just in view at lower left. The plane carries one 250-kg bomb and six 60-kg bombs. Flak bursts show that American AA fire is greeting the arrival of Lieutenant Commander Egusa's dive-bombers.
Konnichi no Wadai-sha

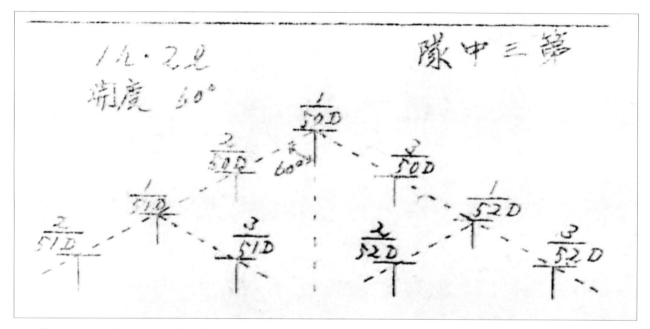

The formation from which the *Shōkaku*'s 3rd *Chūtai* pressed their attack on NAS Pearl Harbor. The designation for Lieutenant Irikiin's lead aircraft—1/50D (first aircraft, 50th Shōtai)—documents Irikiin's decision to command the bomb run personally.
BKS, *Shōkaku* detailed action report

as did a broken layer of cumulus clouds. It being "very difficult to recognize the targets by eye," Irikiin aborted, retreated south, and selected a secondary target that stood clear of the murky billows pouring out to the southwest: the untouched aircraft hangars along the northwest shore of Ford Island. Having reset, Irikiin again traversed the Ewa sugarcane fields and the channel of West Loch at 2,800 meters, with the row of hangars now in his bombsight.[24]

Lookouts on the *Tangier* (AV 8) spotted Lieutenant Irikiin droning toward the harbor from the southwest. Alerted by the earlier dive-bombing attacks, the seaplane tender's mixed battery of two 3-inch/50-caliber guns forward and two 3-inch/23-caliber guns aft took the formation under fire, but the gunners overestimated the range by 3,600 feet.

Initiating the bombing attack at 0916, Irikiin mishandled the run. Whatever the cause—poor visibility and clouds or an inadvertent premature signal—almost all of the bombs from the group's four "pulls" (one for the 250-kg bombs and three

in succession for the pairs of 60-kg bombs) landed across the channel "on Waipio Peninsula about opposite the western end of Ford Island."[25]

What followed the debacle of the "attack" on Waipi'o Peninsula is unclear. Since the required four pulls by each bombardier consumed several seconds, perhaps some of Irikiin's crews realized the error at the last second and saved a few bombs for the hangars. Any subsequent pulls, however, fared little better than the previous ones because the bombs fell hundreds of yards away into the water near the *Tangier* in Berth F-10 (perhaps the intended target) and near the buildings along the northwest shore of Ford Island. Dive-bombers from the *Akagi* and *Sōryū* also subjected the ships in the Middle Loch and those moored along Ford Island to a brief but intense dive-bombing attack, and it cannot be ruled out that some of the bombs that fell near the *Tangier* came from those dive-bombers.[26]

Whatever their origin, bombs bracketed the *Tangier* at about 0913 but inflicted only minor

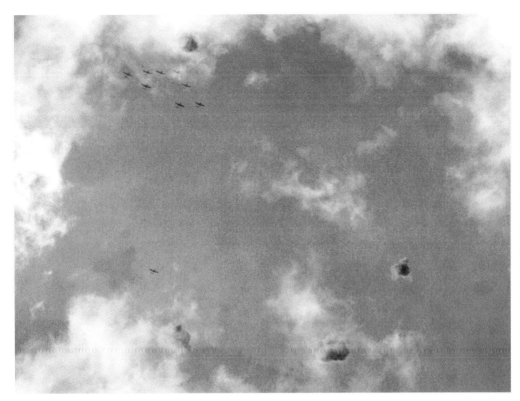

A poorly placed AA barrage greets the horizontal bombers of the second wave over Pearl Harbor. Because all four of the nine-plane units (three from the *Zuikaku* and one from the *Shōkaku*) set up their attack runs with a flight over the harbor, it is impossible to identify the unit at upper left. The formation's number-five aircraft (lower left) has fallen behind.

NARA II, RG 80

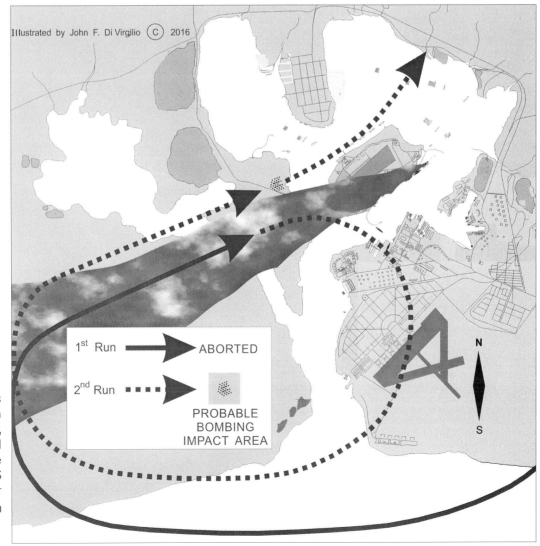

Illustrated by John F. Di Virgilio (C) 2016

1st Run ➡	ABORTED
2nd Run ▪▪▪➤	PROBABLE BOMBING IMPACT AREA

N
S

Lieutenant Irikiin's deployment south of Oʻahu, his abort, and his unit's final approach to the target area of NAS Pearl Harbor

Di Virgilio

第三中隊
「オード島格納庫
附近上空一面雲

Lieutenant Irikiin's ultimate target area (the crosshatched block) was the hangar line along the northwest shore of Ford Island.

BKS, *Shōkaku* detailed action report

near-miss damage. Heavy explosions occurred forward—one bomb hitting about three hundred yards off the port bow (striking Ford Island) and two others off the starboard bow, close aboard. Two other near misses impacted aft on the starboard beam and quarter, both close aboard. Considering the proximity of the impacts, it seemed a miracle that the *Tangier* suffered no more damage than she did. She was struck by splinters in forty-two places but nowhere punctured below the waterline. Fortunately, the *Tangier* sustained no damage to her machinery and equipment and had only three sailors wounded.[27]

Meanwhile, Irikiin ordered PO3c Okiyama Tetsuo to report the results of the attack. The radioman tapped out a tepid—if not somewhat deceptive—report to *Kidō Butai* at 0916 . . .

_ ._ _ . . . . _ . _ _ .
"ユ-ヌ 55 ル" (*Yu-Nu 55 Ru*).

"Results of our bombing on Ford are small."

The *Shōkaku*'s action report stated only: "Ford Island: no confirmation on destruction of the maintenance hangar."[28]

On Ford Island, Irikiin's attack might have gone unnoticed except for the bomb that fell among the storehouses and magazines along the northwest shore. When Japanese aircraft appeared, the sailors from VP-23 dashed back into the small-arms magazine for protection just before a bomb landed fifteen feet off the north corner of Building 170. Flying debris created the illusion of the roof being lifted from the structure, although the building sustained little damage. With the immediate danger past, the VP-23 men jumped into their trucks and raced back to the other side of Ford Island. Although the buildings suffered superficial damage, the detonation broke a water line running from the nearby artesian well. Falling debris and fragments fell on two buildings and punched numerous holes in the roofs.[29]

As the second-wave attack units deployed over Oʻahu, another SBD from the *Enterprise* landed successfully. Lt. Cdr. Hallsted L. Hopping, CO of VS-6, closed on Barbers Point with heavy smoke visible from the direction of Pearl Harbor out to

A geyser of water erupts close aboard the *Tangier*'s starboard side amidships at approximately 0913.
NARA II, RG38

Second-Wave Attack on NAS Pearl Harbor
Lt. Irikiin Yoshiaki
Shōkaku Horizontal Bombing Unit
3rd *Chūtai*

	Pilot	Observer/Bombardier	Radioman/Rear Gunner
50th *Shōtai*	WO Shindō Saburō	Lt. Irikiin Yoshiaki	PO3c Okiyama Tetsuo
	PO1c Iwadate Nisaburō	WO Kawashima Heisaburō	Sea1c Morishita Noboru
	PO2c Hasegawa Tokio	PO2c Yamazaki Saburō	Sea1c Kodama Terumi
51st *Shōtai*	PO2c Seki Tokuji	WO Saitō Masaji	PO2c Kamata Yasuaki
	PO3c Ryōchi Tomotsu	PO1c Ōtake Tomie	Sea1c Takasugi Kyōtarō
	PO2c Ōtsuka Akio	PO3c Aoki Susumu	Sea1c Nomura Osamu
52nd *Shōtai*	PO2c Toda Gisuke	WO Matsumoto Yoritoki	PO2c Abe Akira
	Sea1c Sekifuji Chōji	PO2c Higuchi Kinzō	Sea1c Ōsaka Taisaburō
	Sea1c Satō Katsumi	PO3c Satō Yukiyoshi	Sea1c Inoue Hiroshi

NAS Pearl Harbor, 10 December 1941, with an arrow indicating the crater opened (filled in at that juncture) near the north corner of Inert Storehouse 170 at far left. NARA II, 80-G-387589, cropped

the east. Seeing the Ewa Mooring Mast Field under attack, he dove to low altitude, set 6-S-1 (BuNo 4522) onto Ford Island, and taxied to the control tower "to make arrangements for bombs and to get detailed information to ComTaskFor Eight." ChGun William M. Coles—the station's assistant gunnery officer—appeared and agreed to supply bombs for the three *Enterprise* aircraft and for other SBDs that might arrive. With the transmitter in the Operations Building out, Hopping rushed to his aircraft and "broadcast several times the details of the attack and that Ford Island was usable." At the Administration Building, Rear Admiral Bellinger directed Hopping to send up one of the three SBDs then on the field "to investigate reports of two Japanese carriers southwest or west of Barbers Point between 25 and 40 miles, and to hold remaining planes on [the] ground as [an] attack group."[30]

Back at the seaplane hangars, with water pressure gone, sailors resorted to bucket brigade duty until the Fire Department's pumper drew water from the harbor to battle the blaze at Hangar 6. Other men brought to bear machine guns from improvised mountings on the aprons and from observation floatplanes near Hangar 54. AOM2c Russell P. Josenhans fired from the rear cockpit

Lt. Cdr. Hallsted L. Hopping, CO, VS-6, on board the *Enterprise*, 24 January 1942. That same day, Task Force 8 received the order from Admiral Nimitz to conduct a raid on the Marshall Islands on 1 February 1942—a raid in which Hopping would lose his life. NARA II, 80-G-464484, cropped

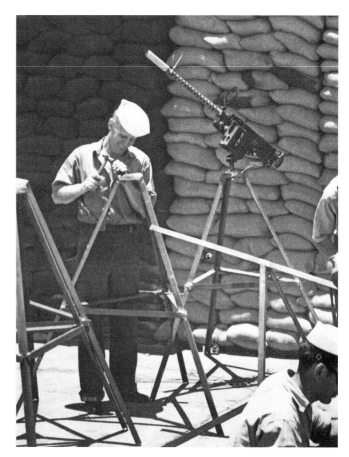

Improvised stand similar to that employed during the attacks of 7 December 1941, in this case mounting a Browning .30-caliber machine gun
NARA II, 80-G-19706

of an OS2U-3 and scored repeated hits on a dive-bomber flying low over Hangar 54 during the attack on the *Nevada*. RM3c Kenneth P. Anderson, who supplied Josenhans with ammunition, stood behind him and saw him adjust his fire so that the tracers struck the wing, which came off just as if it had been "cut away with a pair of scissors."[31]

The men at the utility plane hangars fought back similarly. AOM1c William H. Anderson from VJ-1 spared no effort to support men attempting to lay down fire against the attackers. He organized machine-gun crews and ammunition parties, setting an extraordinary "example of coolness and refusal to seek cover, despite the severe enemy bombing and strafing."[32]

One of three pumpers from the NAS Pearl Harbor Fire Department sits on an incline separating Ramp 2 and Ramp 3, siphoning water needed for fighting fires on the island.
NARA II, 80-G-32714, cropped

AOM2c Russell P. Josenhans,
16 September 1941
NPRC, St. Louis

Lt. (jg) William H. Anderson, circa
November 1944, while serving as
ordnance and gunnery officer with VJ-7
NPRC, St. Louis

The men and equipment attached to the station's Fire Department found themselves under fire as well. As CBM John Burnfin, the station's fire chief, drove about the island and directed firefighting near the hangars, machine-gun fire hit his car in four places, narrowly missing the driver. Two of the station's fire trucks suffered similar damage. A large fragment struck the control panel on a third truck, and the engine of another took a hit on the radiator or water line.[33]

With a substantial portion of the station's firefighting equipment disabled, the officers and men relied on manpower to combat the various blazes. Just as the second-wave attack commenced at about 0900, Ens. Gilbert M. Rice, SC-V(G), the stock control officer in the Supply Department, and Ens. Paul F. Cosgrove Jr. (SC) took a Clark cab and trailer loaded with sand buckets and fire extinguishers to the Kenneth Whiting School, adjacent to aboveground Reserve Storage Tank 63 and Berth F-5 (battleships *Maryland* and *Oklahoma*). A building nearby, across from the playground near the school, was ablaze. The burning *West Virginia* and numerous oil fires threatened nearby structures, although firefighters were containing the blaze, with Ens. Daniel F. Logan, D-V(G), joining in the effort. The fires, however, did not prevent sailors abandoning the *West Virginia* from coming ashore.[34]

Later in the second-wave attacks, burning oil drifting with the current collected along the shore near the small boat landing behind Berth F-2 and along the wharf further southwest. The creosote-impregnated fenders and pilings along Landing A and Berth F-1 ignited, and the flames advanced, enveloping the Administration Building in suffocating smoke. At about 0930 the fires endangered three crates of PBY wings and spare parts. Commander Harter and Lieutenant Mattson of the Supply Department directed a working party under the supervision of CSK (PA) Andrew Callaghan and CSK (PA) Oscar Ledford to move the huge crates to safety with the aid of a truck. Their action saved two of the six-ton crates, although the flames consumed one crate of aircraft wings.[35]

Captain Shoemaker appeared on the scene and found the timbers along Berth F-1 ablaze. He organized the efforts of the Fire Department's pumpers, starting upwind from the fires along Landing A. The required angle to combat the blaze being

ActPayClk Oscar Ledford,
circa August 1942
NPRC, St. Louis

awkward, crews passed hoses down to sailors in boats, who labored to douse the flames. The energetic work of the men under Shoemaker's leadership and direction brought the fires under control in about two hours.[36]

Help came from an unexpected quarter when one of two clipper tenders from the Pan American dock at Pearl City arrived with a crew of three Navy men from the station under CBM (PA) Eddie O. Wiener, a former Pan American employee who was familiar with Pan Am's firefighting equipment. Seeing the oil fires threatening the station, he had located two volunteers, hopped in a motor launch, and headed straight for Pearl City. From there the men took the tender *Panair XP* to the landing, and the boat's powerful pump cast a steady stream of water on the flames for more than two hours.[37]

The pilings at the southern terminus of Landing A were set ablaze by burning oil floating down from the battleships. The main fire area is behind mooring platform F-2-S, where Ford Island juts southeast—a natural collection point for oil drifting down channel with the outbound current. The white craft assisting at center is the clipper tender *Panair XP* from the Pan American docks at Pearl City. The trimmer companion tender, *Panair XXP*, had two fire monitors and assisted with controlling fires on the *West Virginia*'s superstructure.
NARA II, 80-G-32692, cropped

CBM (PA) Eddie O. Wiener, circa 1941
NARA, St. Louis

The smoke from the oil fires on the waterfront disrupted the Communications Department inside the Administration Building. The radio room became almost untenable, with "smoke and fumes . . . soon of a suffocating intensity." Lt. Leroy Watson, the station's communications officer, instructed CRM Giemont to abandon the radio room if necessary and have "the emergency equipment moved out of the building." Knowing that would interrupt communications, however, "Giemont and two operators remained at their posts and successfully carried on . . . in an exhibition of perseverance and devotion over and beyond the call of duty." Bellinger recommended that Giemont be advanced immediately to the warrant rank of chief radio electrician.[38]

After being cooped up all morning in the Enlisted Barracks, SK3c Jacob Rogovsky was nervous and frightened. Hence, when the call went out for volunteers, Rogovsky reported to Landing A to assist swimmers coming ashore. Rogovsky was completely unprepared to face the horrific scene. He helped one man onto the dock whose clothing was black from the oil in the water and who was badly burned on the hands and face. He "half dragged and half carried" the sailor to the Dispensary, but every place seemed to be taken by the dead, wounded, and dying.[39]

For those manning the boats, the task of rescuing the sailors was overwhelming. F1c Henry de Coligny's boat approached the desperate sailors as closely as possible and hauled them on board,

A sailor at Landing A tosses his life jacket aside as oil burns on the water behind him.
NARA II, 80-G-32570, cropped

grabbing them by the hair in some instances: "Whether a fellow was dead or whether he was drowning or what, we retrieved the body and put him down in the boat. We went back . . . and dumped our load of humanity and the bodies and went out again." AMM3c Carl L. Hatcher's experience was similarly grisly. One man in Hatcher's crew grabbed the arm of a sailor and the man's skin and flesh came off in his hands.[40]

Other incidents provided a bit of humor and psychological relief amid the horrors of the rescues. A Marine from the *West Virginia* risked his life going below decks to retrieve three hundred dollars from his locker. He stuffed the money in his pocket, emerged topside, took off his pants, and jumped in the water, not realizing until he boarded the rescue boat that he had left his cash on the blazing battleship. Another man off the *West Virginia*—an older chief—cursed and shook his fist at the

SK2c Jacob S. Rogovsky, circa 1942
Rogo

Japanese aircraft overhead. Somewhat taken aback at the man's vehemence, Sea1c Delia inquired what the problem was. "Them goddamned Japs!" the chief replied. "When they told me to abandon ship I jumped over the side and lost my false teeth!"[41]

A boat crew backs away from the burning *West Virginia*, having thrown a line to a sailor in the water. The wake generated by the boat as it motors aft and the turbulence in the water behind the sailor are indicators that the boat is pulling away.
NARA II, 80-G-474937, cropped

At the Dispensary, doctors forwarded the less serious cases to the Enlisted Barracks, but rescuers began to deliver critical cases straight to the barracks as well. By 0900 Cdr. Jesse D. Jewell (MC) and his staff from the *California* and Lt. DeBert W. Connell (MC) from the *West Virginia* had arrived to assist Lieutenant Schuessler at the barracks. Jewell worked despite suffering from shock and second-degree powder burns to his face.[42]

Sea2c Victor Kamont was present in the mess hall as the casualties arrived. The experience of seeing so many men in agony lingered in Kamont's memory for the remainder of his days: "Some of the men looked beyond help, burned flesh and bone showing through the oily mess. Some of these men were half clothed, raw meat just hanging from their bones. Some cried like babies, babbling for their mother, father, or loved ones. It was a sickening sight."[43]

Overcrowding was soon the least of the problems in the Dispensary. Lieutenant Riggs, having taken flight surgeon training at NAS Pensacola, had developed a good eye for aircraft maneuvers. At 0915 he observed that one of three dive-bombers

Cdr. Jesse D. Jewell, the former senior medical officer on the *California*, circa July 1942
NPRC, St. Louis

attacking the *California* wobbled, "kicked too much left rudder [and] then tried to get back by right rudder." The pilot released the bomb—almost certainly by accident—at an altitude of several thousand feet. The bomb passed high above the battleship, fell into the Dispensary's central tiled patio, and detonated. The blast ejected a mass of concrete shards vertically, leaving a crater seven feet deep and fifteen by twenty feet wide. Miraculously, none of the 150 patients along the perimeter of the 80-by-48-foot patio received additional injuries. The blast shattered windows and the glass doors to the building's western entrance, blew walls and partitions out of plumb, and disrupted water and electrical service.[44]

Lt. Elmer L. Caveny and Lt. (jg) Rodney T. West reported immediately afterward. West climbed the seven steps up to the side door of the Dispensary, walked through the short passageway leading into the courtyard, and stood immobile, gaping in shock and disbelief at the bomb crater in the center of the patio. Hurrying to the dressing station, he found the compartment jammed with injured sailors, many suffering from flash burns. West counted six doctors present at various points in time.[45]

Following the bomb strike in the courtyard Commander Iverson ordered that all ambulatory patients be evacuated to the Marine dormitory in the north wing of the Enlisted Barracks. Major Zuber of the Marine detachment asked for volunteers to assist with the evacuation, and "practically every able-bodied man not engaged in firing at the enemy responded," with guards directing the wounded to specified locations. The casualties soon filled the Marines' quarters too, however, forcing the medical staff to use the already crowded adjacent mess hall. The wet and wounded men appeared to bear up well during the transfer, with few complaints.[46]

First Lieutenant Closser lit cigarettes for those unable to use their arms. Then he routed cases of .30-caliber ammunition to the roof, where the Marine guards had one Lewis machine gun, two

The crater opened by the 250-kg bomb explosion in the central courtyard of the Dispensary. Despite broken windows and fragmentation damage above waist level, there is no such apparent damage closer to the floor. Also, the glass in the windows is not entirely blown out, further evidence that the main force of the blast was deflected vertically.

NARA II, 80-G-32599

BARs, and several rifles laying down fire against the Japanese attackers. In addition, Zuber allowed six to eight of his men to fire from the front porch of the barracks.[47]

The conduct of the Marines was exemplary. Pvt. Donald E. Bramlette "helped many survivors in the water to safety, despite the constant bombing and straffing [sic] of the enemy." Similarly, Sgt. Hubert L. Breneman brought in many badly wounded men from exposed points during the enemy action. Cpl. Clifton Webster, atop the Enlisted Barracks, placed "a large burst of Lewis machine gun fire into the cockpit of a low flying Japanese bomber," which crashed in the main channel.[48]

Lt. (jg) Rodney T. West, MC-V(S), 14 January 1942 NPRC, St. Louis

Pvt. Donald E. Bramlette, USMC, 27 August 1940, one week after his enlistment
NARA, St. Louis

Sgt. Hubert L. Breneman, USMC, 27 December 1941
NARA, St. Louis

By about 0945 about seventy-five men were being treated by the Dispensary staff on mess tables in the Enlisted Barracks. To relieve the congestion, Ensign Osborne moved all the unarmed bystanders to the second level, where they were to make themselves available for work parties, and kept the armed sailors on the first floor. When a call went out for mattresses for the wounded men in the mess hall, sailors loaded the mattresses onto a waiting truck with little apparent regard for their own safety.[49]

In addition to the medical care provided at the Enlisted Barracks, the galley crew made hot coffee for the doctors and wounded sailors in the mess hall. It was also necessary to feed and clothe the hundreds of refugees on the island. Ensign Satchell closed the Pay Office and placed his storekeepers in the charge of CSK (PA) Doc G. Culwell, who was setting up a field kitchen in a building near the station garage. Culwell also put the Luke Field mess hall into operation and prepared flight rations for crews readying for takeoff. Chief Paymaster Pischner directed that issues of clothing be made to men from the battleships, who "in some instances were nude, or nearly so."[50]

During the second wave, men from VJ-1 reported to Hangar 37 from various locations across Oʻahu. RM3c Frederick Glaeser of VJ-1 managed to return despite having spent the night in his car parked at the YMCA in Honolulu. Another returnee from Pearl City was CRM (PA) Gerald M. "Jake" Jacobs, who received orders to assign flight crew radiomen for three utility aircraft assigned to a search mission. Jacobs entered the radio shack and announced, "I want three volunteers to go as radiomen on a search mission. You, you, and (pointing to RM2c Harry Mead) you." The young radioman stammered: "But Chief, I've got the watch." Jacobs snapped back, "I'll relieve you. Get your ass in the plane and pre-flight it!" Mead gathered his gear and went to his aircraft.[51]

Across the Koʻolau Range at NAS Kaneohe Bay, Japanese fighters had just destroyed the two aircraft that Logan Ramsay had ordered prepared for aerial searches. Communications between Pearl and Kaneohe had been severed, and Commander McGinnis (ComPatWing 1) was cut off. Wishing to comply with the order regarding the now-defunct PBYs, McGinnis acted on his own and diverted Ensign Tanner and Ens. Thomas W. "Tommie" Hillis to cover the westerly sectors Ramsey had specified, leaving Ens. Otto F. "Freddie" Meyer to continue his search northwest out to 450 miles. Although Bellinger received notification at 0925 that the aircraft being readied for flight had been destroyed, he was unaware of McGinnis' improvisation for several days—a change that "removed two planes from a sector where the Japanese task

RadElec Gerald M. Jacobs, circa
August 1942, while serving with VJ-1
NPRC, St. Louis

RM2c Harry R. Mead, circa
late 1940
Fiore

force was later determined to be near." Hence, the prospects for locating Nagumo's Carrier Striking Force in a vulnerable position within two hundred miles of O'ahu dimmed considerably.[52]

Shortly before 0900, Bellinger's staff realized that the PBYs from VP-24 over Operating Area C5 had not shifted northeast of O'ahu as Ramsey had ordered at 0800. Due to a communication error, the PBYs circled near Maui until the staff discovered the snafu. Bellinger sent a message at 0853—with a clarification two minutes later—ordering the planes to proceed west of O'ahu and search a sector from 280 to 240 degrees.[53]

Earlier that morning, at 0825, while conducting firing and sweeping exercises twenty miles south of O'ahu, the heavy cruiser *Minneapolis* (CA 36), Capt. Frank J. Lowry commanding, and her screen of four high-speed minesweepers—*Lamberton* (DMS 2), *Boggs* (DMS 3), *Chandler* (DMS 9), and *Hovey* (DMS 11)—received notification of the Japanese attacks. Sounding General Quarters, the force manned its antiaircraft batteries and turned west. "Heavy smoke from the direction of Pearl Harbor and heavy anti-aircraft fire," earlier mistaken for cane fires, darkened the horizon to the north.[54]

As the *Minneapolis* and her screen steamed approximately twenty miles south of Barbers Point, VP-24's PBYs arrived on the scene at about 0930. Shortly thereafter, 24-P-4 sighted a submarine near the cruiser—misidentified as the *Indianapolis* (CA 35)—and the four minesweepers. The submarine, apparently hostile, crash-dived immediately. Unable to attack, the PBY's crew dropped floatlights and signaled the surface force of the submarine's presence. After dropping additional lights, 24-P-4 departed on a course of 245 degrees and began searching to the southwest.[55]

As the Japanese raiders were leaving Hawai'i, the first of the four PBYs from VP-24 took station west of O'ahu and commenced its search at 0945. Though the sector that Ramsey wanted Lieutenant Commander Fitzsimmons' PBYs to cover was 245–285 degrees, the actual area of coverage was somewhat less, only from 243 to 275 degrees. The four crews executed standard crossover patrols out to three hundred miles with a 90-degree turn to port at the end of the outward leg, flying fifteen miles before turning back to O'ahu.[56]

As the drone of Japanese aircraft engines over O'ahu dissipated, NAS Pearl Harbor took stock of

VP-24 Searches, 7 December 1941

Aircraft		Sector	Plane Commanders
24-P-1	(BuNo 2411)	275–270°	Lt. Cdr. John P. Fitzsimmons
24-P-2	(BuNo 2412)	265–260°	*Lt. Eugene Tatom
24-P-5	(BuNo 2428)	255–251°	*Lt. (jg) Thomas S. "Stuart" White
24-P-4	(BuNo 2414)	245–243°	*Ens. Charles P. Hibberd

*Aircraft assignment uncertain

its material losses. The figures were not encouraging. The Japanese strategy of disabling Rear Admiral Bellinger's capability to search for the Carrier Striking Force had worked well; those assets lay disabled or destroyed on the aprons at NAS Pearl Harbor and NAS Kaneohe Bay. Only eleven PBY-5s were operational, with eight of those already airborne. Crews from VJ-1 were in Hangar 37 preparing for takeoff at the earliest practical moment, but prospects for their success—not to mention their survival—appeared dismal. Moreover, communication between the services proved awkward and difficult, hindering any meaningful coordination between the Army and Navy. The Naval Base Defense Air Force on which Kimmel and Bloch had relied so heavily had proved to be little more that a figment of prewar imagination.

Like hundreds of other sailors, AMM3c Carl L. Hatcher did not return that day to his quarters in the barracks. When the rescue activity in the harbor wound down, he returned to his duty station in the Assembly and Repair Department. Although few people appreciated the ramifications of what had occurred on the morning of 7 December 1941 at the time, the sailors and Marines of Ford Island did realize that their world had changed and that America faced a long and difficult road ahead.[57]

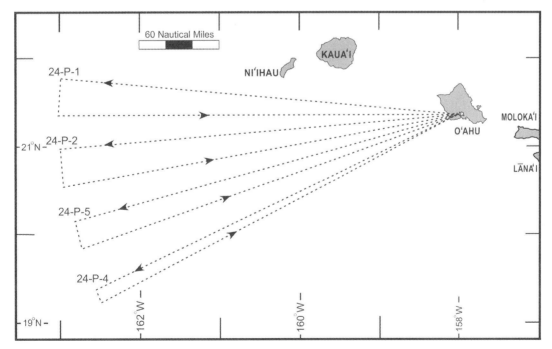

Chart of patrols west of O'ahu flown by VP-24 on 7 December 1941. No charts of the track out to Operating Area C5 exist, nor are there any verified associations of pilots with plane numbers apart from Fitzsimmons.
Di Virgilio

Chapter Nine

"PEOPLE WERE GETTING UP IN ANYTHING THAT THEY COULD THROW A ROCK OUT OF"

As the men of NAS Pearl Harbor worked with single-minded dedication to repair damage, clear aprons, and fight fires, efforts to locate the Japanese carriers took on an air of frantic desperation. With no evidence to suggest that the Japanese would *not* return, it was critical to divine the enemy's intent in order to prepare proper defenses and to neutralize imminent threats. By this time, deep anger had displaced the shock at the unexpected attack, and the desire to retaliate was intense. Any attempts to locate the enemy, however, would demand uncommon courage from the naval aviators and aircrews on Ford Island.

Amid the chaos, the departure of two Curtiss SOC Seagulls from the station during the attack went practically unnoticed. Lt. (jg) Raphael Semmes Jr. and Ens. Maurice J. Thornton, A-V(N)—two pilots from VCS-5 assigned to the *St. Louis* aviation unit—reported to Ford Island of their own accord. All five naval aviators from the *St. Louis* were on authorized leave, but Semmes and Thornton had negotiated the tangled route to Pearl.[1] The cruiser's four Curtiss SOC-3s had been in

overhaul since 28 November, with a detail of fifteen men having reported for temporary duty on Ford Island. Semmes and Thornton strapped themselves into the first available airworthy, gassed, and armed Seagulls and took off, sans radiomen-gunners, on a hunt for the Japanese. Most likely taking off near the end of the raid, the two pilots failed to make contact with the Japanese carrier force but supposedly encountered and attacked—unsuccessfully—a formation of Type 99 carrier bombers returning north to *Kidō Butai*. Ensign Thornton ran out of fuel during the return flight and had to ditch, necessitating his rescue by a destroyer on 9 December.[2]

As the PBY-5s of VP-14 shifted their patrols north and west of O'ahu, the probability was high that their paths would intersect with those of the Japanese aircraft orbiting at the rendezvous west of Ka'ena Point prior to their return flight. Of the three American aircraft lumbering away from the island, it was 14-P-2 (BuNo 2418) that ran afoul of the enemy. At about 1000, Ens. Freddie Meyer and his crew observed nine aircraft "about six miles distant on the bow and crossing [the] flight

Ens. Rafael Semmes Jr.,
28 August 1940, at NAS Pensacola
NNAM

AvCdt. Maurice J. Thornton,
27 February 1940, at NAS Pensacola
NNAM

path from starboard to port." Meyer was cruising at about one thousand feet, bearing 310 degrees from Ka'ena Point, and the enemy formation was five hundred to one thousand feet above and on an opposite course. Increasing power, Meyer put his PBY into a dive and leveled out over the water to deter high-side attacks.[3]

The Japanese aircraft—seven Type 99 carrier bombers from the *Hiryū* led by Lt. Nakagawa Shun—commenced firing passes on the PBY, first from astern but then on the beams at high angles of deflection. At least one attacker dove in vertically from high above. Meyer's decision to take his airplane down to the water reduced considerably the attacks' effectiveness because it forced the Japanese to cease firing early and pull out of what amounted to a strafing attack to avoid crashing into the Pacific. Although a malfunction of a .50-caliber Browning in one of the starboard waist blisters (quickly replaced by the .30-caliber tunnel gun) and problems with the rotating hatch "nose turret" hampered the crew's defensive efforts, the gunners held the Japanese at bay, possibly scoring hits on the aircraft of Sea1c Fuchigami Kazuo (pilot)

and Sea1c Mizuno Yasuhiko (observer). Although gunfire holed their bomber's fuel tanks, Fuchigami and Mizuno returned to the *Hiryū*. Concurrently, 14-P-2's radioman tapped out an uncoded five-fold repetition of "BEING ATTACKED" to NAS Kaneohe Bay.[4]

Meyer's tactics probably saved his crew and aircraft. Enemy fire hit the plane in seven places, though none of the eleven hits affected the PBY's operation. Nonetheless, Meyer retired to within approximately five miles of O'ahu on a heading opposite that of the enemies' return course—probably the reason that the carrier bombers broke off the action. When the skies cleared of the Japanese, he reversed course and proceeded with his 380-mile search to the northwest. After hearing of the PBY's interception, Commander McGinnis at Kaneohe passed along an advisory of his own at 1040 instructing Meyer and company to "take due caution" during their search to the northwest. Meanwhile, at 1128, Rear Admiral Bellinger—after a morning fraught with friendly fire incidents—warned Meyer and Ensign Hillis, in 14-P-3, to "STAY OUT."[5]

Ens. Otto F. Meyer,
pilot of 14-P-2,
30 November 1940
NPRC, St. Louis

Ens. Sylvan Greenberg,
A-V(N), copilot in 14-P-2,
15 September 1941
NPRC, St. Louis

Ens. George E. DeMetz,
A-V(N), navigator in 14-P-2,
15 September 1941
NPRC, St. Louis

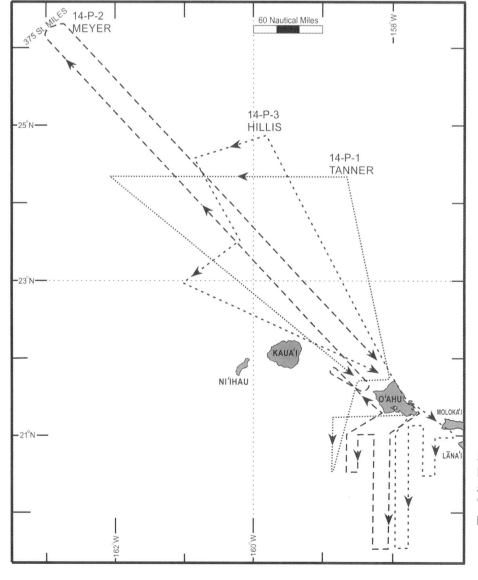

Search patterns flown
by VP-14 on the morning
and afternoon of
7 December 1941
Di Virgilio

Meanwhile, VP-23's maintenance crews in Hangar 54 readied another PBY-5 for flight. In the midmorning hours, beaching crews rolled 23-P-12 (BuNo 2455) down the ramp and into the water, with Ens. Joseph M. Kellam, A-V(N), VP-23's engineering officer, at the controls. After lifting away from the waters north of Ford Island at about 1000, the young ensign, a Davidson College graduate from Biscoe, North Carolina, shaped a course of 260 degrees and embarked on a hunt for the Japanese fleet in a sector that lay just south of the one that the squadron's skipper, Lt. Cdr. Massie Hughes, was searching.[6]

Pressure mounted to launch all available planes to locate the invaders, and with no other PBYs ready to go, the eight utility aircraft at Hangar 37—five Sikorsky JRS-1s and three Grumman J2F Ducks—were next in line. The longer-range Sikorskys were responsible for sectors that Pat-Wing 2 might have searched under normal circumstances. With eight aircraft from VP-24 and VP-23 (some still not ready for flight) earmarked to cover the west and southwest approaches to O'ahu, three JRS-1 crews drew sectors to the northwest, filling the gap between VP-23/24 and where Bellinger and

Ramsey *thought* the three crews from VP-14 were searching up to the north. To reinforce the supposed VP-14 searches, Ramsey assigned two additional crews from VJ-1 to search north of O'ahu.[7]

Among the first utility plane pilots to depart on the search for the Japanese was Ens. Wesley H. Ruth, A-V(N), a native of De Smet, South Dakota. Characterized as thorough, industrious, and quiet, he graduated from South Dakota State College in July 1938 with a B.S. in chemistry, entered flight training at NAS Pensacola in September 1938, and received his wings on 31 October 1939. Because Ruth intended to fly for the airlines eventually, he expressed his preference for a utility squadron and reported to VJ-1 shortly thereafter. Ruth's second pilot was ACMM (PA) (NAP) Emery C. "Pappy" Geise, a steady, mature, twelve-year veteran from Mound City, Iowa, with a decade of flight experience.[8]

After their crew assembled, Ruth and Geise taxied to the south end of Ford Island's runway in 1-J-1 (BuNo 1063), turned their JRS-1 180 degrees, and took off from downwind into the northeasterly trades. Ordered to proceed north and search out to 250 miles, Ruth and Geise flew over O'ahu's

AvCdt. Joseph M. Kellam, circa January 1939, at NAS Pensacola

NPRC, St. Louis

AvCdt. Wesley H. Ruth, first pilot of 1-J-1, circa October 1938, at NAS Pensacola

NPRC, St. Louis

Mach Emery C. Geise, second pilot of 1-J-1, circa April 1942

NPRC, St. Louis

broad central plain of sugarcane and pineapple fields, emerged over the Pacific well west of the Koʻolau Range, and proceeded on a heading of 335 degrees. Although unintended, Ruth's crew actually helped to fill the void left when, due to confusion, two of the PBY-5s from VP-14 rotated their search patterns to the northwest. The real reason for the search to the north was Bellinger's lack of confidence in the Army's ability to mount the searches he had requested in that direction.[9]

Taking off at the same time as Ruth was Ens. Nils R. "Pinky" Larson, A-V(N), a confident and gregarious Worcester, Massachusetts, native just eleven days short of his twenty-eighth birthday. He entered flight training at Pensacola in August 1938, received his ensign's commission and wings twelve months later, and reported to VJ-1, eventually serving as the squadron's assistant engineering officer. His nickname stemmed from his prematurely bald pate and various hijinks during his four years at the University of Alabama. With ACM (PA) (NAP) William P. Byrd as second pilot in 1-J-7 (BuNo 1193), Larson flew generally west,

hoping to uncover any Japanese force approaching from that direction.[10]

Shortly thereafter, having splashed ashore on one of the station's seaplane ramps, junior lieutenants Bolser and Robb noticed intact aircraft on VJ-1's parking apron. The pair burst into Hangar 37, demanded information from the duty officer regarding "where the Japs were coming from," and requested permission to take off and hunt for the carriers. Longtime members of the squadron, the two officers, along with Ens. Richard Chilcott, A-V(N), were renowned as VJ-1's playboys. A Massachusetts native, the "assured, quiet" Bolser was the squadron's personnel officer. He graduated from UCLA in 1933 with a B.A. in economics, but with limited prospects of advancement as assistant superintendent at Forest Lawn Memorial Park in Glendale, California, he applied for flight training in the U.S. Naval Reserve in August 1935. After winning his wings as an ensign in February 1937, Bolser reported to VJ-1 following a stint of duty with the aviation unit on board the heavy cruiser *Tuscaloosa* (CA 37).[11]

Ens. Nils R. Larson, A-V(N),
first pilot of 1-J-7, circa
12 September 1941 at NASPH
NPRC, St. Louis

ACM (PA) (NAP) William P. Byrd,
second pilot of 1-J-7, circa
June 1928
NARA II, 80-G-465573

Lt. (jg) James W. Robb was born on Staten Island, New York, on 15 September 1912 and graduated in 1935 with a B.A. from Wagner Memorial Lutheran College on Staten Island (with concurrent service in the New York National Guard). Robb secured an appointment as an aviation cadet on 12 September and, after receiving his wings, reported to VCS-6 in the heavy cruiser New Orleans (CA 32). Robb was fortunate to survive the capsizing of his SOC-1 floatplane after it bumped the ship's hull during recovery operations. Finally securing an ensign's commission in the summer of 1939, he transferred to VJ-1 on 2 October. An accomplished musician, Robb led the "Windjammers" band on board the New Orleans and wrote songs recorded by the renowned Hawaiian vocalist Ray Kinney. Robb's skill at the piano landed him regular gigs at Shangri La—the house of American tobacco heiress, socialite, and jazz enthusiast Doris Duke—near Diamond Head, a favorite haunt of VJ-1's aviators.[12]

Since Ensign Ruth had just taken off on a search to the north, Bolser drew a sector west by north-west from Oʻahu and hurriedly assembled a radio-man, a mechanic, and a second pilot—AMM1c (NAP) William A. Simpson, a native of Graceville, Florida. After the crew set out from Hangar 37, two Marines from the battleship Oklahoma showed up armed with Springfield '03s and asked to come along. The JRS-1 was unarmed, so Bolser accepted their offer; two rifles were better than no arms at all. After boarding 1-J-6 (BuNo 1057), Bolser warmed up the plane's two Pratt and Whitney R-1690 "Hornets" and taxied to the south end of Ford Island's runway for takeoff. Once airborne he turned northwest up the central plain at low altitude to avoid attracting the attention of Japanese aircraft. Emerging over the water north of Kaʻena Point, he shaped a course of 290 degrees that would carry his impromptu crew over the island of Niʻihau. Lieutenant (jg) Robb's crew in 1-J-4 (BuNo 0506) with second pilot AMM1c (NAP) William R. "Pete" Evans—a five-year veteran from Bement, Illinois—departed on a search sector just north of Bolser's on a course that bisected the island of Kauaʻi.[13]

Lt. (jg) Gordon E. Bolser, first pilot of 1-J-6, circa 31 October 1941 at NAS Pearl Harbor
NPRC, St. Louis

Ens. William A. Simpson, second pilot of 1-J-6, circa April 1942
NPRC, St. Louis

Lt. (jg) James W. Robb, first pilot of 1-J-4, circa 12 September 1941 at NAS Pearl Harbor
NPRC, St. Louis

AMM2c William R. Evans, second pilot of 1-J-4, at NAS Pensacola, circa early 1937
Waalkes

Yet another JRS-1 crew formed under Ens. John P. Edwards, A-V(N), VJ-1's assistant operations officer and a native of Eureka, Kansas, with a business degree from the University of Kansas—a "highly intelligent and forceful officer." Ordered by Lieutenant Commander Richards to prepare 1-J-8 (BuNo 1059) for flight, Edwards selected his crew—an aviation machinist's mate as a second pilot and three sailors standing nearby armed with a meat cleaver, a Colt .45 automatic pistol, and a Browning automatic rifle. Standardizing their armament with Springfield rifles, the men reported to the aircraft, only to discover that the wing had been damaged by machine-gun fire. Next they reported to 1-J-4, but Robb's crew beat them to the punch, leaving Edwards' men to take up 1-J-10 (BuNo 0504?). The last to take off—owing to confusion and a damaged aircraft—the young ensign taxied to the south end of the station's runway and was airborne. Edwards departed on a heading of due north, just east of that flown by Ensign Ruth, accompanied by second pilot ACMM (PA) Donald W. Wright, a stalwart veteran with twenty-four years of naval service.[14]

Ens. John P. Edwards, A-V(N), first pilot of 1-J-10, circa 7 August 1941
NPRC, St. Louis

Mach Donald W. Wright, second pilot of 1-J-10, circa January 1942
NPRC, St. Louis

VJ-1 Searches, 7 December 1941, JRS-1s

Aircraft		First Pilot	Second Pilot	Sector
1-J-10	(BuNo 0504?)	Ens. John P. Edwards	ACMM (PA) (NAP) Donald W. Wright	000–005°
1-J-1	(BuNo 1063)	Ens. Wesley H. Ruth	ACMM (PA) (NAP) Emery C. Geise	335–359°
1-J-4	(BuNo 0506)	Lt. (jg) James W. Robb	AMM1c (NAP) William R. Evans	300–310°
1-J-6	(BuNo 1057)	Lt. (jg) Gordon E. Bolser	AMM1c (NAP) William A. Simpson	290°
1-J-7	(BuNo 1193)	Ens. Nils R. Larson	ACM (PA) (NAP) William P. Byrd	278°

With VJ-1's available long-range aircraft airborne (except for Ensign Edwards), there were still critical gaps in the coverage of the airspace around Oʻahu, so Commander Murphy's utility squadrons summoned the available single-engine aircraft.[15] Again the burden fell on VJ-1, with three J2F Ducks being allocated to search patterns west and west-southwest of the island. The limited range of the diminutive amphibians restricted the outbound legs of their searches to about two hundred miles—better than nothing but hardly enough to ensure a reasonable expectation of making contact unless the Japanese were closing on Oʻahu. The Ducks carried a crew of only two, but in light of the shortage of aircraft, "people were getting up in anything that they could throw a rock out of." Hence, a trio of pilots strode out to the aprons southwest of Hangar 37 to board their aircraft: Des Lacs, North Dakota, native AMM2c (NAP) David L. "Lee" Switzer, AMM1c (NAP) David J. Lesher from Ft. Scott, Kansas (a close friend of Switzer's), and AMM1c (NAP) Robert S. Fauber from Oskaloosa, Kansas. Each pilot had a rear-seater to observe and man the flexible .30-caliber Browning machine gun in the rear cockpit.[16]

Just prior to departing in his J2F-2 (BuNo 1195), which had undergone minor repairs for gunfire damage, Switzer sat and penciled a brief one-page letter to his wife, Doris, in Waikīkī. Deeply troubled over the dim prospect of his survival, Switzer poured out a tender farewell from the depths of his heart, pondering a world turned upside down and wondering what the future might hold for him and his wife. After voicing his hope of getting "one crack at the Yellow dogs that came after us," he sought to console Doris in the event he failed to return: "Just Remember Darling I was a true blue husband and I['m] sorry that you have to be left out here in this hell whole [sic]. Always be your true self Honey and don't let this Harden you. Your [sic] too sweet for that."[17]

Ironically, if Switzer, Lesher, or Fauber were to make contact with the Japanese, their J2Fs probably had a somewhat better chance of survival than the larger Sikorskys. The little Grummans presented a smaller and more nimble target and had the ability to fend off attackers with defensive fire. The three Ducks departed NAS Pearl Harbor and flew out on the southwestern horizon, executing a mix of crossover and out-and-back patterns.[18]

VJ-1 Searches, 7 December 1941, J2Fs

Aircraft		Pilot	Sector
J2F-4, 1-J-20	(BuNo 1665)	AMM1c (NAP) Robert S. Fauber	268–259°
J2F-4, 1-J-18	(BuNo 1649)	AMM1c (NAP) David J. Lesher	250°
J2F-2, 1-J-22	(BuNo 1195)	AMM2c (NAP) David L. "Lee" Switzer	230°?

Note: The aircraft assignments of the three gunners—RM3c Walter G. Schulz, AMM3c Edward L. Frissell, AOM3c Edgar S. Hall—are unknown.

AMM1c (NAP) David L. Switzer and wife Doris
in April 1942 on their first wedding anniversary
Switzer

AMM1c (NAP)
Robert S. Fauber,
20 August 1941
NARA, St. Louis

AMM1c (NAP)
David J. Lesher,
20 August 1941
NARA, St. Louis

From Midway, far to the west, VP-21 sent its PBY-3s on a search for the Japanese carriers. Earlier that morning, however, the squadron had sent five aircraft aloft at 0630 to patrol sectors to the southeast, covering the advance of Task Force 12. Because the *Lexington* was to launch the SB2U-3 Vindicators of VMSB-231 later in the day, two additional PBYs (including skipper Lt. Cdr. George T. Mundorff in 21-P-1) also took off at 0630 to locate and patrol over the task force during launch and then escort the Marine scout bombers into Midway.[19]

Having received notification at 0830 of the attacks on O'ahu, the *Lexington* went to Flight Quarters five minutes later and began the complicated evolution of respotting the flight deck to clear the Marine bombers and send up its first combat air patrol (CAP) of the war. Launch of the CAP and scouting group commenced at 0921. Now alerted, VP-21 received dispatches from CinCPac at 0903 and from Bellinger at 0935 ordering a search for the Japanese carriers. In accordance with those orders, at 1030 the *Lexington* launched another four aircraft to fly search patterns to the east and

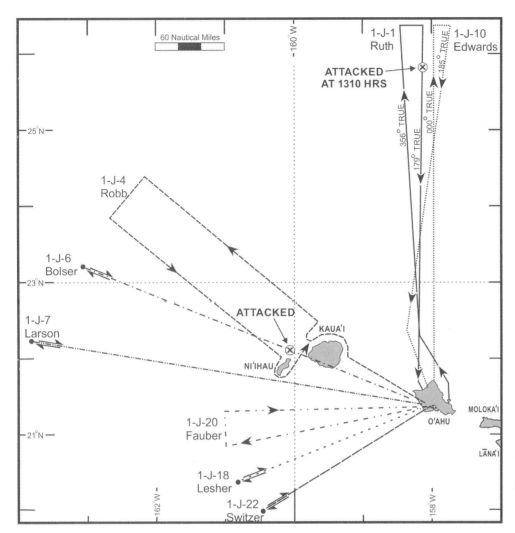

Search patterns flown by VJ-1 on the morning and afternoon of 7 December 1941

Di Virgilio

northeast. The next two hours found the PBYs and the *Lexington*'s patrols groping in the figurative dark, with Mundorff sighting five SBDs at 1115, the *Lexington*'s CAP making contact with one of the PBYs just after 1230, and Task Force 12 canceling the reinforcement of Midway upon receiving Kimmel's 1258 dispatch to do so. With the Japanese Carrier Strike Force far removed from Midway and Task Force 12, Bellinger could expect no useful information from American assets to the west.[20]

Another search related to VP-21 was more notable. Ens. Theodore W. Marshall, A-V(N), VP-21's assistant flight officer, found himself without a plane when the Battle of O'ahu began. Marshall, who began his service career as an aviation cadet in July 1938, received his naval aviator wings on

19 November 1939. Early in the raid he left the New BOQ and commandeered one of VP-21's trucks. During the height of the Japanese first-wave attacks, he shuttled between the officers' quarters, the enlisted men's barracks, and the squadron area ferrying men to their battle stations. Bomb fragments and machine-gun bullets riddled his vehicle. Once he completed his transportation duty, Ensign Marshall spied an unmanned Grumman F4F-3 Wildcat fighter. Despite the fact that he had never flown a service land plane, he climbed up into the cockpit, coaxed the Grumman's engine to life, and began to taxi. The movement apparently attracted unwanted attention because strafing Japanese planes in the second attack wave badly damaged the F4F, leaving it unfit for flight.

Providentially unharmed—and undaunted—the intrepid ensign rushed over to the next carrier plane he saw, a Douglas TBD-1 Devastator, normally used as a torpedo or high-level bomber, "a type [as the F4F had been] with which he was entirely unfamiliar." He managed to get the big aircraft started and took off to follow the retiring Japanese, chasing them for 150 miles. "Because of the slowness of his airplane," however, he proved unsuccessful in his attempt to overtake the enemy. Dwindling fuel compelled Marshall to return to Oʻahu, where "through his skill and ingenuity" he was able to land the airplane without damage. For his heroism that momentous morning Marshall was awarded the Silver Star.[21]

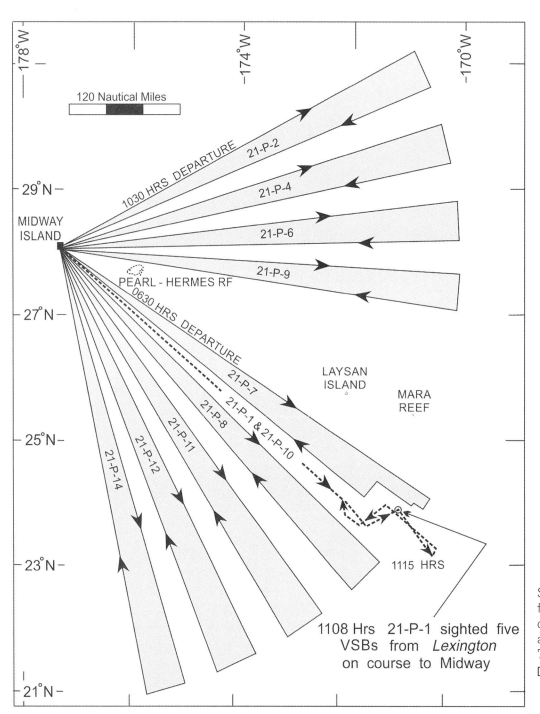

1108 Hrs 21-P-1 sighted five VSBs from *Lexington* on course to Midway

Search patterns flown by VP-21 on the morning and afternoon of 7 December 1941
Di Virgilio

Lt. Cdr. George T. Mundorff Jr.,
CO, VP-21, circa February 1941
NPRC, St. Louis

Ens. Theodore W. Marshall,
A-V(N), of VP-21, circa 1941
NPRC, St. Louis

Over and near Oʻahu, meanwhile, SBD pilots from the *Enterprise* attempted to reunite at NAS Pearl Harbor with their comrades from the early-morning search. Some approached via a direct route into Ford Island, others via fitful detours. Driven off by ground fire during their earlier landing attempt at the station, one group of pilots including Lt. Wilmer E. Gallaher in 6-S-10; Ens.

William P. West, A-V(N), in 6-S-5; and Ens. Cleo J. Dobson, A-V(N), in 6-S-8 set down at Ewa at 0945. Finding the situation there "untenable" and told by the Marines on the ground to leave immediately, the trio took off for NAS Pearl Harbor and landed unhurt at 0955 despite the defenders' efforts to drive them away. Four remaining aircraft fled west, landing once again at Ewa five minutes later.[22]

Lt. Wilmer E. Gallaher
with VS-6 on board the
Enterprise, 24 January 1942
NARA II, 80-G-464484, cropped

Ens. William P. West, A-V(N),
circa 1941
NARA, St. Louis

Ens. Cleo J. Dobson, A-V(N),
on board the *Enterprise*,
24 January 1942
NARA II, 80-G-464484, cropped

Hoping to avoid the near-fatal errors of the morning when gunfire threatened to bring down the approaching friendly aircraft, a chief petty officer in an Operations Department truck passed word to the gun crews that a green light flashed at various positions about the field constituted a signal that incoming aircraft were friendly. The system remained in force for the remaining hours of 7 December.[23]

Shortly after Gallaher, West, and Dobson landed, maintenance crews on Ford Island completed servicing Lieutenant Commander Hopping's SBD-3 and the mounts of the two other early arrivals—Lieutenant Commander Young and Ensign Teaff. With six SBDs now at the station, in accordance with Bellinger's previous instructions, Hopping reserved five planes as a nucleus around which a strike group could coalesce and prepared to set out in 6-S-1 (also in compliance with Bellinger's orders) to reconnoiter the area west and south of Barbers Point. Reports placed two Japanese carriers in the vicinity, and Hopping, accompanied by RM1c Harold "R" Thomas, was to proceed alone to verify the presence of any enemy force before risking the few aerial assets that remained.[24]

Six Sail One took off from the landing field on Ford Island at 1030 and proceeded to Barbers Point. From there, Hopping flew a sawtooth pattern of tracks—west twenty miles, south twenty, west sixty, and south twenty. After a tense outbound leg, Hopping turned back to the east, flew for sixty miles, and returned to the station, reporting "no contacts except with our own ships and sampans." Further, "there were no Japanese surface craft within [the] rectangle covering area 100 miles west and 60 miles south of Barbers Point." Hopping's and Thomas' solo exploration out from Barbers Point required no small amount of courage given the lack of information regarding the location of the Japanese. Having cleared O'ahu's flank to the southwest, however, Hopping had set the stage for the more important activity still to come: a search north of the island by a far more substantial force. After digesting the report, ComPatWing 2 issued a further order "to search sector 330 degrees to 030 degrees (T), attack enemy forces encountered, and return to Ford Island."[25]

During Hopping's search for the carriers off Barbers Point, events moved forward at Ewa and NAS Pearl Harbor. Work proceeded in earnest to arm the five aircraft left behind on Ford Island, and Gunner Coles and his group of volunteers finished loading bombs and ammunition fifteen minutes after Hopping departed. Similar labors were under way with the four scout bombers at Ewa, with work completed for three of the aircraft at about 1105. At that juncture the field's commander, Lt. Col. Claude A. Larkin, USMC, advised Admiral Kimmel and Rear Admiral Bellinger of the planes' availability. Soon afterward orders came back to Lt. (jg) H. Dale Hilton—the senior officer of the pilots then ready for departure on Ford Island—to take off immediately and rendezvous with several of the Army's "heavy bombers" that the beleaguered mechanics at Hickam had finally deemed airworthy. About half a mile west of Ford Island, the trio of aviators found antiaircraft fire directed their way, and Hilton "led the planes down low behind and north of Ford Island" to meet the bombers as they rose from the southwest-northeast runway at Hickam Field. They saw no sign of the Army aircraft, however. Hearing Lieutenant Commander Hopping over the radio as he reported being near Barbers Point, Hilton radioed his chief, who instructed him to return to NAS Pearl Harbor, refuel, and rearm. Hilton landed at 1120 and joined the other surviving crews and aircraft that had struggled onto Ford Island.[26]

Hopping landed soon afterward, at 1145. By noon, ground crews had serviced and armed his aircraft along with Hilton's three machines. In light of the critical situation, Hopping wasted no time in getting his flight of nine SBDs airborne, all armed with 500-pound bombs. This time they ran into little or no AA fire. The crews of eight of the nine planes were unchanged from the early-morning search into Oʻahu. The lone exception was that of Lt. Clarence E. Dickinson in CEAG. Having lost his rear-seater, RM1c William C. Miller, killed when shot down by Type 0 carrier fighters from the *Sōryū* near Ewa, Dickinson acquired AMM3c James L. Young Jr., a volunteer from VP-22, to replace him.[27]

After the second-wave attacks ended, a call went out for volunteers from VP-22 to flesh out crews for the *Enterprise* SBDs that had recently landed because they had just received orders to search for the enemy fleet. Young reasoned there were not enough guns for all of the men at the station, and there seemed no hope of taking up any of VP-22's aircraft, so he volunteered to fly with the carrier group. Only one man was needed to replace RM1c Miller, so Young was ordered to report to Lieutenant Dickinson. Young had no flight jacket—only dungarees, a shirt, and a flying helmet that was too large. After boarding the aircraft, Young unshipped the free gun with orders to fire to suppress friendly fire as the three planes took off.[28]

During takeoff, the gunners on the ground did indeed open fire, but "through the grace of the good lord," the three aircraft escaped harm and headed toward Kaʻena Point, whence the search fanned out to the north. As Lieutenant Dickinson banked the aircraft to port, Young glanced out to the left as all of Pearl Harbor came into view. The enormity of the disaster struck him like a body blow. "They just blew the hell out of us."[29]

Dickinson's drafty SBD was no place for someone wearing just a shirt and dungarees, but Young gritted his teeth in the frigid air of the open rear cockpit. His oversized helmet had no earphones, so Dickinson relayed instructions via hand signals. Young, however, had no experience in the aircraft type and "didn't know what the hell he was talking about." Ultimately, Dickinson turned around and screamed over the engine noise and passed

written notes. Finding nothing in the empty seas below, the two men returned to NAS Pearl Harbor after about four hours, with all nine crews returning by 1545.[30]

Once again the aerial view of the harbor made a deep impression on Young. It was a living hell of gigantic fires and burning ships, buildings, and airplanes, all "torn up or blown to hell and gone." For the first time that day, the youthful aviation machinist's mate felt deep and profound fear.[31]

The day's exertions were not at an end for the SBD crews. Shortly after their return, reports of enemy troop transports off Barbers Point prompted PatWing 2 to dispatch four of the aircraft to "investigate and attack" the supposed invasion force bearing down on southwestern Oʻahu. On their return the pilots reported seeing only four sampans in the vicinity. In the absence of transports, and after a day of frustration and anxiety marked by the inability to land counterblows on the Japanese, the SBD pilots carried out strafing attacks on the defenseless sampans in the water below.[32]

Lt. Clarence E. Dickinson with VS-6 on board the *Enterprise*, 24 January 1942
NARA II, 80-G-464484, cropped

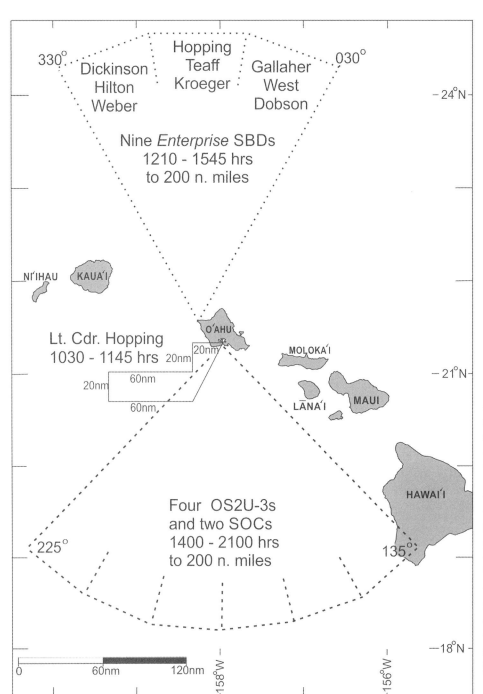

Searches flown during the morning and afternoon of 7 December 1941 by Lieutenant Commander Hopping, SBDs from the *Enterprise*, and a mix of OS2Us and SOCs. Note than the two SOCs shown here (per Bellinger's original chart) probably represent those of Semmes and Thornton. It is far more likely that they followed a flight of Japanese carrier bombers to the west rather than the south. Details of their searches are unknown.

Di Virgilio

Afternoon Search by *Enterprise* SBDs from NAS Pearl Harbor

Plane	Pilot	Radioman	Sector
6-S-1	Lt. Cdr. Hallsted L. Hopping	RM1c Harold "R" Thomas	350–010° (T)
6-S-2	Ens. Perry L. Teaff, A-V(N)	RM3c Edgar P. Jinks	350–010° (T)
6-B-5	Ens. Edwin J. Kroeger, A-V(N)	RM2c Walter E. Chapman	350–010° (T)
6-S-10	Lt. Wilmer E. Gallaher	RM1c Thomas E. Merritt	010–030° (T)
6-S-5	Ens. William P. West, A-V(N)	RM3c Louis D. Hansen	010–030° (T)
6-S-8	Ens. Cleo J. Dobson, A-V(N)	RM3c LeRoy A. Hoss	010–030° (T)
CEAG	Lt. Clarence E. Dickinson	AMM3c James L. Young Jr. (VP-22)	330–350° (T)
6-S-7	Lt. (jg) H. Dale Hilton	RM2c Jack Leaming	330–350° (T)
6-B-12	Ens. Frederick T. Weber, A-V(N)	Sea1c Lee E. J. Keaney	330–350° (T)

In the intervening time, having been airborne for more than an hour, VP-23's Massie Hughes made the first of several PBY contacts with Task Force 8, centered on the *Enterprise* and operating southwest of Kaua'i. In a brief transmission at 1058, the radioman in 23-P-4 made only a vague reference to "investigating a suspicious vessel [latitude] 21 00 [longitude] 159 59," as the PBY probed gingerly along the fringe of Task Force 8's destroyer screen. With the weather conditions hazy and visibility bad, the crew somewhat unexpectedly found themselves over Halsey's force. Hughes' second pilot, Lieutenant Ogden, had had four years of service in the heavy cruisers *Chicago* and *Northampton* (1933–38) and recognized the profiles of Halsey's vessels as they came into view. Hence there was no panic among the PBY crew, although Ogden was preoccupied with the issue of recognition signs in case of a hostile response from below.[33]

At 1103, five minutes after the radio dispatch went out from Hughes' aircraft, a far more ominous message from Ens. Joseph M. Kellam's 23-P-12 arrived at the Administration Building on Ford Island advising that the crew had discovered "two subs unknown nationality," and that the boats submerged upon the PBY's approach. The vague message failed to note the position of the incident, saying only that the submarines were on a course of 271 degrees—an omission that must have frustrated the PatWing 2 staff.[34]

With Task Force 8 operating south-southwest of Kaua'i, it was almost inevitable that one of the PBYs from VP-24 would make contact with the *Enterprise* and her screen. At about 1030, during 24-P-2's outbound search leg of 265 degrees, the crew spied Vice Admiral Halsey's force pressing eastward toward O'ahu, illuminated by sunlight spilling in from the southeast through the three-tenths altocumulus cloud cover. The radioman on board the patrol plane tapped out a brief but relatively accurate assessment of the sighting to

ComPatWing 2: "EIGHT MEN OF WAR LAT 21 10 LONG 160 16 COURSE 90 DEGREES."

Bellinger immediately informed Task Force 3—under Vice Adm. Wilson Brown, ComScoFor, in the heavy cruiser *Indianapolis* (CA 35) screened by the five high-speed minesweepers *Dorsey* (DMS 1), *Elliot* (DMS 4), *Southard* (DMS 10), *Long* (DMS 12), and *Hopkins* (DMS 13)—which had just arrived off Johnston Island to conduct tests of Higgins landing boats on the coral reefs there. Brown was extremely concerned over his "quite exposed position" and the possible presence of Japanese submarines. Acting on orders from CinCPac to join Halsey, Brown recovered his SOC Seagulls and shaped a course toward the rendezvous point five hundred miles to the northwest.[35]

At 1139, very soon after VP-24's 0930 submarine contact, Bellinger sent a message to the squadron on 4105 kilocycles—the tactical frequency being guarded by patrol planes and submarines—reiterating the need for searches out to two hundred miles. With the exception of 24-P-1, then working in the vicinity of the *Minneapolis*, however, the PBYs were already at the three-hundred-mile mark. As soon as the other three patrol bombers received the message from Bellinger, they turned 90 degrees to port for about ten miles before turning again and shaping a course toward Pearl Harbor for the inbound leg of their searches.[36]

North of VP-24's sectors, after reaching the prescribed two hundred miles at 1220, Ensign Kellam in 23-P-12 radioed ComPatWing 2 for instructions. PatWing 2 replied at 1227 that the crew should extend their outbound leg to three hundred miles. Kellam complied and turned north and then west on a course that brought the PBY onto the same track as Hughes. Kellam continued another one hundred miles and again radioed Ford Island offering to fly further but received orders to cross far to the south and proceed to Pearl Harbor, bearing 220 degrees from O'ahu, well north of the projected sectors that VP-23 pilots Lieutenant

Winters and Ensign Wood, neither of whom had yet taken off, would cover.[37]

Back in the Administration Building on Ford Island, at approximately 1200 an increasingly frustrated Bellinger again attempted to dip into the Army's nearly empty well for help with the searches. With little confidence in what might be forthcoming, he requested that the 18th Bombardment Wing conduct a search of the quadrant southeast of O'ahu "as far as practical with planes available." That this sector was considered to be the *least likely* through which the Japanese might approach revealed Bellinger's total lack of confidence in Brigadier General Rudolph's ability to achieve meaningful results. To Rudolph's credit, however, the ground crews at Hickam did manage to send up three surviving B-17Ds (although not until after 1500) to search for "an enemy carrier reported between 165–195 degrees," with no contact being made.[38]

As midday approached, the empty skies above and the vacant seas below revealed no immediate enemy presence to the eight crews from VJ-1. Due north of O'ahu in 1-J-1, Ensign Ruth and Pappy Geise saw nothing on the outbound leg of their search, or on the short ten-mile crossover to the east. Accordingly, Ruth turned south for the return flight to Pearl Harbor. Unknown to the Americans as they proceeded on course 179 degrees, Japanese carrier fighters *were* in the vicinity—two *shōtai*s of three fighters each from the *Zuikaku*'s third combat air patrol guarding the southern perimeter of Nagumo's Carrier Strike Force. Having taken off at 1020, the *kansen*s patrolled south of *Kidō Butai* maintaining a careful watch for American aircraft. Well to the south, meanwhile, a report from one of the *Hiryū*'s returning carrier bombers—who had seen Ruth's JRS-1 plodding north—doubtless intensified the concern on board the *Zuikaku*, although it is not known whether the message was received by, or was relayed to, the Japanese fighters: "It is suspected that an enemy flying boat is tracking us from the rear."[39]

The leaders of the patrol's two sections—PO1c Itō Junjirō and PO1c Iwamoto Tetsuzō—were solid senior NCOs. Itō graduated with the first class of the Kō enlisted reserve program in June 1939 after completing training with the Tsuchiura Air Group. Iwamoto was the more senior, having graduated in December 1936 from the thirty-fourth class of the pilot trainee program. Iwamoto emerged from the war in China as the Imperial Japanese Navy's leading ace, with fourteen victory claims to his credit. Although bitterly disappointed at missing out on the fighting over O'ahu, he nonetheless resigned himself to his situation. Officers on board the carrier seemed confident that the Americans would try to intercept Nagumo's force, so Iwamoto consoled himself with the thought that "it was not so bad to fight over the fleet." Thus, under able leadership and chafing at not being selected for the mission over O'ahu, the pilots of the *Zuikaku*'s third patrol were ready for a scrap.[40]

Meanwhile, as Ruth turned south at low altitude to observe from a position just below the clouds, 1-J-1's silver fuselage and brightly colored wings and empennage stood out brightly against the water one thousand feet below. At about 1310 the lumbering Sikorsky attracted the attention of one or more *Zuikaku* carrier fighters guarding the southern approaches to *Kidō Butai*. The Japanese aircraft accelerated, attempting to intercept what they thought to be a "flying boat" searching for the fleet. Just in time, Ruth and his riflemen spied an approaching *kansen* charging in from astern. Faced with possible destruction, Ruth displayed "cool-headed thinking, courage, and excellent

Combat Patrols over *Kidō Butai*
7 December 1941
Zuikaku Fighter Unit
3rd Patrol, 1050–1420

PO1c Itō Junjirō	PO1c Iwamoto Tetsuzō
PO1c Tsukuda Seiichi	PO3c Kuroki Saneyuki
Sea1c Fujii Kōichi	PO3c Kurata Nobutaka

PO1c Itō Junjirō, section leader, third combat air patrol from the *Zuikaku*

Prange, via Goldstein Collection

PO1c Iwamoto Tetsuzō, section leader, third combat air patrol from the *Zuikaku*

Prange, via Goldstein Collection

piloting ability" and pulled back sharply on the control column of the JRS-1, climbing into the cloud layer above. His "prompt and skillful action" shook off the pursuer. Ruth reset the course for Ford Island, the only American pilot to have made direct contact with patrols from *Kidō Butai*. At 1700 that afternoon, in a visual signal from the 5th Carrier Division to Vice Admiral Nagumo, Rear

Admiral Hara gave Ruth the credit he deserved: "A flying boat was tracked south of the submarines. Fighters pursued it but missed it as it went through clouds."[41]

Lieutenant (jg) Robb and the crew of 1-J-4 covered the sector northwest of Oʻahu. They ran into no opposition but flew the most complex of VJ-1's searches, with the outbound leg taking them

The engines on Ensign Ruth's JRS-1, 1-J-1 (BuNo 1063), undergo maintenance outside the southwest doors of Hangar 37, 8 December 1941. Although the side number and red section leader stripe on the fuselage aft are covered with nonspecular sea blue paint, the large black "1" is still visible at the center of the wing.

NARA II, 80-G-32483, cropped

toward Kaua'i. On reaching the eastern shore Robb circumvented the island and detoured counter-clockwise until he was off the northwest shore, then cut northeast until he closed on his original track and flew on a course of 305 degrees. Three hundred miles out from O'ahu he turned 90 degrees to port and flew fifty miles before making another right-angle turn for the inbound leg of the flight. Heading straight for Ni'ihau, he flew counter-clockwise around the island, intersected his original track around Kaua'i, and returned to Pearl Harbor after a flight of more than five hours.[42]

For all of its navigational gymnastics, 1-J-4 returned with nothing to report. The lack of hard-and-fast action did little, however, to ease the anxiety of the crew. Not until Robb's anger at the Japanese had cooled and the aircraft was two hundred miles out from O'ahu did he fully appreciate the Sikorsky's vulnerability. Back in the passenger compartment, Sea2c John A. Birmingham of VJ-1—a New York City enlistee who had been with the squadron only since 22 July 1941—experienced similar emotions. Though in the service only briefly,

he had already been in serious trouble in November when he was AOL for seven days and sentenced to thirty days' confinement. Perhaps seeking a measure of redemption, he reported to VJ-1's leading chief and volunteered for the mission with Robb. Wielding the aircraft's only armament—a 30.06 Springfield rifle—Birmingham spent the drafty flight perched precariously on the steps leading to the open hatch atop the passenger compartment aft, waiting to ward off any attacking fighters. Like Robb, he had yet to understand the dangers of the flight and how foolish he was to believe that he might shoot down enemy aircraft.[43]

Flying a pattern just south of Robb's, Lieutenant (jg) Bolser and second pilot Simpson flew 1-J-6 on a heading of 290 degrees that passed over Kaulakahi Channel separating Kaua'i and Ni'ihau. Like Ruth, Bolser flew at low altitude just under a broken layer of clouds. The search proceeded uneventfully until Bolser approached Ni'ihau, when a lone Japanese fighter came into view and attempted a firing pass from astern.[44] As Robb had done, Bolser reacted quickly, pulling back on the

Lieutenant (jg) Robb's JRS-1, 1-J-4 (BuNo 0506), rests on the oiled surface of the apron north of Hangar 54, 8 December 1941. The plane has not yet been repainted and still sports white engine cowlings that designate it as the squadron's first aircraft, second section.
NARA II, 80-G-32507, cropped

control column and climbing into the clouds just above. His crew included two leathernecks who had jumped on board the JRS-1 during its taxi, including Sgt. Thomas E. Hailey, a survivor from the *Oklahoma*. Eager to fire on the attacking fighter, one of the Marines lodged a good-natured complaint with Bolser that the ascent into the clouds had spoiled his shot.[45]

There is some debate as to the attacker's identity. One possible culprit was PO1c Nishikaichi Shigenori of the *Hiryū*'s second-wave fighter unit, a graduate of the second class of the Kō enlisted reserve program in December 1939. Nishikaichi was last seen by his comrades in the vicinity of Bellows Field, where Lt. Nōno Sumio led the unit in a strafing attack on the base.[46] It is thought that, after becoming separated from his comrades and unable to navigate back to the *Hiryū*, Nishikaichi decided to fly toward Niʻihau and ditch near the island. The submarine *I-74*, under Cdr. Ikezawa Masayoshi, was on station there to serve as a rendezvous and rescue vessel. Though the sequence of subsequent events is uncertain, it is possible that

Flight reserve enlisted trainee Nishikaichi Shigenori with the second Kō flight class, circa December 1938 at Yokosuka. Nishikaichi was first wingman, 12th Shōtai, second-wave *Hiryū* fighter unit, and the possible interceptor of Lieutenant (jg) Bolser's JRS-1 off Niʻihau.
USAR

Bolser's JRS-1 arrived while Nishikaichi was circling, unable to find the *I-74*. Following this failed interception, Nishikaichi may have force-landed *kansen* BII-120 on Niʻihau. Another possibility is that one of two pilots missing from the *Kaga*'s second-wave fighter unit—PO1c Inanaga Tomio and WO Gotō Ippei—might have been the attacker.[47]

South of Bolser's track, meanwhile, Ensign Larson and second pilot Byrd in 1-J-7 flew from Oʻahu on a course of 278 degrees. In contrast to Ruth and Bolser, they made no enemy contact but doubtless felt a great deal of tension during the long flight. The three J2Fs likewise searched to the southwest and likewise came up empty. Although the aviators in VJ-1 plugged holes and filled gaps in the day's search patterns, they had only two fleeting contacts with Japanese fighters to the north and west to show for their efforts and did not sight the enemy fleet.[48]

Plt.Sgt. Thomas E. Hailey, rifleman on board 1-J-6, pictured 18 May 1942
NHHC, NH 102556

The island of Ni'ihau, property of Aylmer Francis Robinson, looking northeast, 4 April 1940
NARA II, 80-G-411116

The starboard engine of Lieutenant (jg) Bolser's JRS-1, 1-J-6 (BuNo 1057), undergoes maintenance in Hangar 37, 8 December 1941. The side numbers have been painted out, but the white bottom halves of the engine cowlings designate the Sikorsky as third aircraft in the second section. At right is 2-F-12, a Brewster F2A-3 Buffalo of Fighting 2 from the *Lexington*, left behind for maintenance when Task Force 12 sailed from Pearl Harbor on 2 December to ferry VMSB-231 to Midway.
NARA II, 80-G-32483, cropped

Ensign Larson's JRS-1, 1-J-7 (BuNo 1193), rests on the apron north of Hangar 54, 8 December 1941. The plane has yet to be repainted. NARA II, 80-G-32507, cropped

Ens. John P. Edwards' relatively late search in 1-J-10 failed to provide intelligence from what should have been the most promising sector, due north of O'ahu. The JRS-1 could not match the endurance of a PBY because the Sikorskys could carry only enough fuel for a seven-hour flight. Edwards extended the out-and-back search pattern to its very limit, turning back after three and one-half hours. RM2c James O. Jackson worried less about the fuel supply than about whether he could successfully transmit information to Ford Island in the event of a sighting. The plan was to send a brief contact report of "many ships" before the plane went down. If the worst came to pass, the Navy's various radio stations could triangulate to determine the origin point of the message; otherwise, the radioman was free to send amplifying messages. As it turned out, however, there was no reason for Jackson to report and risk detection by the Japanese.[49]

Ensign Edwards' JRS-1, 1-J-10 (BuNo 0504?), on the parking apron west of Hangar 37, 8 December 1941. The Sikorsky's plane number is visible only on the center of the wing. Note the clumsy efforts under way to camouflage the aircraft, with sloppy overpainting of the side numbers on the nose as well as the black section leader fuselage band. NARA II, 80 G 32481, cropped

By about 1300 VP-23 had prepared two additional aircraft to support the search plan PatWing 2 had ordered. At 1330 Lt. Robert C. Winters—a native of Newark, New Jersey, with a diverse background in fighting, scouting, and patrol aviation—took off in 23-P-1 (BuNo 2417). Monticello, Minnesota, native Ens. Robert H. Wood—the squadron's gunnery and assistant flight officer—followed thirty minutes later in 23-P-6 (BuNo 2449).

The two crews undertook searches well to the south of Hughes and Kellam, with Winters flying out to the southwest at 235 degrees and Wood taking the 225-degree sector. Taking into account the outbound legs of all four VP-23 aircraft, the assigned tracks straddled those of VP-24, with those of Hughes and Kellam filling gaps to the north, and those of Winters and Wood doing the same to the south.[50]

Ens. Robert C. Winters in happier days at NAS Pensacola, circa 1929
NARA, St. Louis

Lt. (jg) Robert H. Wood, 6 May 1942
NPRC, St. Louis

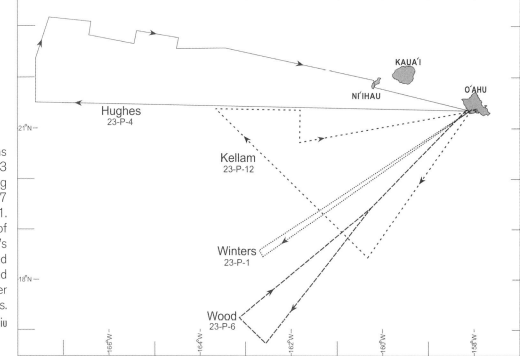

Search patterns flown by VP-23 on the morning and afternoon of 7 December 1941. Note the irregularity of Hughes' and Kellam's sectors compared with the pie-shaped sectors of the other search plans.
Di Virgilio

VP-23 Searches, 7 December 1941

Aircraft		Pilot	Outbound Leg
23-P-4	(BuNo 2447)	Lt. Cdr. Francis M. Hughes	270°
23-P-12	(BuNo 2455)	Ens. Joseph M. Kellam	260°
23-P-1	(BuNo 2417)	Lt. Robert C. Winters	235°
23-P-6	(BuNo 2449)	Ens. Robert H. Wood	225°

Having concluded that the southern approaches were less likely routes of advance toward the island, Ramsey reserved that area for available battleship and cruiser floatplanes to search. Apart from the SOCs Lieutenant (jg) Semmes and Ensign Thornton had taken out earlier that morning, only four OS2U-3 Kingfishers—two each from VO-1 (*Arizona*) and VO-4 (*Maryland*)—were available. Bellinger required outside help to locate crews because the men from the battleships' aviation units were not usually billeted at NAS Pearl Harbor. Accordingly, Rear Adm. Walter S. Anderson, Commander, Battleships and ComBatDiv 4, sent out an order for "all battleships [to] send pilots and aviation personnel to Ford Island immediately." After the crews arrived, they received briefings, took off, and fanned out to cover the quadrant of 135–225 degrees out to two hundred miles. The last plane departed at about 1430.[51]

VO/VCS Searches, 7 December 1941, 135–225°

Aircraft		Pilot	Observer
SOC (earlier flight)		Lt. (jg) Raphael Semmes	N/A
SOC (earlier flight)		Ens. Maurice J. Thornton	N/A
OS2U-3, 1-O-2 (Arizona)	(BuNo 5313)*	unknown	unknown
OS2U-3, 1-O-3 (Arizona)	(BuNo 5333)*	unknown	unknown
OS2U-3, 4-O-7 (Maryland)	(BuNo 5285)	Lt. (jg) James B. Ginn	RM2c William R. Roberts
OS2U-3, 4-O-9 (Maryland)	(BuNo 5287)*	unknown	unknown

* BuNo assignment probable but uncertain.

An OS2U-3, 4-O-9 (BuNo 5287), from the *Maryland* rests on the edge of Ramp 2 adjacent to Hangar 38 during the midmorning of 7 December. That afternoon, an unknown pilot and observer flew this aircraft south of O'ahu in a hunt for the Japanese fleet. NARA II, 80-G-32663, cropped

Meanwhile, as the four OS2U-3 crews flew south, 24-P-1 located Halsey's task force south of Ni'ihau, not surprising given the proximity of the search sector to that of 24-P-2, which had found TF 8 earlier that morning. The radioman on board tapped out an advisory to CinCPac and ComPatWing 2 shortly after 1420 relaying the crew's assessment of the ships below. Flying further east, the crew sighted a land plane at five hundred feet altitude south of Kaua'i and reported it at about 1428. Nine minutes later the relieved crew concluded that the ships reported earlier were friendly, notified the authorities accordingly, and continued on toward O'ahu. By 1545, following their predawn flight to Operating Area C5 and a very full day in the air, VP-24's four flying boats began landing in the waters of Pearl Harbor.[52]

There is no evidence that any VJ-1 aircraft reported either their negative searches *or* contacts with the Japanese fighters before returning to base. Having taken off first, Ensign Ruth and Ensign Larson were likely the first to land at about 1430. Cdr. John L. Murphy of the Base Force Utility Wing greeted Ruth as he taxied up to Hangar 37. After hearing Ruth's account of the flight, Murphy drove the young ensign immediately to the Administration Building to relate his story of the confrontation with the Japanese fighters two hundred miles north of O'ahu to Rear Admiral Bellinger and Commander Ramsey.[53]

Waikīkī roommates Robb and Bolser returned shortly after Ruth and Larson, low on fuel. On board 1-J-6 the situation was particularly critical because Bolser had flown well past Ni'ihau and the calculated point of no return, gambling that he could reach Pearl Harbor by reducing power and using a leaner fuel mixture. When the engines began to sputter intermittently, Sergeant Hailey and the other Marine, with grim humor, drew straws to see who would jump out first to save weight. As 1-J-6 neared O'ahu, Bolser rocked his

wings to extract the last of the fuel from the tanks, then held steady to ensure that every precious drop went into the carburetors. Coming in low and slow, the lumbering Sikorsky landed without incident on Ford Island.[54]

VJ-1's flights for 7 December closed with naval aviation pilots Fauber, Lesher, and Switzer landing their J2Fs, and Ensign Edwards' JRS-1 touching down at about 1730; all reported negative searches. Although none of the eight crews had sighted Nagumo's carriers, the aerial contacts—with the *Zuikaku*'s combat air patrol to the north and perhaps with PO1c Nishikaichi off Ni'ihau—gave Bellinger important insights into the direction and distance from which the morning's attacks might have come. To their credit, the men who took off in the practically defenseless JRS-1s and J2F Ducks exhibited extraordinary courage. In a memo from 15 January 1942 regarding the flights, Lt. Cdr. Thomas G. Richards, ComUtron 1, praised his men to the utmost, saying, "Be it noted that the main difficulty while assembling crews was the necessity to refuse permission to those present to go along. . . . The glorious aspect of this occasion lies in the fact that each and every man was aware that almost certain destruction would result if a contact with enemy aircraft was made while on the search for enemy surface units."[55]

Southwest of O'ahu, Ensign Kellam proceeded in 23-P-12 with his somewhat unorthodox crossover patrol into midafternoon. At 1515 he received permission to use plain-language transmissions to report further sightings in his sector. Just prior to turning 90 degrees for the return to Pearl Harbor at 1542, his flight path intersected with that of the westernmost of the OS2U-3s. Kellam's radioman raised PatWing 2 via a plain-language transmission to report a "small unidentified scout plane 19/00 [latitude] 160/30 [longitude]." The crew made no further sightings and continued to Pearl Harbor.[56]

Grumman J2F-2, 1-J-18, seen circa early 1939. Later replaced by J2F-4
(BuNo 1640), flown by AMM1c David J. Leshcr on 7 December 1941.
Ruth

Grumman J2F-4, 1-J-20 (BuNo 1665), flown by AMM1c Robert S. Fauber
on 7 December 1941, as seen 8 December 1941
NARA II, 80-G-32482, cropped

Grumman J2F-2, 1-J-22 (BuNo 1195), flown by AMM2c David L. Switzer
on 7 December 1941, as seen 7 October 1938
NARA II, 80-G-464994

By late afternoon the four OS2U-3s had concluded their searches south of Oʻahu, having flown south for more than two hours. The experience of the *Arizona*'s 1-O-2 was typical; the crew radioed back to the *Tangier* at 1714 that they had concluded the outbound leg by 1700 with no contacts.[57] One of the Voughts from VO-4 checked in with the *Tangier* three minutes later with similar news.[58]

By 1729 both aircraft from VO-1 had Oʻahu in sight, and the floatplane crews began their final approaches. The crew on board 1-O-2, however, steered clear of Pearl Harbor and landed at NAS Kaneohe Bay instead, probably aware of the indiscriminate AA fire being hurled at anything in the air. At 1746 VP-14 radioed the approaching OS2U that the station was placing landing lights in the bay and to "land as close aboard as possible." With daylight waning, 1-O-2 radioed its sister aircraft at 1800 that it was landing. Soon thereafter, beach crews pulled the plane from the water, moving it well away from the repair and salvage activity on the aprons. Eventually, sailors rolled the aircraft north of Hangar 1.[59]

The pair of Kingfishers from the *Maryland*'s aviation unit attempted to land later that evening. In 4-O-7 south of Oʻahu, Lt. (jg) James B. Ginn and RM2c William R. Roberts became disoriented in the approaching darkness and attempted to raise the *Tangier* on 2562 kilocycles to verify their position. The crew had difficulty establishing contact, however, because the radioman sent at least three messages requesting information. In the last known message from 4-O-7, at 1854, Ginn and Roberts reported their position, which they estimated as twenty miles south of Oʻahu, and once again entreated the *Tangier* to check their position. Meanwhile, off the south coast, the crew of 4-O-9 reported out of the murk at 2036 that they were approaching Barbers Point.[60]

By now Ginn and Roberts were in mortal peril, and Ginn either crash-landed 4-O-7 or decided to set down in the heavy seas while still some distance off Barbers Point. At about 2000, BuNo 5285 hit the swells hard, with the impact knocking both men unconscious. Regaining his senses, Roberts freed himself from the after cockpit, inflated his life

The intersection of Sixth Street and Avenue B northeast of Hangar 1 at NAS Kaneohe Bay on 8 December 1941. Note the OS2U circled at upper right, north of the temporary contractor buildings. The aircraft is probably 1-O-2 (BuNo 5313) from the *Arizona*, moved by ground crews north of the hangar line after it landed the evening of 7 December.
NARA II, 80-G-32943, cropped

jacket, and in the blackness located Ginn trapped in the front cockpit with his right leg pinned between the seat and the side bulkhead. Roberts freed Ginn and inflated his life jacket, then placed the helpless pilot on a wing float while he made repeated dives to free the rubber boat from its housing. Finally succeeding, he placed Ginn in the boat and paddled toward Barbers Point, where the surf capsized the inflatable craft. Ginn disappeared momentarily in the turbulent surf, but Roberts located him, dragged him ashore, and made him as comfortable as possible. Then he hiked inland in search of help and successfully hailed an approaching Army truck—no mean feat for an unidentified flyer given the high tension on Oʻahu that day. The truck moved both men to Tripler General Hospital,

arriving at 0215 on 8 December. Roberts survived his harrowing ordeal, but the severely injured Ginn died at 0250. Roberts required fifteen stitches to close the lacerations to his head. For his strenuous exertions to save his pilot's life, Roberts received the Navy Cross. Ginn's death added his wife, Harriett, to the long list of next of kin to be notified in the days ahead.[61]

The PBY crews from VP-23 also experienced difficulties as they approached Oʻahu in the gathering darkness. One of the crews—probably that of Ensign Kellam in 23-P-12—notified PatWing 2 at 1803 that the aircraft's landing lights could not be turned off and requested permission to land with them on. It is uncertain whether Kellam received authorization, but the plane's electrical problem

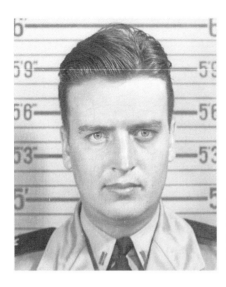

Ens. James B. Ginn, circa early 1941
NARA, St. Louis

RM2c William R. Roberts, 12 January 1942
NARA, St. Louis

greatly concerned the crew as they closed on Oʻahu, unable to conceal themselves from jittery gunners. Following close behind, Lieutenant Winters landed on the waters north of Ford Island at 2020. One hour later, Ensign Wood in 23-P-6, unsure of his position in the darkness, radioed an estimate that he was twenty-five miles off Barbers Point.[62]

Massie Hughes also approached Oʻahu in the murk, following a search that was uneventful after the contact with Task Force 8. During the long hours in the air, Lieutenant Ogden "wondered what the hell was happening back home on both Ford Island and out in town" but heard nothing on the radio during the entire flight. The sight of Lieutenant Commander Hughes in the left seat with his pajamas sticking out from his pants legs provided some diversion, as did the squadron commander's "running remarks," which were of "an obscene nature [and] . . . applied more to U.S. congressmen than they were to the Japanese."[63]

After a 1,400-mile, twelve-hour flight, Hughes arrived over Oʻahu at about 2030 with the weather "as black as the inside of a cow [and] raining like hell." The crew tried unsuccessfully to raise someone on the radio. Hughes turned on every light on the plane. The next issue was where to land, and Hughes opted for the Pearl City Channel. Luckily, much of the debris in the water had been removed or had been swept away by the current. Palpable

relief washed over Ogden at not being targeted by the station's defenders as the PBY taxied toward the ramps. "We went cheerfully along our way, acting friendly as all get-out."[64]

By 2020 all of the search planes that were supposed to return to NAS Pearl Harbor had done so, with two notable exceptions. Lieutenant (jg) Ginn and RM2c Roberts in the *Maryland*'s 4-O-7 were engaged in a life-and-death struggle to gain the shore off Barbers Point, and Ensign Thornton of the *St. Louis* aviation unit was still bobbing up and down in the Pacific swells in his SOC.

After the raid, Rear Admiral Bellinger reflected on those who flew from Ford Island in search of the Japanese fleet that day, all of whom had won his undying thanks and admiration. Given the circumstances and the emergency at hand, it was not possible to recognize all who deserved acclaim. Bellinger's sentiment regarding Lt. Cdr. Massie Hughes was typical of his heartfelt affection for those men. Bellinger praised Hughes effusively as "a fighting man. . . . [He] did not have to go on this flight. He seized the opportunity that was presented and went. I take my hat off to him." Bellinger lauded Hughes' efforts after the raid as well. "His organizing ability and leadership the following days quickly brought order out of chaos. . . . I wish he were twins and both under my command."[65]

Chapter Ten

"HOW IN GOD'S NAME COULD SOMETHING LIKE THIS HAPPEN?"

Despite the destruction visited upon the Pacific Fleet, the facilities at NAS Pearl Harbor sustained remarkably little material damage except for Hangar 6 and the surrounding aprons. At ground level, however, damage to the "industrial area" and seaplane hangars appeared more significant, with debris and wrecked aircraft stark against a backdrop of fires at Hangar 6 and oily smoke from the battleships and the moorings southeast of Ford Island.

There were nine impacts from bombs east and south of the hangar, with the largest crater being twenty feet wide and seven feet deep. Fires ignited by a bomb explosion east of Hangar 6 severely damaged the northeast corner of the building, which, although gutted, retained its steel structure intact. The effects of the attack on Hangar 38 were insignificant by comparison because the bomb that struck the building passed through the roof, penetrated the deck of the Staff Repair Shop in the hangar's west corner, and broke apart.[1]

Losses among the aircraft assigned to PatWing 2 were severe. Although VP-21 at Midway Island was spared (one aircraft was destroyed during the

Japanese shelling there that night), at Pearl Harbor only nine flyable PBYs remained out of thirty from VP-22, VP-23, and VP-24, along with a Dutch PBY-5 awaiting installation of metric instruments. A number of other aircraft were repairable but yet unavailable. VJ-2 was completely out of action, with none of the squadron's PBYs and J2Fs operational at midmorning. A substantial number of the OS2U Kingfishers from the battleships were disabled or destroyed as well. Taken together, Bellinger's air assets on Oʻahu had fared badly. Of the seventy-eight PBY-3s and PBY-5s at Midway, Pearl, and Kaneohe, fifty-six aircraft were out of commission, forty of them completely destroyed or beyond repair.[2]

There were other worrisome matters, including the bomb explosion in the Dispensary courtyard, although not a single person was injured in the blast. The explosion of the *Arizona* and fires along Battleship Row caused great concern for the safety of the aboveground fuel storage system, but the situation was under control—though still dangerous—by the end of the day. By chance, the Luke Field side of the island escaped Lieutenant

Irikiin's intended bombardment, but the single bomb that did strike hit among the storehouses and magazines. The torpedo damage to 1010 Pier and the sunken hulk of the *Arizona* that cut off Ford Island's water supply added to the losses.

In the immediate aftermath of the attack, the lack of more complete destruction on Ford Island was scant comfort. The sailors had occupied an unwilling ringside seat to the greatest naval disaster in American history, and a depressed, almost sick feeling was common among them. AMM2c

Earnest Cochran fancied himself a "tough guy" afraid of nothing, styling himself after the cocky depictions of Navy men by actors James Cagney and Pat O'Brien during the 1930s, but the attack forced him to an unsettling realization: he was very frightened. For nearly a week afterward Cochran had trouble keeping food down. For most it had been "a day of shock, horror and disbelief." Sea2c Houston James' thoughts mirrored those of many shipmates as he asked himself, "How in God's name could something like this happen?"[3]

The seaplane hangars at NAS Pearl Harbor, 10 December 1941. Note damage to the northeast corner of Hangar 6; scorched areas on the pavement mark where aircraft burned during the raid. Many sandbagged positions are still present on the aprons. A large area of wreckage, all PBY-3s from VP-22, lies at lower left. NARA II, 80-G-387579, cropped

Three surviving aircraft—a PBY-3 from VP-22 in the foreground at left and two PBY-5s behind it—rest on the apron north of Hangar 6 in front of the Motor Test Building in the distance. The PBY-5 at left is a Dutch machine with distinctive orange triangles outlined in black atop the wing.
NARA II, 80-G-32505, cropped

The mood of those at command levels was no better. From the windows on the northeast face of the Administration Building, stricken vessels moored alongside Ford Island were clearly visible in an unforgettably dramatic end-on view of Battleship Row. Pat Bellinger, thinking in later years on the day's experience from that vantage point, recorded somberly: "The accumulation of damage caused some ships to settle gradually to the bottom on an even keel and others to turn slowly on the side. I could see some of this happening from my window. It is impossible to describe the feelings of a Navy man watching while a ship receives death blows and sinks, [because] for him death has just claimed a personal friend."[4]

Before the morning's shock dissipated, most of those on Ford Island concluded that another attack was probably in the offing, and the thought of it set nerves on edge. One anonymous sailor declared, "We knew that should the enemy attack the island for the purpose of invasion that we would have to fight to the end." Anxiety mounted as the day wore on, with almost everyone wondering when— and not necessarily whether—the Japanese would return. The chances of mounting a successful defense seemed slender. Cpl. Lawrence Keith of the Marine detachment wrote later that after viewing the harbor while standing guard, "it was like everything had come to an end."[5]

One senior chief petty officer gave voice to a sentiment perhaps not unexpected given the uniformly determined reaction to the attack. Like most "old-timers," CSF Albert Molter—with twenty-one years in the Navy—had complained "many times about 'the Navy's gone to hell with all these kids in it.' I changed my tune after December 7th.

I saw youngsters become men in minutes. I saw them handle whatever needed to be done, with calm deliberation, clear thinking and immediate action."[6]

Rumors ran riot in the hours and days after the attack. Most of the stories that circulated on Ford Island related to threats of invasion, with fears fueled by a feeling of isolation from the other would-be defenders on Oʻahu. The Japanese had landed on the windward side of the island, one rumor said, and American fighter planes were engaged in desperate dogfights with enemy aircraft. Transports were disgorging troops onto Oʻahu, and paratroopers were landing on Barbers Point. The "news" circulating about paratrooper landings was particularly terrifying to the sailors. A general uprising of the island's Japanese population was under way as well, rumor said. With no

facts to squelch any of the rumors, Houston James believed everything he heard. AM1c Thomas Malmin and his shipmates at the station had their guard up, as did Sea1c Kuzma and his friends at the Fire Station, who were convinced that Ford Island would be the site of the last stand on Oʻahu. All of them were prepared to fight to the finish.[7]

Firefighting on Ford Island continued through the day and into the night. Crews from the Fire Station commandeered two or three fire engines parked near the Fuel Pier that were earmarked for delivery elsewhere. When the paint on the old wooden BOQ on Ford Island, in proximity to the *Arizona*, began to smolder, the engine crews sprayed water on the exterior. In the course of protecting the BOQ, the parched firemen entered the building in search of something to drink and discovered a nickel Coca-Cola machine. No one had change, so

Preparing for the return of the Japanese, sailors belt .50-caliber ammunition on the foot of Ford Island, probably near Ramp 5, northwest of Hangar 6. Note the senior petty officer in whites at center with two reenlistment stripes.
NARA II, 80-G-32497, cropped

the men forced open the box and retrieved the soft drinks—the first liquid for many of the men the entire day.[8]

While assisting with efforts to clear debris and wreckage from the aircraft parking aprons, Ens. William A. Keutgen hastened to one of the station's garages in an attempt to locate heavy equipment and badly needed shovels. Several men there remembered seeing a bulldozer on the Luke Field side of the station, and Keutgen dispatched men to find it. Meanwhile, he found a forklift and was fortunate enough to locate an operator as well—a near miracle because none of the men in the clean-up crews knew how to operate heavy equipment.[9]

The forklift was not particularly useful for pushing aside larger pieces of wreckage and rub-ble. The small wheels jammed quickly, fouled by even pebble-sized debris. Fortunately, the men from the north side of the island rumbled onto the scene with their purloined bulldozer, which "did a pretty good job of pushing the stray wings and dirt out of the way." Keutgen secured shovels and sandbags from the contractor's shed; the men there coop-erated fully and even offered the services of their

Ens. William A. Keutgen, circa October 1941
NPRC, St. Louis

Byers crane truck, "which helped immeasurably in removing the engines and larger wing sections."[10]

Meanwhile, now that the vast majority of the men forced to abandon ship had been taken ashore, the boat crews in the harbor transitioned to collecting the dead. There were so many body

At center right, the Byers crane truck Ensign Keutgen obtained from civilian contractors clears aircraft wreckage on the north side of Hangar 6. The fires are out, but the hangar still smolders.
NARA II, 80-G-32565, cropped

parts floating in the water after the attack that boat crews used improvised skimmers made of pipes and chicken wire to facilitate the grisly retrieval. F3c Henry de Coligny pulled in a lower leg and foot in a high-topped black shoe. The realization that the man to whom it belonged was probably dead sickened him. He and BM2c Albert E. Humphrey helped transport the canvas-wrapped torso of a sailor to the landing, where men from the Dispensary were carefully collecting remains for identification. When the two sailors lifted the corpse, its body fluids ran out onto the horrified Humphrey, who immediately stripped and trailed his clothes behind the boat in an attempt to wash them.[11]

With the raid over, Lt. Cdr. James Baldwin went to inspect several houses on the island reportedly hit by splinters and debris to ensure that no fires had broken out. As he was leaving, Baldwin heard a sentry calling him to the shore, where the man "had discovered a dead enemy flier on the beach." Several men nearby joined in to help pull the Japanese man's body completely ashore and commenced a thorough rifling of his clothing, searching for papers and identification. All such material was "cut off or removed" and taken to Lieutenant Black, the station's intelligence officer.[12]

Sea2c Houston James and a shipmate received orders to go to the north end of Ford Island along Battleship Row to investigate the possible presence of a Japanese airman there. Not knowing whether the enemy flyer was dead or alive, the pair set off armed with rifles. They found the aviator, dead, in a clump of bushes. Later, James learned that the aviator did indeed land in the water and swim to shore, where, reportedly, the *Tennessee*'s Marine detachment shot him after he emerged from the water.[13]

The Japanese plane commander and observer, PO2c Matsuda Isamu from the *Kaga*'s torpedo bombing unit, shot down after launching a torpedo against the *Nevada*, was still in his flight gear and wearing his green parachute harness straps ("sashes," according to James) and flight helmet. James and the other sailor lifted the body, placed it into the back of a waiting pickup truck, and climbed into the cab for the short ride to the Dispensary. They dragged the body from the bed of the truck onto the loading dock on the building's northeast side, where Commander Iverson and CPhM (PA) Eugene Griffith pronounced Matsuda dead.[14]

The men at the Dispensary were not quite sure how they should dispose of the body. Finally, someone said, "Well, take him over to Pearl. They're taking everyone else over there." James and his companion pushed the body back into the truck bed, drove to the landing, transferred the body to a motor launch, and instructed the coxswain to head for 1010 Pier. A large number of craft were there evacuating American dead, with an officer on the dock with a bullhorn issuing instructions. After determining what James and the others were doing, the officer instructed them to bring the dead aviator ashore.[15]

The proximity of the Japanese to the American dead being stacked on the pier incensed the officer in charge of the operation. "Don't put that goddamn son-of-a-bitch over there with those dead! Move him over there by himself!" Eventually, the men on 1010 Pier transferred Matsuda to the temporary morgue at the Pearl Harbor Naval Hospital.[16]

Sea2c Houston F. James of VP-24, circa late 1941
NARA, St. Louis

PO2c Matsuda Isamu, plane commander, *Kaga* torpedo bombing unit, circa 5 December 1941

Maeda

At the Dispensary, meanwhile, all officers and men were in place by 1000, and all hands worked to prepare patients for transfer to the Pearl Harbor Naval Hospital, it being obvious that the Dispensary had to be cleared in anticipation of further attacks. The process moved forward quickly, and most patients had been moved out by 1130. Carp Clyde L. Ernst, the station's assistant first lieutenant, supervised movement of the most critical cases via truck to the boat landing and ferry slip. Eventually, the hospital sent word that they could accept no more men, and the Dispensary transferred the additional cases to the Navy's new hospital at 'Aiea, although that facility was not yet in full operation.[17]

Bungalows built for the station's senior chief petty officers, looking southeast, 10 July 1924

NARA II, 71-CA-152A-9-PH458, cropped

The service entrance and loading dock at the Dispensary on 1 December 1940. Houston and other sailors delivered Matsuda's body there for examination.
NARA II, 71-CA-152C-14009, cropped

Cdr. Louis Iverson (MC), 14 January 1942
Sherrard

CPhM (PA) Eugene Griffith, 14 January 1942
Sherrard

Sailors transfer bodies from boats onto 1010 Pier, probably during the late morning or early afternoon hours of 7 December. Sea2c Houston James encountered this scene as he departed from Ford Island's boat landing to deliver Matsuda's corpse. The *Argonne* (AG 31), flagship of the Base Force, Pacific Fleet, lies on the opposite side of the pier, with the *YSD 27* at far left.
NARA II, 80-G-32604, cropped

Although all the radio transmitters and receivers on Ford Island were back online by 1025, concern regarding further outages led the Communications Department to set contingencies in place. At about 1045 the department scrounged extra equipment to establish a signal watch in the tower of the Fire Station. Crews installed a battery-powered TBP portable transmitter and receiver and placed the equipment in operation. Several aircraft radios from VJ-1, equipment on board the *Tangier*, and relays of message-bearing runners functioned as additional backups, easing the burden on the Pat-Wing 2 Communications Department.[18]

The station also faced the difficult challenge of feeding all those present, many of whom had missed two meals that day. The Enlisted Barracks' mess hall was completely unfit for food service and required a thorough cleaning, so preparations moved forward to set up open-air messes. At about 1400 Major Zuber obtained 3 field kitchens and 1,500 cots from the Navy Yard and established messes for the survivors crowded onto Ford Island.[19]

Ensign Reed and Chief Pay Clerk Pischner took charge of the general mess on the seaplane hangar side of the island, and CCStd (AA) Peter L. Gauthier of VP-24 was in charge of the Luke Field side. CCStd (PA) John M. Roberts of VP-21 supervised at the garage field kitchen, and CCStd (PA) Norman L. Carlton and MAtt2c Edward L. Washington tended the mess hall at the BOQ. Storekeepers and cooks divided into teams and drew provisions for feeding the 12,000 refugees. While the interrupted water supply handicapped the efforts in the field kitchens and galleys, Reed, Pischner, CCStds (PA) Carl J. Johnson, Gauthier, Roberts, SK1c Raymond W. Sorensen, and Bkr1c Earl E. Wood brought in water from the swimming pools and other sources.[20]

Robert W. Reed, circa
late 1940, upon his application
to the U.S. Naval Reserve
NPRC, St. Louis

ChPayClk Clifford B. Pischner,
11 September 1934
NARA, St. Louis

ActPayClk Peter L. Gauthier,
circa August 1942
NPRC, St. Louis

The crushed water mains—one from the Navy Yard and another crossing from Kūāhua Island—left several wells, three swimming pools, and a water tank as the only supplies on Ford Island. Commander Harter of the Supply Department drained the pools into some storage tanks with instructions to ration and boil the water for cooking and drinking, a condition that lasted for two days. The swimming pool water could not be replenished because Lieutenant Irikiin's bomb strike had broken the six-inch line running from the artesian well on the north side of the island.[21]

The water at one of the wells was brackish and renowned for its unfitness, but crews pumped the water into five-hundred-gallon tanks, purified it with a healthy dose of Clorox and iodine from the Medical Department, stirred it with a board, and declared it fit for consumption. "What gosh-awful tasting stuff that was!" CSF Molter remembered. The chlorinated water from the swimming pools tasted almost as bad, but there was little choice in the matter.[22]

Meanwhile west of Oʻahu, the *Enterprise* had conducted air operations for much of the day in search of the Japanese fleet. A supposed sighting at 1630 of a *Sōryū*-class aircraft carrier prompted quick action. The *Enterprise* launched a strike group of thirty-one aircraft at 1642—nineteen torpedo-laden TBD-1s under Lt. Eugene E. Lindsey, six SBDs to lay a smoke screen for the torpedo attack, and six F4F fighters led by Lt. (jg) Francis F. "Fritz" Hebel to protect the strike group.[23]

Fritz Hebel was a Janesville, Wisconsin, native and graduate of the California Institute of Technology. After enlisting on 7 October 1935 he entered the Aviation Cadet Program, winning his wings on 25 February 1937. Following service with the *Nevada*'s aviation unit, he reported to VF-6 on board the *Enterprise* on 1 April 1941. Hebel's wingman, the quiet and unassuming Ens. Herbert H. Menges, A-V(N), was a native of Louisville, Kentucky, who had attended the University of Louisville before enlisting in the Naval Reserve on 3 July 1939. He won his wings in 1940, joined VF-6 on 28 November, and was the squadron's assistant navigator and communications officer.

Ens. James G. Daniels led the second section. He attended the University of Kansas and the

University of Southern California before his family's financial situation forced him to drop out and enlist in the Naval Reserve. He received the designation of naval aviator in August 1939, an ensign's commission one month later, and joined VF-6 in October 1939. Daniels' wingman, Lt. (jg) Eric "Ethan" Allen, was a native of Palmer, Massachusetts, and the only U.S. Naval Academy (class of 1938) graduate among the six fighter pilots. After completing flight training at NAS Pensacola, he joined VF-6 on board the *Enterprise* on 1 April 1941, the same day as Fritz Hebel.

Commanding the third section was Ens. Gayle L. Hermann, A-V(N), a Duke University graduate and native of New Britain, Connecticut. After winning his wings on 6 July 1939, "Hermann the German" (as Daniels called him) joined VF-6 on 3 August 1939. Of the six pilots, Hermann had been with the squadron the longest. His wingman was another reservist, Ens. David R. Flynn, A-V(N), who had attended Cornell and enlisted on 15 October 1939, shortly after the outbreak of war in Europe. Flynn won an ensign's commission on 10 August 1940 and transferred into VF-6 from Fighting 3 in December 1940.[24]

Back at NAS Pearl Harbor, CRM Farrow had returned to his duty station in the control tower at about 1600 when the *Enterprise* radioed and inquired as to the best time to send aircraft into the station. Farrow suggested that twilight—about 1900—would be the optimum time. Very importantly, Farrow added that the aircraft should approach from downwind out of the southwest, rendezvous at 1,500 feet off Barbers Point, turn on their running lights, use a steady approach, and *come right in*. The jittery nerves on O'ahu that evening might be trouble for aircraft returning to Ford Island that deviated from the prescribed protocol.[25]

CinCPac Headquarters retransmitted an 1848 advisory from Halsey regarding the incoming

planes to all ships present, to PatWing 2, and to the Fourteenth Naval District. Charlie Coe made all the necessary arrangements with the Defense Center in the Navy Yard to ensure that the AA batteries would not fire. Lt. Cdr. Earl B. Wilkins, the station's inspection and survey officer, sent out men "in cars, motorcycles, etc. to warn all riflemen, machine gun nests, etc. to hold fire." After passing word of the flight a second time, particularly to the men on the southwest end of Ford Island, he went to the warming-up platform in front of Hangar 133—the center building of the three remaining old Luke Field hangars—to direct the incoming aircraft to their parking area.[26]

At about that same time, the strike group from the *Enterprise*, having found nothing, reversed course for the flight back to Task Force 8. Just after nightfall, Hebel's fighters became separated from Lindsey's TBDs but arrived directly over the carrier nonetheless. At about 1950, Halsey instructed the six F4Fs to fly to Ford Island because of his reluctance to turn on the carrier's lights.[27]

Back at Pearl Harbor, Captain Shoemaker went to the control tower in the Operations Building and summoned Commander Young, CEAG, to guide in his pilots by voice, reasoning that they would recognize their air group commander and that Young was best able to bring in the approaching aircraft. Two floodlight trucks parked at the southern end of the landing field were shining their lights in a northeasterly direction to illuminate the runway, with green lights at the northeast end of the field intended as the signal that friendly aircraft were approaching. At that juncture, some of the men of Ford Island were aware of the incoming flight, but others clearly were not. Despite warnings and admonitions regarding the friendly aircraft, the men on Ford Island—and all over Pearl Harbor—were in a foul mood, trigger-happy, and had instructions to shoot to kill. To a man, they expected trouble.[28]

As the time of VF-6's arrival approached, an uneasy Pat Bellinger mounted the roof of the Administration Building to observe the landings. His apprehension was well placed. The defenders on Ford Island and across the harbor—nerves raw from the harrowing ordeal that morning—kept up intermittent fire. In such a situation it would be very difficult to land any aircraft that evening, preparations and instructions notwithstanding.[29]

Meanwhile, Hebel was having difficulty "locating" O'ahu, thinking that the smoke and fires from the harbor were cane fires on Kaua'i. Confused, he turned east, but he realized his mistake when he reached Moloka'i and reversed course toward O'ahu. Making landfall near Koko Head, the F4Fs curved clockwise around Fort Kamehameha and headed up the entrance channel toward the harbor, with each section in echelon right. In coming

Evening Flight into O'ahu, VF-6, 7 December 1941

Aircraft		Pilot	
F4F-3A	6-F-1	(BuNo 3906)	Lt. (jg) Francis F. Hebel
F4F-3A	6-F-15	(BuNo 3935)	Ens. Herbert H. Menges
F4F-3A	6-F-5	(BuNo 3916)	Ens. James G. Daniels III
F4F-3A	6-F-12	(BuNo 3938)	Lt. (jg) Eric Allen Jr.
F4F-3	3-F-15	(BuNo 3982)	Ens. Gayle L. Hermann
F4F-3A	6-F-4	(BuNo 3909)	Ens. David R. Flynn

Ens. Gayle Hermann's F4F-3 (BuNo 3982) on board the *Saratoga* (CV 3) in early October. When Hermann flew it as a "loaner" from VF-3, the side number was 3-F-15. NARA II, 80-G-81391

from the east, however, Hebel had failed to set up properly for the specified direct approach to the runway on Ford Island.[30]

As the fighters approached the station, they contacted the tower by radio. The tower instructed, "Turn on your running lights, make approach from Barbers Point. Come in low as possible." One of the pilots, presumably Hebel, responded, "Am making one pass at the field," contradicting the instructions passed to the *Enterprise* earlier in the afternoon. The tower reiterated, quite clearly, the previous instructions: "Do not make pass at field.

Turn on running lights and come in as low as possible." Again, the flight leader passed his own contradictory instructions to the flight, which was then approaching the dry dock channel. "Close in, I am going to make one pass at the field." The tower again instructed, "Do not make pass at field, *come straight in.*"[31]

At some point between 2115 and 2120, just as the tower advised Hebel (then abreast the Dispensary at three hundred feet altitude) for the third time, firing started, "apparently from the surface vessels." Almost immediately a voice crackled over

The Operations Building on 8 December. Because the large control tower (seen rising at center) was unfinished, the observation platform atop the building served as a control tower on the evening of 7 December. NARA II, 80-G-32483, cropped

the radio, "What in hell is wrong down there?" The tower offered no explanation, merely gave the curt order to "turn off running lights and beat it."[32]

From Lieutenant Commander Wilkins' vantage point near Hangar 133, within five seconds the entire harbor seemed to open up on the F4Fs flying up the channel and kept firing until the fighters disappeared near the Administration Building. From the building's roof, Bellinger saw some AA guns "cut loose," prompting guns in the harbor to open fire. Even before Bellinger could hurry off the roof, "tracer fire covered the entire heavens." Rushing inside and down the stairs toward the naval base defense phone, he found Charlie Coe already talking. Bellinger grabbed the phone and yelled at the party on the other end to stop the firing, cursing at the top of his lungs. Antiaircraft fire, including 3- and 5-inch guns, still lit up the sky. Although machine-gun fire and splinters from the aerial bursts splashed in the water all around Massie Hughes' PBY—still sitting off the seaplane ramp despite having landed fifty minutes earlier—no one was hurt, and 23-P-4 sustained no damage.[33]

The sailors fired at their imaginary foes with wild abandon. RM2c Harry Mead recalled a sky "filled with tracers. . . . Every conceivable angle of trajectory imaginable was displayed. One of the officers in our squadron was running back and forth between sandbag emplacements (set up that afternoon) shouting, 'Hold your fire! Hold your fire! Those are our planes!' It did no good."[34]

Coming in low and slow over the channel, it was almost impossible for the six *Enterprise* pilots to evade the fire directed at them. Gunners probably hit Ensign Menges first, disabling him or killing the young Kentuckian outright. His F4F arched northward, lost way, and slammed into the veranda of the Palm Lodge in Pearl City, "on the east waterfront of the peninsula on Kirkbride Avenue, near Palm Avenue." The conflagration completely destroyed the building—a popular lodging for Pan Am Clipper passengers awaiting transportation

to the next stop along their route. The flames badly scorched nearby structures as well.

The men of Battery F, 64th Coast Artillery (AA) took note of the crash site, most likely having fired on Menges themselves with .30- and .50-caliber machine guns. The battery commander, Capt. Philip N. Gallagher, had transferred the unit from Fort Shafter to its assigned "AA defense position" on Pearl City Peninsula earlier in the day. Almost a week later, on 13 December, Gallagher approached Lt. Richard Black, officer in charge of intelligence for NAS Pearl Harbor, and reported that the wreckage was still present, as were Menges' remains. Black investigated and had the remains "wrapped in a sheet and buried temporarily in the shallow hole under a marker." The naval authorities finally collected the rest of Menges' mangled and charred body on 14 December and summoned Ens. David Flynn to identify his friend's wristwatch. For some time the crash site was a popular gathering spot for locals, although guarded by a sentry during the daylight hours.[35]

Fritz Hebel managed to clear the harbor and decided to fly up the valley between the Koʻolau and Waiʻanae mountain ranges, intending to land at Wheeler Field. The men there—almost surely unaware of the provisions made to receive the

AvCdt Herbert H. Menges, 15 December 1939, at NAS Pensacola
NHHC, NH 96616

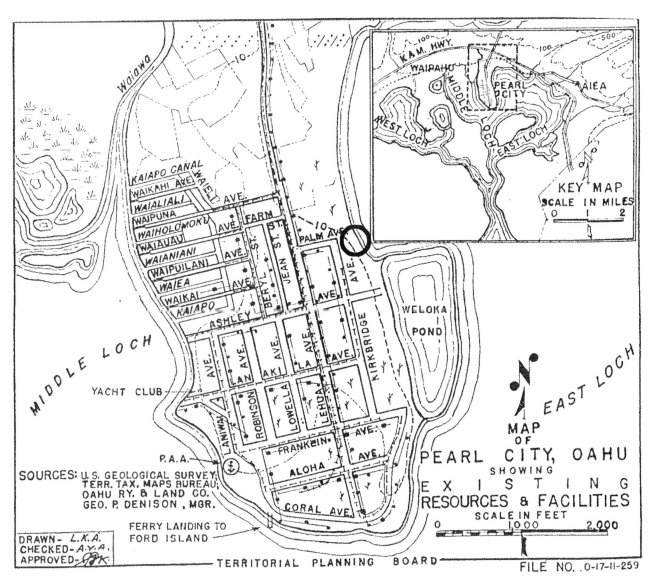

Map of Pearl City Peninsula created by the Territorial Planning Board in 1939, showing the location of the Palm Lodge, where Ensign Menges crashed
HABS

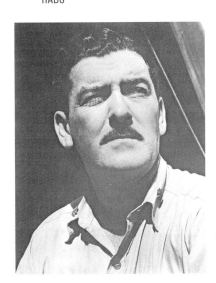

Lt. Cdr. Richard B. Black, circa 1945
Prince William County [Va.] Historic Preservation Division

Enterprise planes—supposed Hebel to be Japanese and opened fired at full deflection. Hebel struggled to maintain control of his aircraft, but it hit the ground and came to rest "in a gulch 200 yards west of Kunia Road just northwest of Wheeler Field." The F4F had no shoulder harness, and Hebel's head struck the gunsight, which inflicted a severe skull fracture. Soldiers nearby rushed to the crash only to find an American pilot. Lifting him gingerly from the wreck of 6-F-1, they conveyed Hebel to Tripler General Hospital, where he survived only a brief time. His body was interred at Schofield Barracks.[36]

After a dud 5-inch shell passed through the engine of 3-F-15, Ens. Gayle Hermann took the only option open—a dead-stick landing at the station. Gliding toward Ford Island, he landed on the station's golf course in a hail of gunfire, which continued even after the F4F-3 came to rest. Hermann retrieved his seat parachute pack and trudged toward the old land plane hangars on the northwest side of Ford Island—a very risky thing to do on that dark night.[37]

Ens. David Flynn had a harrowing time that evening as well. After turning off his running lights, he sped away from the harbor and flew ten miles out to sea past Ewa Mooring Mast Field. Possibly intending to land at Ewa, he reversed course in the vicinity of Barbers Point. However, the F4F-3A's Pratt and Whitney died, either from fuel starvation or gunfire damage. At 1,200 feet Flynn abandoned 6-F-4 and bailed out over land. The aircraft exploded when it hit the ground about one mile north of Barbers Point near Ewa Beach. In the darkness Flynn could not see to guide his parachute and landed in a tree. Releasing the harness of the parachute, which he had borrowed from squadronmate Lt. (jg) Wilmer E. Rawie, Flynn fell to the ground and wrenched his back. Meanwhile, soldiers from the 35th Infantry Regiment spied his slow descent and converged on the injured naval aviator, intent on capturing, or skewering, one of their erstwhile tormentors. As they rushed the downed flyer the soldiers heard Flynn lambasting them with profanity that no Japanese could possibly know. The infantrymen placed Flynn in an ambulance headed for Tripler, ironically the same vehicle carrying Lieutenant (jg) Ginn and RM2c Roberts after their ordeal.[38]

Lt. (jg) Eric Allen fared poorly. His aircraft was hit at about the same moment as that of Ensign Menges. Although 6-F-12 caught fire in an instant and exploded, Allen managed to bail out but was struck by a rifle bullet during his very short descent. Injured and probably unable to prepare for the low-altitude, high-speed impact with the water, he very nearly came down onto the minesweeper *Vireo* (AM 52), which had moored alongside the *California* at 2100. Around 2115 the crew pulled on board what they assumed to be a Japanese aviator but quickly identified him as an *Enterprise*

Lt. (jg) Francis F. Hebel, circa March 1941, shortly before joining the *Enterprise* and VF-6
NARA, St. Louis

Ens. Gayle L. Hermann on board the *Enterprise*, circa January 1942
NARA II, 80-G-464482, cropped

Ens. David R. Flynn on board the *Enterprise*, circa January 1942
NARA II, 80-G-464482, cropped

pilot. They transferred Allen—in tremendous pain—to the *California* and finally to the Dispensary and Lieutenant Riggs for examination. Riggs treated Allen for burns on his legs from "a tracer exploding in [the] cockpit" and, thinking that the severely injured aviator might also have a ruptured liver, ordered his transfer to the Naval Hospital, where Allen died that evening.[39]

Ensign Daniels' F4F-3A, 6-F-5, was the last aircraft of the flight still aloft. Prudently, he waited for the AA fire to die down before making another attempt to land. Very nearly out of fuel and with not a moment to spare, Daniels contacted the tower via radio and began a cat-and-mouse game with Cdr. Howard Young, who was still present. Based on the hot reception by the island's defenders, and possibly thinking that the Japanese might already

Ens. Eric Allen on 12 August 1940 at NAS Pensacola
NHHC, NH 96617

At left, the minesweeper *Vireo* assists with salvage operations under way on the *California* at right. Note that salvagers have removed the main battery directors from the upper level of the battleship's control tops as well as the secondary battery directors from the lower platforms.
NARA II, RG19, cropped

have occupied the station, Daniels refused to identify himself until Young did the same, prompting an exchange of Daniels' middle name (Ganson) and Young's nickname (Brigham), which the Japanese could not possibly know. With that established, Daniels roared in for a fast landing, sans flaps. When he flew into the spotlight illumination, the men on the ground saw the American insignia and the firing abated somewhat. Avoiding obstructions, he ground-looped the Wildcat but recovered to taxi back toward his assigned hangar only to be fired at by a Marine from a sandbagged position. Ensign Flynn, still en route afoot to the hangar, persuaded the Marine to cease fire with the help of a gun butt. Near Hangar 133, Lieutenant Commander Wilkins heard Daniels taxiing and, at considerable personal risk, flagged him down with a flashlight.[40]

The loss of five additional aircraft and the death of three more naval aviators was a sad end to a terrible day and the beginning of a period of profound uncertainty for the men of VF-6. A considerable time was to pass before the squadron

Ens. James G. Daniels III, on board the
Enterprise, circa January 1942
NARA II, 80-G-464482, cropped

learned the fate of their squadronmates, and the manner of Hebel's, Menges', and Allen's deaths did nothing to comfort or inspire them. A glum Jim Daniels confided later in his diary: "Hermann and I were taken to the tower to report to the Group Commander. It's awful—Ens. Gonzale[z], Ens Vogt, LT(JG) Patriarca [actually safe], Willis from Scouting six and Bombing Six beside LT(JG) Hebel, Ens Flynn [actually safe], and Ens Menges from our own outfit. Some of the Japs got it, but our outfit was shot up by our own guns."

The eruption of AA fire as the *Enterprise* pilots tried to land exacerbated the fear and apprehension among Ford Island's defenders. With the panic surrounding the arrival of the flight, not to mention the rumors passing among the sailors, there was little sleeping done on the night of 7–8 December.

The burning fenders and pilings in the vicinity of the Administration Building, set ablaze by burning oil, provided the only light that night. The scene reminded Rear Admiral Bellinger of a Fourth of July bonfire. Despite the darkness, however, Bellinger carefully negotiated the cordon of trigger-happy sentries at about midnight and returned to Quarters K to check on his family. When he arrived he beheld "a weird sight" in the dim blue light emanating from the shelter: "The basement was filled with women and children all stretched on the floor in an effort to rest, mothers trying to keep their young ones quiet and trying to make the best of an awful situation." He returned to his office and slept on a cot there for several nights.[41]

With the entire island edgy, afraid, and on guard, the men were frequently more of a danger to themselves than the Japanese were. Word passed around that anyone with a lit cigarette would be shot. Many vehicles on Ford Island had their headlights and taillights broken out deliberately in an attempt to prevent any light from guiding in would-be invaders. Any slight noise or disturbance in front brought screams of, "Who is there?" followed by wild gunfire.[42]

All the men—officers included—found rest elusive. Anticipating that the Japanese would renew their attacks, the doctors at the Dispensary tried to get some sleep, a number of them bedding down on the floor of Lieutenant Riggs' office. At some point during the night Lt. Cdr. George W. Dickinson, the station's assistant medical officer, startled by one of the many firing incidents during the night, jumped up and accidentally kicked Riggs in the face.[43]

As the intensity of their fear and desperation abated over the next few days, the men of Ford Island reflected on the disaster and how it might have been averted, or its impact lessened. Bellinger mused that he was almost relieved that he was ill on the night of 6 December. "I thank God for the flu, otherwise I and my staff would have been wrongly accused of sobering up from a hangover on the morning of [December] 7th."[44]

In his testimony before the Hart Inquiry and the Joint Committee investigating the attack, Bellinger deflected some of the blame toward the Army, which, he said, "was not ready to perform their part in the protection of Pearl Harbor." Feeding that notion was the Army's reluctance to hold air raid drills prior to 7 December, citing interference with critical training. Bellinger felt that "the quality of the general run of their pilots" was poor, although prior to the war the Army was trying to use its best pilots and crews to fly the B-17s. From conversations with Martin, Bellinger was aware that his counterpart experienced great difficulty finding competent crews for the B-17s because many of the best crews had transferred to the Philippines. Regarding the number of aircraft available, there were simply not enough of them to support the activities of the Search and Attack Group, although this issue was beyond Martin's control.[45]

Admiral Kimmel harbored no illusion that the facilities, equipment, and personnel available to the Naval Base Defense Force were adequate to the task of continuous air defense. However, according to Bellinger, the "main idea was to evolve a plan and organization that would make the most of the tools that were available." Believing firmly that Kimmel viewed the picture from a realistic perspective, Bellinger testified later, "I know of no man who, under the circumstances, could have done more."[46]

For the enlisted men, however, there were few strategic views from Mount Olympus. Following a day of coping with the emotional hangover left by mortal danger and little food and water, RM3c Glenn Pennock's perspective bore on the more practical matters at hand. He wrote shortly after the attack:

Be it ever resolved:

1. We must make every effort to get enough food to sustain life.
2. We must make every effort to stay alive.
3. We must not go to the Waikiki Tavern on Saturday nights and then do battle the next morning.
4. We must stop drinking the damn swimming pool water.[47]

In a spare moment soon after the attack, Lt. Jackson D. Arnold penned an angry letter to Washington demanding a squadron. Having flown with VT-6 from the *Enterprise*, with VCS-8 on the *Savannah* (CL 42) as senior aviator, and having endured "the working over the Japs gave that day," Arnold had his fill of flying a desk at a naval air station. His letter expressed his desire "to lead an air group against the biggest Jap base I could find." And Lieutenant Arnold got his wish. From May 1942 through March 1943 he formed and trained VT-2 at NAS Quonset, Rhode Island, and embarked with the squadron in the new *Hornet* (CV 12). During March and April 1943 he participated in the raids against Palau, Woleai, Hollandia,

Truk, and Pohnpei. From June 1943 through September of the following year, as commander, Air Group 2 in the *Hornet* (and following another promotion), he continued to lead air strikes from the Mandates to the Philippines and flew in the "Marianas Turkey Shoot."[48]

Other men from NAS Pearl Harbor were just as eager to take the fight to the Japanese and exact vengeance. Such opportunities came within a matter of weeks or months for some. Others, who did not engage in direct combat against the enemy, would have to wait more than three years to savor America's ultimate victory over Japan.

Unquestionably, Pat Bellinger and the other officers at NAS Pearl Harbor did all within their power and authority to prepare and train their commands for a coming conflict with Japan. Those commanders strove mightily and tirelessly to provide their men with every possible advantage. Sadly, despite their dogged perseverance, they labored under a set of assumptions, judgments, and circumstances shaped by poor intelligence, underestimation of a formidable foe's capabilities, matériel and personnel shortages, a Navy Department that was sympathetic but unable to respond adequately to the service's requirements in Hawai'i, and a war plan that did not envision the lightning-like strike that would descend on O'ahu.

Lt. Jackson D. Arnold, circa 1941, while serving as accessories officer in the Assembly and Repair Department at NAS Pearl Harbor
NPRC, St. Louis

The seventh of December 1941 was a day that none of the individuals present on Ford Island would forget—the memories etched into their souls as words graven into stone. In the succeeding months, years, and generations, the survivors needed no prompting to "Remember Pearl Harbor." The experiences of that day had become part of their lives forever.

NOTES

Chapter 1. "An Island in Pearl River Covered with Goats, Hogs, and Rabbits"

1. Unpublished history of Naval Air Station Pearl Harbor (hereinafter NAS Pearl Harbor history) section 2, "A Narrative," 1, Quarters K Binder, courtesy of Daniel Martinez, World War II Valor in the Pacific National Monument (hereinafter Quarters K Binder); William H. Dorrance, "Moku'ume'ume," *Historic Hawai'i* 17, no. 12 (December 1991): 4.

2. NAS Pearl Harbor history, section 2, "A Narrative," 1; Donald Cutter, "The Spanish in Hawaii: Gaytan to Marin," *Hawaiian Journal of History* 14, no. 21 (1980): 23; Michael Pietrusewsky et al., "The Search for Don Francisco de Paula Marin: Servant, Friend, and Advisor to King Kamehameha I, Kingdom of Hawai'i," in *Studies in Forensic Biohistory: Anthropological Perspectives*, ed. Christopher M. Stojanowski and William N. Duncan (Cambridge, U.K.: Cambridge University Press, 2016), 67; Jan Becket and Joseph Singer, comps., *Pana O'ahu: Sacred Stones, Sacred Land* (Honolulu: University of Hawai'i Press, 1999), 38; Catherine C. Summers and Elspeth P. Sterling, *Sites of Oahu* (Honolulu: Bishop Museum Press, 1988), 58; Wenger analysis; Peter Corney, *Early Northern Pacific Voyages* (Honolulu: Thos. G. Thrum, 1896), 115.

3. NAS Pearl Harbor history, section 2, "A Narrative," 1; Storrs L. Olson, "The Contribution of the Voyage of H.M.S. *Blonde* (1825) to Hawaiian Ornithology," *Archives of Natural History* 23, no. 1 (1996): 1–42; "Index of 19th Century Naval Vessels," *Blonde*, http://www.pbenyon.plus .com/18-1900/B/00602.html, accessed 27 October 2017; Andrew Bloxam, *Diary of Andrew Bloxam, Naturalist of the "Blonde" on Her Trip from England to the Hawaiian Islands, 1824–25* (Honolulu: The Museum, 1925), 44.

4. NAS Pearl Harbor history, section 2, "A Narrative," 2; Navy Department, Office of the Chief of Naval Operations, Naval History Division, *Dictionary of American Naval Fighting Ships*, vol. 2: *1963* (Washington, D.C.: Government Printing Office, 1963), 284, entry for *Dolphin*; Rebecca Paulding Meade, *Life of Hiram Paulding, Rear Admiral, U.S.N.* (New York: Baker and Taylor, 1910), 17; Linda McKee, "Mad Jack and the Missionaries," *American Heritage* 22, no. 3 (April 1971): 30–37, 85–87.

5. David B. Tyler, *The Wilkes Expedition: The First United States Exploring Expedition (1838–1842)* (Philadelphia, Pa.: American Philosophical Society, 1968), 219.

6. NAS Pearl Harbor history, section 2, "A Narrative," 2.

7. Ibid., 2–3; Eliakim Reed Ford, *Ford Genealogy* (Oneonta, N.Y.: self-published, 1916), 21; "Historical Collections of the Hawaiian Islands—Kamehameha IV," entry for Dr. Seth Porter Ford, http://files.usgwarchives.net/hi/keepers/koc52.txt, accessed 28 October 2017; "Dr Seth Porter Ford," http://findagrave.com/cgi-bin/fg.cgi?page=gr&GRid=43364622, accessed 7 August 2015; Dorrance, "Moku'ume'ume," 4.

8. NAS Pearl Harbor history, section 2, "A Narrative," 3.

9. "Organizational History, 6th Fighter Squadron, 15th Fighter Group, VII Fighter Command, Seventh Air Force" (hereinafter Organizational History, 6th Fighter Squadron), Air Force History Support Office, Bolling AFB (hereinafter AFHSO), reel A0716, file SQ-FI-6-Hi, 1–2; untitled chronology, 6th Fighter Squadron, VII Fighter Command History of, vol. 1, AFHSO, reel A7586, file 741.01, 1.

10. "Organizational History, 6th Fighter Squadron, 1–2; Station Plan 1405-6-63, "Army and Navy Holdings, Ford Island," 18 April 1938 (hereinafter Luke Field station plan, 18 April 1938), in the microfilmed records of the Bureau of Yards and Docks (hereinafter BuYards & Docks microfilm), RG 71I, series I, reel 1168, NARA II, original generated by the Department Engineer Office, Headquarters, Hawaiian Department, Fort Shafter; photographs at "Hawaii Aviation," http://hawaii.gov/hawaiiaviation/aviation-photos/1910-1919/luke-field, accessed 10 August 2015.

11. NAS Pearl Harbor history, section 2, "A Narrative," 5–6; Organizational History, 6th Fighter Squadron, 3; "Luke Field Passes On," *Honolulu Star-Bulletin*, 4 November 1939; John T. Correll, "The Legend of Frank Luke," *Air Force Magazine* 92 (August 2009): 48, 50; "Hall of Valor, Frank Luke, Jr.," http://valor.militarytimes.com/recipient.php?recipientid=896, accessed 28 October 2017.

12. NAS Pearl Harbor history, section 2, "A Narrative," 7; correspondence, JMW and RJC, 18 August 2015; Station Plan 1400-3-106, "Navy Yard, Pearl Harbor, T.H., Fourteenth Naval District, Showing Conditions on June 30, 1941" (hereinafter NASPH station plan, 30 June 1941), Records of the Bureau of Yards and Docks, RG 71, NARA II; photographs 71-CA-165A-PH53 and 71-CA-152A-PH1114-5-21, Still Picture Branch, NARA II.

13. Memorandum, "Navy Property on Ford's Island, Hawaii," circa September 1935, copy of unknown origin in the authors' collection.

14. Biographical files, History and Archives Division, Naval History and Heritage Command, Washington Navy Yard (hereinafter HAD, NHHC), "Captain Robert D. Kirkpatrick, U.S. Navy, Retired," 18 June 1958, 1; "Captain Robert Dudley Kirkpatrick, U.S.N.," 25 November 1958, 1; "Biography of Captain Robert D. Kirkpatrick, USN, Ret.," 7 December 1944, 2, 4; Reginald W. Arthur, *Contact!: Careers of US Naval Aviators Assigned Numbers 1 to 2000*, vol. 1 (Arlington, Va.: Cooper-Trent, 1967), 30–31.

15. The hangars were manufactured in Angers, France, by Etablissements Bessonneau, headed by Julien Bessonneau, a maker of rope and canvas. See bond certificate in "Galerie Numistoria," https://numistoria.com/en/maine-et-loire-49/10738-etablissements-bessonneau.html, accessed 28 October 2017; and biographical data in "Julien Bessonneau (1842–1916)," http://data.bnf.fr/10797578/julien_bessonneau/, accessed 28 October 2017.

16. NAS Pearl Harbor history, section 2, "A Narrative," 7.

17. Although we know of no single document that details the development of NAS Pearl Harbor, we have constructed a narrative from contemporary photographs, plans, and contracts.

18. NAS Pearl Harbor history, section 1, "A Chronology," 1; biographical file, "Captain Robert D. Kirkpatrick, U.S. Navy, Retired," 18 June 1958, HAD, NHHC, 1, authors' collection.

19. NAS Pearl Harbor history, section 2, "A Narrative," 8.

20. Willis E. Hurd, "North Pacific Ocean," *Monthly Weather Review* 51, no. 1 (January 1923): 36, http://docs.lib.noaa.gov/rescue/mwr/051/mwr-051.01.0036.pdf, accessed 27 August 2015; Department of the Interior, *Report of the Governor of Hawaii to the Secretary of the Interior 1921* (Washington, D.C.: Government Printing Office, 1921), 101; NAS Pearl Harbor history, section 2, "A Narrative," 8.

21. "History of the 5th Bombardment Group (H)" (hereinafter 5th Bombardment Group History), AFHSO, reel B0051, file GP-5-Hi, 17 May 1918–31 December 1943, 1.

22. NAS Pearl Harbor history, section 2, "A Narrative," 10.

23. Ibid.; Station Plan 1405-3-15, "Naval Air Station, Ford Island, Showing Developments to June 30, 1928," BuYards & Docks microfilm, RG 71I, series I, reel 1167, NARA II; photographs 71-CA-153B-PH2411 and -5622, Still Picture Branch, NARA II.

24. Station Plan 1405-3-22, "Fleet Air Base, Ford Island, Showing Developments to June 30, 1932" (hereinafter NASPH station plan, 30 June 1932), BuYards & Docks microfilm, RG 71I, series I, reel 1167, NARA II; photographs 71-CA-153B-9665, -9809, -9860, and -9861, Still Picture Branch, NARA II.

25. Photographs 71-CA-153E-10518/10519 (collage), -10864, 71-CA-152A-PH17495, 71-CA-153E-10517, -10864, and -5495, Still Picture Branch, NARA II.

26. Station Plan 1405-3-23, "Pearl Harbor, T.H. Fleet Air Base, Showing Conditions on June 30, 1933," BuYards & Docks microfilm, RG 71I, series I, reel 1167, NARA II; photographs 71-CA-154C--PH16939, -PH17107, and -10471, Still Picture Branch, NARA II.

27. Station Plan 1405-3-24, "Pearl Harbor, T.H. Fleet Air Base, Showing Conditions on June 30, 1934," BuYards & Docks microfilm, RG 71I, series I, reel 1167, NARA II; Station Plan 1405-3-25, "Pearl Harbor, T.H. Fleet Air Base, Showing Conditions on June 30, 1935" (hereinafter NASPH station plan, 30 June 1935), BuYards & Docks microfilm, RG 71I, series I, reel 1167, NARA II; photographs 71-CA-154D-SLIDES2, Still Picture Branch, NARA II.

28. NASPH station plan, 30 June 1935; Station Plan 1405-3-28, "Pearl Harbor, T.H. Fleet Air Base, Showing Conditions on June 30, 1936," BuYards & Docks microfilm, RG 71I, series I, reel 1167, NARA II; photographs 71-CA-153B-11658, and -11727, Still Picture Branch, NARA II.

29. Telephone conversation, 22 August 2016, JMW and Jeffrey Dodge; Station Plan 1405-3-26, "U.S. Naval Fleet Air Base, Ford Island, Pearl Harbor, T.H. Officers & Married C.P.O. Qtrs, Barracks & Mess Hall," proposed upgrades on 20 August 1935, BuYards & Docks microfilm, RG 71I, series I, reel 1167, NARA II; Station Plan 1405-3-29, "Fleet Air Base Pearl Harbor, T.H. 14th Naval District Showing Conditions on June 30, 1937," BuYards & Docks microfilm, RG 71I, series I, reel 1167, NARA II; photographs 71-CA-152A-13, 71-CA-152C-PH312861, 71-CA-152B-2, 71-CA-152C-11908, and 80-G-32501, Still Picture Branch, NARA II.

30. Station Plan 1405-3-30, "Naval Fleet Air Base, Pearl Harbor, T.H. 14th Naval District, Showing Conditions on June 30, 1938" (hereinafter NASPH station plan, 30 June 1938), BuYards & Docks microfilm, RG 71I, series I, reel 1167, NARA II; telephone conversation, JMW and Jessie Higa of Honolulu, Hawaii, 5 September 2015.

31. Navy Department, Office of the Chief of Naval Operations, Naval History Division, *Dictionary of American Naval Fighting Ships*, vol. 5: *1970* (Washington, D.C.: Government Printing Office, 1970), 537–38, 583–87; NASPH station plan, 30 June 1938, BuYards & Docks microfilm, RG 71I, series I, reel 1167, NARA II; photographs 71-CA-153B-12871 and -12935, Still Picture Branch, NARA II.

32. Leatrice Arakaki and John R. Kuborn, *7 December 1941: The Air Force Story* (Washington, D.C.: Government Printing Office, 1991), 18; Maurer Maurer, *Aviation in the U.S. Army, 1919–1939* (Washington, D.C.: Government Printing Office, 1987), 371, 569; Office of the Chief of the Air Corps, *Air Corps News Letter* (hereinafter *ACNL*) 18, no. 18 (1 October 1935): 7; *ACNL* 18, no. 19 (15 October 1935): 9; Franklin D. Roosevelt, Executive Order [7215], "Interchange of Certain Property between the War and Navy Departments[,] California, Hawaii, and District of Columbia," 26 October 1935, Executive Orders and Presidential Proclamations, 1933–36, Franklin D. Roosevelt Presidential Library and Museum, http://www.fdrlibrary.marist.edu/_resources /images/eo/eo0033.pdf, accessed 2 October 2015.

33. "Administrative History of Headquarters, Seventh Air Force, APO953" (hereinafter Administrative History, Seventh Air Force), AFHSO, reel A7532, file 740.01.2, 4–5; various microfilmed reports and histories of the squadrons involved from the AFHSO and NARA, St. Louis.

34. Record of Equipment and Condition of Buildings, Luke Field, Pearl Harbor, T.H., 30 June 1940 (hereinafter Record of Equipment, Luke Field),

2–5, Records of the Chief of Engineers, RG 77, NARA II; Station Plan 1405-3-33, "Naval Air Station Pearl Harbor, T.H. 14th Naval District Showing Conditions on June 30, 1940," BuYards & Docks microfilm, RG 71I, series I, reel 1167, NARA II.

35. "Hawaiian Air [Depot] Material Area History" (hereinafter HAD History), vol. 1, July 1931 to 6 December 1941, AFHSO, reel A7374, file 723.401, 141.

36. Ibid., 142; Headquarters, Hawaiian Air Depot, Information Bulletin 13, 12 August 1940 (hereinafter HAD Bulletin 13), appended to HAD History; Headquarters, Hawaiian Department, General Orders No. 28, 13 September 1940, appended to HAD History; Record of Equipment, Luke Field, 1.

37. NASPH station plan, 30 June 1940; photographs 71-CA-153B-PH312856, -13599, and -13600, Still Picture Branch, NARA II.

38. NASPH station plan, 30 June 1940; NASPH station plan, 30 June 1941; photographs 342-FH-3B-47449 and 71-CA-152A-46-PH114124, Still Pic-ture Branch, NARA II.

39. NASPH station plan, 30 June 1940; NASPH station plan, 30 June 1941; photographs USAR-14ND-Box85-TEMP-NO-795, Fourteenth Naval District Collection, World War II Valor in the Pacific National Monument; 80-G-32483, Still Picture Branch, NARA II.

40. Luke Field station plan, 18 April 1938; NASPH station plan, 30 June 1941; photographs 80-G-279375, -279385, and 71-CA-153B-14825, Still Picture Branch, NARA II; Record of Equipment, Luke Field, 1; Robert A. Oborne Jr., account, n.d., 3, Lord Collection, HAD, NHHC (hereinafter Oborne, Lord account); Quartermaster Corps Form 117, Building 77, Luke Field, Pearl Harbor, T.H., circa 4 June 1938, Records of the Chief of Engineers, RG 77, NARA II.

Chapter 2. "We Are Facing a Very Tough Proposition"

1. Chief of Bureau of Navigation to Capt. Patrick N. L. Bellinger, "Change of Duty," 30 October 1940, Official Military Personnel File (hereinafter OMPF), RG 24, NARA, St. Louis; Patrick N. L. Bellinger, Report of Compliance with Orders, 1 November 1940, OMPF, RG 24, NARA, St. Louis; Chief of Bureau of Navigation to Capt. Patrick N. L. Bellinger, "Transportation," 12 October 1940, OMPF, RG 24, NARA, St. Louis; testimony of Patrick N. L. Bellinger before the Joint Committee, 31 January 1946 (hereinafter Bellinger testimony, Joint Committee), *Pearl Harbor Attack: Hearings before the Joint Committee on the Investigation of the Pearl Harbor Attack* (hereinafter *PHA*) (Washington, D.C.: Government Printing Office, 1946), part 8, 3451; Patrick N. L. Bellinger, "The Gooney Birds" (unpublished manuscript, n.d.), 300–301, HAD, NHHC; "Admiral Aubrey W. Fitch, USN (1883–1978)," http://www.ibiblio.org/hyperwar/OnlineLibrary/photos/pers-us/uspers-f/aw-fitch.htm, accessed 14 October 2015; Patrick N. L. Bellinger, Acceptance/Oath of Office, 1 November 1940, OMPF, RG24, NARA, St. Louis; correspondence with historian Jessie Higa, 16 October 2015.

2. Patrick N. L. Bellinger, Record of Officers, U.S. Navy, various entries, OMPF, RG 24, NARA, St. Louis; Bellinger testimony, Joint Committee, *PHA*, part 8, 3492–94.

3. Charles F. Coe, interview, 23 January 1963 (hereinafter Coe, Prange interview), 3, Prange Papers in the Goldstein Collection, Archives Service Center, University of Pittsburgh, UA-90/F-78, box 23, FF-14; James M. Shoemaker, interview no. 1, 31 January 1963 (hereinafter Shoemaker, Prange interview no. 1), 1, Prange papers in the Goldstein Collection, Archives Service Center, University of Pittsburgh, UA-90/F-78, box 23, FF-106; Wenger analysis and informal conversations with veterans of the period.

4. Testimony of Patrick N. L. Bellinger before the Navy Court of Inquiry, 25 August 1944 (hereinafter Bellinger testimony, Navy Court of Inquiry), *PHA*, part 32, 498; testimony of Logan C. Ramsey before the Navy Court of Inquiry, 23 August 1944 (hereinafter Ramsey testimony, Navy Court of Inquiry), *PHA*, part 32, 449; Bellinger testimony, Joint Committee, 31 January 1946, *PHA*, part 8, 3486.

5. CinCPac to ComPatWing 2, "Patrol Wing Organization, Hawaiian Area," Serial 0914, 14 June 1941, CinCPac Operation Orders, RG 38, NARA II.

6. This date is unknown.

7. Testimony of Patrick N. L. Bellinger before the Roberts Commission, 31 December 1941 (hereinafter Bellinger testimony, Roberts Commission), *PHA*, part 22, 554; testimony of Patrick N. L. Bellinger before the Army Pearl Harbor Board, 24 August 1944 (hereinafter Bellinger testimony, Army Board), *PHA*, part 28, 828.

8. Bellinger testimony, Navy Court of Inquiry, *PHA*, part 32, 497; Bellinger testimony, Roberts Commission, *PHA*, part 22, 555.

9. Bellinger testimony, Navy Court of Inquiry, *PHA*, part 32, 498; Bellinger testimony, Army Board, *PHA*, part 28, 828.

10. Bellinger testimony, Joint Committee, *PHA*, part 8, 3451; "Administrative History of Headquarters, Seventh Air Force," AFHSO, Bolling AFB, reel A6532, file 740.01-2, 35; "Major General Frederick Martin," http://www.af.mil/About Us/Biographies/Display/tabid/225/Article /108125/major-general-frederick-martin.aspx, accessed 16 February 2015.

11. Bellinger testimony, Joint Committee, *PHA*, part 8, 3451; Bellinger, "The Gooney Birds," 303–4; "Administrative History of Headquarters, Seventh Air Force," AFHSO, Bolling AFB, reel A6532, file 740.01-2, 35.

12. Testimony of Claude C. Bloch before the Roberts Commission, 29 December 1941 (hereinafter Bloch testimony, Roberts Commission), *PHA*, part 22, 461–62; Pacific Fleet Confidential Letter 2CL-41, Proceedings of the Roberts Commission, *PHA*, part 22, 338; testimony of Claude C. Bloch before the Hart Inquiry, 7 March 1944 (hereinafter Bloch testimony, Hart Inquiry), *PHA*, part 26, 12, 16.

13. Com 14 to CinCPac et al., "Operation Plan No. 1-41," 27 February 1942, *PHA*, part 24; Exhibits of the Roberts Commission, Exhibit 45 (Navy Packet No. 2), 1622–24.

14. Bellinger, "The Gooney Birds," 303–4; ComPat-Wing 2, "Annex Baker to Commander Naval Base Defense Operation Plan No. 1-41 Dated February 27, 1941" (hereinafter Annex Baker to Operation Plan No. 1-41), 28 February 1942, *PHA*, part 24; Exhibits of the Roberts Commission, Exhibit 45 (Navy Packet No. 2), 1629–30.

15. Annex Baker to Operation Plan No. 1-41, *PHA*, part 24, 1629–30.

16. Testimony of Patrick N. L. Bellinger before the Hart Inquiry, 15 March 1944 (hereinafter Bellinger testimony, Hart Inquiry), *PHA*, part 26, 140; Commander, Naval Base Defense Air Force and Commanding General, Hawaiian Air Force, "Joint estimate covering Joint Army and Navy air action in the event of sudden hostile action against OAHU or Fleet Units in the Hawaiian area," 31 March 1941 (hereinafter Joint Estimate/ Martin-Bellinger Report), Proceedings of the Roberts Commission, *PHA*, part 24, Exhibits of the Roberts Commission, Exhibit 45 (Navy Packet No. 2), 1630–34. For further discussion of Martin-Bellinger, see Gordon W. Prange et al., *At Dawn We Slept: The Untold Story of Pearl Harbor* (New York: McGraw-Hill, 1981), 93–97.

17. ComPatWing 2 to OpNav, Dispatch 290424, Serial 8-674, 29 August 1941, CinCPac dispatch files, Pearl Harbor Liaison Office, RG 80, NARA II (hereinafter CinCPac dispatches, PHLO).

18. OpNav to ComPatWing 2, Dispatch 302130, Serial 8-721, 30 August 1941, CinCPac dispatches, PHLO; letter, Logan C. Ramsey, staff, ComPatWing 2 to Matthias B. Gardner, staff, ComAirScoFor, 3 September 1941 (hereinafter Ramsey to Gardner), 1, uncataloged papers of Rear Adm. Logan C. Ramsey, HAD, NHHC.

19. Ramsey to Gardner, 2; Joseph H. Strittmatter, interview with Dr. Ronald Marcello, 8 June 1974, OH 0210 (hereinafter Strittmatter NTU interview), 17, University of North Texas Oral History Collection, Denton, Texas (hereinafter UNTOHC); JMW and James Sawruk, e-mail correspondence, 2 May 2009.

20. Ramsey testimony, Navy Court of Inquiry, *PHA*, part 23, 441–42, 456.

21. Ramsey to Gardner, 1–2; Ramsey testimony, Navy Court of Inquiry, 23 August 1944, *PHA*, part 32, 441–42, 447.

22. Prange et al., *At Dawn We Slept*, 212–14, 278–79.

23. OpNav to CinCLant, CinCPac, CinCAF, Dispatch 162203, Serial 10-340, 16 October 1941, CinCPac dispatches, PHLO.

24. Com 14 to Naval Air Stations, Dispatch 170356, Serial 10-304, 17 October 1941; Com 14, Dispatch 170319, Serial 10-350, 17 October 1941; CinCPac to ComSubScoFor, Dispatch 170354, Serial 10-352, 17 October 1941; CinCPac to

ComSubScoFor, Dispatch 170426, Serial 10-357, 17 October 1941; CinCPac to ComPatWing 2, Dispatch 170429, Serial 10-358, 18 October 1941; all of the above CinCPac dispatches, PHLO.

25. ComPatWing 2 to ComPatron 22, Dispatch 170555, Serial 10-363, 17 October 1941; ComSubScoFor to *Swordfish* and *Sturgeon*, Dispatch 180510, Serial 10-424, 18 October 1941; CinCPac to MarDet Wake, Dispatch 190729, Serial 10-471, 19 October 1941; all of the above, CinCPac dispatches, PHLO.

26. OpNav to CinCPac, Dispatch 170458, Serial 10-385, 17 October 1941, CinCPac dispatches, PHLO. Bellinger's involvement in the movement of the B-17s was considerable. As ComTF9 he was responsible for placing seaplane tenders along a portion of the route for plane guard duty. For details, see CinCPac to ComAirScoFor, Dispatch 082117, Serial 10-137, 8 October 1941, CinCPac dispatches, PHLO; ComAirScoFor to CinCPac, Dispatch 092333, Serial 10-183, 9 October 1941, CinCPac dispatches, PHLO; ComAirScoFor to ComPatWing 2 et al., Dispatch 140330, Serial 10-304, 14 October 1941; CinCPac Message Files, NARA II via John Lundstrom (hereinafter CinCPac dispatches, Lundstrom).

27. Copies of microfilmed movement cards, VP-12; VPB-120 [VP-24 in December 1941], HAD, NHHC; "Employment Schedule, Aircraft, Task Force One, U.S. Pacific Fleet," Exhibits of the Hart Inquiry, Exhibit 27, Item 60, p. 4, *PHA*, part 26; U.S. Navy Aircraft History Cards, PBY-3 and PBY-5, courtesy of Eric Mitchell on www.pby.com, accessed 6 November 2015; Thomas S. White, "Temporary Additional Duty in Connection with the Ferrying of Aircraft," 10 July 1941, OMPF, RG 24, NPRC, St. Louis; Kenneth K. Anderson, interview with Dr. Ronald Marcello, 18 September 1988, OH 0755 (hereinafter Anderson NTU interview), 4–5, UNTOHC.

28. So described by Cdr. Logan C. Ramsey in his correspondence with Cdr. Matthias B. Gardner, chief of staff for ComAirScoFor.

29. ComAirScoFor to CinCPac, "Service of U.S.S. *Wright* for movement of Patrol Wing One to Kaneohe; Request For" (hereinafter Service of U.S.S. *Wright*) 30 August 1941, RG 313, Records

of Naval Operating Forces (Pre–World War II), entry 299, U.S. Fleet, Scouting Force: Commander Aircraft; General Correspondence, 1937–1942, file A4-3, Employments, box 35, NARA I.

30. Service of U.S.S. *Wright*; ComAirScoFor, Movement Order 1-41, 18 February 1941, Operational Plans & Orders, RG 38, NARA II; ComTF 7, ComAirScoFor to ComScoFor, "Proposed Schedule of Employment, Aircraft, Scouting Force, Pacific Fleet, Second Quarter, Fiscal Year 1942," 23 August 1941, RG 313, Records of Naval Operating Forces (Pre–World War II), entry 299, U.S. Fleet, Scouting Force: Commander Aircraft; General Correspondence, 1937–42, file A4-3, Employments, box 35, NARA I.

31. Robert J. Waters, "Temporary Additional Duty," 2 October 1941, OMPF, RG 24, NARA, St. Louis; *Wright* deck log, 29 September–8 October 1941, RG 24, NARA II; Otto V. Horky, interview with Dr. Ronald Marcello, 17 May 1974, OH 0203, 15–16, UNTOHC.

32. BuNos 2411–2414, 2416, 2428. Effective 1 September, CNO reduced VP-12's operating strength from twelve aircraft to six, although the Bureau of Aeronautics' "Monthly Status of Naval Aircraft" indicates that the squadron did not lose its aircraft until October, prior to its departure for Hawai'i as the new VP-24. *Wright* deck log, 17–27 October 1941, RG 24, NARA II; *Ballard* deck log, 20–29 October 1941, RG 24, NARA II; JMW telephone interview with Capt. Charles P. Muckenthaler, USN (Ret.), 20 December 2009. The departure of VP-12 is based on the *Wright*'s deck log entry for the midwatch on 28 October.

33. Maurice H. Meister, interview with Dr. Ronald Marcello, 10 April 1991, OH 0836 (hereinafter Meister NTU interview), 20–21, UNTOHC.

34. *Wright* deck log, 27 October–1 November 1941, RG 24, NARA II; JMW telephone interview with Capt. Charles P. Muckenthaler, USN (Ret.), 20 December 2009, 6–7, Wenger Collection; microfilmed Movement Card, PatWing 1, HAD, NHHC.

35. PatWing 2 Operation Schedule No. 42-41, 4 November 1941, Exhibits of the Joint Committee, Exhibit 113-C, *PHA*, part 17, 2563; Bureau of Aeronautics, "Monthly Status of Naval Aircraft," 31 August 1941, 10, HAD, NHHC; Bellinger, "The Gooney Birds," 315a–316.

36. VP-14 was to upgrade by exchanging its early-production PBY-5s (nearly a year old) with aircraft fresh off the assembly line.

37. PatWing 2 Operation Schedule No. 42-41; Bureau of Aeronautics, Aircraft History Cards, PBY-5, courtesy of Eric Mitchell on www.pby.com; PatWing 2 Operation Schedule No. 43-41, 11 November 1941, Exhibits of the Joint Committee, Exhibit 113-C, *PHA*, part 17, 2558; PatWing 2 Operation Schedule No. 44-41, 18 November 1941, Exhibits of the Joint Committee, Exhibit 113-C, *PHA*, part 17, 2554; correspondence with Mr. James Sawruk, 12 February 2009, regarding his research in the microfilmed records of the Bureau of Aeronautics (hereinafter Sawruk correspondence).

38. PatWing 2 Operation Schedules Nos. 43-41 and 44-41; Sawruk correspondence; Bellinger testimony, Hart Inquiry, 15 March 1944, *PHA*, part 26, 125; Bellinger, "The Gooney Birds," 315a–316.

39. OpNav to CinCPac and CinCAF, Dispatch 272337, Serial 11-856, 28 November 1941, CinCPac dispatches, PHLO.

40. CNO to CinCPac, "The U.S. Pacific Fleet Operating Plan, Rainbow No. 5 [hereinafter Navy Plan O-1, Rainbow No. 5] WPPac-46, review and acceptance of," 9 September 1941, Annex I, I-6, Records of the Strategic Plans Division, RG 38, NARA II; OpNav to CinCPac, Dispatch 170458, Serial 10-385, 17 October 1941, CinCPac dispatches, PHLO.

41. CinCPac to ComAirBatFor and ComPatWing 2, "Naval Air Station Wake and Naval Air Station Midway—Basing of Aircraft At," Serial 01825, 10 November 1941, Operational Plans & Orders, CinCPac, box 19, RG 38, NARA II.

42. CinCPac to Com TF2 and Com 14, Dispatch 280447, Serial 11-860, 28 November 1941; CinCPac to ComPatWing 2, Dispatch 280450, Serial 11-861, 28 November 1941, both CinCPac dispatches, PHLO.

43. ComTF 9 to VP-21, VP-22, and ComTG 9.2, "Operation Order 981," Secret Mailgram 292103, Serial 11-974, 30 November 1941; ComTF 9 to VP-21, "Operation Order 982," Secret Mailgram 292101, Serial 11-973, 30 November 1941; NAS Midway to ComTF 9, Dispatch 020330, Serial 12-30, 2 December 1941; Wake (Aero) to Com TF9 and Midway (Aero), Dispatch 020530, Serial 12-46, all CinCPac dispatches, PHLO.

44. CinCPac to ComTF 3, Com 14, and ComPatWing 2, Dispatch 040237, Serial 12-110, 4 December 1941, CinCPac dispatches, PHLO; *Lexington* deck logs, 5 December 1941, Exhibits of the Joint Committee, Exhibit 102, *PHA*, part 16, 2108.

45. That Kimmel's response to the "War Warning" message was a knee-jerk reaction is clearly a misconception because the movement of PBYs and Marine aircraft had been contemplated for some time according to Kimmel's letter to Halsey and Bellinger from 10 November.

46. Wenger analysis of aircraft available October–December 1941.

47. Testimony of Arthur C. Davis before the Hart Inquiry, 13 March 1944 (hereinafter Davis testimony, Hart Inquiry), *PHA*, part 26, 106; Wenger analysis.

48. Coe, Prange interview, 5–6; Prange et al., *At Dawn We Slept*, 357–58; George W. Bicknell, interview, 7 September 1967 (hereinafter Bicknell, Prange interview), 8–9, Prange Papers in the Goldstein Collection, Archives Service Center, University of Pittsburgh, UA-90/F-78, box 23, FF-8; Bicknell, Prange interview, 12 September 1967, 8–11; Vernon Reeves, interview, 27 October 1969 (hereinafter Reeves, Prange interview), 5, Prange Papers in the Goldstein Collection, Archives Service Center, University of Pittsburgh, UA-90/F-78, box 23, FF-92; "Martin M-130 Flying Boat: China Clipper's Trans-Pacific Flights," http://www.historynet.com/martin-m-130-flying-boat-china-clippers-trans-pacific-flights.htm, accessed 8 November 2015; SecNav to NAS Wake/NAS Midway/Com 14/Governor of Guam, Dispatch 072116, no serial, 7 November 1941.

49. Coe, Prange interview, 5–6; Davis testimony, Hart Inquiry, *PHA*, 105; Wenger analysis.

50. Ramsey testimony, Navy Court of Inquiry, *PHA*, part 32, 451–52; Com PatWing 2 to ComPatrons, "Watch and Duty Schedule for December 1, 1941 to January 1, 1942," 25 November 1941, Enclosure A, Exhibits of the Joint Committee, Exhibit 113-C, *PHA*, part 17, 2548; Bellinger testimony, Joint Committee, *PHA*, part 8, 3457, 3480. The number of aircraft from each squadron participating in the long-distance patrols of 2–5 December

is uncertain, although it was probably low. To conserve aircraft for operations on subsequent days, it would be logical if Commander Ramsey had sent up no more than a section from each squadron.

51. Shoemaker, Prange interview no. 1, 9–10; James M. Shoemaker, interview no. 2, 31 January 1963 (hereinafter Shoemaker, Prange interview no. 2), 7, Prange Papers in the Goldstein Collection, Archives Service Center, University of Pittsburgh, UA-90/F-78, box 23, FF-106; testimony of James M. Shoemaker before the Roberts Commission, 3 January 1942 (hereinafter Shoemaker testimony, Roberts Commission), *PHA*, part 23, 729.

Chapter 3. "Pearl Harbor . . . Where the Hell Is That?"

1. John Kuzma, interview with Dr. Ronald Marcello, 5 December 1974, OH 0256 (hereinafter Kuzma, NTU interview), 2, 4–5, 13–14, UNTOHC. Although Kuzma referred to *Follow the Fleet* (1936) in his interview, the motion picture to which he alluded was more likely *Wings over Honolulu* (1937), in which then-captain Bellinger made an uncredited cameo appearance.

2. Houston F. James, interview with Dr. Ronald Marcello, 26 May 1983, OH 0600 (hereinafter James, NTU interview), 11, UNTOHC; James L. Young Jr., interview with Dr. Ronald Marcello, 17 August 1974, OH 0244 (hereinafter Young, NTU interview), 5–6, UNTOHC.

3. John W. Kuhn, interview with Dr. Ronald Marcello, 26 October 1976, OH 0346 (hereinafter Kuhn, NTU interview), 3–6, 8–9, UNTOHC; John W. Kuhn, service record form, OMPF, RG 24, NPRC, St. Louis.

4. Shoemaker testimony, Roberts Commission, *PHA*, part 23, 735; Shoemaker, Prange interview no. 1, 19.

5. Glennon J. Ryan, interview with Dr. Ronald Marcello, 16 September 1988, OH 0769 (hereinafter Ryan, NTU interview), 11–12, UNTOHC; James, NTU interview, 17–18; architectural drawings 1405-30-82 through 1405-30-87, "U.S. Fleet Air Base, Ford Island, Pearl Harbor, T.H., Barracks and Mess Hall" [various floors, with all drawings ca. 1935], in BuYards & Docks

microfilm, RG 71I, series I, reel 1170, NARA II; photograph 80-G-32501, RG 80, Still Picture Branch, NARA II; Shoemaker testimony, Roberts Commission, *PHA*, part 23, 735.

6. Various OMPFs, RG 24, NARA and NPRC, St. Louis.

7. Architectural drawing 1405-31-2, "2nd Floor Plan, Dispensary, 14th Naval District, Pearl Harbor T.H.," in the microfilmed records of the Bureau of Yards and Docks, RG 71I, series I, reel 1170, NARA II; architectural drawing 1405-24-2, "Fourteenth Naval District, Fleet Air Base—Pearl Harbor, T.H., Fire Station, Plans & Details," in BuYards & Docks microfilm, RG 71I, series I, reel 1169, NARA II; Henry L. de Coligny, interview with Dr. Ronald Marcello, 17 November 1987, OH 0719 (hereinafter de Coligny, NTU interview), 15–17, UNTOHC.

8. Aircraft History Cards (microfilm), PBY-1, BuNo 0102, 1911–1949, reel 7, HAD, NHHC, copies courtesy of Eric Mitchell on www.pby.com; Bureau of Aeronautics, "Monthly Status of Naval Aircraft," 29 November 1941, 3, 18, HAD, NHHC; Bureau of Aeronautics, "Monthly Status of Naval Aircraft," 31 December 1941, 2, HAD, NHHC.

9. Virgle A. Wilkerson, interview with Dr. Ronald Marcello, 28 January 1977, OH 0368 (hereinafter Wilkerson, NTU interview), 14–15, UNTOHC; Herschel W. Blackwell, interview with Dr. Ronald Marcello, 26 April 1986, OH 0975 (hereinafter Blackwell, NTU interview), 10–11, UNTOHC.

10. Patrol Wing Two Watch and Duty Schedules, Exhibit 113-C (hereinafter PatWing 2 Watch and Duty Schedules), Exhibits of the Joint Committee, *PHA*, part 17, 2547–67; John S. Kennedy, *The Forgotten Warriors of Kaneohe* (Oakland, Calif.: East Bay Blue Print & Supply, 1996), account of Murray Hanson, 359; Arthur R. Grace Jr., interview with Dr. Ronald Marcello, 14 October 1977, OH 0394 (hereinafter Grace, NTU interview), 10–13, UNTOHC; ComBatFor to U.S. Fleet, "Operating Area Chart, Hawaiian Area," 10 November 1941, RG 313, Records of Naval Operating Forces (Pre–World War II), Entry 299, U.S. Fleet, Scouting Force: Commander Aircraft; General Correspondence, 1937–1942, file A4-3, Employments, box 35, NARA I.

11. PatWing 2 Watch and Duty Schedules, *PHA*, part 17, 2547–67; testimony of Patrick N. L. Bellinger before the Hart Inquiry, 15 March 1944, *PHA*, part 26, 130–31.

12. Bellinger, "The Gooney Birds," 306; PatWing 2 Watch and Duty Schedules, *PHA*, part 17, 2563; "Operating Areas Hawaiian Area," chart, *PHA*, part 21, Exhibits of the Joint Committee, Item 9.

13. James A. Caudel, interview with Dr. Ronald Marcello, 17 August 1974, OH 0238 (hereinafter Caudel, NTU interview), 9, UNTOHC; Bellinger testimony, Joint Committee, *PHA*, part 8, 3464; Jack Rogo [Jacob S. Rogovsky], letter, 2 September 1962 (hereinafter Rogo, Prange letter), 3, Prange Papers in the Goldstein Collection, Archives Service Center, University of Pittsburgh, UA-90/F-78, box 23, FF-97.

14. Earnest A. Cochran, interview with Dr. Ronald Marcello, 20 December 1974, OH 0262 (hereinafter Cochran, NTU interview), 11, UNTOHC. The comparison with RAF practice comes from Capt. Archer M. R. Allen's "Intelligence Report: British Far East Command—RAF, 4 August 1941," 6.

15. Cochran, NTU interview, 14–15, 18; Kuhn, NTU interview, 12; Strittmatter, NTU interview, 11–12, 18; Carl L. Hatcher, interview with Dr. Ronald Marcello, 18 May 1974, OH 0196 (hereinafter Hatcher, NTU interview), 25, UNTOHC.

16. Kuhn, NTU interview, 13; Cochran, NTU interview, 19–20; Hatcher, NTU interview, 15–16, 26.

17. Cochran, NTU interview, 17; Hatcher, NTU interview, 28–29; de Coligny, NTU interview, 18; George M. Hemingway, interview with Dr. Ronald Marcello, 18 May 1974, OH 0206 (hereinafter Hemingway, NTU interview), 15, UNTOHC; Strittmatter, NTU interview, 10.

18. John N. Delia, interview with Dr. Ronald Marcello, 6 May 1984, OH 646 (hereinafter Delia, NTU interview), 16–17, UNTOHC; telephone conversation, JMW and John N. Delia, 13 April 2013. Mike and Julia Stapleton married on 25 March 1942.

19. Lawrence J. Keith, interview with Dr. Ronald Marcello, 13 November 1987, OH 0729 (hereinafter Keith, NTU interview), 8–9, 12, UNTOHC.

20. Cochran, NTU interview, 13; James, NTU interview, 24.

21. Robert J. Peth, questionnaire, n.d. (hereinafter Peth, Lord questionnaire), 1, Lord Collection, HAD, NHHC; Kuzma, NTU interview, 3.

22. Coe, Prange interview, 2–3.

23. Bellinger testimony, Navy Court of Inquiry, *PHA*, part 32, 518; Bellinger testimony, Roberts Commission, *PHA*, part 22, 587; Bellinger testimony, Hart Inquiry, *PHA*, part 26, 130; Bellinger testimony, Joint Committee, *PHA*, part 8, 3489, 3498.

24. Shoemaker testimony, Roberts Commission, *PHA*, part 23, 733–34.

25. De Coligny, NTU interview, 25–27.

26. Kuzma, NTU interview, 38–39.

27. Young, NTU interview, 27–29; James E. McColgan, questionnaire, n.d. (hereinafter McColgan, Lord questionnaire), 1, Lord Collection, HAD, NHHC.

28. Paul J. Sherrard, interview with Dr. Ronald Marcello, 17 September 1988, OH 0756 (hereinafter Sherrard, NTU interview), 30, UNTOHC; e-mail correspondence, Debbie Sherrard (granddaughter) and JMW, 7 March 2016.

29. Caudel, NTU interview, 14–15.

30. Kuhn, NTU interview, 20–23.

31. Bellinger testimony, Hart Inquiry, *PHA*, part 26, 127–28; Bellinger testimony, Joint Committee, *PHA*, part 8, 3488; Bellinger, "The Gooney Birds," 317; Mary Ann Ramsey, "Only Yesteryear," *Naval History* 5, no. 4 (1991), reprinted in *Pearl Harbor–Gram* 116 (November 1993): 1–2, 18–19.

Chapter 4. "From Peace to Hell in a Matter of Seconds"

1. Strittmatter, NTU interview, 20–21.

2. Meister, NTU interview, 37.

3. ComPatron 24 to CinCPac, "Report of Offensive Measures Taken during December 7 Raid—Losses and Damage to Enemy—Distinguished Conduct of Personnel," 15 December 1941 (hereinafter VP-24 action report), 1, RG 38, NARA II; Meister, NTU interview, 38.

4. *Gudgeon* deck log, 4–7 December 1941, RG 38, NARA II; also Vice Adm. Elton W. Grenfell, U.S. Navy (Ret.), biography dated 20 October 1964; *Seagull* deck log, 4–5 December 1941, RG 38, NARA II; Lt. Cdr. Daniel Beville Candler, biography sheet, 26 December 1941; *The Lucky Bag*, U.S. Naval Academy class of 1922.

5. Thomas E. Farrow, interview, 16 August 1964, 1, Prange Papers in the Goldstein Collection, Archives Service Center, University of Pittsburgh, UA-90/F-78, box 23, FF-45 (hereinafter Farrow, Prange interview); architectural floor plans of the Operations Building, authors' collection.

6. Cochran, NTU interview, 21–22, 24–25.

7. Lester E. Robinson, interview with Dr. Ronald E. Marcello, 23 April 1988, OH 0743 (hereinafter Robinson, NTU interview), 10–11, UNTOHC.

8. Albert H. Molter, letter, 11 March 1956 (hereinafter Molter, Lord letter), 2, Lord Collection, HAD, NHHC.

9. Hubert D. Gano and Margaret Ellen Gano, "Interview with Eyewitnesses Johnie and Dale Gano," December 1996, http://teacher.scholastic .com/pearl/transcript.htm, accessed 15 November 2013; Hubert D. Gano and Margaret Ellen Gano, "Their Story," circa 1994, courtesy of son Richard D. Gano.

10. Lt. Jay H. Mattson to CO, NAS Pearl Harbor, "Air Raid attack by Japanese," 14 December 1941, Quarters K Binder, World War II Valor in the Pacific (hereinafter Mattson report, Quarters K Binder), 1; Lt. Joseph B. Musser to CO, NAS Pearl Harbor, "Report on air raid attack by Japanese," 15 December 1941, Quarters K Binder, World War II Valor in the Pacific (hereinafter Musser report, Quarters K Binder), 1.

11. Ens. "D" Arnold Singleton to CO, NAS Pearl Harbor, "Japanese air attack Sunday, Dec. 7, 1941—report on," 14 December 1941, Quarters K Binder, World War II Valor in the Pacific (hereinafter Singleton report, Quarters K Binder), 1; "D" Arnold Singleton, duty recommendation form, 25 September 1945, OMPF, RG 24, NPRC, St. Louis.

12. Lt. Leroy F. Watson to CO, NAS Pearl Harbor, "Personal Observation," n.d., Quarters K Binder, World War II Valor in the Pacific (hereinafter Watson report, Quarters K Binder), 1.

13. Shoemaker, Prange interview no. 1, 5, 11.

14. ComPatWing Two to CinCPac, "War Diary of Commander Patrol Wing TWO for December, 1941," 21 January 1942 (hereinafter PatWing 2 war diary), 1, HAD, NHHC; CO, Task Force 9 to CinCPac, "Operations on December 7, 1941," 20 December 1941 (hereinafter TF 9 Operations), 1–2, HAD, NHHC.

15. PatWing 2 war diary, 1–2; ComSubron 6 to distribution, Mailgram 300145, Serial 11-982, 1 December 1941, CinCPac dispatches, PHLO; VP-24 action report, 1, RG 38, NARA II.

16. CinCPac to ComPatWing 2, Dispatch 280450, Serial 11-861, 28 November 1941, CinCPac dispatches, PHLO; NAS Midway to ComTF 9, Dispatch 020330, Serial 12-30, 2 December 1941, CinCPac dispatches, PHLO; CinCPac to ComTF 3, Com 14, ComPatWing 2, Dispatch 040237, Serial 12-110, 4 December 1941, CinCPac dispatches, PHLO; PatWing 2 war diary, 1, ComTF 9 to NAS Midway, Dispatch 050323, Serial 12-206, 5 December 1941, CinCPac dispatches, PHLO; "Status of Navy and Marine Corps Aircraft in Hawaiian area, Dec. 7, 1941," Exhibits of the Joint Committee, Exhibit 6, Item 12, PHA, part 12, 352; Bellinger testimony, Navy Court of Inquiry, PHA, part 32, 516; Bellinger testimony, Hart Inquiry, PHA, part 26, 131; chart provided by Rear Adm. Patrick N. L. Bellinger showing aerial searches undertaken on 7 December 1941 from Oʻahu and Midway Island, Roberts Commission Exhibits, Exhibit 43 (hereinafter Bellinger chart of aerial searches), Records of the Pearl Harbor Liaison Office, Entry 167J, box 66, RG 80, NARA II.

17. Genda Minoru, Prange interview 25, 28 December 1947 (hereinafter, Genda, Prange interview 25), 1, Prange Collection, University of Maryland, box 19; Opana plot chart, Treasure Vault, NARA II.

18. Reconstruction of coded message based on fragmentary codebooks recovered from Japanese aircraft wreckage (hereinafter Japanese codebooks, NARA II). See Pearl Harbor Liaison Office, Entry 167F, RG 80, NARA II. Dr. Timothy P. Mulligan provided copies to the authors.

19. Genda, Prange interview 25, 3; Mifuku Iwakichi, Prange statement, 6 March 1951, 2, Prange Collection, University of Maryland, box 19; Fuchida Mitsuo, Prange conference 3, 11 December 1963, 2, Prange Collection, University of Maryland, box 19 (hereinafter Fuchida, Prange conference 3); Fuchida Mitsuo, Prange interview 14, 29 February 1948, 10, Prange Papers in the Goldstein Collection, Archives Service Center, University of Pittsburgh, UA-90/F-78, box 21 (hereinafter Fuchida, Prange interview 14); Fuchida Mitsuo,

Prange interview 19, 6 January 1949, 1, Prange Collection, University of Maryland, box 19. Two accounts exist of the transmission of the code word "トツレ" (*to-tsu-re*). See Yoshino Haruo, "*Kaga Dengekitai, Senkan Okurahoma Ni Shiro-o Tore,*" comp. Fujita Iyozō, *Shōgen Shinjuwan Kōgeki* (Tōkyō: Kōjin-sha, 1991), 42; Matsuda Norio, "*To Renso,*" *Rekishi-to Jinbutsu* (Tōkyō: Chūō Kōron-sha, 20 January 1983), 246.

20. Fuchida, Prange conference 3, 2; Fuchida, Prange interview 14, 9; Genda, Prange interview 25, 28; *Shōkaku* detailed action report (hereinafter *Shōkaku* DAR, Atene Shobo), Yamagata Tsunao, comp., *Kaigun: Kūbo-Kan Sentō Kiroku* (Atene Shobō, 2002), 200.

21. *Shōkaku* DAR, Atene Shobō, 198; authors' analysis.

22. Actually, Takahashi did not exercise direct command over a *chūtai*. His "Special Command *Shōtai*" fronted the 3rd Chūtai composed of six aircraft under Lt. Hira Kuniyoshi.

23. *Shōkaku* DAR, Atene Shobō, 200.

24. Genda, Prange interview 25, 3; chart of first wave deployment and tactical analysis by John Di Virgilio.

25. Di Virgilio, chart of first wave deployment and tactical analysis; *Hikōkitai Sentō Kōdōchōsho* (hereinafter *Kōdōchōsho*), War History Office, Japan Defense Agency, *Shōkaku, Zuikaku,* 8 December 1941; Detailed Action Report 1, Car-Div 5 (trans.), 15, Prange Collection, University of Maryland, box 21 (hereinafter CarDiv 5 DAR); Fuchida deployment map. The final authority on the direction of attacks is the *Shōkaku*'s DAR, Atene Shobō, 200. Also see Fuchida, Prange interview 14, 10.

26. Shiga Yoshio, "*Seikutai kara Mita Shinjuwan Kōgeki,*" comp. Fujita Iyozō, *Shōgen Shinjuwan Kōgeki* (Tōkyō: Kōjin-sha, 1991) (hereinafter Shiga, *Shōgen Shinjuwan Kōgeki*), 111–12; *Kōdōchōsho, Akagi,* 8 December 1941.

Chapter 5. "Air Raid Pearl Harbor X This Is No Drill"

1. It is uncertain whether the message from 14-P-1 was coded or uncoded. Ramsey's recollection was that Ballinger informed him that it was *not* coded. However, the timeline Bellinger provided to the Joint Committee (*PHA*, part 8, 3467–68) reported that the 0715 message was coded, a contention supported by Ensign Tanner's action report. See Ens. William P. Tanner to CO, VP-14, "Narrative of Engagement with enemy submarine on December 7, 1941," 28 January 1942, authors' files.

2. ComPatWing 2 to CinCPac, "War Diary of Commander Patrol Wing TWO for December, 1941," 21 January 1942 (hereinafter PatWing 2 war diary), RG 38, NARA II; telephone directory, U.S. Naval Air Station Pearl Harbor, T.H., September 1941 (hereinafter telephone directory, NASPH), 9, HAD, NHHC; Ramsey testimony, Navy Court of Inquiry, *PHA*, part 32, 444; Ramsey, Prange interview, 1; Logan C. Ramsey, untitled account of the Japanese attack, 7 December 1941 (hereinafter Ramsey account), 1, Ramsey Papers, uncataloged, HAD, NHHC; M. Ramsey, "Only Yesteryear," 1; radio logs, 14-P-1 and NAS Kaneohe Bay, 7 December 1941, Ramsey Papers (uncataloged), HAD, NHHC; VP-24 action report, 1.

3. CO, Task Force 9 to CinCPac, "Operations on December 7, 1941," 20 December 1941 (hereinafter Task Force 9 operations), 2, RG 38, NARA II; Ramsey testimony, Navy Court of Inquiry, *PHA*, part 32, 444; testimony of Vincent R. Murphy before the Hart Inquiry, 23 March 1944, *PHA*, part 26, 209; Ramsey, Prange interview, 1; Ramsey account, 1. What Ramsey referred to as the "Operations Center" was likely the suite of offices and compartments on the north end of the Administration Building's second floor.

4. Ramsey testimony, Navy Court of Inquiry, *PHA*, part 32, 444; Ramsey, Prange interview, 1; Ramsey account, 1; Task Force 9 operations, 2. Although Ramsey estimated his arrival at 0755, other evidence suggests that he arrived at about 0745.

5. Ramsey, Prange interview, 1; Ramsey account, 1; Ramsey testimony, Navy Court of Inquiry, *PHA*, part 32, 452.

6. Ramsey, Prange interview, 2. We have reconstructed Ramsey's movements by using the architectural plans of the Administration Building.

7. Lt. Frank Erickson, USCG, undated speech in support of the Fourth War Bond Drive (hereinafter Erickson speech), 1, authors' collection.

8. Ryan, NTU interview, 13–14; Victor A. Kamont, letter, 4 November 1964 (hereinafter Kamont, Prange letter), 1, Prange Papers in the Goldstein Collection, Archives Service Center, University of Pittsburgh, UA-90/F-78, box 23, FF-63.

9. Āliamanu Crater was the location of the Hawaiian Department Command Post.

10. Tactical analysis by Di Virgilio and Wenger; interview 16, Fuchida Mitsuo, 4 March 1948, 2, Prange Collection, University of Maryland, box 19.

11. Tactical analysis by Di Virgilio and Wenger.

12. Prior to the Hawaiian Operation, tactics called for the "ready" and "drop" signals to be given at 800 and 600 meters respectively. The need for greater accuracy caused a shift in the signals to 600 and 400 meters, the additional danger notwithstanding.

13. Shōkaku DAR, Atene Shobō, 199; tactical analysis by Di Virgilio and Wenger. Takahashi's bombs employed a Type 97 Otsu ground fuse that provided for a relatively long 0.1-second delay. Although intended to allow deeper penetration, the fusing might have caused a very large proportion of duds and partial detonations, possibly as much as 40–50 percent.

14. No other deck log or action report mentions Takahashi's deployment and movements until he passed over 'Aiea.

15. CO, Allen to Commander, Inshore Patrol, Fourteenth Naval District, "Air Raid by Japanese—Report On," 14 December 1941, RG 38, NARA II; "War Diary of U.S. Naval Air Station, Pearl Harbor, T.H.," 25 January 1942, Quarters K Binder, World War II Valor in the Pacific (hereinafter NASPH war diary, Quarters K Binder), 1; CO, Zane to CinCPac, "Air Raid on Pearl Harbor, Report Of," 10 December 1941, RG 38, NARA II; CO, Pennsylvania to CinCPac, "U.S.S. Pennsylvania's Report of Action during Enemy Air Attack morning of Sunday 7 December 1941," 16 December 1941, RG 38, NARA II; St. Louis deck log, 7 December 1941, RG 24, NARA II.

16. Charles A. Flood, letter to Walter Lord, 8 March 1956, Walter Lord Papers, HAD, NHHC; CO, Helena to CinCPac, "Brief Report of the Japanese Attack of December 7, 1941," 14 December 1941, RG 38, NARA II; decoration citation, Ens. William J. Jones, 3 April 1946, HAD, NHHC, authors'

collection; Henry D. Davison, "Statement of Ensign H. D. Davison, U.S. Navy, U.S.S. Arizona," Enclosure F to CO, Arizona to CinCPac, "Action Report U.S.S. Arizona (BB 39), December 7, 1941," 13 December 1941, RG 38, NARA II.

17. Ramsey account, 1; Ramsey, Prange interview, 2; Ramsey testimony, Navy Court of Inquiry, PHA, part 32, 444, 458.

18. Bellinger testimony, Roberts Commission, PHA, part 22, 565; Bellinger, "The Gooney Birds," 318.

19. Ramsey account, 2.

20. St. Louis deck log, 7 December 1941.

21. Kōdōchōsho, Shōkaku, 8 December 1941; Shōkaku DAR, Atene Shobō, 200; dive-bombing strike chart on page 16 in the original copy of Shōkaku's detailed action report in the War History Library at the Japanese Defense Agency (hereinafter Shōkaku dive-bombing strike chart); ComPatron 22 to CinCPac, "Summary of Action and Damage during Air Raid on December 7, 1941," 13 December 1941 (hereinafter VP-22 action report), 1–2, RG 38, NARA II; Cdr. Louis Iverson to CO, NASPH, "Addenda to Memorandum Report to Commanding Officer Dated December 15, 1941," 20 December 1941, Quarters K Binder, World War II Valor in the Pacific (hereinafter Iverson report, Quarters K Binder), 1; Wilkerson, NTU interview, 50; CO, NAS Pearl Harbor to SecNav, "Damage resulting from Air Raid Attack by Japanese on 7 December 1941," n.d. (hereinafter Shoemaker damage report), 1, authors' collection.

22. Shōkaku DAR, Atene Shobō, 200; John Di Virgilio, recollection of undated interview with Abe Zenji, 24 January 2016.

23. Shōkaku dive-bombing strike chart; Kōdōchōsho, Shōkaku, 8 December 1941; Shoemaker damage report, 1, and appended chart.

24. Shōkaku dive-bombing strike chart; Kōdōchōsho, Shōkaku, 8 December 1941; Shoemaker damage report, 1, and appended chart; Cdr. Karl Schmidt to CO, NASPH, "Air Raid Attack by Japanese—Report on," n.d., Quarters K Binder, World War II Valor in the Pacific (hereinafter Schmidt report, Quarters K Binder), 3; anonymous questionnaire, n.d. (hereinafter anonymous Lord questionnaire), 1, Lord Collection, HAD, NHHC; Lt. Edward D. Killian to CO, NAS Pearl

Harbor, "Air Raid Attack by Japanese, Report on," n.d., Quarters K Binder, World War II Valor in the Pacific (hereinafter Killian report, Quarters K Binder), 3. Captain Shoemaker suggested in his report that "the after body of a bomb" was responsible for the hole in the roof of Hangar 38.

25. James S. Layman, questionnaire, n.d. (hereinafter Layman, Lord questionnaire), 1, Lord Collection, HAD, NHHC; *Shōkaku* dive-bombing strike chart; Kōdōchōsho, *Shōkaku*, 8 December 1941; Shoemaker damage report, 1, and appended chart; Cdr. Karl Schmidt, Quarters K Binder, 3; VP-24 action report, 1; James, NTU interview, 38–41; Young, NTU interview, 36.

26. Shiga, *Shōgen Shinjuwan Kōgeki*, 112.

27. Strafing attack chart on page 17 in the original copy of the *Shokaku's* detailed action report in the War History Library at the Japanese Defense Agency. Although no reports are known to exist for VJ-1 or VJ-2, no aircraft from VJ-2 participated in the 7 December searches. It thus seems certain that Takahashi's other seven bombers shot up VJ-2 rather thoroughly. See Item 51, Exhibits of the Roberts Commission, *PHA*, part 25.

28. *Shōkaku* DAR, Atene Shobō, 200, 202, 204; Detailed Action Report No. 1, CarDiv 5 (trans.) (hereinafter CarDiv 5 DAR), 15, Prange Collection, University of Maryland, box 21; Yokosuka Naval Air Corps, "Lessons (air operation) of the Sea Battle Off Hawaii, Vol. 1" (trans.) (hereinafter Yokosuka NAC, "Lessons of the Sea Battle Off Hawaii"), 40, Prange files, authors' collection; Kōdōchōsho, *Shōkaku*, 8 December 1941.

29. Tactical analysis by John Di Virgilio; CarDiv 5 DAR, 17–18; Yokosuka NAC, "Lessons of the Sea Battle Off Hawaii," 21. Per Di Virgilio, only seven of Takahashi's bombs detonated.

30. Ibusuki Masanobu, account provided to Walter Lord via the Tōkyō Bureau of *Life* magazine, 30 October 1956, 4, Lord Collection, HAD, NHHC.

31. Exhibits of the Roberts Commission, Exhibit 39 (Navy Packet 2), CinCPac, "Disposition of Task Forces," 20 December 1941 (hereinafter "Disposition of Task Forces"), *PHA*, part 24, 1606.

32. Exhibits of the Roberts Commission, Exhibit 44, untitled chart of aerial searches undertaken on 7 December 1941 (hereinafter chart of aerial

searches), which includes Commander Ramsey's original search plan, RG 80, NARA II; "Disposition of Task Forces," 1607; Task Force 9 operations, 2.

33. Ramsey account, 4; radio log, NAS Kaneohe Bay, 7 December 1941, Ramsey Papers (uncataloged), HAD, NHHC; VP-24 action report, 3; Bellinger testimony, Joint Committee, *PHA*, part 8, 3467.

34. Ryan, NTU interview, 13–14; Kamont, Prange letter, 1; anonymous Lord questionnaire, 1.

35. Ryan, NTU interview, 14; Lloyd B. Osborne, Pearl Harbor Commemorative Medal application/information, 20 July 1991, OMPF, RG 24, NPRC, St. Louis; Chief Paymaster Clifford R. Pischner to CO, NASPH, "Air Raid Attack by Japanese—Observations thereto," n.d., Quarters K Binder, World War II Valor in the Pacific (hereinafter Pischner report, Quarters K Binder), 2; Lt. William R. Kane to CO, NAS Pearl Harbor, "Air Raid on Pearl Harbor by Japanese Aircraft, Sunday 7 December, 1941, Report On," 17 December 1941, Quarters K Binder, World War II Valor in the Pacific (hereinafter Kane report, Quarters K Binder), 1; Killian report, Quarters K Binder, 1–2; Lt. Frank A. Erickson to CO, NAS Pearl Harbor, "Air Raid Attack by Japanese, December 7, 1941," 17 December 1941, Quarters K Binder, World War II Valor in the Pacific Binder (hereinafter Erickson report, Quarters K Binder), 1; Kamont, Prange letter, 2; anonymous Lord questionnaire, 1.

36. Shoemaker, Prange interview no. 1, 11–12; Shoemaker, Prange interview no. 2, 7–8; Erickson report, Quarters K Binder, 1; Capt. James M. Shoemaker, USN, "Memorandum for File . . . Japanese Air Raid on 7 December [1941]" [22 December 1941], SA-SL Miscellaneous, box 3, Adm. Claude C. Bloch Papers, Library of Congress Manuscript Division, Washington, D. C. (hereinafter Shoemaker account), 1.

37. Erickson speech, 1; Adolph Zuber, "Report of Action of Marine Barracks during Japanese Air Raid of December 7, 1941," 16 December 1941, Quarters K Binder, World War II Valor in the Pacific (hereinafter Zuber report, Quarters K Binder), 1; decoration citations for Frank Dudovick, James D. Young, and Pvt. Paul O. Zeller, HAD, NHHC.

38. Don Klotz, *On Hell's Perimeters: Pacific Tales of PBY Patrol Squadron 23 in World War II* (Austin, Tex.: Sunbelt Eakin, 2002), 17.

39. Kenneth K. Anderson, interview with Dr. Ronald Marcello, 16 September 1988, OH 0755 (hereinafter Anderson, NTU interview), 17–18, UNTOHC.

40. Harry R. Mead, letter, 27 March 1956 (hereinafter Mead, Lord letter), 2–3, Lord Collection, HAD, NHHC.

41. Farrow, Prange interview, 1–2. The building's floor plans of the period have no compartment labeled "Central Control."

42. Lt. Joseph B. Musser to CO, NAS Pearl Harbor, "Report on air raid attack by Japanese," 15 December 1941, Quarters K Binder, World War II Valor in the Pacific (hereinafter Musser report, Quarters K Binder), 1.

43. Lt. Elmer W. Schuessler to CO, NAS Pearl Harbor, "Air Raid Attack by Japanese," 15 December 1941, Quarters K Binder, World War II Valor in the Pacific (hereinafter Schuessler report, Quarters K Binder), 1.

44. Ibid.

45. Sherrard, NTU interview, 31, 44.

46. Lt. Richard B. Black to CO, NAS Pearl Harbor, "Air Raid Attack by Japanese," 16 December 1941, Quarters K Binder, World War II Valor in the Pacific (hereinafter Black report, Quarters K Binder), 1.

47. "Witnesses Share Memories" (hereinafter Edwards account), *Miami County Republic* (Paola, Kans.), 4 December 1991, 1A; "Pearl Harbor Attack Remembered," *Hawaii Navy News* 2, no. 49, 7 December 1977, 1.

48. Lt. Frederick Volbeda (ChC) to CO, NAS Pearl Harbor, "Air Raid Attack by Japanese," n.d., Quarters K Binder, World War II Valor in the Pacific (hereinafter Volbeda report, Quarters K Binder), 1; Edwards account, 1A; "Pearl Harbor Attack Remembered," 1.

49. Gordon E. Bolser, letter to Wyatt Blassingame, 17 February 1965 (hereinafter Bolser letter), 1, courtesy of Gordon M. Bolser; telephone conversation, JMW and Shannon Bolser Gault, 27 July 2012.

50. Black report, Quarters K Binder, 1.

51. Molter, Lord letter, 2–3.

52. Ibid.

53. George W. Edmondson, account, n.d. (hereinafter Edmondson, Lord account), 1, Lord Collection, HAD, NHHC; Jacob S. Rogovsky [aka Jack Rogo], account, 28 April 1956 (hereinafter Rogo, Lord account), 1, Lord Collection, HAD, NHHC.

54. Kuhn, NTU interview, 27–29.

55. Young, NTU interview, 31–33.

56. Ibid., 33–34. Lemmon was a veteran of World War I. He received high praise from Lt. Cdr. James W. Baldwin—commanding officer of the *Camanga* (AG 42) in June 1942—as "dignified, well read, highly intelligent, and extremely loyal."

57. Russell C. Morse, questionnaire, 18 June 1956 (hereinafter Morse, Lord questionnaire), 1-1C, Lord Collection, HAD, NHHC.

58. Bellinger, "The Gooney Birds," 318–19; Glen Williford and Terrance McGovern, *Defenses of Pearl Harbor and Oahu 1907–50* (Oxford, U.K.: Osprey, 2003), 17, 29, 60.

59. Coe, Prange interview, 6–7.

60. Ibid., 7–8.

61. Zuber report, Quarters K Binder; telephone directory, NASPH.

62. Klotz, *On Hell's Perimeters*, 17; James R. Ogden, "Airborne at Pearl," Naval Institute *Proceedings* 110, no. 1090 (December 1993): 61.

63. Daniel P. Closser, "Report of Air Raid by 1st Lieutenant Daniel P. Closser, USMC," n.d., Quarters K Binder, World War II Valor in the Pacific (hereinafter Closser report, Quarters K Binder), 1; Cdr. Daniel P. Closser Jr., USN (Ret.) (son of Daniel P. Closser Sr.), telephone conversation with JMW, 7 February 2012 (hereinafter Closser conversation, 7 February 2012).

64. Lt. (jg) Jaroud B. Smith Jr. to CO, NAS Pearl Harbor, "Air Raid Attack by Japanese—Report Of," 16 December 1941, Quarters K Binder, World War II Valor in the Pacific (hereinafter Smith report, Quarters K Binder), 1.

65. Lt. Magruder H. Tuttle to CO, NAS Pearl Harbor, "Observations Noted during Air Raid on 7 December, 1941," n.d., Quarters K Binder, World War II Valor in the Pacific (hereinafter Tuttle report, Quarters K Binder), 1.

66. Ibid.

67. Wesley H. Ruth, interview with JMW, 12 August 2005 (hereinafter Ruth interview), 4, Wenger

Collection. Ruth's yellow Pontiac convertible was a source of envy among the junior officers, most of whom could not afford a late-model car. The downside to the flashy vehicle was its dyed red leather seats, which ruined Ruth's whites when he first used the car.

68. Ogden account, 60–61.

69. McColgan, Lord questionnaire, 1.

70. Ens. William G. Boynton to Captain Shoemaker's yeoman, "Japanese Air Raid on Naval Air Station—December 7, 1941," n.d., Quarters K Binder, World War II Valor in the Pacific (hereinafter Boynton report, Quarters K Binder), 1.

71. Mattson report, Quarters K Binder, 1.

72. Delia, NTU interview, 22, 24–25.

73. Edwards account, 1A, 3A; "Pearl Harbor Attack Remembered," 1; Black report, Quarters K Binder, 1.

74. Edwards account, 3A; "Pearl Harbor Attack Remembered," 1; Black report, Quarters K Binder, 1; Volbeda report, Quarters K Binder, 2.

75. Lt. Cdr. James W. Baldwin to CO, NAS Pearl Harbor, "Air Raid Attack by Japanese—Request for Report On," 16 December 1941, Quarters K Binder, World War II Valor in the Pacific (hereinafter Baldwin report, Quarters K Binder), 1; Robert J. Cressman, telephone conversation with JMW, 2 February 2016.

76. Baldwin report, Quarters K Binder, 1.

77. Ibid., 2.

78. Rodney T. West, MD, *Honolulu Prepares for Japan's Attack: The Oahu Civilian Disaster Preparedness Programs, May 15, 1940 to December 8, 1941* (privately printed, 1993), 66.

79. Ibid., 66–67; Virginia M. Cowart, *Gas Masks and Palm Trees: My Wartime Hawaii* (Victoria, B.C.: Trafford Publishing, 2006), 12.

80. West, *Honolulu Prepares*, 67.

81. Anonymous, Lord questionnaire, 2–3; Hemingway, NTU interview, 25.

Chapter 6. "We Are Now in a State of War"

1. Cochran, NTU interview, 27–28.

2. Young, NTU interview, 35–36; Hemingway, NTU interview, 19–20.

3. Zuber report, Quarters K Binder, 1; Keith, NTU interview, 17–18.

4. Hemingway, NTU interview, 21–22.

5. VP-24 action report, 2.

6. Iverson report, handwritten memo, Quarters K Binder; certificate of death for Theodore Wheeler Croft, 7 December 1941, OMPF, RG 24, NARA, St. Louis (hereinafter Croft death certificate).

7. Anderson, NTU interview, 19; Hatcher, NTU interview, 35; Layman, Lord interview, 3; Hemingway, NTU interview, 23; Klotz, *On Hell's Perimeters*, 15–16.

8. Strittmatter, NTU interview, 23–27; analysis of aircraft history cards by Mr. Jim Sawruk; VP-24 action report, 1–2; Paul E. Bos, questionnaire, 23 March 1956, Lord Collection, (hereinafter Bos, Lord questionnaire), 2, HAD, NHHC; commendations for Albert P. Ferguson, James M. Gibson, Joseph A. Howard, Leif I. Larson, Roy R. Bratton, Frank S. Evans, and Burt L. Swisher, all in HAD, NHHC, authors' collection.

9. Mead, Lord letter, 3; Erickson report, Quarters K Binder, 1.

10. Hamway report, Quarters K Binder, 1; Erickson report, Quarters K Binder, 1.

11. Cochran, NTU interview, 29–33; Oborne, Lord letter, 1; Wenger analysis.

12. Cochran, NTU interview, 34, 39.

13. ComPatWing 2 to Chief of BuNav, "Giemont, Andrew John, 213-22-941, CRM (PA), U.S.N.—Advancement to Chief Warrant Rank for Meritorious Conduct—Recommendation For," [?] January 1942, photostatic copy in the authors' collection (hereinafter Giemont recommendation), 1.

14. Ens. William A. Keutgen to CO, NAS Pearl Harbor, "Air Raid Attack by Japanese, Report On," n.d., Quarters K Binder, World War II Valor in the Pacific (hereinafter Keutgen report, Quarters K Binder), 1.

15. Raymond D. Strong, interview with Dr. Ronald Marcello, 16 December 1995, OH 1124 (hereinafter Strong, NTU interview), 18–19, UNTOHC; James C. Lagerman, questionnaire, n.d., Lord Collection (hereinafter Lagerman, Lord questionnaire), 1–2, HAD, NHHC.

16. Meister, NTU interview, 38–39; VP-24 action report, 3; "Messages and Orders from Headquarters of the Commander in Chief Pacific Fleet, December 7, 1941," Exhibits of the Roberts Commission, Exhibit 8 (Navy Packet 2), *PHA,*

part 24, 1370; *Gudgeon* deck log, 7 December 1941, RG 38, NARA II.

17. Meister, NTU interview, 39–40.

18. John W. Burton, questionnaire, 1 March 1956, Lord Collection (hereinafter Burton, Lord questionnaire), 1, HAD, NHHC.

19. George A. Carroll, "Eyes of the Fleet" (unpublished manuscript), excerpts from chapter 9, "Day of Infamy—7 December 1941," 2–3, courtesy of Mr. Don Montgomery.

20. Mattson report, Quarters K Binder, 1; Ens. Rolland A. Helsel to CO, NAS Pearl Harbor, "Report on Air Raid by Japanese on December 7, 1941," n.d., Quarters K Binder, World War II Valor in the Pacific (hereinafter Helsel report, Quarters K Binder), 1; Musser report, Quarters K Binder, 1–2. Foamite was an improbable mixture of licorice and bicarbonate of soda.

21. Musser report, Quarters K Binder, 2; Mead, Lord letter, 4.

22. Lt. Walter F. Arnold to CO, NAS Pearl Harbor, "Memorandum to the Commanding Officer," 16 December 1941, Quarters K Bender, World War II Valor in the Pacific (hereinafter Arnold report, Quarters K Binder), 1; Smith report, Quarters K Binder, 1.

23. Peth, Lord questionnaire, 1.

24. De Coligny, NTU interview, 30–31, 28; Baldwin report, Quarters K Binder, 2.

25. Shoemaker, Prange interview no. 2, 7–8; Shoemaker, Prange interview no. 1, 11–12; McColgan, Lord questionnaire, 2–3.

26. Shoemaker, Prange interview no. 1, 7, 12; Shoemaker account, 1.

27. Coe, Prange interview, 8.

28. Ibid., 8; Bellinger, "The Gooney Birds," 319.

29. Coe, Prange interview, 8–10.

30. Ibid., 10.

31. Ryan, NTU interview, 15.

32. Ruth interview, 3–4.

33. Kane report, Quarters K Binder, 1; Chief Machinist Joseph A. Sanders to CO, NAS Pearl Harbor, "Air Raid Attack by Japanese on 7 Dec. 1941," 16 December 1941, Quarters K Binder, World War II Valor in the Pacific (hereinafter Sanders report, Quarters K Binder), 1; Public Works Officer (Yard) to Commandant [Pearl Harbor Navy Yard], "Report of Air Raid by Japanese on December 7, 1941," 15 December 1941 (hereinafter Public Works Officer report, PHNYd), 2, Enclosure B to Com 14 to CNO, "Report on the Battle of Pearl Harbor," 24 December 1941, RG 38, NARA II; Lt. Thomas L. Davey to CO, NAS Pearl Harbor, "Air Raid Attack by Japanese (7 Dec. 1941)—Report On," 17 December 1941, World War II Valor in the Pacific Binder (hereinafter Davey report, Quarters K Binder), 1; NASPH war diary, Quarters K Binder, 1; Shoemaker damage report, 2.

34. Bellinger, "The Gooney Birds," 320; Zuber report, Quarters K Binder, 1; Bellinger testimony, Joint Committee, *PHA*, Part 8, 3472; Bellinger testimony, Roberts Commission, *PHA*, part 22, 582–83.

35. Coe, Prange interview, 10, 13.

36. Delia, NTU interview, 31–32.

37. Ens. Guy R. Nance to CO, NAS Pearl Harbor, "Air raid attack by Japanese, report on," 15 December 1941, Quarters K Binder, World War II Valor in the Pacific (hereinafter Nance report, Quarters K Binder), 1; Schmidt report, Quarters K Binder, 3.

38. Cecil D. Riggs, interview, 14 January 1964 (hereinafter Riggs, Prange interview), Prange Manuscripts/Goldstein Collection, University of Pittsburgh, Archives Service Center, UA-90/F-78, box 23, FF-95, 2–3, 7.

39. George W. Dickinson to CO, NAS Pearl Harbor, "Memorandum to the Commanding Officer, Naval Air Station, Pearl Harbor, T.H.," 16 December 1941, Quarters K Binder, World War II Valor in the Pacific (hereinafter Dickinson report, Quarters K Binder), 1.

40. Riggs, Prange interview, 4.

41. Iverson report, Quarters K Binder, handwritten memo; Croft death certificate; Theodore Wheeler Croft, beneficiary slip, 1 October 1941, OMPF, RG 24, NARA, St. Louis; Donald A. Morton, telephone interview with JMW, n.d.

42. *Neosho* deck logs, 28–30 November 1941 and 6–7 December 1941, RG 38, NARA II.

43. Singleton report, Quarters K Binder, 1–2; CO, NAS Pearl Harbor to Chief of the Bureau of Navigation, "Recommendation for immediate promotion to rank of Lieutenant (junior grade) in the case of Ensign D. A. Singleton, A-V(S), U.S. Naval Reserve," 5 January 1942 (hereinafter Shoemaker, Singleton recommendation), OMPF,

RG 24, NPRC, St. Louis; Molter, Lord letter, 3–4; de Coligny, NTU interview, 28; Malmin, Lord questionnaire, 3; Cdr. Charles J. Harter to CO, NAS Pearl Harbor, "Air Raid Attack by Japanese—Report On," 14 December 1941, Quarters K Binder, World War II Valor in the Pacific (hereinafter Harter report, Quarters K Binder), 1.

44. Harter report, Quarters K Binder, 1. The nature of the sprinkler system for the aboveground tanks is unclear because the authors found no such details in the records of the Bureau of Yards and Docks.

45. Lieutenant (jg) Osborne's background included service with Pan American Airways, for whom he made fourteen flights in the *China Clipper* as copilot and navigator.

46. Singleton report, Quarters K Binder, 2; Shoemaker, Singleton recommendation; decoration citation, Navy Cross, "D" Arnold Singleton, 18 March 1942, HAD, NHHC, authors' collection; Albert L. Hansen, Notice of Separation from the U.S. Naval Service, 25 July 1946, RG 24, NARA, St. Louis.

47. Keutgen report, Quarters K Binder, 1; Ens. Lester D. Satchell to CO, NAS Pearl Harbor, "Air Raid by Japanese—Report On," 17 December 1941, Quarters K Binder, World War II Valor in the Pacific (hereinafter Satchell report, Quarters K Binder), 1; Closser report, Quarters K Binder, 1.

48. Solomon S. Isquith, account, n.d., 4, Lord Collection, HAD, NHHC; Ens. James W. Cronenberg to CO, NAS Pearl Harbor, "Report on Air Raid Attack by Japanese," n.d., Quarters K Binder, World War II Valor in the Pacific (hereinafter Cronenberg report, Quarters K Binder), 1.

49. Boynton report, Quarters K Binder, 1; Ens. John McCormack to CO, NAS Pearl Harbor, "Air Raid Attack by Japanese—Report On," 14 December 1941, Quarters K Binder, World War II Valor in the Pacific (hereinafter McCormack report, Quarters K Binder), 1; Hamway report, Quarters K Binder, 1.

50. Ens. Guilbert S. Winchell to CO, NAS Pearl Harbor, "Japanese Air Raid on Ford Island—Report On," 17 December 1941, Quarters K Binder, World War II Valor in the Pacific (hereinafter Winchell report, Quarters K Binder), 2–3; Closser report, Quarters K Binder, 1; Closser telephone conversation, 7 February 2012; BuNav, *Navy Directory: Officers of the United States Navy and Marine Corps* (Washington, D.C.: Government Printing Office, 1941); McCormack report, Quarters K Binder, 1.

51. Bellinger testimony, Roberts Commission, *PHA*, part 22, 565, 581–82; Bellinger, "The Gooney Birds," 321; Bellinger testimony, Joint Committee, *PHA*, part 8, 3467; Bellinger chart of aerial searches; Coe, Prange interview, 10; Ramsey account, 4–5.

52. Schuessler report, Quarters K Binder, 1–2; Riggs report, Quarters K Binder, 1. Crawford served in the Army's Medical Department during World War I and enlisted in the U.S. Naval Reserve on 4 October 1940. See Verne G. Crawford, various documents, OMPF, RG 24, NARA, St. Louis.

53. Riggs report, Quarters K Binder, 1; NASPH war diary, Quarters K Binder, 1; Helsel report, Quarters K Binder, 1.

54. Ryan, NTU interview, 18, 20.

55. NASPH war diary, Quarters K Binder, 1; Farrow, Prange interview, 2.

56. Ens. Henry T. Bultman Jr. to CO, NAS Pearl Harbor, T.H., "Air Raid Attack by Japanese—report on," 15 December 1941, Quarters K Binder, World War II Valor in the Pacific (hereinafter Bultman report, Quarters K Binder), 1; Ens. Francis S. Woods to CO, NAS Pearl Harbor, "Air Raid by Japanese—Request for Report On," n.d., Quarters K Binder, World War II Valor in the Pacific (hereinafter Woods report, Quarters K Binder), 1.

57. Shoemaker account, 1.

58. Yokosuka Naval Air Corps, "Lessons of the Sea Battle Off Hawaii," 40; Young, NTU interview, 38–39; VP-22 action report, 1; Cochran, NTU interview, 33.

59. Young, NTU interview, 42.

Chapter 7. "Well, There's Nothing Left, so I Guess It's Going to Be Every Man for Himself"

1. Shoemaker, Prange interview no. 1, 13; Shoemaker account, 1.

2. Keutgen report, Quarters K Binder, 2; VP-24 action report, 2.

3. Cochran, NTU interview, 35, 49.

4. Coe, Prange interview, 11–12; Bellinger chart of aerial searches.

5. Bellinger, "The Gooney Birds," 325; Bellinger chart of aerial searches; Ramsey account, 5–6.

6. Bellinger, "The Gooney Birds," 321–22; Ramsey account, 5; Bellinger testimony, Joint Committee, *PHA*, part 8, 3467; Exhibits of the Roberts Commission, Exhibit 8, "Messages and Orders from Headquarters of the Commander in Chief Pacific Fleet, December 7, 1941," *PHA*, part 24, 1373.

7. Bellinger, "The Gooney Birds," 323a.

8. Robert J. Cressman and J. Michael Wenger, *Steady Nerves and Stout Hearts: The* Enterprise *(CV6) Air Group and Pearl Harbor, 7 December 1941* (Missoula, Mont.: Pictorial Histories, 1989), 10–11, 25, 27; reports of Lt. Cdr. Howard L. Young (hereinafter CEAG report), 1–2, and Ens. Perry L. Teaff (hereinafter Teaff report), 1, both from HAD, NHHC; Bromfield B. Nichol, Rotary Club talk, circa 7 December 1959, 6–7, authors' collection.

9. Bellinger, "The Gooney Birds," 323a.

10. Riggs, Prange interview, 11; Bellinger, "The Gooney Birds," 324; CEAG report, 2.

11. Shoemaker, Prange interview no. 1, 14; Shoemaker account, 1.

12. Teaff report, 1; Erickson report, Quarters K Binder, 2.

13. Klotz, *On Hell's Perimeters*, 17; Ogden, "Airborne at Pearl," 61.

14. Ogden, "Airborne at Pearl," 61; Bellinger chart of aerial searches.

15. Ogden, "Airborne at Pearl," 61.

16. Ibid.; Klotz, *On Hell's Perimeters*, 18–19.

17. Francis M. Hughes, BuNav biographical data sheet, 4 December 1937, OMPF, RG 24, NPRC, St. Louis; transcript of naval service, Rear Adm. Francis Massie Hughes, OMPF, RG 24, NPRC, St. Louis; Report of Compliance with Orders from 12 August 1940, OMPF, RG 24, NPRC, St. Louis.

18. James P. Ogden, officer biography sheet, 4 November 1953, NHHC, authors' collection.

19. Theodore S. Thueson, enlistment paper, 23 April 1934, OMPF, RG 24, NPRC, St. Louis; recommendation for flight training at Pensacola, Florida, 1 November 1937, OMPF, RG 24, NPRC, St. Louis; summary of service, OMPF, RG 24, NPRC, St. Louis.

20. Molter, Lord letter, 4; Allan G. MacKay, "Statement of A. G. MacKay, CRM (PA), U.S. Navy," n.d., OMPF, RG 24, NPRC, St. Louis.

21. Molter, Lord letter, 4–5.

22. Farrow, Prange interview, 3; Layman, Lord questionnaire, 2.

23. Lt. (jg) Lloyd B. Osborne to CO, NAS Pearl Harbor, "Air Raid Attack by Japanese—Report On," n.d., Quarters K Binder, World War II Valor in the Pacific (hereinafter Osborne report, Quarters K Binder), 1.

24. McColgan, Lord questionnaire, 2; *Monaghan* deck log, 7 December 1941, RG 24, NARA II.

25. Shoemaker account, 1–2.

26. Ibid., 2.

27. Shoemaker, Prange interview no. 1, 13–14.

Chapter 8. "Get Your Ass in the Plane and Pre-Flight It!"

1. Sherrard, NTU interview, 33–34.

2. Baldwin report, Quarters K Binder, 1–2.

3. Thomas S. Malmin, questionnaire, 9 March 1956, Lord Collection (hereinafter Malmin, Lord questionnaire), 2, HAD, NHHC.

4. Bellinger, "The Gooney Birds," 323; PatWing 2 war diary, 2.

5. Lt. (jg) Kenneth L. Longeway to CO, NAS Pearl Harbor, untitled report, 7 December 1941, Quarters K Binder, World War II Valor in the Pacific (hereinafter Longeway report, Quarters K Binder), 1; Lt. Jackson D. Arnold to CO, NASPH, "Air Raid Attack by Japanese, Report on," n.d., Quarters K Binder, World War II Valor in the Pacific (hereinafter Jackson Arnold report, Quarters K Binder), 1–2.

6. Bolser letter, 1; West, *Honolulu Prepares*, 67; Lt. Marshall Hjelte to XO, NAS Pearl Harbor, "Air Raid by Japanese—Report On," 16 December 1941, Quarters K Binder, World War II Valor in the Pacific (hereinafter Hjelte report, Quarters K Binder), 1.

7. Kuzma, NTU interview, 48, 50.

8. Ibid., 50–52. Kuzma received a medical discharge in 1944, citing the aftereffects of the concussion he suffered on 7 December 1941.

9. Bolser letter, 1; West, *Honolulu Prepares*, 67–68.

10. Edward P. Waszkiewicz, questionnaire, n.d., Lord Collection (hereinafter Waszkiewicz, Lord questionnaire), 2, HAD, NHHC.

11. Bolser letter, 1; telephone conversation notes, JMW with Shannon Bolser Gault, 27 July 2012; West, *Honolulu Prepares*, 67–68; Kuzma, NTU interview, 54–56.

12. Oborne, Lord letter; Hemingway, NTU interview, 25; Wilkerson, NTU interview, 35–36, 38–40, 48; Cochran, NTU interview, 37.

13. Wilkerson, NTU interview, 48–50, 55; Ens. Norton J. Arst to CO, NASPH, "Japanese air raid Sunday, Dec. 7, 1941," 14 December 1941, Quarters K Binder, World War II Valor in the Pacific (hereinafter Arst report, Quarters K Binder), 1; Rice report, Quarters K Binder, 1; Musser report, Quarters K Binder, 2.

14. Carroll, "Eyes of the Fleet," 3; Burton, Lord questionnaire, 2.

15. Leroy E. Bartels, decoration citation for commendation ribbon and "V," 7 December 1941, HAD, NHHC, authors' collection; various photographs, RG 80, Still Picture Branch, NARA II; Carroll, "Eyes of the Fleet," 2; correspondence with Mr. Don Montgomery.

16. Shoemaker testimony, Roberts Commission, *PHA*, part 23, 736; Lt. Samuel M. Randall to CO, NAS Pearl Harbor, "Memorandum for Commanding Officer [NASPH], 15 December 1941, Quarters K Binder, World War II Valor in the Pacific (hereinafter Randall report, Quarters K Binder), 1–2; Cdr. Harry F. Carlson to CO, NAS Pearl Harbor, "Air Raid Attack by Japanese—Report On," 18 December 1941, Quarters K Binder, World War II Valor in the Pacific (hereinafter Carlson report, Quarters K Binder), 1.

17. Carlson report, Quarters K Binder, 1; Anderson, NTU interview, 21; James, NTU interview, 49; Keith, NTU interview, 21.

18. Strittmatter, NTU interview, 27–28; Ens. James R. Garrett to CO, NASPH, "Air Raid Attack by Japanese—Report On," 17 December 1941, Quarters K Binder, World War II Valor in the Pacific (hereinafter Garrett report, Quarters K Binder), 2.

19. Lt. Leroy F. Watson [to CO, NASPH], "Personal Observation," n.d., Quarters K Binder, World War II Valor in the Pacific (hereinafter Watson report, Quarters K Binder), 1–2; Shoemaker damage report, 3; Task Force 9 report, 2–3; Kane report, Quarters K Binder, 1; ComPatWing 2 to Chief, BuNav, "Giemont, Andrew John, 213-22-94, CRM (PA), U.S.N.—Advancement to Chief Warrant Rank for Meritorious Conduct—Recommendation For," 10[?] January 1942 (hereinafter Giemont recommendation), 1, authors' collection.

20. Frank R. DeAugustine, citation for meritorious performance of duty, 25 May 1942, OMPF, RG 24, NPRC, St. Louis; Frederick W. Glaeser, questionnaire, 9 March 1956, Lord Collection (hereinafter Glaeser, Lord questionnaire), 3, HAD, NHHC.

21. Giemont recommendation, 2; Shoemaker damage report, 3; PatWing 2 war diary, 2; Andrew John Giemont, commendation, 7 April 1942, OMPF, RG 24, NPRC, St. Louis.

22. Watson report, Quarters K Binder, 1.

23. *Shōkaku* DAR, Atene Shobō, 217; chart of Lieutenant Irikiin's formation on page 39 in the original copy of the *Shōkaku* detailed action report in the War History Library at the Japanese Defense Agency in Tōkyō; map, 2nd Attack Wave Deployment, John Di Virgilio; *Kōdōchōsho*, *Shōkaku*, 8 December 1941; Boeicho Kenshujo Senshishitsu, *Senshi Sōsho* [War History], vol. 10, *Hawai Sakusen* (hereinafter *Hawai Sakusen*) (Tōkyō: Asagumo Shimbun-sha, 1967), 608.

24. *Shōkaku* DAR, 217.

25. XO, *Tangier*, to CO, *Tangier*, "Report of Engagement between the USS *Tangier* (AV8) and Japanese Airplanes on December 7, 1941," 11 December 1941, 2, RG 38, NARA II (hereinafter *Tangier* XO report); *Kōdōchōsho*, *Shōkaku*, 8 December 1941; *Shōkaku* DAR, 217.

26. The *Tangier* incident has produced considerable disagreement among the three coauthors. Perhaps the best explanation is that one or two dive-bombers targeted the *Tangier* just as a number of others crossed over simultaneously from the east after expending their ordnance elsewhere. If Irikiin missed badly and/or inadvertently dropped near the *Tangier*, the splashes—simultaneous with the appearance of the dive-bombers—would certainly have strengthened an impression of a large-scale dive-bombing attack. The issue with the dive-bombing scenario is that there are simply not enough attacking aircraft that are unaccounted for to explain the reported bomb splashes around

the *Tangier*, *Curtiss*, and even the *Medusa* (AR 1). This issue will likely never be resolved satisfactorily.

27. Mailgram, Serial 132130, *Tangier* to CinCPac, 13 December 1941, 3, CinCPac dispatches, Lundstrom; CO, *Tangier* to CinCPac, "Raid, Air, December 7, 1941, U.S.S. *Tangier* (AV8)—Report On," 2 January 1942, 3–4, RG 38, NARA II; CO, *Tangier* to Chief, Bureau of Ships, "War Damage Reports," 19 January 1942, 1–2, RG 38, NARA II; *Tangier* deck logs, 7 December 1941, RG 24, NARA II.

28. CarDiv 5 DAR, 15; *Shōkaku* DAR, 217, 220.

29. Wilkerson, NTU interview, 39; Tuttle report, Quarters K Binder, 1; Chief Gunner William M. Coles to CO, NASPH, "Air Raid Attack, Report on," 17 December 1941, Quarters K Binder, World War II Valor in the Pacific (hereinafter Coles report, Quarters K Binder), 1.

30. Lt. Cdr. Hallsted L. Hopping to CO, *Enterprise*, "Report of Action with Japanese at Oahu, T.H., December 7, 1941," 15 December 1941, Enclosure C to *Enterprise* action report (hereinafter Hopping report), 1–2, HAD, NHHC.

31. McColgan, Lord questionnaire, 2; Ens. William S. Tenhagen to CO, NASPH, "Air Attack by Japanese," n.d., Quarters K Binder, World War II Valor in the Pacific (hereinafter Tenhagen report, Quarters K Binder), 1; Keutgen report, Quarters K Binder, 2; VP-24 action report, 2–3; Anderson, NTU interview, 22–23.

32. William H. Anderson, commendation, 22 April 1942, OMPF, RG 24, NPRC, St. Louis.

33. Baldwin report, Quarters K Binder, 3; Kuzma, NTU interview, 68.

34. Ens. Gilbert M. Rice, SC-V(G), to CO, NAS Pearl Harbor, "Air raid attack by Japanese on Ford Island," 14 December 1941, Quarters K Binder, World War II Valor in the Pacific (hereinafter Rice, Quarters K report), 1.

35. Bellinger, "The Gooney Birds," 324; Logan report, Quarters K Binder, 1–2; Musser report, Quarters K Binder, 1–2; war diary, NASPH, Quarters K Binder, 2.

36. Shoemaker account, 2.

37. *New Horizons*, January 1942, 17; Report of Changes, NAS Pearl Harbor, 31 December 1941.

38. Caudel, NTU interview, 18, Giemont recommendation, 2.

39. Rogo, Prange letter, 2.

40. Hatcher, NTU interview, 38–39; de Coligny, NTU interview, 32.

41. Delia, NTU interview, 32–33.

42. Iverson report, Quarters K Binder, 3; Riggs report, Quarters K Binder, 1.

43. Kamont, Prange letter, 3.

44. Riggs report, Quarters K Binder, 1; Riggs, Prange interview, 6–7; Lt. Rush L. Canon to CO, NAS Pearl Harbor, "Observations of Air Raid Attack by Japanese on Pearl Harbor," 14 December 1941, Quarters K Binder, World War II Valor in the Pacific (hereinafter Canon report, Quarters K Binder), 1; Iverson report, Quarters K Binder, 1; Longeway report, Quarters K Binder, 2.

45. Riggs report, Quarters K Binder, 1; West, *Honolulu Prepares*, 69.

46. Canon report, Quarters K Binder, 1; Zuber report, Quarters K Binder, 1.

47. Closser report, Quarters K Binder, 2.

48. Zuber report, Quarters K Binder, 2.

49. Osborne report, Quarters K Binder, 1.

50. Satchell report, Quarters K Binder, 1–2; Pischner report, Quarters K Binder, 3.

51. Glaeser, Lord questionnaire, 1; Harry R. Mead, *20 Was Easy: Memoirs of a Pearl Harbor Survivor* (North Charleston, S.C.: BookSurge, 2005), 37.

52. Bellinger testimony, Joint Committee, *PHA*, part 8, 3467, 3471; PatWing 2 war diary, 2.

53. ComPatWing Two to VP-24, text of message at 0855 (no number or serial), radio log, NAS Kaneohe Bay, 7 December 1941, Ramsey Papers (uncataloged), HAD, NHHC.

54. *Boggs* deck log, 7 December 1941, RG 24, NARA II; CO, *Minneapolis* to CinCPac, "Offensive Measures on Seven December," 13 December 1941, enclosure to CinCPac to SecNav, "Report on Japanese Raid on Pearl Harbor, 7 December, 1941," 15 February 1942, RG 38, NARA II; questionnaire, Enrique S. M. Aflague, circa 31 May 1956, 1, Lord Collection, HAD, NHHC.

55. VP-24 action report, 3; Bellinger chart of aerial searches. The PBY probably saw *I-16* or *I-24*.

56. Bellinger chart of aerial searches; CinCPac, "Disposition of Task Forces," 20 December 1941, *PHA*, part 24, 1606; research by James C. Sawruk.

57. James, NTU interview, 53, Hatcher, NTU interview, 40–41.

Chapter 9. "People Were Getting Up in Anything That They Could Throw a Rock Out Of"

1. The other three aviators from VCS-5 were Lt. (jg) Richard G. Jack (whose Waikīkī apartment at 2221-A Waikolu Way was six blocks from Semmes' and one block from several VJ-1 pilots), Ens. James D. McMillan, A-V(N), and Ens. Raymond E. Moore, A-V(N).

2. *St. Louis* deck log, 28 November 1941, 7–10 December 1941, RG 24, NARA II; *St. Louis* war diary, 7 December 1941, 6, RG 24, NARA II; *St. Louis*, "History of the U.S.S. St. Louis Aviation Unit," 2, World War II Command Files, HAD, NHHC.

3. Bellinger chart of aerial searches; Ens. Otto F. Meyer to CO, VP-14, "Report of Engagement with Hostile Aircraft," 25 December 1941 (hereinafter Meyer report), 1, authors' files. According to James Sawruk's interviews of veterans from the first year of the war, one thousand feet was the normal altitude for searches of this period.

4. Meyer report, 1–2; radio logs, Naval Air Station Kaneohe Bay, 7 December 1941, Ramsey Papers (uncataloged), HAD, NHHC; *Kōdōchōsho*, *Hiryū*, 8 December 1941.

5. Bellinger chart of aerial searches; Meyer report, 3; ComPatWing 1 to 14-P-2, 2121/7Dec41, Dispatch 072110, no serial, 7 December 1941, CinCPac dispatches, PHLO; ComPatWing 2 to 14-P-2 and 14-P-3, 2158/7Dec41, no message number, no serial, 7 December 1941, CinCPac dispatches, Lundstrom. Dispatches with no message number or serial will have time stamps consisting of Greenwich Civil Time (GCT) and the date.

6. Bellinger chart of aerial searches; Joseph M. Kellam, officer biography sheet, 2 October 1956, OMPF, RG 24, NPRC, St. Louis. An admittedly rough estimate of 1000 for Kellam's takeoff time is based on a plain-language message from him at 1101.

7. Bellinger chart of aerial searches.

8. Wesley H. Ruth, officer biography sheet, 31 October 1939, OMPF, RG 24, NPRC, St. Louis; Ruth interview, 5; Emery C. Geise, officer biography sheet, 23 October 1957, RG 24, OMPF, NPRC, St. Louis.

9. Ruth interview, 5; Bellinger chart of aerial searches; Bellinger, "The Gooney Birds," 323; PatWing 2 war diary, 2.

10. Nils R. Larson, officer biography sheets, 1 March 1954 and 30 June 1960, OMPF, RG 24, NPRC, St. Louis; Nils R. Larson, application for aviation training in the U.S. Naval Reserve, 16 March 1938, OMPF, RG 24, NPRC, St. Louis; JMW correspondence with son Niles R. Larson from August 2012; Ruth interview, 5; Nils R. Larson, flight log entry for 7 December 1941, courtesy of son Niles R. Larson; Bellinger chart of aerial searches.

11. Bolser letter, 1–2; Ruth interview, 9, 11–12; Gordon E. Bolser, statement of personal history, n.d., OMPF, RG 24, NPRC, St. Louis; Gordon E. Bolser, application for flight training in the U.S. Naval Reserve, 24 August 1935, OMPF, RG 24, NPRC, St. Louis; Gordon E. Bolser, officer biography sheet, 18 September 1953, OMPF, RG 24, NPRC, St. Louis.

12. Ruth interview, 9; James W. Robb, "Commander James William Robb, Jr., U.S. Navy, Active, Deceased, Re: Service of," 28 May 1946, OMPF, RG 24, NPRC, St. Louis; JAG to SecNav, "Claim of Aviation Cadet James W. Robb, Jr., U.S.N.R., for reimbursement for personal effects lost in the disaster to U.S.S. *New Orleans* Plane 6-CS-10, No. 9873 on January 10, 1939," 27 February 1939, OMPF, RG 24, NPRC, St. Louis; James W. Robb, officer biography sheet, 26 November 1940, OMPF, RG 24, NPRC, St. Louis; William R. Evans, flight log entry for 7 December 1941, courtesy of Diane Clark.

13. Gordon E. Bolser, flight log entry for 7 December 1941, courtesy of son Donald Bolser; Bellinger chart of aerial searches. Conflicting sources and lack of official reports make it very difficult to determine Edwards' position in the order of takeoff.

14. John P. Edwards, officer biography sheet, 9 March 1954, OMPF, RG 24, NPRC, St. Louis; John P. Edwards, officer data card, 28 September 1955, OMPF, RG 24, NPRC, St. Louis; Edwards account, 3A; "Pearl Harbor Attack Remembered," 1.

15. Bellinger chart of aerial searches; Commander, Utility Squadron One to Commander, Utility

Wing, Serial 30, "Performance of Duty during Air Raid on 7 December 1941—Recommendations for Awards to Personnel Involved" (hereinafter ComUtron One, Serial 30), 15 January 1942, excerpts contained in the OMPFs (S-2 filing) of Wesley H. Ruth, James W. Robb, Gordon E. Bolser, Nils R. Larson, and John P. Edwards, NPRC, St. Louis; Nils R. Larson, flight log entry, 7 December 1941; Gordon E. Bolser, flight log entry, 7 December 1941; research by James C. Sawruk.

16. Bellinger chart of aerial searches; Ogden, "Airborne at Pearl," 62.

17. David L. Switzer to Doris Switzer, letter, 7 December 1941, courtesy of son Roger B. Switzer.

18. Bellinger, "The Gooney Birds," 325; testimony of Patrick N. L. Bellinger before the Joint Committee, 31 January 1946, *PHA*, part 8, 3468.

19. Bellinger chart of aerial searches.

20. *Lexington* deck log, 7 December 1941, Exhibit 101, Exhibits of the Joint Committee, *PHA*, part 16, 2113; Bellinger chart of aerial searches; CinCPac to Midway, 1933/7Dec41, no message number, no serial, "Narrative of Events Dec 7–14 1941," 1, CNO Security Documents, Entry 167F, box 48, RG 80, NARA II (hereinafter CinCPac Narrative of Events); ComTF 9 to CO, VP-21, 2045/7Dec41, no message number, no serial, CinCPac dispatches, PHLO; 12-P-1 to NAS Midway, Dispatch 072350, no serial, CinCPac dispatches, Lundstrom ; John B. Lundstrom, *The First Team: Pacific Naval Air Combat from Pearl Harbor to Midway* (Annapolis, Md.: Naval Institute Press, 1984), 22; CinCPac to Com TF12, Dispatch 072328, Serial 12-304, 7 December 1941, CinCPac dispatches, Lundstrom.

21. Robert J. Cressman, "Ens. Theodore W. Marshall, A-V(N), USNR: Perseverance at Pearl Harbor, 7 December 1941," copy of MS monograph, authors' collection.

22. Lt. Wilmer E. Gallaher to CO, VS-6, "Report of Action with Japanese on Oahu on 7 December, 1941," 13 December 1941, Enclosure A1 to *Enterprise* action report (hereinafter Gallaher report), 1–2, HAD, NHHC; Ens. William P. West to CO, VS-6, "Report of Action with Japanese on Oahu on 7 December, 1941," 14 December 1941, Enclosure A7 to *Enterprise* action report, 1, HAD,

NHHC; Ens. Cleo J. Dobson to CO, VS-6, "Report of Action on Oahu on 7 December, 1941," 12 December 1941, Enclosure A5 to *Enterprise* action report, 1, HAD, NHHC; Hopping report, Enclosure C, "Task Organization PM Search"; Cressman and Wenger, *Steady Nerves and Stout Hearts*, 34–35, 40, 43–44. Ramsey account, NAS Pearl Harbor timeline, 7 December 1941, 1.

23. Erickson report, Quarters K Binder, 2.

24. Hopping report, 2, and its Enclosure C, "Task Organization PM Search."

25. Hopping report, 2.

26. Hopping report, "Task Organization PM Search"; Lt. (jg) H. Dale Hilton to CO, VS-6, "Report of Action with Japanese on Oahu on 7 December, 1941," 1, Enclosure A3, Hopping report. It is uncertain which aircraft from Hickam were the objects of Hilton's rendezvous because there were two flights out of the field at about that time—four A-20As under Maj. William J. Holzapfel taking off at 1127 and two B-17s getting off the ground at 1140. See "Time of Takeoffs by Airfield after Beginning of Attack, 7 Dec. 1941," Exhibit no. 5, Section VI, Exhibits of the Joint Committee, *PHA*, part 12, 323.

27. Hopping report, "Task Organization PM Search."

28. James L. Young Jr., NTU interview, 39–41.

29. Ibid., 44–45; Gallaher report, 2.

30. James L. Young Jr., NTU interview, 45; Hopping report, 2, and its Enclosure C, "Task Organization PM Search."

31. James L. Young Jr., NTU interview, 47.

32. ComTF 9 to CinCPac, "Operations on December 7, 1941," 20 December 1941, 4, unlabeled enclosure to Admiral Nimitz' action report. See CinCPac to SecNav, "Report of Japanese Raid on Pearl Harbor, 7 December, 1941," 15 February 1942, RG 38, NARA II.

33. 23-P-4 to ComPatWing 2, 2128/7Dec41, no message number, no serial, CinCPac narrative of events, 7; Ogden, "Airborne at Pearl", 62; James R. Ogden, officer biography sheet, 4 November 1953, HAD, NHHC, authors' files. Note that the recipient of the message at 1058 appears as PatWing 1 but was almost surely PatWing 2.

34. 23-P-12 to ComPatWing 2, 2133/7Dec41, no message number, no serial, CinCPac dispatches, PHLO. At the time, this message was thought to

have originated from 23-P-11 (heavily damaged during the attack) rather than Ensign Kellam in 23-P-12. The identity of the submarines Kellam's crew located is unclear, but the most likely candidates are the *I-8* under Cdr. Emi Tetsushirō and the *I-74* under Cdr. Ikezawa Masayoshi. See chart in *Hawai Sakusen*, 249; and "List of Sub COs," box 33, Prange Collection, University of Maryland.

35. 24-P-2 to ComPatWing 2, 2200/7Dec41, no message number, no serial, CinCPac dispatches, PHLO; *Enterprise* deck log, 7 December 1941, RG 24, NARA II; testimony of Wilson Brown before the Roberts Commission, 3 January 1942, *PHA*, part 23, 759. It is not clear whether Bellinger was aware that the force sighted was Task Force 8. The only known message from Halsey that indicated his position early in the morning was sent at 0830 and addressed only to CinCPac on 4205 kilocycles. It is not known whether PatWing 2's radiomen in the Administration Building at NAS Pearl Harbor were guarding that frequency early in the attack. See Lt. (jg) Frank M. Hoak Jr.'s note regarding frequencies used on 7 December 1941 in "To Whom It May Concern," 22 October 1945, CinCPac dispatches, PHLO.

36. ComTF 9 to all VP-24 aircraft, 2209/7 Dec41, no message number, no serial, CinCPac dispatches, PHLO; VP-24 action report, 3.

37. 23-P-12 to ComPatWing 2, 2250/7Dec41, no message number, no serial, 7 December 1941; 23-P-12 to ComPatWing 2, 2314/7Dec41, no message number, no serial, 7 December 1941; ComPatWing 2 to 23-P-12, Dispatch 072256, no serial, 7 December 1941, all three messages from CinCPac dispatches, Lundstrom; ComPatWing 2 to 23-P-12, Dispatch 072330, no serial, 7 December 1941, CinCPac dispatches, PHLO. The sender and recipient in the message at 2250/7Dec41 are almost certainly reversed on the dispatch.

38. PatWing 2 war diary, 3; Maj. George R. Bienfang, Operations Officer, 18th Bombardment Wing to Commander, Naval Base Defense Air Force, "Operations on 7 December 1941," 20 December 1941, 1, AFHSO, reel A7627, file 742.674-1, 17 May 1918–31 Dec 1943, 7th Bomber Command, Reports of the December Attacks.

39. Ruth interview, 5; *Kōdōchōsho*, *Zuikaku*, 8 December 1941; CarDiv 5 DAR, 16; Takeuchi Masato, "*Hawai Shutsugeki Kikki*" *Rekishi-to Jinbutsu* (Tōkyō: Chūō-Kōron-sha), 10 September 1985, 385.

40. Hata Ikuhiko and Izawa Yasuo, *Japanese Naval Aces and Fighter Units in World War II* (Annapolis, Md.: Naval Institute Press, 1989), 241, 413, 417, 420; Iwamoto Tetsuzo, *Zerosen Gekitsui-ō* (Tōkyō: Konnichi no Wadai-sha, 1972), based on Iwamoto's dairies; *Kōdōchōsho*, *Zuikaku*, 8 December 1941.

41. Ruth interview, 5; Bellinger chart of aerial searches; *Kōdōchōsho*, *Zuikaku*, 8 December 1941; ComUtron One, Serial 30; CarDiv 5 DAR, 17. While the entry from Iwamoto's diary is vague, it seems to indicate that a single fighter pilot (unidentified) gave chase to the JRS-1. When questioned why he was at such a low altitude, Ruth said that he did not want enemy aircraft to get underneath him, and further, "I wouldn't have so far to fall in case I was shot down."

42. William R. Evans, flight log entry for 7 December 1941, courtesy of daughter Diane Clark. Robb perished in an accidental bombing incident on 4 April 1946 and left no known account of the mission.

43. "Navy Cross Is Given Daring Pilot for Pearl Harbor Heroism," *Galveston Daily News*, 26 April 1942, 17; "Ford Islsand," *Pearl Harbor–Gram*, no. 118, May 1994, 4; Report of Changes, VJ-1, 30 November 1941, www.fold3.com, accessed on 21 March 2016.

44. It is unknown whether the interception occurred during Bolser's inbound or outbound search leg.

45. Bolser letter, 2; telephone conversation, JMW and Shannon Bolser Gault, 27 July 2012.

46. The portion of *Hiryū*'s *Kōdōchōsho* from 8 December 1941 that deals with this point is practically illegible.

47. *Kōdōchōsho*, *Hiryū*, 8 December 1941; Hata and Izawa, *Japanese Naval Aces*, 421; Shibuya Matsuwaka, interview 4, 2, Prange Collection, box 33, University of Maryland; *Kōdōchōsho*, *Kaga*, 8 December 1941; Yoshio Shiga, interview for Walter Lord, 9 July 1956, 3, Lord Collection, HAD, NHHC; CO, *Northampton* to Commander, Task Force 8, "Narrative of Air Scouting Conducted on December 7, 1941," 18 December

1941, RG 38, NARA II. Lt. Shiga Yoshio, commander of the *Kaga* fighter squadron, stated in a postwar interview that WO Gotō went missing subsequent to strafing attacks on NAS Pearl Harbor. Hence it is plausible that PO1c Inanaga, unable for reasons unknown to return to the carrier, flew west toward a rendezvous with the *I-74*. The authors believe that this pilot engaged, unsuccessfully, two SOC-1 scout planes from the *Northampton* and thus might be Bolser's attacker as well.

48. Bellinger chart of aerial searches.

49. Ibid.; Edwards account, 1A, 3A; "Ford Island," *Pearl Harbor–Gram*, no. 118, May 1994, 4.

50. PatWing 2 war diary, 3; Ramsey account, NAS Pearl Harbor timeline, 7 December 1941, 1; Robert H. Wood, officer biography sheet, 16 July 1958, OMPF, RG 24, NPRC, St. Louis; Bellinger chart of aerial searches.

51. Bellinger chart of aerial searches; Ramsey account, NAS Pearl Harbor timeline, 7 December 1941, 1; Commander, Battleships to Batships in Company, Dispatch 072219, no serial, 7 December 1941, CinCPac dispatches, PHLO. Dispatches and message traffic provide only a rough picture for the OS2U flight apart from 4-O-7.

52. Bellinger chart of aerial searches; 24-P-1 to CinCPac, Dispatch 080045, no serial, 7 December 1941, CinCPac dispatches, PHLO; 24-P-1 to CinCPac, Dispatch 080109, no serial, 7 December 1941, CinCPac dispatches, PHLO; 24-P-2 to ComPatWing 2, 0215/8Dec41, no message number, no serial, CinCPac narrative of events, 22. Similarly, 24-P-5 located Halsey's force later in the afternoon, though it reported sighting two battleships and many destroyers. See 24-P-5 to CinCPac, 070158, no serial, 7 December 1941, CinCPac dispatches, PHLO.

53. Ruth interview, 5–6.

54. Gordon M. Bolser, letter from Bolser's son relating his father's exploits.

55. ComUtron One, Serial 30, 1.

56. ComPatWing 2 to 23-P-12, Dispatch 080145/8, no serial, 8 December 1941; 23-P-12 to ComPatWing 2, Dispatch 080205, no serial, 8 December 1941, both messages from CinCPac dispatches, Lundstrom; 23-P-12 to ComPatWing 2, 0214/8Dec41, no message number, no serial,

7 December 1941, CinCPac Dispatch Files, Entry 167F, box 45, PHLO, RG 80, NARA II.

57. The *Tangier* assisted with aircraft communications at this juncture, perhaps as a result of the interrupted communications of the morning.

58. 1-O-2 to *Tangier*, 0340/8Dec41 and 0347/8Dec41, no message numbers, no serials, 8 December 1941 CinCPac narrative of events, 26.

59. VP-14 to 1-O-2, 0416/8Dec41, 8 December 1941; 1-O-2 to 1-O-3, 0430/8Dec41, 7 December 1941; no message numbers, no serials, both messages from CinCPac dispatches, Lundstrom.

60. 4-O-7 to *Tangier*, 0521/8Dec41, 8 December 1941; 4-O-7 to *Tangier*, 0524/8Dec41, 8 December 1941; 4-O-9 to *Tangier*, 0706/8Dec41, 8 December 1941, no message numbers, no serials, all three messages from CinCPac dispatches, Lundstrom.

61. Robert J. Cressman and J. Michael Wenger, "This Is No Drill: U.S. Naval Aviation and Pearl Harbor, December 7, 1941," *Naval Aviation News*, November–December 1991, 25; Donald K. Ross and Helen L. Ross, *"0755": The Heroes of Pearl Harbor* (Port Orchard, Wash.: Rokalu Press, 1988), 48–49; *Maryland* deck log, 1138, 9 December 1941, RG 24, NARA II; James Blackburn Ginn, certificate of death, OMPF, RG 24, NARA, St. Louis.

62. VP-23 to ComPatWing 2, 0433/8Dec41, 7 December 1941; 23-P-6 to ComPatWing 2, 0731/8Dec41, 7 December 1941, no message numbers, no serials, both messages from CinCPac dispatches, Lundstrom; Ramsey account, NAS Pearl Harbor timeline, 7 December 1941, 1.

63. Ogden, "Airborne at Pearl," 62.

64. Ibid.; Francis M. Hughes, "Biography of Rear Admiral Francis Massie Hughes, U.S. Navy," circa 1953, OMPF, RG 24, NPRC, St. Louis.

65. PatWing 2 war diary, 3; Bellinger, "The Gooney Birds," 324–25.

Chapter 10. "How in God's Name Could Something Like This Happen?"

1. Davey report, Quarters K Binder, 1; anonymous, Lord questionnaire, 1; Cdr. Karl Schmidt, "Memorandum to Commanding Officer" [NAS Pearl Harbor], n.d., Quarters K Binder, World War II Valor in the Pacific (hereinafter Schmidt

report, Quarters K Binder), 3; Ryan NTU interview, 19; Killian report, Quarters K Binder, 3.

2. Bellinger testimony, Army Board, *PHA*, part 28, 854–55. Wenger modified Bellinger's totals somewhat in a white paper prepared for the National Park Service. See J. Michael Wenger, "Whitepaper No. 14: Navy Aircraft Losses—Attacks on Oʻahu," 28 March 2016, authors' files.

3. Anderson, NTU interview, 24; Cochran, NTU interview, 37, 41, 47; Glaeser, Lord questionnaire, 2; James, NTU interview, 65.

4. Bellinger, "The Gooney Birds, 324.

5. Anonymous, Lord questionnaire, 3; Keith, NTU interview, 25–26.

6. Molter, Lord questionnaire, 9.

7. Gerald M. Jacobs, questionnaire, n.d., 3, Lord Collection, HAD, NHHC (hereinafter Jacobs, Lord questionnaire); Edmundson, Lord account, 1; James, NTU interview, 61; Malmin, Lord questionnaire, 3; Kuzma, NTU interview, 67.

8. Kuzma, NTU interview, 59–60.

9. Keutgen report, Quarters K Binder, 2.

10. Ibid.

11. De Coligny, NTU interview, 38, 40–42.

12. Baldwin report, Quarters K Binder, 3. It is likely that Matsuda came ashore on the small peninsula between Berths F-6 (*West Virginia* and *Tennessee*) and F-5 (*Oklahoma* and *Maryland*), particularly because Lieutenant Commander Baldwin was inspecting quarters in that vicinity.

13. James, NTU interview, 44–46.

14. Keith, NTU interview, 22; James, NTU interview, 45–47. See drawing 1405-31-1, "1st Floor Plan, Dispensary, 14th Naval District, Pearl Harbor T.H.," 15 December 1939, BuYards & Docks microfilm, RG 71I, series I, reel 1170, NARA II.

15. James, NTU interview, 47–48.

16. Ibid., 48; Iverson report, Quarters K Binder, 2.

17. Arnold report, Quarters K Binder, 1; Riggs, Prange interview, 7–8; Iverson report, Quarters K Binder, 2.

18. Watson report, Quarters K Binder, 1–2; Sanders report, Quarters K Binder, 1; Ramsey testimony, Navy Court of Inquiry, *PHA*, part 27, 458; Ogden, "Airborne at Pearl," 62.

19. James, NTU interview, 63; Ryan, NTU interview, 20; Zuber report, Quarters K Binder, 1.

20. Satchell report, Quarters K Binder, 2.

21. Shoemaker, Prange interview no. 1, 12; Church report, Quarters K Binder.

22. Molter, Lord letter, 7.

23. Cressman and Wenger, *Steady Nerves and Stout Hearts*, 47–49.

24. Ibid., 51.

25. Farrow, Prange interview, 5.

26. ComTF 8 to CinCPac, 0518/8Dec, no message number, no serial, 7 December 1941, CinCPac incoming message files, Lundstrom; Bellinger, "The Gooney Birds," 327; Lt. Cdr. Earl B. Wilkins to CO, NAS Pearl Harbor, "Attack by Japanese Planes December 7, 1941," 17 December 1941, Quarters K Binder, World War II Valor in the Pacific (hereinafter Wilkins report, Quarters K Binder), 2.

27. Cressman and Wenger, *Steady Nerves and Stout Hearts*, 51–52; Lundstrom, *The First Team*, 18.

28. Erickson report, Quarters K Binder, 3; Morse, Lord questionnaire, 2C; Layman, Lord questionnaire, 2; Shoemaker, Prange interview no. 1, 16–17.

29. Bellinger, "The Gooney Birds," 327.

30. Cressman and Wenger, *Steady Nerves and Stout Hearts*, 55.

31. Erickson report, Quarters K Binder, 3.

32. Ramsey account, NAS Pearl Harbor timeline, 7 December 1941, 1; Erickson report, Quarters K Binder, 3; Riggs, Prange interview, 9.

33. Wilkins report, Quarters K Binder, 2; Bellinger, "The Gooney Birds," 327; Shoemaker testimony, Roberts Commission, *PHA*, part 23, 731; Ogden, "Airborne at Pearl," 62.

34. Mead, Lord letter, 5.

35. Cressman and Wenger, *Steady Nerves and Stout Hearts*, 55, interviews with Dorinda Nicholson, 1941 resident of Pearl City; morning reports, 64th Coast Artillery Regiment (AA), Battery F, December 1941, RG 64, NARA, St. Louis; "Coast Artillery Orders," *Coast Artillery Journal* (September–October 1941): 516; Officer in Charge, Intelligence Field Unit, NAS Pearl Harbor, T.H., to District Intelligence Officer, "Burned American Aircraft on Pearl City Peninsula," 14 December 2016, RG 313, L11-1 files, NARA I.

36. Cressman and Wenger, *Steady Nerves and Stout Hearts*, 55, 57; memorandum to CO, *Enterprise*, "Burned American Aircraft on Pearl City

Peninsula," n.d., RG 313, L11-1 files, NARA I; Francis Frederick Hebel, certificate of death, 7 December 1941, OMPF, RG 24, NARA, St. Louis.

37. Cressman and Wenger, *Steady Nerves and Stout Hearts*, 57.

38. Ibid.; Structures Officer for Aircraft to CO, *Enterprise*, "Location of Missing Aircraft," 29 December 1941, RG 313, L11-1 files, NARA I.

39. Cressman and Wenger, *Steady Nerves and Stout Hearts*, 58; *Vireo* deck log, 7 December 1941, RG 24, NARA II; CO, *Vireo* to CinCPac, "Action taken by this vessel during Air Raid, 7 December, 1941—Report of," 10 December 1941, RG 38, NARA II; Riggs, Prange interview, 10; Black report, Quarters K Binder, 3.

40. Wilkerson, NTU interview, 55; Cressman and Wenger, *Steady Nerves and Stout Hearts*, 57; Wilkins report, Quarters K Binder, 2.

41. Bellinger, "The Gooney Birds," 320, 324.

42. James, NTU interview, 58; Hemingway, NTU interview, 31.

43. Riggs, Prange interview, 11.

44. Bellinger testimony, Hart Inquiry, *PHA*, part 26, 127–28; Bellinger testimony, Joint Committee, *PHA*, part 8, 3488; Bellinger, "The Gooney Birds," 317.

45. Bellinger testimony, Hart Inquiry, *PHA*, part 26, 137; Bellinger testimony, Joint Committee, *PHA*, part 8, 3460, 3501.

46. Bellinger testimony, Hart Inquiry, *PHA*, part 26, 140.

47. Glenn Pennock, "On Wings of Thunder," *Fort Collins* (Colo.) *Review*, 5 December 1991, 9.

48. Jackson D. Arnold, officer biography sheet, with attachment, "Naval Service," 24 November 1971, OMPF, RG 24, NPRC, St. Louis.

BIBLIOGRAPHY

Military Records

ACTION REPORTS (U.S. NAVY), NATIONAL ARCHIVES AND RECORDS ADMINISTRATION (II), MODERN MILITARY BRANCH, COLLEGE PARK, MD. [HEREINAFTER NARA II], RECORDS OF THE CHIEF OF NAVAL OPERATIONS, RG 38

CO, *Allen* to Commander, Inshore Patrol, Fourteenth Naval District. "Air Raid Attack by Japanese—Report on." 14 December 1941.

CO, *Enterprise* to CinCPac. "Report of Action with Japanese Air Force at Oahu, T.H., December 7, 1941, and with Submarine on December 10, 1941." 16 December 1941.

CO, *Helena* to CinCPac. "Brief Report of the Japanese Attack of December 7, 1941." 14 December 1941.

CO, *Minneapolis* to CinCPac. "Offensive Measures on Seven December." 13 December 1941.

CO, NASPH to SecNav. "Damage resulting from Air Raid Attack by Japanese on 7 December, 1941." N.d.

CO, *Neosho* to CinCPac. "Raid on Pearl Harbor, T.H., December 7, 1941—Report on." 11 December 1941.

CO, *Northampton* to Commander, Task Force 8. "Narrative of Air Scouting Conducted on December 7, 1941." 18 December 1941.

CO, *Pennsylvania* to CinCPac. "U.S.S. *Pennsylvania*'s Report of Action during Enemy Air Attack morning of Sunday 7 December 1941." 16 December 1941.

CO, *Tangier* to Chief, Bureau of Ships. "War Damage Reports." 19 January 1942.

CO, *Tangier* to CinCPac. "Raid, Air, December 7, 1941, U.S.S. *Tangier* (AV8)—Report on." 2 January 1942.

CO, *Vireo* to CinCPac. "Action taken by this vessel during Air Raid, 7 December, 1941—Report of." 10 December 1941.

CO, VP-22 to CinCPac. "Summary of Action and Damage During Air Raid on December 7, 1941." 13 December 1941.

CO, VP-24 to CinCPac. "Report of Offensive Measures Taken During December 7 Raid—Losses and Damage to Enemy—Distinguished Conduct of Personnel." 15 December 1941.

CO, *Zane* to CinCPac. "Air Raid on Pearl Harbor, Report of." 10 December 1941.

Com 14 to CNO. "Report on the Battle of Pearl Harbor, 7 December 1941." 24 December 1941, Enclosure D, CO, NASPH to Com 14, "Air Attack by Japanese on 7 December, 1941, Report On." 21 December 1941.

ComTF 9 to CinCPac. "Operations on December 7, 1941." 20 December 1941.

Davison, Henry D. "Statement of Ensign H. D. Davison, U.S. Navy, U.S.S. *Arizona*." Enclosure F to CO, *Arizona* to CinCPac. "Action Report U.S.S. *Arizona* (BB 39) December 7, 1941." 13 December 1941.

Detailed Action Report No. 1, CarDiv 5 (trans.) via Cressman. Prange Collection, University of Maryland.

Dobson, Cleo J., to CO, VS-6. "Report of Action on Oahu on 7 December, 1941." 12 December 1941.

Gallaher, Wilmer E., to CO, VS-6. "Report of Action with Japanese on Oahu on 7 December, 1941." 13 December 1941.

Hilton, H. Dale, to CO, VS-6. "Report of Action with Japanese on Oahu on 7 December, 1941." 13 December 1941.

Hopping, Hallsted L., to CO, *Enterprise*. "Report of Action with Japanese at Oahu, T.H., December 7, 1941." Enclosure C, "Task Organization PM Search." 15 December 1941.

Meyer, Otto F., to CO, VP-14. "Report of engagement with hostile aircraft." 25 December 1941.

Teaff, Perry L., to CO, VS-6. "Report of Action on Oahu on 7 December 1941." 13 December 1941.

West, William P., to CO, VS-6. "Report of Action with Japanese on Oahu on 7 December, 1941." 14 December 1941.

XO, *Tangier* to CO, *Tangier*. "Report of engagement between the USS *Tangier* (AV8) and Japanese airplanes on December 7, 1941." 11 December 1941.

Young, Howard L., to CO, *Enterprise*. "Report of Action with Japanese Air Force at Oahu, T.H., December 7, 1941." 15 December 1941

ARCHITECTURAL PLANS AND DRAWINGS (U.S. NAVY), MICROFILM, NARA II, CARTOGRAPHIC BRANCH, COLLEGE PARK, MD., RECORDS OF THE BUREAU OF YARDS AND DOCKS. RG 71, SERIES I

"Administration Building, 14th Naval District, Fleet Air Base, Territory of Hawaii." Architectural drawing 1405-34-93, all floors and elevations.

"Dispensary, 14th Naval District, Pearl Harbor T.H." Architectural plan 1405-31-2, all floors.

"Fourteenth Naval District, Fleet Air Base—Pearl Harbor, T.H., Fire Station." Architectural drawings 1405-24-2 (plans) and 1405-24-3 (elevations).

"Navy Yard, Pearl Harbor, T.H. Additional Fuel Storage, Ford Island Diagram, Gasoline Lines." No number.

Station Plans, NAS Pearl Harbor, various. Drawings 1405-3-2 through 1405-3-41.

"U.S. Naval Fleet Air Base Ford Island, Pearl Harbor, T.H., Barracks and Mess Hall." Architectural drawings 1405-30-82 through 1405-30-87, plumbing plans, all floors.

"U.S. Naval Station Pearl Harbor, T.H. Additional Gasoline Storage, Gasoline & Wiring Layout to Thermostats and Master Fire Alarm Boxes." Architectural drawing 1405-43-38.

"U.S. Naval Station Pearl Harbor, T.H. Map of Station Showing Improvements to June 20, 1921." Drawing 1400-3-56.

BIOGRAPHICAL FILES, HISTORY AND ARCHIVES DIVISION, NAVAL HISTORY AND HERITAGE COMMAND, WASHINGTON NAVY YARD

Daniel Beville Candler

Elton W. Grenfell

Robert D. Kirkpatrick

James R. Ogden

BUREAU OF AERONAUTICS, HISTORY AND ARCHIVES DIVISION, NAVAL HISTORY AND HERITAGE COMMAND, WASHINGTON NAVY YARD

Aircraft Trouble Analysis cards (microfilm).

COMMAND FILES (U.S. NAVY), NARA I, OLD MILITARY BRANCH, WASHINGTON, D.C., RECORDS OF NAVAL OPERATING FORCES. RG 313

Commander Aircraft, Battle Force, L11–1 files, 1941.

Commander Aircraft, Scouting Force, A4–3 files, 1941.

Commander Aircraft, Scouting Force, A16–3 files, 1941.

DECK LOGS (U.S. NAVY), NARA II, RG 24

Ballard (AVD 10)

Boggs (DMS 3)

California (BB 44)

Enterprise (CV 6)

Gudgeon (SS 211)

Maryland (BB 46)

Monaghan (DD 354)
Neosho (AO 23)
Seagull (AM 30)
St. Louis (CL 49)
Tangier (AV 8)
Vireo (AM 52)
Wright (AV 1)

DECORATION CITATIONS, HISTORY
AND ARCHIVES DIVISION, NAVAL
HISTORY AND HERITAGE COMMAND,
WASHINGTON NAVY YARD

William H. Anderson
P. W. Ashworth
Lawrence J. Baker
LeRoy Everett Bartels
Oscar W. Benefiel Jr.
John A. Birmingham
Robert D. Bissell
Roy Raymond Bratton
George Francis Browning
Jack R. Brumbaugh
William P. Byrd
Lowell W. Cain
Rush L. Canon
Elmer L. Caveny
William Chrastina
Robert Booth Clarke
Ralph P. Dean
Frank R. DeAugustine
George J. Devita
Alfred Doren
Frank Dudovick
Jones Eldreth
Henry Sedgewick Brand Elsee
Edward T. Estrada
Frank Shupe Evans
William R. Evans
Robert S. Fauber
Albert P. Ferguson
Kurt Otto Flechell
Edward L. Frissell
Albert S. Gallupe
Amos R. Gallupe Jr.
Emery C. Geise
James Nelson Gibson
Andrew John Giemont
Frederick W. Glaeser
Thomas E. Hailey

John D. Hammonds
James B. Hanson
Robert Clinton Harp
Joseph A. Howard
Jack H. Johnson
William J. Jones
Lewis A. Kammerer
Eugene V. Karr
Hugh S. Kenney
Leif I. Larson
Franklin Hale Lemmon
David J. Lesher
Dwight W. Lister
Kenneth L. Longeway
William D. Manning
Harry R. Mead
Robert C. Miles
Loyal Ross Neal
Albert S. Pagliochini
William G. Richards
James J. Rose
Wesley H. Ruth
Walter G. Schultz
Paul Jackson Sherrard
William C. Shute Jr.
William A. Simpson
"D" Arnold Singleton
Jaroud B. Smith Jr.
Burt Legrand Swisher
Donald F. Webster
Rodney T. West
"E" "S" White Jr.
Donald H. Wright
James D. Young
Leroy Young
Paul O. Zeller

DISPATCHES (U.S. NAVY), COURTESY
JOHN D. LUNDSTROM
CinCPac Dispatch Files, Tactical Incoming and Out-
    going, 1941 (microfilm).

DISPATCHES, JOURNALS, PERSONNEL
RECORDS, WAR DIARIES, AND WAR PLANS
Chart provided by Rear Adm. Patrick N. L. Bellinger
    showing aerial searches undertaken on 7 December
    1941 from O'ahu and Midway Island. Original
    Exhibits, Roberts Commission, NARA II, Records
    of the Pearl Harbor Liaison Office. RG 80.

CinCPac Dispatch Files, 1941 (originals and photostats). NARA II, Records of the Pearl Harbor Liaison Office. RG 80.

CinCPac to ComAirBatFor and ComPatWing 2. "Naval Air Station Wake and Naval Air Station Midway—Basing of Aircraft At." NARA II, Operational Plans and Orders, CinCPac. RG 38. Serial 01825, 10 November 1941.

CinCPac to ComPatWing Two. "Patrol Wing Organization, Hawaiian Area." 14 June 1941. NARA II, Operational Plans and Orders, CinCPac. RG 38.

CNO/OpNav Dispatch Files (photostats). NARA II, Records of the Crane Group. RG 38.

CNO to CinCPac. "The U.S. Pacific Fleet Operating Plan, Rainbow No. 5 (Navy Plan O-1, Rainbow No. 5) WPPac-46, review and acceptance of." 9 September 1941. NARA II, Records of the Strategic Plans Division. RG 38.

ComPatWing Two War Diary. NARA II, Records of the Chief of Naval Operations. RG 38.

"Lessons (air operation) of the Sea Battle off Hawaii Vol. I." August 1942 (est.), (trans.) via Cressman. Prange Collection, University of Maryland.

Personnel records of officers and men from the U.S. Navy and U.S. Marine Corps and personnel records of civilian contractors working for the Navy. Official Military Personnel Files, Records of the Bureau of Naval Personnel, RG 24; Records of the U.S. Marine Corps, RG 127; Records of Naval Districts and Shore Establishments, RG 181, NARA, St. Louis and National Personnel Records Center.

St. Louis (CL 49) War Diary. NARA II, Records of the Chief of Naval Operations. RG 38.

U.S. Army, 24th Infantry Division. Journal. Topographical map of Schofield Barracks. NARA II, Division Records. RG 407, file 324–0.3.0.

War Diary, CarDiv 5, 1 December 1941–31 December 1941 (trans.) via Cressman. Prange Collection, University of Maryland.

ENGINEERING RECORDS (U.S. ARMY), NARA II, RECORDS OF THE CORPS OF ENGINEERS, RG 77

Quartermaster Corps Forms 117, Luke Field
> Building 24
> Building 36
> Building 77
> Building 79
> Building 81
> Building 82
> Night Lighting System

Record of Equipment and Condition of Buildings. Luke Field, Pearl Harbor, T.H., 30 June 1940.

FLIGHT LOG BOOKS

Gordon E. Bolser
William R. Evans
Robert S. Fauber
Nils R. Larson
David L. Switzer

JAPAN DEFENSE AGENCY REPORTS, TŌKYŌ

Detailed Battle Report, Aircraft Carrier *Shōkaku*, 8 December 1941.

Hikōkitai Sentō Kōdōchōcho (Aircraft Group Battle Action Reports)
> *Akagi*
> *Hiryū*
> *Kaga*
> *Shōkaku*
> *Sōryū*
> *Zuikaku*

LOGAN C. RAMSEY UNCATALOGED PAPERS, HISTORY AND ARCHIVES DIVISION, NAVAL HISTORY AND HERITAGE COMMAND, WASHINGTON NAVY YARD

Letter, Logan C. Ramsey to Matthias B. Gardner, 3 September 1941.

Radio message logs from NAS Kaneohe Bay and VP-14.

Untitled and undated account of the Japanese attack.

MORNING REPORTS AND ROSTERS (U.S. ARMY), NARA ST. LOUIS, RG 64

4th Reconnaissance Squadron
26th Bombardment Squadron
31st Bombardment Squadron
64th Coastal Artillery (AA) Regiment
72nd Bombardment Squadron

MUSTER ROLLS (U.S. MARINE CORPS)

Marine Detachment, NAS Pearl Harbor, 1–31 December 1941. Marine Corps History Division, Marine Corps Base Quantico.

REPORTS AND DOCUMENTS FROM AUTHORS' FILES

Allen, Archer M. R. "Intelligence Report: British Far East Command—RAF." 4 August 1941.

Bureau of Aeronautics. "Monthly Status of Naval Aircraft." August–December 1941.

CO, NAS Pearl Harbor to SecNav. "Damage resulting from Air Raid Attack by Japanese on 7 December, 1941."

Com 14 to CNO. "Suspected Japanese Unexploded Bombs at the Naval Air Station, Ford Island, Oahu, T.H." 4 January 1942.

ComPatWing 2 to Chief of BuNav. "Giemont, Andrew John, 213-22-94, CRM (PA), U.S.N.—Advancement to Chief Warrant Rank for Meritorious conduct—Recommendation for." Circa January 1942.

Cressman, Robert J. "Ens. Theodore W. Marshall, A-V(N), USNR: Perseverance at Pearl Harbor, 7 December 1941." Manuscript copy of monograph.

Erickson, Frank A. Fourth War Loan Drive speech.

"History of the U.S.S. St. Louis Aviation Unit." World War II Command Files, HAD, NHHC. RJC.

"Navy Property on Ford's [sic] Island, Hawaii." Memorandum, circa September 1935, copy of unknown origin.

Nichol, Bromfield B. Rotary Club talk. Circa 7 December 1959.

Passenger manifests (via Jessie Higa)
    Anzac Clipper
    China Clipper
    SS *Lurline*
    SS *Mariposa*
    SS *Matsonia*

Shoemaker, James M. memorandum to file: "Japanese Air Raid on 7 December, Statement on." 22 December 1941.

Tanner, William P. to CO, VP-14. "Narrative of Engagement with Enemy Submarine on December 7, 1941." 28 January 1942.

Wenger, J. Michael. "Whitepaper No. 14: Navy Aircraft Losses—Attacks on O'ahu." 28 March 2016.

REPORTS OF STATION OFFICERS TO CO, NASPH, QUARTERS K BINDER, WORLD WAR II VALOR IN THE PACIFIC

Lt. Jackson D. Arnold
Lt. Walter F. Arnold
Ens. Norton J. Arst
Lt. Cdr. James W. Baldwin
Lt. Richard B. Black
Ens. William G. Boynton
Ens. Henry J. Bultman Jr.
Lt. Rush L. Canon
Lt. Cdr. Harry F. Carlson
Lt. (jg) William C. G. Church
1st Lt. Daniel P. Closser
ChGun William M. Coles
ChRadElect Francis L. Cook
Ens. Raymond W. Cope
Ens. James W. Cronenberg
Lt. Thomas L. Davey
Lt. Cdr. George W. Dickinson
Lt. Frank A. Erickson
Ens. James R. Garrett
Ens. Hugh G. Gribbin
Ens. Daniel S. Hamway
Cdr. Charles J. Harter
Lt. (jg) William J. Held
Ens. Rolland A. Helsel
Lt. Marshall C. Hjelte
Ens. Raymond A. Hubbard
Cdr. Louis Iverson
Lt. William R. Kane
Ens. William A. Keutgen
Lt. Edward D. Killian
Ens. Daniel F. Logan
Lt. (jg) Kenneth L. Longeway
Lt. (jg) Kenneth C. Lovell
Lt. Jay H. Mattson
Ens. John McCormack
Ens. Stuart B. McKinney
Ens. James M. Murray
Lt. Joseph B. Musser
Lt. (jg) Lloyd B. Osborne
Ens. Guy R. Nance
ChPayClk Clifford R. Pischner
Ens. John S. Pritchard
Lt. Samuel M. Randall
Ens. Robert W. Reed
Ens. Gilbert M. Rice
Lt. Cecil D. Riggs
Ens. Fredrick G. Robinson
ChMach Joseph A. Sanders
Ens. Lester D. Satchell
Cdr. Karl Schmidt
Lt. Elmer Schuessler
Capt. James M. Shoemaker
Ens. "D" Arnold Singleton
Lt. (jg) Jaroud B. Smith Jr.
Ens. William S. Tenhagen
Lt. Magruder H. Tuttle

Lt. Frederick Volbeda
Lt. Leroy F. Watson
Ens. Spencer F. Weaver Jr.
Lt. (jg) Rodney T. West
Lt. Cdr. Earl B. Wilkins
Cdr. Errol W. Willett
Ens. Guilbert S. Winchell
Ens. Francis S. Woods
Maj. Adolph Zuber

Correspondence and Interviews
AUTHORS' CORRESPONDENCE AND
MISCELLANEOUS INTERVIEWS
Ann Barnhill
Linda Black
Gordon, Mimi, and Michael Bolser
Daniel P. Closser Jr.
John N. and Nick Delia
Paul W. "Doc" Doolittle
Jim Duty
Joan Earle
Perry and Andy Edwards
Toni Espinoza
Carol Fauber, Lynne Erdahl, and Tracy Rossello
Janice Fiore
Richard D. Gano
Shannon Bolser Gault
Joanne Herrera
Robert Hanson
Niles Rodney Larson
Janet K. Lesher
John B. Lundstrom
Allan G. MacKay Jr.
Capt. Donald Morton, USN (Ret.)
Dorinda Nicholson
Thomas W. Richards
James C. Sawruk
Debbie Sherrard
Roger and Rick Switzer
Christopher Waalkes
Daniel Young

INTERVIEWS AND STATEMENTS IN THE
PAPERS OF WALTER LORD. HISTORY
AND ARCHIVES DIVISION, NAVAL HISTORY
AND HERITAGE COMMAND, WASHINGTON
NAVY YARD
Anonymous respondent
Paul E. Bos

John W. Burton
Carlos J. Cunningham
George W. Edmundson
Charles A. Flood
Frederick W. Glaeser
Ibusuki Masanobu
Gerald M. Jacobs
James C. Lagerman
James S. Layman
Thomas S. Malmin
James E. McColgan
Harry R. Mead
Alfred H. Molter
Russell C. Morse
Robert A. Oborne Jr.
Logan C. Ramsey
Jack Rogo (aka Jacob S. Rogovsky)
Shiga Yoshio
Earle K. Van Buskirk
Edward P. Waszkiewicz

INTERVIEWS AND STATEMENTS IN
THE PAPERS OF GORDON W. PRANGE,
GOLDSTEIN COLLECTION, ARCHIVES
SERVICE CENTER, UNIVERSITY OF
PITTSBURGH
George W. Bicknell
Charles F. Coe
Thomas E. Farrow
Victor A. Kamont
Vernon H. Reeves
Cecil D. Riggs
Jack Rogo [aka Jacob S. Rogovsky]
James M. Shoemaker

INTERVIEWS BY THE AUTHORS:
AMERICAN VETERANS
Capt. Charles P. Muckenthaler, USN (Ret.)
Jack Rogo [aka Jacob S. Rogovsky], USN (Ret.)
Cdr. Wesley H. Ruth, USN (Ret.)

INTERVIEWS BY THE AUTHORS:
JAPANESE VETERANS
Abe Zenji
Fujita Iyozō
Harada Kaname
Satō Zenichi
Ushijima Shizundō

INTERVIEWS, STATEMENTS, AND
PAPERS IN THE PRANGE COLLECTION,
UNIVERSITY OF MARYLAND

Fuchida Mitsuo (*Akagi*). Map of deployment over
O'ahu; interview 14; interview 19; conference 3

Genda Minoru, interview 25

Ibusuki Masanobu, questionnaire

Mifuku Iwakichi, statement

Muranaka Kazuo, questionnaire

Okajima Kiyokuma, statement

Logan C. Ramsey, interview

Shibuya Matsuwaka, interview 4

Shiga Yoshio, statement

Photography

NATIONAL ARCHIVES AND RECORDS
ADMINISTRATION (II), STILL PICTURE
BRANCH

RG 19: Bureau of Ships

RG 71: Bureau of Yards and Docks

RG 72: Bureau of Aeronautics

RG 77: Corp of Engineers

RG 80: Department of the Navy

RG 111: Signal Corps

RG 208: Office of War Information

RG 226: Office of Strategic Services

NATIONAL ARCHIVES AND RECORDS
ADMINISTRATION/NATIONAL PERSONNEL
RECORDS CENTER, ST. LOUIS, MISSOURI

Service photography, U.S. Navy and U.S. Marine
Corps.

NATIONAL NAVAL AVIATION MUSEUM,
PENSACOLA, FLORIDA

NAVAL HISTORY AND HERITAGE
COMMAND, PHOTOGRAPHIC SECTION,
WASHINGTON NAVY YARD

PRIVATE COLLECTIONS

Linda Black

Daniel P. Closser Jr.

Robert J. Cressman

Paul W. "Doc" Doolittle

Toni Espinoza

Robert Hanson

Joanne Herrera

Izawa Yasuo

Maru magazine

Al Makiel

Gordon W. Prange Papers, via Wenger

Gordon W. Prange Papers, Goldstein Collection,
Archives Service Center, University of Pittsburgh

Gordon W. Prange Papers, University of Maryland,
Hornbake Library

Thomas W. Richards

Debbie Sherrard

Christopher Waalkes

Kathy Weeks

J. Michael Wenger

WORLD WAR II VALOR IN THE PACIFIC
NATIONAL MONUMENT, HONOLULU, HAWAII

Curator's Office, 14th Naval District Collection

Historian's Office, Photo Archives

Congressional Hearings

U.S. Congress, 79th Congress, 1st Session. *Pearl Harbor Attack: Hearings before the Joint Committee on the Investigation of the Pearl Harbor Attack*, 39 parts, plus Joint Committee Report and General Index. Washington, D.C.: Government Printing Office, 1946.

TESTIMONY

Patrick N. L. Bellinger

Claude C. Bloch

Wilson Brown

Howard C. Davidson

Arthur C. Davis

Husband E. Kimmel

Frederick M. Martin

James A. Mollison

Vincent R. Murphy

Logan C. Ramsey

James M. Shoemaker

U.S. Air Force Reports, Histories, and Correspondence Files

Bienfang, George R. (Operations Officer, 18th Bombardment Wing to Commander, Naval Base Defense Air Force). "Operations on 7 December 1941." U.S. Air Force, Air Force Historical Support Division, Bolling AFB, Washington, D.C. Reel A7627, file 742.6741.

Hawaiian Air Depot. "Hawaiian Air [Depot] Material Area History." Vol. 1, July 1931–6 December

1941. U.S. Air Force, Air Force Historical Support Division, Bolling AFB, Washington, D.C. Reel A7374, file 723.401.

5th Bombardment Group. "History of the 5th Bombardment Group (H)." Reel B0051, file GP-5-Hi, 17 May 1918–31 Dec 1943. U.S. Air Force, Air Force Historical Support Division (formerly Air Force Historical Support Office), Bolling AFB, Washington, D.C.

6th Fighter Squadron. "Organizational History, 6th Fighter Squadron, 15th Fighter Group, VII Fighter Command, Seventh Air Force." U.S. Air Force, Air Force Historical Support Division (formerly Air Force Historical Support Office), Bolling AFB, Washington, D.C. Reel A0716, file SQ-FI-6-Hi.

VII Fighter Command. Untitled chronology, 6th Fighter Squadron, History of VII Fighter Command. Vol. 1. U.S. Air Force, Air Force Historical Support Division (formerly Air Force Historical Support Office), Bolling AFB, Washington, D.C. Reel A7586, file 741.01.

7th Air Force. "Administrative History of Headquarters, Seventh Air Force, APO953." U.S. Air Force, Air Force Historical Support Division, Bolling AFB, Washington, D.C. Reel A7532, file 740.012.

31st Bombardment Squadron. "Historical Supplement—26 June 1917–1 January 1944." U.S. Air Force, Air Force Historical Support Division, Bolling AFB, Washington, D.C. Reel A0546, file SQ-Bomb-31-Hi.

Books

Arakaki, Leatrice, and John R. Kuborn. 7 December 1941: The Air Force Story. Washington, D.C.: Government Printing Office, 1991.

Arthur, Reginald W. Contact!: Careers of US Naval Aviators Assigned Numbers 1 to 2000. Vol. 1. Arlington, Va.: Cooper-Trent, 1967.

Becket, Jan, and Joseph Singer, comps. Pana Oʻahu: Sacred Stones, Sacred Land. Honolulu: University of Hawaiʻi Press, 1999.

Bloxam, Andrew. Diary of Andrew Bloxam, Naturalist of the "Blonde" on Her Trip from England to the Hawaiian Islands, 1824–25. Honolulu: The Museum, 1925.

Bōeichō Kenshūjo Senshishitsu. Senshi Sōsho. Vol. 10: Hawai Sakusen. Tōkyō: Asagumo Shimbun-sha, 1967.

Campbell, Douglas E. Volume 3: U.S. Navy, U.S. Marine Corps and U.S. Coast Guard Aircraft Lost during World War II—Listed by Aircraft Type. Washington, D.C.: Syneca Research Group, 2011.

Coletta, Paolo E. Patrick N. L. Bellinger and U.S. Naval Aviation. New York: University Press of America, 1987.

Corney, Peter. Early Northern Pacific Voyages. Honolulu: Thos. G. Thrum, 1896.

Cowart, Virginia M. Gas Masks and Palm Trees: My Wartime Hawaii. Victoria, British Columbia: Trafford Publishing, 2006.

Creed, Roscoe. PBY: The Catalina Flying Boat. Annapolis: Naval Institute Press, 1985.

Cressman, Robert J. A Magnificent Fight: The Battle for Wake Island. Annapolis: Naval Institute Press, 1995.

Cressman, Robert J., and J. Michael Wenger. Steady Nerves and Stout Hearts: The Enterprise (CV6) Air Group and Pearl Harbor, 7 December 1941. Missoula, Mont.: Pictorial Histories, 1989.

Ford, Eliakim Reed. Ford Genealogy. Oneonta, N.Y.: self-published, 1916.

Fuchida Mitsuo and Okumiya Masatake. Midway: The Battle That Doomed Japan. Annapolis: Naval Institute Press, 1955.

Fujita Iyozō, comp. Shōgen Shinjuwan Kōgeki. Tōkyō: Kōjin-sha, 1991.

Hara Tameichi et al. Destroyer Captain: Pearl Harbor, Guadalcanal, Midway—the Great Naval Battles as Seen through Japanese Eyes. Annapolis: Naval Institute Press, 2011.

Hata Ikuhiko and Izawa Yasuo. Japanese Naval Aces and Fighter Units in World War II. Annapolis: Naval Institute Press, 1989.

Iwamoto Tetsuzō. Zero-sen Gekitsui-ō. Tōkyō: Konnichi no Wadai-sha, 1972.

Kennedy, John S. The Forgotten Warriors of Kaneohe. Oakland, Calif.: East Bay Blue Print & Supply, 1996.

Klotz, Don. On Hell's Perimeters: Pacific Tales of PBY Patrol Squadron 23 in World War II. Austin, Tex.: Sunbelt Eakin, 2002.

Lord, Walter. Day of Infamy. New York: Henry Holt, 1957.

Lundstrom, John B. The First Team: Pacific Naval Air Combat from Pearl Harbor to Midway. Annapolis: Naval Institute Press, 1984.

Maurer, Maurer. *Aviation in the U.S. Army, 1919–1939.* Washington, D.C.: Government Printing Office, 1987.

Mead, Harry. *20 Was Easy: Memoirs of a Pearl Harbor Survivor.* North Charleston, S.C.: BookSurge, 2005.

Meade, Rebecca Paulding. *Life of Hiram Paulding, Rear Admiral, U.S.N.* New York: Baker and Taylor, 1910.

O'Neill, P. G. *Japanese Names: A Comprehensive Index by Characters and Readings.* New York and Tōkyō: John Weatherhill, 1972.

Prange, Gordon W. *At Dawn We Slept: The Untold Story of Pearl Harbor.* New York: McGraw-Hill, 1981.

Roberts, Michael D. *Dictionary of American Naval Aviation Squadrons.* Vol. 2: *The History of VP, VPD, VP(HL) and VP(AM) Squadrons.* Washington, D.C.: Government Printing Office, 2000.

Ross, Donald K., and Helen L. Ross. *"0755": The Heroes of Pearl Harbor.* Port Orchard, Wash.: Rokalu Press, 1988.

Summers, Catherine C., and Elspeth P. Sterling. *Sites of Oahu.* Honolulu: Bishop Museum Press, 1988.

Tyler, David B. *The Wilkes Expedition: The First United States Exploring Expedition (1838–1842).* Philadelphia: American Philosophical Society, 1968.

United States Department of Commerce. *United States Coast Pilot: The Hawaiian Islands, 1933.* Washington, D.C.: Government Printing Office, 1933.

United States Department of the Interior. *Report of the Governor of Hawaii to the Secretary of the Interior 1921.* Washington, D.C.: Government Printing Office, 1921.

United States Naval Academy. *Lucky Bag.* U.S. Naval Academy class of 1922.

United States Naval Institute. *The Bluejackets' Manual: United States Navy 1940.* Annapolis: U.S. Naval Institute, 1940.

United States Navy Department. *Ships' Data U.S. Naval Vessels, January 1, 1938.* Washington, D.C.: Government Printing Office, 1938.

United States Navy Department, Office of the Chief of Naval Operations, Naval History Division. *Dictionary of American Naval Fighting Ships,* various volumes. Washington, D.C.: Government Printing Office, 1959–81.

West, Rodney T., MD. *Honolulu Prepares for Japan's Attack: The Oahu Civilian Disaster Preparedness Programs, May 1, 1940 to December 7, 1941.* Privately published, 1993.

Williford, Glen, and Terrance McGovern. *Defenses of Pearl Harbor and Oahu 1907–50.* Oxford, U.K.: Osprey Publishing, 2003.

Yamagata Tsunao, comp. *Kaigun: Kūbo-Kan Sentō Kiroku.* Tōkyō: Atene Shobō, 2002.

Articles and Manuscripts

Bellinger, Patrick N. L. "The Gooney Birds." Unpublished manuscript in the Bellinger Papers, History and Archives Division, Naval History and Heritage Command.

Carroll, George. "Eyes of the Fleet." Unpublished manuscript furnished to Mr. Don Montgomery.

"Coast Artillery Orders." *Coast Artillery Journal,* September–October 1941.

Correll, John T. "The Legend of Frank Luke." *Air Force Magazine* 92, no. 8 (2009): 48–51.

Cressman, Robert J., and J. Michael Wenger. "'This Is No Drill.' U.S. Naval Aviation and Pearl Harbor, December 7, 1941." *Naval Aviation News,* November–December 1991.

Cutter, Donald. "The Spanish in Hawaii: Gaytan to Marin." *Hawaiian Journal of History* 14 (1980): 16–25.

Dorrance, William A. "Moku'ume'ume." *Historic Hawai'i* 17, no. 12 (1991): 4–6.

"Fire Fight." *New Horizons* (January 1942). 17.

"Ford Island." *Pearl Harbor–Gram,* no. 118 (May 1994): 4.

Garrett, Ruth (Snodgrass). "A Date with a Bombing." *American Heritage* 42, no. 8 (December 1991): 36–39.

"History of NAS Pearl Harbor." Quarters K Binder, World War II Valor in the Pacific, 1 January 1945.

Hurd, Willis E. "North Pacific Ocean." *Monthly Weather Review* 51, no. 1 (January 1923).

"Luke Field Passes On." *Honolulu Star-Bulletin,* 4 November 1939.

Matsuda Norio. "To Renso." *Rekishi-to Jinbutsu.* Tōkyō: Chūō Kōron-sha, 20 January 1983.

McKee, Linda. "Mad Jack and the Missionaries." *American Heritage* 22, no. 3 (April 1971): 30–37, 85–87.

"Navy Cross Is Given Daring Pilot for Pearl Harbor Heroism." *Galveston Daily News,* 26 April 1942.

Office of the Chief of the Air Corps. *Air Corps News Letter* 18, no. 18, 1 October 1935, and no. 19, 15 October 1935.

Ogden, James B. "Airborne at Pearl." U.S. Naval Institute *Proceedings* 119, no. 1090 (December 1993): 60–62.

Olson, Storrs L. "The Contribution of the Voyage of H.M.S. *Blonde* (1825) to Hawaiian Ornithology." *Archives of Natural History* 23, no. 1 (February 1996): 1–42.

"On Wings of Thunder." *Fort Collins* (Colo.) *Review*, 5 December 1991.

"Pearl Harbor Attack Remembered." *Hawaii Navy News* 2, no. 49, 7 December 1977.

Pietrusewsky, Michael, et al. "The Search for Don Francisco de Paula Marin: Servant, Friend, and Advisor to King Kamehameha I, Kingdom of Hawai'i." In *Studies in Forensic Biohistory: Anthropological Perspectives*, ed. Christopher M. Stojanowski and William N. Duncan, 67–88. Cambridge, U.K.: Cambridge University Press, 2016.

Ramsey, Mary Ann. "Only Yesteryear." *Naval History* 5, no. 4 (winter 1991). Reprinted in *Pearl Harbor–Gram* 116 (November 1993): 1–2, 18–19.

Shiga Yoshio. "Seikutai kara Mita Shinjuwan Kōgeki." Comp. Fujita Iyozō, *Shōgen Shinjuwan Kōgeki*. Tōkyō: Kōjin-sha, 1991.

———. "Sonohi Watakushi Wa, Tsunenogotoku Shutsugekishita." *Mikōkai Shashin No Miru: Shinjuwan Kōgeki*, 12 July 1990.

Tagaya, Osamu. "Aichi 99 Kanbaku 'Val' Units of World War II." A portion of Mr. Tagaya's unpublished manuscript furnished to Wenger for review and comment.

Takeuchi Masato. "Hawai Shutsugeki Kikki." *Rekishi-to Jinbutsu*. Tōkyō: Chūō Kōron-sha, 10 September 1985.

Wise, James E. Jr. "Ford Island." U.S. Naval Institute *Proceedings* 90, no. 740 (October 1964).

"Witnesses Share Memories." *Miami County Republic* (Paola, Kans.), 4 December 1991.

Yoshino Haruo. "Kaga Dengekitai, Senkan Okurahoma Ni Shiro-o Tore." Comp. Fujita Iyozō, *Shōgen Shinjuwan Kōgeki*. Tōkyō: Kōjin-sha, 1991.

Internet Sources

Julien Bessonneau (1842–1916). http://data.bnf.fr/10797578/julien_bessonneau/.

Galerie Numistoria. https://numistoria.com/en/maine-et-loire-49/10738-etablissements-bessonneau.html.

Historical Collections of the Hawaiian Islands-Kamehameha IV-(Part 3). http://files.usgwarchives.net/hi/keepers/koc52.txt.

IJN *Izumo*: Tabular Record of Movement. http://www.combinedfleet.com/Izumo_t.htm.

IJN *Yakumo*: Tabular Record of Movement. http://www.combinedfleet.com/Yakumo_t.htm.

Interview with Pearl Harbor Eyewitnesses. http://teacher.scholastic.com/pearl/transcript.htm.

[Luke Field photography] 1910–1919. http://aviation.hawaii.gov/aviation-photos/1910-1919/.

Frank Luke, Jr. Hall of Valor. http://valor.militarytimes.com/recipient.php?recipientid=896.

Major General Frederick Martin. http://www.af.mil/About-Us/Biographies/Display/Article/108125/major-general-frederick-martin/.

Martin M-130 Flying Boat: China Clipper's Trans-Pacific Flights. http://www.historynet.com/martin-m-130-flying-boat-china-clippers-trans-pacific-flights.htm.

Muster Rolls and Records of Changes (U.S. Navy) for NAS Pearl Harbor, VJ-1, VJ-2, VP-21, VP-22, VP-23, VP-24. www.fold3.com.

Naval Database, HMS *Blonde* (1819). http://www.pbenyon.plus.com/18-1900/B/00602.html.

Franklin D. Roosevelt, Executive Orders 7201–7241. http://www.fdrlibrary.marist.edu/_resources/images/eo/eo0033.pdf.

U.S. Navy Aircraft History Cards (BuNos 0102–0501). http://www.pby.com/ArchiveDatabase/USN.AHC-08793.00577.php.

U.S. Navy Aircraft History Cards (BuNos 0842–1244). http://www.pby.com/ArchiveDatabase/USN.AHC-00578.01302.php.

U.S. Navy Aircraft History Cards (BuNos 2289–2488). http://www.pby.com/ArchiveDatabase/USN.AHC-02025.02819.php.

INDEX

151, 159–60; submarine sighting during, 177, 232–33n34; Task Force 8 operations, 128–29, 177, 190; VCS-5 operations, 162, 231n1; VJ-1 operations, 128, 159, 161, 165–69, 171, 178–83, 186–87, 188, 233n41; VO/VCS operations, 185, 188–89, 190; VP-11 operations, 122, 131; VP-12 operations, 122; VP-14 operations, 122, 162–64, 165–66, 188, 231n3; VP-21 operations, 170–72; VP-23 operations, 126, 128, 131, 165, 177, 184–85, 189–90; VP-24 operations, 122, 128, 160, 161, 177–78, 186

Seattle, 12

Seki Masao, 82, 85, 87

Sekifuji Chōji, 151

Semmes, Raphael, Jr., 162, 163, 185, 231n1

Senior Officer Quarters, 16, 17, 23, 98, 116, 118

Sever, Earl, 111, 143–44

Shacklett, Francis, 131

Shaw, 137, 139, 141–43, 144

Sherrard, Alma, 60, 94, 136

Sherrard, Paul J., 60, 94, 136, 137

Shiga Yoshio, 69, 86, 233–34n47

Shimazaki Shigekazu, 68, 136, 137, 145

Shindō Saburō, 136, 151

Shinohara Kazuo, 80, 87

Ship Services (Building 17), 95

ships: names and identification numbers of, xvii; vessels moving in harbor after attack, 134

Shoemaker, James M.: antisabotage drills and sabotage attack simulation, 48; *Arizona* explosion and sinking, eyewitness to, 113; *Arizona* explosion concussion and sinking experienced by, 113–14; bucket brigade organization by, 135; checking on family after attack, 135; commendation for courage and bravery of photographers from, 144; damage inspection tour of, 123–24, 126; damage report of, 84; dive-bombing attacks, observation of technique of Japanese pilots, 144–45; *Enterprise* incoming planes, arrangements to land, 201; firefighting organization by, 153–54; Hangar 38 damage from bomb body, 222–23n24; liberty policy and schedule, 59; office of, location of, 73; photo of, 113; praise for sailors at fuel facility, 118; reflection on the start of the Pacific War, 135; response to attack, 112–13; response to opening moments of attack, 91–92; Sunday morning activity of, 63; wounded survivors transport by,

130, 135; Young and Nichol transport to Landing A, 130, 135

Shōkaku (Japan): action report on dive-bombing attack, 84; aircraft formation for attack, 148; attack on Hickam Field from, 91; attack on NAS Kaneohe Bay by, 90–91; attack on Pearl Harbor and Hickam Field plan, 65, 67, 68–69; attack on Pearl Harbor from, 74–82, 84–87, 94; command of, 65; dive-bomber group on, 65; number of aircraft on, 65; second attack wave from, 136, 145, 147–50, 151, 229–30n26; strafing runs on aircraft from, 106, 107–8

Sikorsky JRS-1 amphibians: Marines with rifles on, 167; paint scheme on, 183; radio communications from during power failure, 145, 146; range of, 183; search operations with, 128, 165–69, 178–81, 182, 183, 186, 233n41; strafing runs on, 86, 88; vulnerability of, 128, 180, 186

Silver Star, 172

Simpson, William A., 167, 169, 180

Singleton, "D" Arnold, 63, 118, 120, 134

Small Arms Magazine No. 1 (Building 168), 143

Small Arms Magazine No. 2 (Building 169), 143

Smith, Jaroud B., Jr., 100, 112, 117

Smith, William W., 37

SOC Seagulls, xvii; attacks on, 82; firefighting to save, 106; *Kaga* second-wave fighter contact with, 233–34n47; location of at Pearl Harbor, 64; photo of, 34; search operations with, 128, 162, 167, 177, 185, 190; survival of after attack, 127; Thornton ditching after running out of fuel, 162, 190

Sorensen, Raymond W., 199

Sōryū (Japan): attack on fisherman by aircraft from, 95; second attack wave from, 148; shoot down of Miller by aircraft from, 175; torpedo bombers from, 82, 87, 93

Southard, 177

Spanfelner, Perry B. F., 106

Sparks, Jack, 105

Staff Repair Shop, 82, 191

Stapleton, Mike, 54, 102

Stark, Harold R. "Betty," 28, 29

Storehouse (Building 26): annex to (Building 26-A), 14, 143; arms and ammunition for women seeking refuge at loading platform, 143; distribution of weapons, blankets, and towels from, 107; Sunday morning activity in, 63

Strittmatter, Joseph H., 61, 106

Strong, Raymond D., 109

Sturgeon, 36

submarines: antisubmarine patrols, 52; attacks on Oʻahu by Japanese submarines, possibility of, 45, 52, 59; bombing and sinking of midget submarine, 70–73, 221n1; coordination of locations for patrol squadron operations, 52; operating areas for submerged operations, 52, 53, 61, 62; sighting during search for Japanese fleet, 177, 232–33n34; sighting of hostile submarine, 160; sinking of midget submarine by *Monaghan*, 134; VP-24 patrol and training exercise with *Gudgeon*, 61, 63, 72–73, 89, 109–10; war patrols near Midway and Wake islands, 36–37

Supply Department, 54, 63, 111, 122–23, 143, 153, 200

survivors: from *Arizona*, 116, 120; assistance to survivors at Landing A, 155; from Battleship Row, 120–22; blankets, towels, sheets, mattresses, and cots for, 107, 122–23, 133, 159; emotional reactions, fear, and shock after attack, 123, 157, 192–93, 208–10; feeding and clothing survivors, 159, 199; first-aid stations for, 120, 122–23, 133; memories of and "Remember Pearl Harbor," 210; from *Oklahoma*, 133; rescue of from harbor, 116, 155–56, 158; trench excavation for cover after coming ashore, 120, 121; from *Utah*, 116, 120, 121; from *West Virginia*, 120, 153

Sutherland, Will R., 144

Suzuki Mitsumori, 104

Suzuki Toshio, 81–82, 87

swimming pool water, 199–200

Swisher, Burt L., 106, 107

Switzer, David L. "Lee," 169, 170, 186, 188

Switzer, Doris, 169, 170

Swordfish, 36

T4M-1 floatplanes, 15

Taiyo Maru (Japan), 37

Takahashi Kakuichi: attack plan and approach to Pearl Harbor for attack, 65–69, 221n22; bomb and fuse types used by, 76, 222n13; damage to and destruction estimates, 87, 124; detonation rate of bombs, 223n29; dive-bomber force command by, 65; dive-bombing attacks by, 74–76, 79–81, 82, 86, 87, 88; machine-gun fire as soon as bombs released, 81; photo of, 86; report about movement

ABOUT THE AUTHORS

Military historian **J. Michael Wenger** lives in Raleigh, North Carolina, and has been conducting research since the 1970s at repositories in the United States from St. Louis to Washington, and also in Tōkyō, Berlin, and London. He has co-written eleven books and numerous journal articles, newspaper features, and reviews. His main interest is Japanese carrier aviation and doctrine in World War II.

Naval historian **Robert J. Cressman** lives in Silver Spring, Maryland. His *The Official Chronology of the United States Navy in World War II* received a John Lyman Book Award (1999), and his body of work on U.S. naval aviation history was recognized with the Admiral Arthur W. Radford Award (2008).

Military historian **John Di Virgilio** lives in Honolulu, Hawaii. He has conducted research for forty years in repositories across the United States and Japan. He is the author of two groundbreaking articles related to Pearl Harbor and is recognized for his extensive research on Japanese naval ordnance and for his illustrated Pearl Harbor battleship damage profiles.